Salish Etymological Dictionary

UM

Occasional Papers in Linguistics No. 16, 2002

Salish Etymological Dictionary

Aert H. Kuipers

First Published December 2002

UMOPL — A series dedicated to the study
of the Native languages of the Northwest.

SERIES EDITORS
Anthony Mattina, University of Montana (mattina@selway.umt.edu)
Timothy Montler, University of North Texas (montler@unt.edu)

Address all correspondence to:
        UMOPL — Linguistics Laboratory
        The University of Montana
        Missoula, MT 59812

Aert H Kuipers
        Salish Etymological Dictionary
        UMOPL No. 16

ISBN 1-879763-16-8

Library of Congress Control Number: 2002114544

CONTENTS

ACKNOWLEDGMENTS

Warm thanks are due to the Netherlands Organization for the Advancement of Pure Research (Z.W.O., now renamed N. W. O.) which financed research on Salish and Wakashan in the 1970s. This made possible the work of H. Nater on Bella Coola, J. van Eijk on Lillooet, J. Timmers on Sechelt and Comox, and of F.H.H. Kortlandt, J. Rath and H. Vink on Wakashan. In addition, a grant to M. Dale Kinkade made possible extensive consultations with the latter, besides furthering his work on Tsamosan.

Special thanks are also due to the editors of the *UMOPL* series, whose experience in publishing Salish material has greatly improved the design of the dictionary, originally submitted as a camera-ready MS. In particular, the author is grateful to dr. Mattina for overcoming his initial objections to submitting an electronic version and for doing most of the extra work this entailed.

ABBREVIATIONS

(For abbreviations of language names see p. viii)

borr.	borrowing	o.s.	oneself
dial.	dialect	pl.	plural
e.o.	each other	poss.	possible/y
fr.	from	red.	reduplication/-ted
geogr.	geographic name	sb.	somebody
imp.	imperative	st.	something
Intro	Introduction	suff.	suffix
irreg.	irregular	tr.	transitive
itr.	intransitive	unid.	unidentified
lit.	literally	w.	with
LR	see Bibliography		

SALISH AND NEIGHBORING LANGUAGES

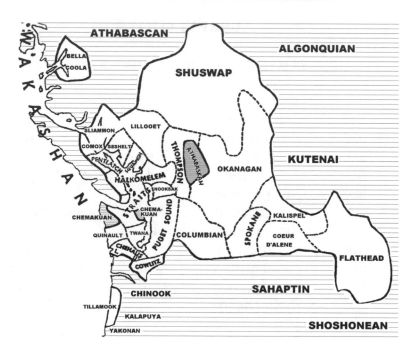

ABBREVIATIONS OF LANGUAGE NAMES

Be	Bella Coola	IS	Interior Salish	S...	Southern...
CeS	Central Salish	KUT	Kutenai	Se	Sechelt
Cb	Columbian	KWA	Kwakiutl	Sg	Songish
Ch	(Upper) Chehalis	Ka	Kalispel	Sh	Shuswap
CJ	Chinook Jargon	Ld	Lushootseed	Si	Siletz
Ck	Chilliwack	Li	Lillooet	Sl	Sliammon
Cl	Clallam	Lm	Lummi	Sm	Samish
Cr	Coeur d'Alene	Ms	Musqueam	Sn	Saanich
CS	Coast Salish	N...	Northern...	So	Sooke
Cv	Colville	Ne	Nehalem	Sp	Spokane
Cw	Cowichan	Nk	Nooksack	Sq	Squamish
Cx	Comox	NOO	Nootka	St	Straits
Cz	Cowlitz	Ok	Okanagan	Th	Thompson
E...	Eastern...	OOW	Oowekyala	Ti	Tillamook
Fl	Flathead	P...	Proto...	Ts	Tsamosan
HAI	Haisla	PS	Proto-Salish	Tw	Twana
HEI	Heiltzuk	Pt	Pentlatch	W...	Western...
Hl	Halkomelem	QUI	Quileute	WAK	Wakashan
		Qu	Quinault		

viii

CLASSIFICATION OF SALISH LANGUAGES

I. COAST SALISH
  A. Bella Coola (= Nuxalk)
  B. Central Salish
      B1. North Georgia Branch
          Comox-Sliammon
          Pentlatch
          Sechelt
      B2. South Georgia Branch
          Squamish
          Halkomelem (dialects: Cowichan, Musqueam,
              Chilliwack)
          Nooksack
          Northern Straits (dialects: Samish, Sooke,
              Songhish, Saanich, Lummi)
          Clallam (= Southern Straits)
      B3. Puget Sound Branch
          Lushootseed (dialects N and S)
      B4. Hood Canal Branch
          Twana
  C. Tsamosan (= Olympic)
      Quinault
      Lower Chehalis
      Upper Chehalis (dialects Satsop, Oakville, Tenino)
      Cowlitz
  D. Tillamook (dialects: Nehalem, Tillamook, Siletz)

II. INTERIOR SALISH
  A. *Northern Branch*
      Lillooet (dialects Fountain, Mt.Currie)
      Thompson
      Shuswap (dialects W and E)
  B. *Southern Branch*
      Columbian
      Colville-Okanagan
      Kalispel-Spokane-Flathead
      Coeur d'Alene

PS PHONEMES

p	t		c		k		k^w	q	q^w	
p'	t'		c'	ƛ'	k'		k'^{w}	q'	q'^{w}	ʔ
		s		ł	x		x^w	x̌	x̌^{w}	h
m	n			l	y	γ	w	ʕ	ʕ^w	
m'	n'			l'	y'	γ'	w'	ʕ'	ʕ'^{w}	

	i	i̧		u	u̧	
			ə ə̧			
			a ạ			

γ	velarized y (functioning as a resonant).
ạ i̧ u̧ ə̧	retracted (darkened) vowels, phonetically [a ɪ o ʌ] as opposed to plain [æ i u ə].

In individual languages:

ç'	glottalized apico-interdental affricate.
θ	apico-interdental fricative.
3 3̌	voiced dental resp. palatal affricate.
ḥ ḥ^w	voiceless pharyngeal fricatives.
ḷ ṣ ç	are [l s c] pronounced with retracted tongue-root. In NIS the phonemes s c are phonetically [š č], whereas ṣ ç are close to [s c].
z z'	lax voiced apico-dental continuants (similar to English voiced th) functioning as resonants.
ŋ ŋ'	velar nasals.
G	voiced uvular stop (Wakashan only).

INTRODUCTION

1. THE GEOGRAPHICAL DISTRIBUTION AND A CLASSIFICATION of the Salish languages are given on p. viii-ix. Several of the languages have died out, many are close to extinction, none have more than a few hundred speakers left, of varying fluency, and most if not all of these use English in everyday life. The classification is that of Swadesh 1950, with a primary CS-IS division added. For general data on Salish and in particular a history of Salish comparative phonology see Thompson 1979. The reconstruction of the PS system of phonemes is that of Kuipers 1981.

Material for a Salish etymological dictionary has been collected by the author since the late 'sixties. Intensive study of a Coast Salish language (Squamish) and an Interior Salish one (Shuswap) created favorable conditions for such an enterprise. From the beginning, lexical material in reliable notations was available for Coeur d'Alene (Reichard 1939), Kalispel (Vogt 1940), Halkomelem (Elmendorf-Suttles 1960) and Puget Sound Salish (= Lushootseed, Snyder 1968), and a first list of etymologies was published under the title *Towards a Salish etymological dictionary* in 1970. In 1972 I arranged for my students Nater, Timmers and Van Eijk to work on Bella Coola, Sechelt and Lillooet respectively, providing them with a classified 1800-word list to be used in their field work and to facilitate comparison. These lists yielded many additional etymologies, enough to arrive at a reconstruction of the Proto-Salish sound system (Kuipers 1981) and a continuation of the abovementioned *Towards...* (1982). As more lexical material became available the series was continued in ICSNL (III 1995, IV 1996, V 1998); here only new reconstructions were listed, so that the older work is out of date. These gaps are filled in the present dictionary, which also contains revisions and new material.

1

The Salish languages are unevenly documented. Extensive lexica exist for Bella Coola (= Nuxalk), Squamish, the Cowichan and Chilliwack dialects of Halkomelem, Lushootseed, Upper Chehalis, Lillooet, Thompson, Shuswap, Colville-Okanagan, Kalispel, Spokane and Coeur d'Alene. Shorter dictionaries, word- and stemlists are available for Comox, Sechelt, the Musqueam dialect of Halkomelem, the Songish, Samish, Saanich and Clallam dialects of Straits, Twana and Columbian. For Sliammon the material im Hagège 1981 and Grenier and Bouchard 1971 has been included. A special case is Tillamook, for which there is the beginning of a dictionary (M.T. Thompson, n.d.); because of the importance of this isolated Coast language, the Tillamook material in Boas' Comparative Salishan Vocabularies (1925) is included in the present dictionary.

Comparative Salish is faced with the difficulties presented by language families the members of which have remained in close contact with each other. In phonology we find multiple correspondences, in lexicon isoglosses not corresponding to language- and even language-branch borders. The reason is not just borrowing in the narrow sense but interpenetration of languages resulting from bi- and even trilingualism in contact areas (and where groups are mobile any area can be a contact area). Of prehistoric migrations and fusions of Salish (and possibly non-Salish) groups we know nothing beyond what the languages themselves can tell us.

In what follows, first the regular phonetic changes leading to the individual languages are given, next sporadic and special developments are treated.

2

2. REGULAR DEVELOPMENTS

*p *p' *m > č č̓ ŋ in St (besides frequent borrowed p p' m);
   > h h w in Ti.

*m *n > b d in Ld Tw; *n > l in Ck.

*t' *ƛ' both > ƛ' in Li Th Sh (in Sh written t'); > t' in Cr.

*c > θ in Sl Cw Ms Ck; > s in Cx Lm Sg So (occasionally in
   Be); > s/θ in Sn.

*c' > ç' in Sl Cw Ms Ck Sn.

*c *s > c̣ ṣ after retracted vowels in Li Th Cb (occasionally in
   Sh).

*k *k' *x > č č̓ š in Cx Sl Se Sq Ld Tw Ch Ti Ka Sp Cr; in
   Cz this shift takes place in certain positions only;
   > c c' š in Cw Ms; > c c' x in Ck (for *c *c' see
   above);
   > c c' s in Cl Sm (coinciding w. original *c *c' *s);
   > s c' s in Lm Sg So (coinciding w. original *s *c');
   > s/θ ç' s in Sn.

   NB. In St and recent Ck often borrowed č č̓.

*γ > ǯ in Cr; > y in Cb Cv Ka Sp (etymologies limited to IS).

*q *qʷ > q/x̌ qʷ/x̌ʷ in Be.

*ʕ *ʕʷ > x̌ x̌ʷ in CS; > ḥ/ʕ ḥʷ/ʕʷ in Cb.

*l > y in Cx Sl Sq So Cl Th (called y-languages, the rest
   l-languages);[1] > w in labialized surroundings in Cx Sl;
   > r after original retracted vowels in Cb Ok Cv Sp Cr.

*y *w > ǯ g in Cx Sl; > č kʷ (*alternating w.* y w) in St; > ǯ/ʒ
   gʷ in Ld; > y gʷ/g in Ti; > d gʷ in Cr (besides frequent
   y w).

---

[1] A special case is Sq, which is considered a y-language because it has y in
grammatical morphemes, though the l-forms outnumber the y-forms by 2 to
1.

*y *y' > z c' in Th; > z z' in Li.

*ạ *ụ *ị > *a *u *i in CS;

    CS *a > e in Hl Nk NSt;

    CS *u > a in Hl NSt.

The development of the vowels in IS, where the retracted ones remain distinct, calls for a few comments. (1) Different transcriptions are used: where Li Cb write a ạ u ụ, Th Sh Ka Sp Cr write e a u o. (2) The development of the vowels has been different in neutral (N) and in retracting (Q) environments; the latter are: an immediately following uvular in Li Th Sh Cb Ok Cv, and any uvular (in Cr also a retracted vowel)[2] later in the word in Ka Sp Cr. In environment Q all vowels are phonetically more or less retracted and in Li Th Sh Ka Sp Cr have the same timbre as the retracted vowels in N, except that Th Ka Sp i is not affected (at least not in the transcription). (3) In Li Sh plain vowels are written for the automatically retracted ones in Q; in Th Ka Sp Cr retracted vowels are written here, except that in Th there is a distinction eQ - aQ with a very low functional yield (mostly they are in free variation). Apart from notational conventions, the real changes are the following:

*a > iN aQ in Ok Cv Cr.

*ạ *ị *ụ > *a *i *u before *l (which > r) in Ok Cv Sp.

*ạ *ụ > ʕa in Ok Cv.

*i > iN eQ in Cr (eQ > aQ if a suffix with a uvular follows).

*ị > e/i in Sh; *ịl > iḷ > ir in Ok Cv, > iḷ > er in Cr.

---

[2] As this point has not been made, here follow examples: from Reichard 1938 sect. 374 syanc'áw'm *dishwasher* (sye- *agent*), sect. 382 at'apsčént *he customarily shoots* (e(c)- *customary*), sect. 736 ła sc'am' *the bones* (łe *article*), from Nicodemus 1975 acp'át' *blob*, syaat'ápm *archer,* syaapón'eʔ *bully,* čatpoʔsák*ʷ*eʔ *to bubble* (čet- *on, over*); the rule includes Cr er < *ịl, eg. čatp'ért *the floor was flooded* (Nicodemus).

*ə́ *ą́ > é á in Sh Ka Sp Cr. Possibly PS *ə and *ą were not distinct.

Roots with nonautomatic retracted vowels (ie. in N) require them in suffixes; the retracted vowels survive here even if the root vowel is reduced to zero.

In all the Salish languages borrowings from neighbors are found. The very numerous *l*-forms in Sq (a *y*-language), the frequent occurrence of p p' m instead of č č̓ ŋ < *p *p' *m in Straits and the Cr occurrence of w besides gʷ < *w were already mentioned in the list above. In Cx Sl Se Sq where the original velars become palatals there are words with k k' (seldom x). Occasional forms with kʷ < *w, which are typical of St, occur in Hl Sq Se (see PS *way). The CS languages which retain *u* < *u have borrowed forms with *a* from Hl and/or St. Forms with i < *a as found in Ok Cv Cr occasionally occur in other IS languages. In St *k *k' *x, besides their regular reflexes, often appear as č č̓ š. The reflexes č č̓ are also found in recent recordings of Ck (eg. Galloway 1980 čéləx *hand* < *kalax), they are absent from older recordings (El-mendorf-Suttles 1960 céləx). In Cx Sl *ł is reflected by ł or λ (voiceless lateral affricate), the latter undoubtedly under Wakashan influence (substratum?) – For interchange l/y and u/a see also 3C and 3I below.

3. Sporadic And Special Developments

A. Inversion of root-elements (eg. $C_1VC_2 > C_2VC_1$) is remarkably frequent in Salish. When one or a few languages have a form deviating from all others they are considered the innovators (such cases are marked "(inv.)" in the dictionary). Otherwise both forms are listed, eg. for *pitch* NIS points to *c̓it̓, SIS to *t̓ic̓.

B. *l is devoiced to ł sporadically all over the Salish area, most often word-finally but also in other positions (l and ł often alternate). For an example see PS *c'u̱/a̱l.[3]

C. All the l-languages have occasional forms with y instead, and the y-languages forms with l. Many but by no means all of these can be explained as loans from present-day neighbors, cf. the Tw forms under PS *t'əl, the Ka Sp ones under PIS *sul, the Ch form under PCS *t'əlqay; cf. also PS *q'al/y.

D. Somewhat less frequent are parallel forms with l and n; these, too, are found all over, cf. the comments under PS *yəl, the Sn Ld Tw forms under PS c'u̱/a̱l, the PS suffix *-n/lup.

E. Glottalization in resonants (for some CS languages interpreted as mʔ, wʔ, etc) is unstable and of limited etymological significance (see L below). It is written in reconstructions if a majority of languages have it.

F. Occasionally roots are found with a velar in some, a uvular in other languages (in IS w acting as the velar counterpart of ʕʷ). The two sometimes alternate with a sound-symbolic function, the uvular form having the connotation *large, strong, loud,* etc. For another source of a velar-uvular correspondence see G. below. There remain unexplained cases. Especially for Tw often a uvular was recorded where other languages have a velar (occasionally the opposite occurs).

G. Retracted vowels are found in IS only, as are uvular resonants (of which they are historically the syllabic variants).[4] The feature of retraction has often been transferred to a preceding velar, changing it into a uvular, or has affected a following c s l changing these to c̣ ṣ ḷ, with ḷ becoming r in Cb Ok Cv Sp Cr. For examples see PS *xa̱l, *xʷəl, *la̱xʷ/xʷa̱l, *kʷəl, *wəl. The change of a preceding velar to a uvular is common in Th, and sharply distinguishes it from closely related Sh, cf. Th x̌ʷyekst *do st. fast, speedy w. one's hands* Sh

---

[3] As the Cb forms under this heading show, Cb is no exception here (thus Thompson 1979:719).

[4] In WSh the root *bend* is niʕʷ- or noy-, a case of inversion where i : y = o : ʕʷ.

xʷəl'akst (Cv xʷrrapp *be in a hurry*), Th (n)ʕʷyən *stomach* Sh wlank (Sp ʔurín), Th x̌iʔx̌áy't *steep* Sh xlxalt (Cb x̌ə́r'xər't / x̌ə́l'xəl't Ka Cr šáršart), Th x̌y'əpt *take a shortcut* Sh xlapt.[5] – In individual languages retraction has sometimes been eliminated in individual words. In a few cases retracted and unretracted forms exist side by side (see PS *mạl, *xạl). It is possible that the unretracted forms are due to CS influence; this would also account for occasional IS forms with x̌ʷ < *ʕʷ (eg. the Cb form under *səʕʷ) and for some lexical items with a limited distribution in IS (eg. PS *ƛ'apat).

H. In a few cases plain and labialized velars have to be reconstructed side by side (see PS *manəxʷ/x, *-mixʷ/x); the labialized forms are probably old, as delabialization is observed elsewhere, eg. in Cx and (dialectically) Ti g < *w, in Cx č'áč'at'an? *mouse,* where the other languages point to *k'ʷat'an, in the PS suffix -kʷa/-qʷa *water* which appears in Cw as -cə/-qə. Roots beginning in *kʷu kʷu xʷu mostly retain labialized velars but in individual words in individual languages shift to ču č'u šu, c.q. with further fronting of the consonant and shifting of the vowel to *a*. Curiously, in the latter case the original consonant may reappear in re-duplications, eg. from *kʷum *go up/inland* Ms has caːm, continuative cakʷm.

I. A number of roots have forms with the reflexes of both *a and *u and of *ạ and *ụ. Some cases of *u* may result from the influence of a neighboring labialized consonant, some cases of *a* are borrowings from Hl or NSt (where *u > a), but there remain cases that cannot be explained this way. In Se both vowels occur in lulx̌ʷ *fishtrap*, lax̌ʷls *Indians from up-country*

---

[5] These cases show that one cannot posit a PS phoneme *r on the basis of a correspondence Th l ~ Cv etc. r. Thompson's statement (1979:711) that in the Th shift *l > y 'no cases of original *r are involved' is based on incomplete data. In the r-languages r is a *consequence* of retraction in a vowel, not the *cause* of it, as has been usually assumed.

(poss. *Lillooet*)[6], Sq has lux̌ʷls *Lillooet people* (the Ck name for the Lillooet is sç'k̓ʷał). Co-occurrence of *ạ and *ụ is the rule rather than the exception. In dictionary entries *u/a and *ụ/ạ are written. – In the same way *i/a is written where the material points both ways; here, too, different explanations are possible in individual cases (borrowing from i-languages, plural or diminutive forms with i). A special case is unstressed final -a(?), -i(?), the two forms being irregularly distributed over the languages. Both could continue an older *-ay(?), see PS *ʔask'ay', *-ask'ay' and PIS *c'awa(y'), but these are the only examples of this kind. Here, too, we write *i/a(?).

J. In Sh only the last oral plosive of a root retains glottalization, eg. *k'ip' *squeeze, pinch* is Sh kip'-, besides Li p'c'iq'ʷ- *to spit* we have Sh pciq'ʷ-, in Sh reduplications only the last consonant remains glottalized (and Sh t' [λ'] is reduplicated by t [t]). Sh ʔ does not have this deglottalizing effect. This "Grassmann's law" for Salish[7] is observed in a weakened form in Be (where it is common but does not affect reduplications) and occasionally in the languages of the North Georgia branch, more regularly in Ti, where it seems to be universal in roots and is common in reduplications. Irregularities in glottalization occur also in the zero grade of roots, and occasionally alternative forms must be reconstructed (see eg. PS *cək̓ʷ, *pəq'ʷ).

K. A number of roots occur both with and without an initial hV or ʔV (V = vowel). Both forms may occur in the same language, eg. Sq hiʔq̓ʷ- and yəq̓ʷ- *burn* (in different derivatives), Sn ʔəšes and šes *sea-lion*. In Hl certain roots beginning in a resonant form the continuative with an initial hə or he (Galloway 1993:60-1, 272-3). The initial syllable may at least in some cases have been part of the root, and was reduced as the result of a stress-shift, cf. Cx ʔə́x̌tay *act (thus)* Se sʔəx̌tl

---

[6] These words have parallels in Wakashan, cf. Haisla łax̌ú *get trapped*, Kwakiutl łax̌ʷlis *man from the Interior*. For a semantic parallel cf. Sq č'iaq *salmon weir,* č'iaqməš *Cheakamus (people).*
[7] The parallel was pointed out by E.P. Hamp, see Kuipers 1970:48.

be called (name), sx̌ətál *be same, alike*; PS *huy *finish*, *-cin *mouth*, *huy-cin *finish eating* Sn hay, hačθn Cv wiʔ, wiʔcín. In the dictionary both forms are listed, one with a reference to the main entry.

L. A root-final *-um' > -ap' in Hl and NSt, see PS *ɬum', *sum'. This is one of the two cases where glottalization in a resonant shows a special development (the other one is Th c' < *y').

4. FROM THE OUTSET the guiding idea in establishing cognate sets and reconstructing PS forms has been a primary division between Coast and Interior Salish, Bella Coola being regarded as belonging to CS. Thompson (1979:695) suggests that Bella Coola became isolated from the main body of Salish before the ancestors of IS moved to the Interior. Here follows evidence ranging Be firmly with the other Coast languages. (1) Be, like the other CS languages, lacks retracted vowels and merges the uvular resonants ʕ ʕʷ with the fricatives x̌ x̌ʷ (see the Be forms under PS *c'uʕʷ, *laʕʷ, *λ'əʕʷ, *pəʕʷ, *yəʕ, ʕʷəy). (2) Be words with cognates in the rest of CS and unattested for IS are three times as numerous as those with cognates in IS only. (3) Newman (1980:165) finds innovations in the Be pronominal system shared with the other northern Coast languages, and non-participation of Be in any of the pronominal changes in the Interior. (4) Be shares with other CS the existence of gender in articles (absent from IS); moreover, the consonants t for unmarked and c ɬ for feminine gender are widespread in CS including Be. (5) The number of Be ~ other CS cognates increases with geographical proximity. (6) Among the roots with IS cognates there are some which have survived in Be and in the North Georgia branch independently (ie. not as a result of borrowing) as they are found in quite different formations (see PS *kʷʷaxʷ, *yman).

5. WITH CERTAIN EXCEPTIONS to be mentioned presently a root or suffix is reconstructed for PS if it is found in both CS and IS and shows the regular phonological developments. There will be a certain excess in the totality of reconstructions because (1) some items are found in a limited area and may have spread from an unknown center to neighboring CS or IS languages, and (2) older borrowings from one of the two groups into the other are not always recognizable as such; where they are, they are not given PS status. As more lexical material was gathered by Salishists it became evident that Lillooet and to a lesser extent Thompson (both bordering on CS) contain many loans from CS. This is particularly clear where a Li or Th word has cognates in a range of CS languages, the rest of IS using a different word. These entries were removed from the PS file; where they qualify for the PCS one reference is made to the Li and/or Th (in a few cases Cb) borrowings.

6. IT REMAINS TO COMMENT on a few points raised in Thompson 1979.

1) The curious development of PS *p *p' *m to Straits č č̓ ŋ leads Thonpson (p. 716) to the following proposal: PS lacked labials; all present-day labials developed from PS *kʷ *k̓ʷ ŋʷ, the phonemes *kʷ k̓ʷ being preserved only in certain (yet to be specified) positions to account for contemporary all-Salish kʷ k̓ʷ not attributable to secondary rounding. This proposal creates more problems than it aims to solve (see Kuipers 1981 sect. 6 p. 332ff.). The supporting argument that "the cases in which *kʷ and k̓ʷ are clearly to be reconstructed from historic labiovelars are surprisingly few" is based on insufficient evidence, cf., with vowels other than u and labiovelar cognates in Straits, PS *kʷan *take*, *k̓ʷə́c *bend, twist*, *k̓ʷən *look at*, *k̓ʷin *how many?*, *cəkʷ *straight(en)*, *c̓ikʷaʔ *left (side)*, *ɬikʷ *hook up*, *xʷi/akʷ *wipe, clean, bathe*, PCS *k̓ʷim *red*, *k̓ʷəx *count*, *makʷ *eat*, *p̓akʷ *float*. These core-lexicon items have labiovelars in root-initial and -final position, with various vowels, so that the proposal cannot be maintained.

2) On p. 723 Thompson tentatively reconstructs a retracting feature (written γ with superscribed dot)[8] to account for the retracted vowels a̱ u̱, but it is simpler to regard these as vocalic

---

[8] In Kuipers 1981 p. 324 r.c. the dotted gammas are misinterpreted; they represent the "darkening feature" proposed in Kuipers 1973.

ʕ ʕʷ (and the rare i̯ as vocalic γ): This brings the retracted cases in line with the plain ones i/y u/w a/h and simplifies the Cr retracting rule (see fn. 2 on p. 4), cf. also the statement of a native speaker that Sh i̯ "has a γ in it" (Kuipers 1989:16, sect. 11).

3) On p. 724 Thompson states that "the l > r theory faces considerable conflicting evidence and does not explain why the environment for the shift was so limited". But the entire evidence for a separate PS phoneme *r consists of eight of the words where Th has l rather than y (the others necessarily being loans). Moreover, seven of these have either a retracted vowel or a uvular as C_2, so that at most the shift from *l to y tended to be blocked in a retracted environment (a separate phoneme would be expected to have a less limited distribution). And there is decisive evidence against a phoneme r: in the r-languages themselves one finds alternants with ł (devoiced l, see sect. 3B above) besides r, see PS *tu̯/a̯l, *la̯xʷ. As for the limited environment for the shift *l > r, it is the same as that for *c *s > c̣ ṣ (not accounted for by Thompson), and there are many examples of shifts taking place in limited environments (eg. that of IE *s to x/š in Indo-Iranian and Balto-Slavic).

Thompson's table of PS phonemes (l.c. 725) is related to the one given on p. x as follows: retain parenthesized p p' m m'; eliminate parenthesized r r'; eliminate boxed ŋ ŋʷ ŋ'ʷ and the four cases with dotted γ; add i̯ u̯ a̯ ə̣.

DICTIONARY

Separate listings are given of roots and of suffixes, and within these categories of PS, PCS and PIS elements. The order of the languages is CS - IS and within these roughly from north to south (except that Cb is placed before Ok-Cv). In the PS root list the symbol ~ separates the CS from the IS cognates. The PCS lists contain elements found (1) from Be down to Ld and (2) minimally from Sq/Hl down to Ts and/or Ti.

Reconstructions are printed in heavy type, meanings in italics. Square brackets indicate that a possible cognate is either formally deviating or semantically doubtful. Where no meaning of a word in an individual language is given, this meaning is that of the reconstructed entry. Meanings given as *id.* are the same as the last meaning given previously (including bracketed ones). If of one language several words are quoted they are separated by commas, and if the meaning of the first word is that of the reconstructed entry this word is followed by a semicolon. A forward slash separates alternatives; here phonemes such as m', k'ʷ are treated as units.

Adjustments have been made to the transcription of some of the sources. The lower mid vowel written ɛ/æ/ä/e is uniformly written e;[1] where a vowel system is rendered e a o ə the symbols e o have been replaced by i u. The voiceless uvular fricative, often written x with a subscribed dot or χ is written x̌. The symbol t'θ for the glottalized apico-interdental affricate is replaced by ç'. The automatic ə before a word-final m m' n n' l l' is omitted throughout. Long vowels are marked with a following colon. Stress is not written in words with only

---

[1] In Kinkade and Sloat 1972 a distinction is made between Cr ɛ (= Reichard's ä) and e, the latter reflecting **i**. A spectrographic analysis gives little support for this distinction (see N.J. Bessel in Czaykowska-Higgins and Kinkade 1998 p. 135f.); it is not made by Nicodemus (1975).

one full vowel (ie. vowel other than ə) when this vowel carries the stress (as is almost always the case). Reconstructions are given without stress-mark. Double parentheses mark words quoted from older (pre-phonemic) sources, with certain adjustments ("c tc" replaced by š č, etc.). Lincoln and Rath's z for Wakashan 3 is replaced by 3.

For Ch the main entries of Kinkade 1991 are quoted, for Cr the forms given in Reichard 1939 (mostly bare roots). For the other languages full words are quoted as given in the sources. The Ok Cv words in Mattina 1987 are listed as Cv unless the author explicitly identifies them as Ok.

In translations the English dictionary form is given for verbs (*to walk, to cut,* etc.) In Salish a root which allows a transitivizing suffix by itself usually suggests an object rather than a subject, so that a translation *be cut* would be more exact. Note that for transitive verbs (ie. roots with a transitivizing suffix) the Th Sh dictionary form is the 3sg. subj. and obj. one ending in -s, the Cb Ka Sp one has the corresponding 1sg. subj. form ending in -n.

The alphabetic order is based in the first place on the *consonants* (other than ʔ) of a root or suffix; roots with initial ʔ are quoted at the beginning, otherwise ʔ is disregarded for alphabetic purposes. The order is as follows:

ʔ c c' h k k' kʷ k'ʷ l ł ƛ' m n p p' q q' qʷ q'ʷ s t t' w x xʷ x̌ x̌ʷ y γ ʕ ʕʷ

(vowels: ə ə̣ a ạ i ị u ụ)

In the PCS and CeS root lists, if of roots beginning with č č' š no cognates with k k' x are attested, they are quoted with č č' š, alphabetically after c c' s respectively.

The nominalizing prefix *s- and the local prefix *n- are disregarded for alphabetic purposes.

NOTE. Many words relating to flora and fauna are listed in Kinkade 1991 and 1995, in the latter article with comments and quotations of both newer and older (pre-phonemic) recordings.[2] Explicit reference to this and other articles is made only where the occasion calls for it.

---

[2] For Shuswap both phonemic and practical transcriptions are quoted, and in the latter case t's is written for both practical t's [ƛ's] and ts' [c']. In all cases the phonemic form (t's resp. c') is also quoted. On p. 46 (no. 58) for st'él'se read sts'él'se.

PROTO-SALISH (PS) ROOTS

ʔ

*ʔacq *to be outside,* *ʔucq *to go outside.* Be ʔasqa *be outside,* ʔusqa *go outside* Sq ʔacq *outside,* ʔucq *go outside* (cf. Sq ʔay- *in, at,* ʔuy- *into)* ~ [Li ʔúc'qaʔ *go outside,* ʔálc'qaʔ *be outside* Th ʔéyc'qeʔ *outside, outdoors* Cb lʔál'sqaʔ *be outside*] Cv ʔácqaʔ *go out* Ka Sp ʔócqeʔ *id.,* [Sp č'ólsqeʔ *outside*]. – See *ʔuɬ-(t)xʷ, PCS *ʔu/as-txʷ and the Be forms under *ʔamut.

*ʔacaʔqʷ *to roast, bake.* Sq ʔácaqʷ *roast* Cw ʔáθaʔqʷ *bake* Ck ʔacəqʷ *id.* Ch ʔácaqʷi- *bake in ashes* ~ Li ʔácaqʷ *anything baked as a whole (apples, potatoes, etc.),* sʔácaqʷ *roast potatoes* Th ʔecqʷ *bake, roast in ashes* Sh ʔecqʷm *bake,* sʔecqʷ *roast potatoes* Cv sʔacqʷ *roasted or baked (as potato).*

*ʔic'am *to cover with a blanket, dress;* *s(ʔ)íc'am *blanket, clothing, covering.* Be ʔic'ama *blanket,* ʔic'amni *id.,* sic'm *leather, banknote,* sic'maaɬ *moccasins* Cx ʔíc'am *clothing, dress* Sl ʔiç'm *blanket* Se sʔíc'am *id.* Sq ʔíc'am *get dressed,* sʔíc'am *attire* Cw Ms sʔiç'm *id.* Ck ʔiç'm *get dressed* Sm ʔic'n̓ *id.,* ʔəc'/ç'enəstxʷ *dress sb.* Sn ʔiç'n̓ *id.* Sg ʔic'n̓ *be dressed,* ʔəc'en̓ *get dressed* Cl ʔic'n̓ *get dressed,* sʔic'n̓ *clothes* Ld sʔic'əb *blanket* (Snyder c'íc'ab) Tw sʔíc'əbəɬqʷay *clothes* Si "se:ca:'o:" CV *blanket* ~ Th ʔic'msc *dress sb.,* sic'm *blanket,* sʔíc'eʔ *cottonwood bark* Sh Cv Ka Sp Cr sic'm *blanket.* – Cf. PS *-ic'aʔ.

*ʔakan see *ka(n).

*ʔal *to be alive, move the body,* (w. suff. *hand:)* *to work.* Se ʔayʔəy *be alive* (borr.) Sq ʔaynəxʷ *id.* [Cw helíʔ *id.*] Ck ʔay(ə)ləxʷ *id.* [Sn həli *id.* Cl həyi *id.* Ld həlíʔ *id.*] ~ Li ʔalkst *to work* Sh ʔelkst *id.* Cr el *move body,* Nicodemus: ʔelmíčtm *move/stir the hand,* ʔelmšínm *id. foot.* – The initial h of the Cw Sn Ld items is unexplained. A homophonous root

15

in words for *house, home* Cx ʔáyaʔ Se ʔə́lwim Sn ʔeʔlŋ Cl ʔaʔyəŋ Ld ʔálʔal, doubtfully connected via a development *alive > live > dwell > dwelling.*

    *ʔul, *ʔuy I *to gather.* Cx ʔúʒut Se ʔuyút, ʔuyáš Cw ʔaləx̌ət Ld ʔuləx̌ *obtain, gather (as clams)* Tw sʔúlax̌ *property, money,* biʔúlax̌čəd *I'm gathering/saving st.* Ch ʔúlax̌i- *gather, pick (as berries)* ~ Li ʔúlʔus *get together, have a meeting* Th ʔuy'm *gather, collect* Cv ʔúllus *be gathered,* ʔúlułt *gather (things for sb.)* Sp ʔul- *meet,* nʔúluʔsm *be united.*

    *ʔi/alk *unid. plant.* Be ʔilk *mission bells (plant and edible bulbs)* = *Indian rice, Fritillaria camschatcensis* ~ Th ʔeyk *kinnikinnick berry* = *Arctostaphylos uva-ursi* Sh ʔelk *id.* Cr ʔilč *id.* -- See comment under ***p'u/an.**

    *ʔalasik *turtle.* Ld ʔaləšək Ch ʔalašík ~ Li ʔalsíkʷ CV Th ʔəl'sikʷ Cb ʔarasíkʷ Cv ʔar'síkʷ Sp ʔer'síkʷ. -- This un-Salish looking root is borrowed from Sahaptin (ʔ)alašík (Kinkade 1991:3, 1995:38). IS retraction as often in borrowings; final kʷ may be due to initial borrowing by a č-language. Cf. PIS ***sp'əlqʷ-aqs.**

    *ʔił(t)n *to eat.* [Be ʔałps] Cx Sl Se ʔiłtn Se sʔiłtn *food* Sq ʔiłn; sʔiłn *food,* ʔiłtántn *medicine to restore appetite* Cw Ms ʔəłtn Ck ʔəłtl Nk ʔiłn Sm Sn Sg ʔiłn; sʔiłn *food* Sm sʔəłtənŋ *berry (generic)* Sn sʔəłtənŋ' *id.* Sg sʔəłtənŋ *id.* Cl ʔiłn Ld ʔə́łəd; sʔə́łəd *food,* ʔəłtxʷ *to feed* Tw ʔiład Ch ʔiłn Ti ʔiłn ~ Li ʔiłn; sʔiłn *food* Th nʔiłn *to graze, forage, eat (of animals)* Sh ʔiłn; sxʔiłn *meal,* Cb Cv Ka Sp ʔiłn; sʔiłn *food* Cr ʔiłn; y'iłn *food.* -- Cf. ***s-ciłn.** For the forms in -tn cf. the Se Ck items under ***kʷul.** Cf. also Cv -iltn *stomach, food, eat* Cr -iln *food.*

    *ʔuł-(t)xʷ *to enter.* Cx Se ʔułtxʷ (Cx ʔałtxʷ *inside*) Tw ʔúltxʷdəxʷ *come in!* ~ Li Th Sh Ka ʔułxʷ Cr n'ułxʷ (Ka Cr *sg.*). -- Cf. ***ʔu/acq, PS *-txʷ** and **PCS *ʔu/as-txʷ.**

    *ʔu/am, m- *to feed, food; to provide, deliver.* Be ʔamuł *get one's share of food* Se ʔamaqáš *return, give back* Sq ʔamʔəq *deliver* Cw xʷʔiʔməqnect *id.,* ʔeʔməqt *return st., take* *it back*, [maʔcəp *start a fire (by transferring coals)*] Ck ʔaːm *give*, mə́stəxʷ *deliver* Sm ʔənaʔt *give st. to sb.* Sn ʔaŋəs *give*, ʔəmniʔŋ *hunt deer, moose, elk*, [ʔam *be fed up*] Sn Sg ŋetxʷ *distribute wealth* Sg ŋetŋ *id.*, ʔaŋəst *to give* Cl ʔə́ŋat *give to sb.*, ʔamxʷúcn *pick berries*, ŋə/aʔtxʷ *distribute goods* Ld ʔab *extend, give, deliver* Tw ʔabšəd *deliver*, ʔábšiləb *bringing, return*, ʔúbatbəš *feed me!*, biʔúbac *sb. gave it to me*, bibátaxʷ *he's giving sb. food* Ch ʔám- *take to, deliver*, ʔúm-n *give food*, sumt *the food given* ~ Li ʔum'n *present a gift to sb.*, ʔamləx *get food for root cellar*, ʔám'can' *feed*, ʔam'stəxʷ *be left in sb.'s care* Th ʔémix *get food supplies for cellar*, ʔémes *go and look after sb.*, ʔém'estxʷ *look after, take care of sb.*, m'ən/n' *give st., make donation*, [metkʷ *transport fire*] Sh cʔemlx *get food out of root cellar*, ʔemstxʷ *stock up on food*, ʔemstxʷns *supply sb. w. food*, cʔemstxʷ *stay in absent owner's house*, mtes *to feed* (customary form cmətstes), smn'sqéx̌eʔ *horsefeed* Cb ʔəmtn *to feed* Cv ʔamnám *id.* Ka Sp ʔem'tm *id.* Cr em *id.*

*ʔimac *grandchild.* Be [ʔimc *nephew, niece*], sɬʔimc *grandchild* Cx ʔímas Sl ʔiməθ Se Sq ʔímac Sq ʔim' *little boy*, ʔim'šn *little girl* Cw Ms ʔiməθ Ch ʔiːməθ Nk ʔímec Sm Sn Sg ʔiŋəs Cl ʔiŋəc Ld ʔíbac Tw ʔíbac Ch ʔímac- ~ Li ʔímac Th Sh ʔimc Cb ʔaʔím'caʔ. – Final -(a)c may be a petrified hypocoristic suffix, cf. PS *s-muɬac, PCS *kapc, *kʷ-tam-c, cf. also its use in words for *husband* derived from words for *man*, eg. Ck sweqəθ (θ < c) besides swiːqə.

*ʔamut, *mut *to sit; to be at home.* Be ʔmt *sit, assume sitting position*, ʔamat *where st. is*, ʔumat *where st./sb. is going/taken to* Cx ʔámut *be/stay at home* Sq ʔmut *assume a sitting position*, ʔm'ut *be sitting down, be at home* Cw Ms ʔəmət *sit* Ck ʔaːmət *id.* Sm ʔə́mət *sit, sit up/down*, ʔam'ət *sitting down* Sn ʔamət *sit up* Sg ʔə́mət *sit, squat* Cl ʔə́mət *sit* Tw ʔabút *assume sitting position*, ʔaʔábat *sit down!*, ʔábətəbid *chair, seat* Ch ʔáːmaq'i- *wait* ~ Th ʔem'cín' *lie in wait* Sh mut *be at home, camped, live somewhere, sg.*, mtəmiʔ *remain seated*, mtep *sit under or at the bottom (foot) of st.*, mtikn' *sit on the ice*, tmətew's *be on horseback*, ʔəmut *sit* *down, sg.,* xʔəmut/xəm'ut *sit up, get up (in the morning),* xʔəmə[t]cin *lie in wait for game,* tʔəm(ə)tew's *mount (a horse)* Cb k'ɬʔamn *wait for* Cv mut *sit,* ʔə/amut *id.,* kʔmtalqʷ *sit on a log,* kʔmtiw's *be on horseback* Ka ʔemút *sit, be at home, sg.,* nʔemtéʔusn *wait for sb.* Sp ʔemút *sit, stay, sg.,* ʔemtép *stay at bottom,* nʔemtéw'sm *wait.* Cr ʔémiš *sit, sg.*

*ʔumat *to name, call.* Tw sʔúbat *name* Ch ʔúmati- ~ Th ʔúmes Sh ʔəmetns Cv ʔumnt.

*ʔa̧n (red.) *magpie.* Ck ʔə́ləl/ʔeləl/ʔə́l'əl Nk ʔénʔen Ld ʔádʔad Ch ʔánaʔàna ~ [Th ʕin'ʕn'] Sh sʔ(a)nʔán'se [Cb ʕ"ʷən'ʕ"ʷán'ps] Sp ʔan'n'. – Cf. KUT ánʔan *id.*

*ʔinwat, *ʔinwa-n- *say what?/something,* resp. itr. and tr. to sb. (obj.). Be ʔinut-ʔiks *what did he say?* Cx ʔínat Sl ʔíʔinət Se ʔínat Sn ʔin'ət Cl ʔeʔnət Ld ʔídigʷat Ch ʔínwat Ti nígʷat ~ Li ʔínwat Th ʔínuns/ʔinwns Sh ʔnwet, ʔnwens [Cv ʔanwínt *sense, feel, hear st.* Ka enuwén *id.* Sp ʔenwén *id.*] Cr ʔíngʷet *be who, what.*

*ʔup *to eat.* Tw ʔúpaɬ Ch ʔupál- Ti ʔəhaləw ~ Th ʔúpis.

*ʔupan, *pan *ten.* Cx Sl ʔupn Se ʔúpan Sq ʔupn Cw Ms ʔapn Ck ʔaːpl Sm Sn Sg ʔapn Cl ʔupn Ld pádac Tw ʔupdəčs Ch pánačs Ti ʔəhančs ~ Th ʔúpnekst Sh ʔupəkst Cv ʔupnkst Ka Sp ʔupn Cr ʔupn(čt).

*s-up-s, *s-up-aʔ *tail.* Cx súpənač Sl supnəč Se súpnač Sq -iʔ-ups Nk c'úpec Tw qʷil'ʔúpsəbəd Ch súpsn'č Ti suhəs (Reichard), ssuhs (Thompson) ~ Li súspaʔ Th Sh súpeʔ Sh suff. -upeʔ, -ups Cb suff. -ups *tail, rump* Cv syups Ka Sp sups Cr čsups, suff. -ups. – See PS suff. *-ups, *-up-aʔ.

*ʔapxʷ, *xʷəp *to lift up.* Be ʔapxʷ ~ Li xʷəpn. – Inversion in either direction.

*ʔap' *to wipe.* Cw ʔeç'ət (borr. fr. Straits) Ms ʔep'ət Ck ʔeːp'ət Sn Sg ʔeč'ət Cl ʔač't Tw ʔasʔáp' *wiped off* Ch ʔáp'a-*brush, caress, slide off* ~ Li ʔáp'an' Th ʔép'es Sh ʔep'm Cb ʔap'n Cv ʔip'm Ka Sp ʔep'n Cr ʔip'.

*ʔiqʼ see *yǝqʼ.

*ʔuqʷ see *qʷuʔ.

*ʔi/aqʷ *to scrape, shave, sweep, rub, pass net through water.* [Be ʔiqʷuc(a) *to rasp, file (prob.* belongs under *yaqʼ)] Cx ʔíqʷumixʷ *sweep floors,* [ǯǝkʷt *rub*] Se ʔíqʷit *sweep,* [yǝkʷt *rub*] Sq ʔiqʷ *be rubbed* Cw ʔiqʷǝt *scrub (w. cedar boughs, for purification)* Ck ʔiqʷǝt *rub st. off, wipe it,* Nk ʔekʷn *wipe* Ld ʔiqʷ *wipe, mop* Tw ʔiqʷíd *sweep it!* Ch ʔaqʷ-*brush, clean* ~ Li ʔiqʷ *get bruised slightly (not drawing blood),* ʔíqʷcamʼ *shave o.s.* [ʔíqʼinʼ *scrape a hide*] Th ʔíqʷes *scrape, shave,* [ʔiqʼm *scrape a hide*] Sh ʔiqʷm *to fish w. a dragnet,* ʔiqʷcnm *shave,* tʔiqʷlʼqʷm *extract sap of jackpine,* [ʔiqʼm *scrape a hide*] Cb ʔaqʷsn *scrape, shave* [Sp ʔaqʼn *scrape*]. – The meanings *grind, rub, polish, file, whet, scrape, scratch, shave, sweep* are distributed irregularly over the roots *yaqʼ, *yǝʕ, *ʔi/aqʷ and *ʔi/ax̌ʷ, locally also *ʔiqʼ (Li Th Sh *scrape a hide,* see above), *ʔix̌ (Se Sq Th *scratch,* see under *yǝʕ).

*ʔuqʷay *(younger) sibling, cousin.* Be suux̌i *younger sibling,* susqʷi(i) *id.,* ʔuux̌i *display jealousy towards one's younger sibling* Sq ʔǝqʷiʔtl *siblings and cousins,* sʔáyʔaqʷa *group of younger siblings* Cw sʔaʔlǝqʷa (pl. of *s-ʔaqʷaʔ) *younger siblings and cousins* Nk súqʷay(ʔ) *younger sibling* Sm šxʷʔaqʷǝʔ *brother* (others: šxʷáqʷaʔ *any relative),* ʔǝqʷǝ́/íyʼtlʼ *be related together* Sn šxʷʔaqʷǝʔ *sibling,* ʔǝqʷeʔtlʼ *siblings* Sg šxʷáʔqʷaʔ *sibling* Cl sʔuqʷǝʔ *id.* Ld súqʷaʔ *younger sibling/cousin, child of parent's younger sibling* Tw súqʷay *younger sibling of same sex* [Ti húkʷi *baby*] ~ Li súqʷazʼ/sǝ́sqʷǝzʼ *younger sibling,* súqʷi *id. (hypocoristic),* sqʷǝzǝ́zwʼǝs *siblings (collectively)* Th sqʷóqʷzeʔ *younger sibling or cousin* Sh ʔuqʷy *sibling of same sex,* also *fellow Indian,* ʔǝqʷyews *siblings and cousins of same sex (collectively).* – Cf. NWAK wʼa(ʔ)qʷa-, wʼqʷ-*sibling of opposite sex* (LR no. 1915).

*ʔus, *ʔisuʔ *to dive.* Ld ʔus Tw ʔusíl Ch ʔisuʔ- Ti cʔúsil
~ [Li ʔustək *catch fish w. dipnet* Th nˤʷus *sink,* ʔiswet *loon*]
Sh ʔust, [wʔus; ʔísut/ʔíswət *loon*] Cb nʔuslx; [ʔswat *loon* Cv
ʔaʔsíw't *id.*] Ka ʔust Sp nʔust; [w'suʔt/w'siw't *loon*] Cr ʔuslš.

*ʔus(-aʔ) *egg; berry.* Cx ʔúsaʔ *blueberry sp.* Se ʔúsa
valley blueberry Sq ʔuʔús *eggs,* ʔúsaʔ *large blueberry* Ld
ʔaʔús *egg* (Snyder) Tw ʔaʔús *ling cod eggs* ~ Li ʔúsaʔ
huckleberry, ʔúʔsa *egg* Th -useʔ *fruit,* ʔeʔúseʔ *egg* Sh ʔúʔse
id. Cb Cv ʔaʔúsaʔ *id.* Ka Sp ʔuʔúseʔ *id.* Cr ʔúseʔ *id.* – Cf. PIS
*-us-aʔ.

*ʔask'ay' *throat, breath, (voice, song).* Ne "asčáe:"
breath (Haeberlin 345), see further PS *-ask'ay'.

*ʔəsal(i/a) *two.* Cx Sl sáʔa Cw yəseʔlə Ms iséʔlə Ck
ise:lə Nk séli Sm čə́sa/e/əʔ Sn Sg Cl čəsəʔ Ld sáliʔ Tw ʔəsáli
Ch sáli ~ Th séye Sh səséle Cb nʔassál'l' Cv ʔasíl Ka Sp ʔesél
Cr ʔésel. – See comments under *x̌əc.

*ʔit *to sleep.* Se Sq ʔítut Cw Ms ʔitət Ck ʔi:tət Nk ʔítut
Sm ʔit(ə)t; ʔətatn̩' *sleepy* Sn Sg ʔitət *go to bed* (Sg *sleep*),
ʔətatn̩ *sleepy* Cl ʔitt; ʔaʔtútn̩ *be sleepy* Ld ʔítut [Ch -it'-] ~ Sh
ʔitx, ʔətix Cb Cv ʔitx Ka Sp Cr ʔitš.

*ʔaw I *to follow.* Be ʔawt Cx ʔáʔawt *the last* Se
sʔawtšn *part of leg directly above heel* Sq ʔawʔt *be behind,
after* [Cw ʔewə *come here*] Ld sʔəgʷač *back of head* Tw ʔáwat
behind, ʔáwad/ʔáwatəb *be last* Ti ʔaʔgʷə́tet *after a while,
soon, next,* dəʔagʷət- *follow, be behind, be the last* ~ Li ʔaw't
get/come behind, come late(r) Th weʔít (inv.) *later, last,*
weʔwít *behind, following* Sh ʔəwit *the last, behind* Cb lsʔawt
behind, ʔaw'tápn *to follow* Cv sʔiwt *behind,* ʔawtpátq *follow,*
ʔawqn(n)wíxʷ *follow one another* Ka eʔutépn *id.* Sp ʔew'étn
sneak up on, [ʔew'tús *enemy*] Cr igʷ *set out for,* [ew(-t)
oppose].

*ʔaw II see *ʔaˤʷ.

*ʔawkʷ see *yəw'kʷ.

*ʔaxʷ *(land-, rock-, snow)slide.* [Cx Sl ʔaxʷ *to snow*] Sq sʔaxʷ [Ch ʔəx̣ʷá- *bank caves in*] ~ Li ʔaxʷ *to slide (rocks, snow),* sʔáxʷa *a slide* Th ʔexʷt *avalanche* Sh sʔexʷt *rock- or snowslide.* – Cf. ***yəxʷ.**

*ʔuxʷ *to freeze.* Sq sʔuxʷn *ice,* ʔuxʷnántm *be frozen* ~ Li ʔuxʷn *frozen, frost-bitten* Th ʔúxʷes *freeze st.,* ʔuxʷt *frozen* Sh ʔuxʷkst *hand is frozen,* ʔuxʷxn' *foot id.* Sp ʔuxʷn *freeze,* ʔuxʷt *frozen.*

*ʔi/axʷəl *some, different.* Be ʔaxʷɫ *some* Ch ʔuxʷ-*different,* ʔuxʷɫ *id., stranger,* ʔuxʷtq *foreigners, different (language)* ~ Li sʔixʷɫ *other, different,* [nʔixʷxʷəz' *make a mistake*] Th sʔixʷɫ *some,* ƛ'íxʷeɫ *different, other, strange* Sh sʔiʔɫxʷ (inv.) *different, several,* t'íxʷət *different, strange* Cv t'ixʷlm *different* Cr ʔixʷəl *id.* – The forms with initial *t' have parallels in ***t'əyqʷ** (see ***həyqʷ**) and in the Sq item under ***yəxʷ.**

*s-ʔixʷal *baby, child.* Be ʔixʷuɫ *mother of illegitimate child,* sʔixʷuɫɫ *illegitimate child* Cx təgixʷaɫ *children, descendants* (see ***taw** II), Se táwixʷal *id.* (id.) Sq sʔixʷəɫ *baby* Nk sʔíxʷuɫ *id.* ~ Li sʔíxʷaɫ *id.* Sh (s)yxʷlscut *illegitimate child,* yxʷelt *bear young, be delivered* Cb sʔixʷl' *siblings (collectively)* [Sp snkʷsixʷxʷ *sibling, cousin, relative*] – Cf. QUI ʔixʷáɫkʷal *(to give) birth.*

*ʔax̌il see ***x̌il.**

*ʔi/ax̌ʷ I *to throw (away).* [Be ʔux̌ʷm *have a miscarriage*] Cx ʔáx̌ʷəyʔ *be left over* Nk ʔíx̌ʷin *throw* Ld ʔíx̌ʷ(i) *throw away* Ch ʔáx̌ʷa- *throw (away)* ~ Li sʔáx̌ʷil *junk, leavings, chips,* ʔax̌ʷəlx *to spawn* Th ʔax̌ʷms *sweep st. out of house, discard, throw away* Sh ʔex̌ʷmns *to throw,* ʔex̌ʷlx *to spawn* Cv sʔax̌ʷlx *salmon after spawning.*

*ʔi/ax̌ʷ II *to sweep.* Sq ʔíx̌ʷinʔ; ʔíx̌ʷtn *broom* Cw ʔíx̌ʷ; ʔax̌ʷtn *broom* Ck ʔíx̌ʷət; ʔəx̌ʷtl *broom* Sn ʔəx̌ʷisət *sweep floor* Cl ʔəx̌ʷict *sweep,* ʔəx̌ʷənukʷn *broom* Ld ʔíx̌ʷicut; səxʷʔíx̌ʷicut *broom* ~ Th ʔax̌ʷm Sh ʔix̌ʷm; ʔíx̌ʷleʔp *broom* Cb ʔáx̌ʷin *seine* Cv ʔax̌ʷmn *brush,* ʔax̌ʷlpm *sweep the floor.*

21

*ʔax̌ʷ-ayan *seine, fishing net.* Ch ʔáx̌ʷyanm *set out a large net* Cz ʔax̌ʷyn *fishing net* ~ Cb ʔáx̌ʷin *id., seine* Cv ʔax̌ʷyn *id.* – See PS *-ayan *net, (fish)trap;* the root may be *ʔi/ax̌ʷ II.

*ʔəx̌ʷuʔ *to cough.* Be ʔax̌x̌ut Se ʔə́x̌ʷut Sq ʔə́x̌ʷuʔn Ch x̌ʷó:ʔi- ~ Li ʔə́x̌ʷʔun; ʔəx̌ʷʔunám *have a cold* Th x̌ʷʕʷəp Sh x̌ʷəx̌ʷuʔ *a coughing cold* [Cb ʔə́ḥʷaʔ *have a cold, cough* Cv həhuʔ *catch cold,* sʕáhaʕ *id.* Sp ʔahóʔ *cough, have a cold* Cr ohiʔt (stress?) *have a cold*].

*ʔáx̌ʷaʔ *clam, mussel.* Sq sʔáx̌ʷaʔ *medium-sized clam, horseclam* Cw sʔáx̌ʷaʔ *butterclam* Ck sʔáx̌ʷə *id., fresh water clam/mussel* Sm sʔáx̌ʷaʔ *butterclam* Sn sʔax̌ʷəʔ *id.* Ld sʔáx̌ʷuʔ *butterclam, clam (generic)* Tw sʔáx̌ʷuʔ ~ Th sƛ̓əƛ̓l̓áx̌ʷeʔ *clam shell* Sh sət̓yéx̌ʷeʔ *id., clam* Cb sʔáx̌ʷuʔ. – Th initial ƛ̓l- also in ƛ̓lems *freshwater mussels/clams (including lake mussels of the Okanagan).*

*ʔay *to (ex)change, barter, pay; meet.* Be ʔayam *to trade,* ʔayawcut *to change, itr.* Cx ʔáǯamat *change, replace* Se ʔáyam *be changed,* ʔayʔíwa(n)t *change st. into st.,* ʔayə́m *exchange, trade,* ʔáyqʷust *go and meet* Sq nəx̌ʷʔayʔs *to exchange, trade in,* nəx̌ʷʔayʔn *change, replace* Cw ʔəyeʔqt *id.* Ck ʔiyéqt *exchange* [Sn ʔeʔaqtl̓ *exchange, trade*] Sg ʔáyeq *to trade* Cl ʔəčšt *change st. into st.,* ʔəčšíti *exchange, trade,* nəx̌ʷsʔáʔi *imitate, copy,* sʔaʔyístxʷ *lend* Ld ʔay̓ *change* Tw ʔáyaq̓ad *change it!,* ʔayʔúčəd *I paid it* Ch ʔáy- *(ex)change* Ti ʔaynə́x̌ʷ *go to meet sb.,* ʔayš *reciprocate* ~ Li ʔaz̓ *buy,* ʔaz̓n/ʔay̓n *pay sb.,* ʔay̓c *to answer,* ʔay̓cán̓ *id. sb.* Th ʔeycn *agree,* ʔazm *buy, trade,* ʔe/əzkst *take revenge* Sh ʔey *pay,* ʔeyns *id. sb.,* t̓eyns *meet,* ʔeycns *answer sb.* Cb kɬʔays *change st. into st.,* nʔays *pay* Cv k̓ɬʔiys *change st. into st.,* nʔiysnt *buy* Cr id *exchange, barter.*

*ʔuy I see *ʔul.

*ʔuy II see *yaw.

*ʔaʔyx̌, *c̓a/uʔyx̌ *crab, crayfish.* [Cx x̌íx̌əyiq̓ Se x̌iyq̓] Sq ʔayʔx̌ Cw ʔeyʔx̌ Ck ʔe:yx̌ Sm ʔečəx̌ Sn Sg ʔeʔčəx̌ Cl ʔaʔčx̌

Ch sc'al'x̌ Ti ʔayx̌ ~ Th ʔey'x̌ Sh c'éy'x̌e Cb c'uy'x̌ Cv c'áyx̌aʔ Ka c'oʔix̌éʔ Sp c'óy'x̌eʔ Cr ay'x̌. – See comment to *c'ik*aʔ.

*ʔiʕ see *yəʕ.

ʔaʕ, *ʔaw *to call, howl.* Se ʔut *to call* Sq ʔu(ʔ)t *call in, invite* Cw ʔaʔət *id.* Ch ʔə́w- *howl* ~ Th ʔaʕ*t *id.,* ʔumt *howl (of wolf)* Sh ʔeʕ*t/ʔawt *id.* Ka ʔáu *to name, call by name* Sp ʕawn *to name,* sʔaww *name.*

c

*cək *to adze, whittle, carve.* Cx sə̌čt *to adze* Se cə̌čt *to sharpen on the end (as wood)* [Ch cíči- *rub, scrub*] ~ Li cíkin' *pick at st.,* cikmn *a pick* Th ckəm *chop, hew* Sh ckem *hew, carve, whittle,* ckmékeʔ *adze,* xckékɫc'etn *id.* [Cb cəkn *hit by throwing*].

*cak *mother-in-law.* Tw cač ~ Sh ɫcəcek Cb cak *(id. of woman),* cákaʔ *older sister (of man)* Cv ɫcick Cr neɫcič *mother-in-law (of woman).*

*ck'aln *woodtick.* Ch ck'aln ~ [Th k'ec'éyn'] Sh ck'eln. – See *k'əc' II.

*ck'alp *rib.* Be ck'ɫp [Ch k'atp] ~ Cb ck'aɫp Cv ck'iɫp.

cək, *cək** I *to pull (out), drag.* Be ck*m, ck**m; cik*m *move* Sq cək*n, k**əcn (inv.) *pluck, pull out (feathers),* [ck**ácut *run*] Cw Ms Ck θk**ət Ld cík*(i) *move, jerk, tug* Ch cik*i- *twitch* Ti ck*ə́win *pull/haul st. out of the water* ~ Li cək*n; cək*ayúʔ *tug-of-war* Th cək*tes; [c'ək**tes *push, propel (w. canoe pole)*] Sh ck*um Cb cə́k*n Cv ck*am Ka Sp ck*um Cr cek*; [Nicodemus c'ek*c'ək*ín'm' *to practice running*]. – The bracketed Th word has a parallel in Sp c'k**um *poke, prod* Cr c'ek** *id.*

cuk *to be all there is (left).* Ld cuk*, cug*- *it is only* Tw cuq* *only* ~ Li cuk* *be finished, stop, quit* Th cuk* *be completed, finished, be all there is* Sh cuk*.

*cək** II, *c'ək** (the latter in SIS) *straight(en), stiff.* Be cak** *straight* [Cx sək' *id.*] Se cák**aw *straightened out* Cw

23

θəkʷ *straight* Ms sθəθikʷ *id.* Ck sθəθe:kʷ *id.* Sn sθakʷʷəɬ *straight,* θkʷʷət *stretch out (arm, rope)* Sg sqʷʷət (poss. kʷʷ) *stretch* Ld cəkʷ *straight, right* ~ Li kʷʷəcp (inv.) *stiff* Th kʷʷəct (inv.) *id.* Sh cəkʷckʷʷenm *get/do better, recover,* cəkʷukʷ *getting stiff* (the Sh forms may reflect *cʼəkʷ as well as *cəkʷʷ) Cb kʷʷacʼ (inv.) *recover, get well,* kʷʷacʼkʷʷácʼt *strong (person)* Cv kʷʷckʷʷact (inv.) *id., stiff,* ckʷʷap *stiff,* cʼukʷ *id.,* cʼkʷʷap *id.,* cʼakʷʷt *id.* Sp cʼukʷ *id.,* cʼkʷʷukʷ *get hard/straight* Cr cʼekʷ *be stiff (as bones).* – Cf. NWAK ʒakʷ- *straighten, extend* (LR no. 638).

cil *five* (w. suff. **-ak-is(t)** *hand*). Cx síyačis Sl θíyačəs Se cílačis Sq cíačis Ld c(ə)lác Ch cílačs Cz cilks- ~ Li cilkst Th ciykst Sh Cb Cv cilkst Ka Sp cil, cəlčst- Cr cil(čt). – For Be Tw Ti see CS **cʼixʷ**. A connection w. **kalax** *hand* is improbable; a possible cognate is Sh ciclm *new,* cf. the IE words for 'nine' and 'new' (Pokorny 1959:319).

ciɬn *fish, food.* [Se sčáliɬtn *fish* Sq sčáyiɬn *id.* (a "high" word) Cw Ms sceɬtn *id.* Ck sce:ɬtl *id.*] Ch ciɬn *fish, food* Ti (ʔ)ciɬn *to eat* ~ [Li cíɬnəqstn *deerlick*] Th cecíɬn *store food,* cʼək(e)ɬcíɬn *use up stored food, be out of food* Sh sciɬn *food* Sp scʔiɬn *a particular kind of food.* – Cf. **ʔiɬ(t)n**.

ci(m) *small; children.* Be caaci *a little bit,* caacti(i) *youth, youngster* Se cúciy *small,* cicicuyálšn *having small feet* Sq ʔəcim *small* ~ Li scmaɬʼt *children* Th cmíʔmeʔ(t) *small, pl.* Sh cəcícmeʔt *cut up in tiny pieces,* scmelt *children* Cb ccə́maʔt *small, pl.,* scəmʼalt *children* Cv ccámʼaʔt *small,* cmʼilt *child* Ka cim- *small, pl,* sccəmelʼt *children* Cr cɪcɪmʼ *be small, pl.,* cɪcemʼeʔ *pl. are small,* scɪcɪmíɬteɬʼt *children in relation to parents.*

cəpɬ *eyebrow, eyelash.* Sq cipɬtn *eyelashes* ~ Cb cəpɬayʼ *id.* Cv cpɬan/nʼ *id.* Sp cpɬenʼ *eyebrow* Fl *id.* – Cf. **ɬip**.

cip(wn) *pithouse, cellar,* **pwan** *cover (a cellar)* w. *dirt.* Be cipa *pithouse* [Se čipwn *cellar* (borr. fr. Li)] ~ Li cipwn/cípun *roothouse, larder* Sh xcipwn *root cellar* (suff. -ipwn). – There are forms lacking initial c(i)-: Be ʔipacut *store* *food*, ʔipu *to hide*, Th npwentn *storage pit* Sh pwénm *cover root cellar*, cpwen *cellar covered w. dirt*; the initial itself is reminiscent of that in PIS *citxʷ.

*cəq *to be in position, stand; tree;* ***cq-al-** *lie on the back.* Cx sə́qat *prop up* Se cəqát *erect (as pole)* Sq scəq *tree*, cqálačn *lie on the back* Cw θqet *tree* Ck θəqet *id.* Nk cqet *id.* Tw cəqə́nəxʷ *stick it in the ground!*, cə́qtəd *support post, tent post*, [c'əq'áp *fish spear, harpoon shaft*, c'ə́q'api *tree (esp. Douglas fir]* Ch cə́q- *be setting, vessel stands*, caqáɫ *spruce tree* ~ Li cə́qn *put down upright* [cəqcaq *tame*, caqcqət *fool hen, spruce grouse]* Th cəqtes *put bulky object*, ʔescáq *be put/placed/stuck in position*, [ca/eʔqstés *to tame*, caqcəqt *fool hen]*, nceqáɫ'qsm *lie on one's back* Sh cqem *put, place, set (upright)*, [cəqciq *tame*, cicqcəqt *fool hen]* Cb sncqikn' *(pack)basket*, cəqqcin *land on the shore*, kɫcaqm'ín'tn *saucer* Cv Ka Sp cq- *be laid/put in position* Ka cqal *lie down on the back* Cr caq *solid object stands upright.* – SIS has a √caqʷ with a similar meaning: Ka ʔesəncáqʷ *it is planted, stuck* Sp caqʷn *I put it there*, poss. in Cv ciqʷlx *tamarack* Sp caqʷlš *id.* Cr ceqʷlš *id.*

*ciq *to dig, stab.* Be ciix̌, ciiqnk *dig up roots* Cx síqit Sl θíqit Se cíqit Sq ciq *stab* [ciqʷ *dig*, Cw θəyqʷ *id.* Ck çiy(ə)qʷt *id.*, θq'ət *stab]* Cl ciqt *poke sb.* Ld ciq *poke, jab*, [ciqʷ *dig roots]* Tw ciqíd *stick st. w. the end of a pole*, dəxʷciqbəd *harpoon head*, [ʔascíqʷ *dug up*, c'íqaš *spearing fish fr. canoe* Ch cíqʷi- *dig]* Ti ciqey'ísn *stir around in the fire* ~ Li cíqin' *stab* Th Sh Cb Ka ciqm *dig* Sp ciqn *id.* Cr ciq *id.*

*cəq' see *c'əq'.

*cəqʷ/*qʷəc *to begin, set out.* Be cqʷ *begin, start on st.* ~ Li qʷəcac *set out, leave*, qʷə́cəc *have started on st., be busy with*, qʷəcn *shake st.*, qʷəcpulm'əxʷ *earthquake* Th qʷəctes *activate, operate, make move*, qʷəctem *have convulsions* Sh qʷəcec *set out, depart, begin*, ʔstqʷic *stir, make movements*, qʷəcpul'əxʷ *earthquake.*

*ci/aqʷ see *cay.

*cəw, *cu(-t, -ł, -n) *to point, show, display behavior; say, order, think, intend, try, want.* Be cut *say, think* Se cut *say* Sq cut *say, think, go through motions, try,* cun *tell, order* Cw θət *say* Nk cúʔut *he answered/decided,* cúʔunm *he got called* Tw cutdəxʷ *she said* Ch cún- *tell, say, order,* cút *say, wonder, think, decide* Cz co:- *plan, think, have an idea* ~ Li scə́cəwʼ *design,* cut *say, think,* cúłunʼ *point at,* Th scuw *work, st. done, made,* cu(we)tés *make st.,* céwʼes *discuss,* scumín *equipment,* cut *say st.,* cuns *say, tell,* scutə́n *custom,* cuł *point out,* cułmn *index finger* Sh xcwum *hint, suggest,* cuwət *behavior,* cut *want, intend, be going to, say,* cuns *tell, order, invite, want, expect, think,* tkcułmns *point at,* cúcłkeʔ *seven* Cb cunn *say,* cunməʔn *teach (how to do)* Cv cawt *one's (way of) doing,* cut *say, tell,* cun *id.,* cułt *id.* Ka Sp cut *say, behave* Ka cun *say, tell* Cr cegʷ *behave, have character,* cun *point, show.*

*caw see ***caʕʷ**.

*cíx-ups *fisher (zool.).* Be cipsx (inv.) ~ Cr cišps. – For the suffix cf. Cv crʼtups *fisher* with a different root and the suffix -ups *tail.*

*caxʷ *be glad, happy, enjoy.* [Se cxʷinám *be like,* scəxʷín *likeness*] Sq cáʔcaxʷ *be glad, happy* Ld caxʷ *type of mind power* ~ Li caxʷ, cáʔcaxʷ Th ceʔcʼéxʷ Sh cʼexʷ; cəxʷílʼe *enjoy one's children* Cv cxʷiltm *id.* [Cr cexʷ *pet, caress*]. – For Se cf. the semantics of Engl. *like.*

*cix̌ʷ *waterfall, mountain stream.* [Be cax̌ʷm *to wade*] Sq scəx̌ʷm *waterfall* ~ Th ncəx̌ʷcəx̌ʷpáqs *have nose continually running* Sh kʷəłcəx̌ʷcíx̌ʷ *waterfall* Cr hın-céx̌ut *stream, river* (Nicodemus has cʼ).

*cay *blood,* ***ciʕʷ** *to bleed,* ***ci/aqʷ** *to bleed, red.* Sq scáciʔn *blood* (√cay), [cəcix̌ʷ *girl's puberty*], caqʷ *bleed* Cw Ms sθéθiyn *blood* Ck sšéθiyəl *id.* Sm s/θeščn *blood,* nəsə́qʷ *bright red* Sn θəyəŋ/θəčəŋ *bleed,* θescn (<*θeθyn) *blood* Sg sescn *id.* Cl ʔənəcə́qʷ *red* Ch cáqʷ- *to paint* Cz scáqʷusm *red face powder* ~ Li cíʔiʕʷ *bleed,* cəqʷciqʷ *red,* cəqʷcaqʷ reddish, cqʷas *flesh of fish is still pink (before spawning)* Th cʔiʕʷ *bleed*, ʔescíʕʷ *already bleeding*, ʔescíqʷ *red*, ʔescáqʷ *red, reddish*, céqʷes *paint red*, cʔaqʷ *turn brown* Sh cʔiʕʷ *bleed*, cʕʷeqs *nosebleed*, ciqʷ *red*, ciqʷsm *paint one's face* Cb cíqʷ- *copper-colored* [Sp ncx̌ʷum *blood is gathered there, bloodclot*] Cr ceqʷ *be bright pink*.

*caʕʷ, *caw *to reach for, stick out; fringe, stripe.* Sq cáx̌ʷam *stick out hand, reach out* Ch cax̌ʷá- *stick out (as fr. window)* ~ Li scuʕʷ *stripe* Th céwix *reach for*, ʔescóʕʷ *striped* Sh cewkstm *reach*, cʕʷum *make a stripe*, cʕʷłniw't *spring salmon* Cb scəʕʷʕʷakst *fingers* Cv kcwcwʕax̌n *fringe on sleeve* [scaʕʕikst *finger*, scaʕʕxən *toe*] Ka esənco:co:łníʔut *he has fringes on both sides* Cr caʕʷ *fringe*.

*ciʕʷ see ***cay**.

c'

*c'iʔ *loot from raid, game bagged.* Sq sc'iʔ *loot from raid* Cw Ms ç'iʔ *id.* Ck ç'i *id.* Tw √c'i *game* in bipíwc'i *he's chasing a seal* (piw- *follow, chase*), dəxʷpíwʔc'i *duck hunter* ~ Li Sh c'iʔ *deer, meat* Cv sc'ʔikst *hind quarter, limb* Ka c'uʔúlixʷ *deer* Sp c'ʔúlixʷ *whitetail id.* Cr c'iʔ *deer.* – The root may be present in the PS suffixes ***-ał-c'aʔ** *game, meat*, ***-ic'aʔ** *hide* (the main products of hunting) and in ***tíxʷ-c'i** *kill game.*

*s-c'ik'/k *fir or pine cone, acorn, nut.* Sq c'ičn *hazelnut*, [sč'íč'inu *fir cone*] Cw Ms sç'icm *hazelnut* Ck sç'i:cm *id.*, sc'ək' *pinecone* (borr.) ~ Li sc'ək' *id.* Th sc'ək' *edible seeds, nuts of conifer*, sc'ək'qínkeʔ *pinecone*, [cəkcəklóle *cedar cones*] Sh scik' *edible acorn*, scək'qin' *fir or pinecone*, ʔəscek' *squirrel* Cb sc'c'ək'l' *cone (of most trees)* Cv sc'c'ák'aʔ *fir or pine cone*, ʔaʔísck' *pine squirrel* Ka sčc'ic'eʔ/scčíc'eʔ/scč'íc'eʔ *pinecone*, ʔiscč *squirrel* Sp cč'eyłp *white pine*, ʔisc'č/ʔistč *pine nut, tree squirrel.*

*c'ikʷ (NCS ***c'iwq'**) *elderberry.* Cx c'iwq' Se sc'iwq' *red id..* Sq sc'iwʔq' Cw ç'iwəq' *red id.* Ck sç'íwəq' *id.* Sn

27

çʼiwəqʼ *id.* Ld cʼíkʷikʷ *blue id.* Tw cʼiqʷíqʷ *id.* Ch cʼkʷikʷ *id.* [Ti scʼúkʷanəsu *thimbleberry*] ~ Li Th cʼiwqʼ (borr. fr. CS) Sh cʼkʷikʷ *red elderberry* Cb Cv Sp cʼkʷikʷ *blue id.* Cr cʼekʷəkʷ *elderberry.* – See comment under **cʼikʷaʔ.*

*cʼikʷaʔ *left side.* [Cx cʼikʷuǯaʔ *left hand(ed)* Sl çʼíkʷuʔǯa] Se cʼikʷá *left handed* Cw Ms sçʼíkʷa Ck çʼíkʷa Sm cʼəkʷəʔiwʼs/sçʼəkʷəʔiwʼs *left arm and hand* Sn çʼəkʷəʔiwʼs Sg scʼkʷaʔíʔws Tw cʼíkʷači *left hand,* cʼíkʷašəd *left leg,* cʼikʷášəd *left foot* [Ch cʼiwqʼ- Ti yəkʷ-] ~ Li ncʼíkʷʔaq *left leg,* ncʼəkʷʔákaʔ *left hand* Th scʼəkʷʔekst *id.* Sh s(tk)cʼəkʷeʔékeʔ *left side* Cb kcʼíkʷaʔ Cv skcʼíkʷaʔ Cr cʼíkʷeʔ. – The deviating Ch form has a parallel in **cʼikʷ* (NCS **cʼiwqʼ*). The Ti form suggests that cʼ- (< cʔ) may be an old prefix; for a parallel see **ʔaʔyx̌.*

*cʼakʷ *light, bright.* Cx cʼukʷ *day(light)* Sl çʼukʷ *id.* Se scʼukʷ *sky, weather, a (nice, etc.) day* Cw çʼekʷət *shine a light on* Tw cʼakʷáb *flare and shadow-screen hunting* ~ Li scʼakʷ *light, illumination* Th scʼekʷ *torch, lamp, light,* cʼekʷm *pit-lamping* Sh cʼekʷ *bright* (ESh *to bloom*), cəkʷcekʷt *bright,* cəkʷckʷesqʼt *clear day* ESh scʼeʔkʷ *flower* Cb cʼaʔákʷm *to bloom,* scʼaʔákʷ *flower(s)* Cv cʼikʷm *make light,* cʼikʷsxn *lantern* Sp cʼekʷ *shine,* cʼʔekʷ *start to bloom,* cʼekʷsšnʼ *lamp,* sncʼʔekʷ *flower.*

*cʼkʷəy see **cʼyaqʷ.*

*cʼəl *to stand; (a stand of) trees, rushes..* Sn sçʼəlʼəl *round cattail* Cl cʼeʔyəŋ *get up on st.* Tw ʔascʼəl *stuck in the ground (post, stick)* Ch cʼəlápi- *stand up* ~ Li scʼalqʷ *stick used in lahal game,* cʼiʔcʼlʼ *picket fence* Th cʼi(ye)tés *set stakes for fish weir,* cʼəlxʷiyx *to squat,* cʼəlxʷám *to erect (squat object)* Sh scʼil̓/scʼel *standing up,* sclcʼi/el *trees,* cʼlem *to plant stalks,* cʼlilx *get up,* cʼlewt *to stand,* cʼlut *rushes,* cʼlxʷum *raise a structure (eg. tent),* scʼluxʷ *standing* Cb scʼəlut *standing, sg.,* ʔascʼálcʼl *trees,* cʼəlix *stop, stand up, sg.,* ncʼəlʼxwikəntn *saddle* Cv cʼlam *stand st. upright,* cʼlcʼal *timber, trees,* kcʼlmint *go stand by sb. (after running up),* Sp c'il- *stand, stick out, pl.,* hesc'íl *trees; they stick out,* c'lc'il *trees,* sc'lalq^w *stick game* Cr c'al *stand, sg.,* c'el *id.*

*c'al (red.) *cricket, grasshopper.* Ch c'alásc'aləs *a small cricket* ~ Sh cilc'l *cricket* Cb c'an'c'an' *grasshopper* Cr c'án'c'n' *id.* – Note Ch and NIS l vs. SIS n; for another SCS - NIS parallel see ***q^watix̌-a?**.

*c'i/al *shade, shadow; outline, similar; shelter.* Be c'ł *to shelter, cover, shade off* Cx c'áǯit *shade, shady* (borr. fr. an older y-dialect, as are the Se forms) Se c'ay *there is no sun,* sc'ayít *shade(d),* c'ac'iymín *shadow* Sq c'ay? *be sheltered (fr. wind, sun, rain),* c'ay?tn *umbrella,* ?əsc'ác'i *be in the shade,* c'ay?áncut *get into the shade* Ld c'álbid *shadow,* c'álbiȝ *reflection,* c'alič̌təd *(stress?) umbrella* Tw ?asc'ál *shade, shady (place)* Ti "scłó:uš" *shadow* (Haeberlin) ~ Li c'íla *be like,* c'əln'akstm *shade eyes w. hand* Th c'íye *same, similar,* Sh c'ilm *id.,* cətc'íte *the same,* cətc'itm *to measure,* cətc'ítke? *pattern* Cb ?asc'al'l' *shade,* sc'əl'l' *id.,* c'ál'c'al't *shady,* sc'əl'c'l'/sc'ál'c'al' *shadow* Cv sc'il' *shade* Cr c'il' *be outline, shadow,* sc'él'c'el't *shadow, contour,* [scíl'eł *substitute*].

*c'u/al *to hurt, smart; cold; tart, bitter, sour, salty.* Sq c'útum *be cold,* c'łuł *cold* Cw sç'eç'ət *cool, cooling off (outside)* Ck ç'eł *cool down (of person),* ç'ełm *be chilled,* [ç'ó:lç'iy *Oregon grape*] Sm c'ałŋ/ç'ałŋ *cold (weather)* Sn ç'a?łŋ *feel cold* Sg c'a?łŋ *id.,* ç'anŋ *cold (as water)* Ld c'ud *cold* Tw ?asc'úd *feel cold* ~ Li c'átan' *cool st. off,* c'útum' *cold (body),* c'əl'c'úl' *sour, bitter,* [c'úl'c'l' *Oregon grape*], Th c'əłt *cold (weather),* c'étes *to cool, chill,* c'?al *to sting, tingle,* c'ol't *tart, sour,* [c'ol'se? *Oregon grape berry*] Sh c'ełt *cold,* c'?al *hurt, throb,* c'alt *bitter, sour, salty,* [sc'al's *Oregon grape berry*] Cb c'əłt *cold,* c'ałn *to cool (solids),* c'ər *salty, sour,* c'art *salt* Cv c'ałt *cold weather,* nc'a?r- *ache (eg.* nc'a?rína? *ear ache),* c'ar *salt,* nc'ritk^w *salt water,* [sc'irws *golden currant,* sc'ars/sc'c'ris *Oregon grape berries*], c'rc'ir'kstmnt *tease* Ka c'alt *cold,* c'ol *salt, sour* Sp c'er(ə)t *cold,* c'?eł *cool off,* c'ur *salty, sour* Cr c'ar *feel cold to the touch, be ill, hurt, ache,* c'or *sour.* – The Sn Ld and Tw forms show the

occasional shift l > n. For the berry names see comment under
*c'a̱l(s).

c'a̱l(s) *shiny, oily, wet.* Sq c'als *be shiny*, c'lsan *shine
up* Cw c̣'al?x̌ʷm? *shiny* Ck c'elc'm (borr.) *id.* [Ld c'əlc'əlkáyus
chickadee] Ch c'ələ́m *kingfisher*, [c'alíčn *swallow, sparrow*] ~
Li c'ə̱ls *kingfisher* Th c'lə̱ṣ *kingfisher* Sh c'lsam *to oil*, [sc'al's
Oregon grape], c'las *kingfisher*, tkc'last *soaking wet* Cv
[sc'írws *golden currant*, sc'ars/sc'ris *Oregon grape berries*] Ka
c'alís *kingfisher* Sp c'ris *id.* Cr c'álus *id.* – The Oregon grape
could be named after its shiny leaves or its tart flavor (see
under *c'u̱/a̱l*); the original form may have been *s-c'a̱ls, with
secondary replacement of final s by the PIS suffix *-us-a?
berry, leaving the meaning *tart* for the root. For the semantics
oily - wet cf. *nu̱/a̱s.

c'əm *sharp pointed.* Be c'm *forefinger* Cx
c'ə́malə/c'əmálə *id.* [Se sc'úmals *whetstone*] Sq c'm?al?
arrow, [c'm?il *thin, flat*] Cw c̣'əme:n(?) *arrow* Sm c'/c̣'əm'e:n'
id. Sn c̣'m'e:n *id.*, c̣'əm'əqən *scissors*, c̣'əṇsistəṇ *get pinched by
crab* Tw ?asc'əm?áxʷaqs *sharp-nose*, ?asc'əmáxʷqəd *pointed
head* ~ Li c'ə́m'c'm'əqs *sharp (point)*, c'əm'qsán' *sharpen a
point* Th ?es(c'əm)c'máqs *sharp (pointed)* Sh cmc'meqs *id.*,
c'meqsns *give st. a sharp point* Cv c'mc'mípa?ɬxn
sharp-heeled shoes, [c'mtus *sturgeon*] Sp čc'em'épl'e? *pear* Cr
c'am *be nearly pointed (as football or lemon).* – Cf. NWAK
c'm- *index finger, nails, point, poke* (LR no. 724), QUI c'a?b
sharp. See also PIS *c'mixʷ.

c'u̱/a̱m *to suck,* **s-c'u̱/a̱m** *bone.* Be c'um *to kiss* Cx
c'əmtn *woman's breast* Cw Ms sc̣'am? *bone* Ck sc̣'a:m *id.* Nk
sc'úmiqʷ *skull* Sm sc'/c̣'am/m' *bone* Sn sc̣'am? *id.* Sg sc'am?
id. Cl sc'um? *id.*, sc'a?méqʷ *skull* Ld c'ú(?)bid *fishbone* Ch
c'amí- *suckle* Ti c'áw'il *bone*, sc'əwəwágʷəs *backbone, spine
(of elk or person)*, c'awúh *fish spine (removed fr. fish)*, sc'úwa
CV *breast (female)*, sc'əwə?ə́win *to nurse (a baby)* ~ Li sc'am'
fishbone, nc'úm'qsan' *to kiss*, [c'am'án *to lick*] Th sc'em'
(small) bone (of human or animal), fishbone, c'úm'es *suck*,
[c'əm'tes *eat soapberry confection*] Sh c'mntes/c'emns *suck a*

bone, bite and suck blood (mosquito), sc'em *fishbone*, c'um'qsn *to kiss* Cb c'əm'm *suck*, sc'ạm' *bone*, Ok xʷaʔɫc'ám' *geogr. Sixmile Creek*, lit. *many bones* Cv c'mc'um'nt *suck*, sc'im *bone* Ka Sp sc'om' *id*. Cr sc'am' *bone*, c'om' *suck on solid object*. – Cf. NWAK ʒam'- *(suck at the) breast* (LR no. 636). The bracketed Li form has parallels with i in CS words for *lick*: Cx c'ímit Se c'imít Sq c'im?ín? Ld c'íbid; this Ld word also means *dip into*, cf. Sq c'im? *eat grease, dip dried salmon in oil*. Cf. further *c'uqʷ.

*c'əmx̌ *disappear, wear away*. Cx Se c'əmx̌ ~ Li c'əmx̌ *worn out* Th c'əmx̌atés *wear out* Sh c'mex̌ *id., spoil*. – Cf. KWA c'm'a *dissolve, wear away* (LR no. 731).

*s-c'nay' *bullhead*. Sq (s)c'nay? ~ Li sc'anáz' Th sc'enéc' Sh sc'néy'e *fish w. head like frog*.

*s-c'ipəq *skunk*. Cw Ms spəpəç'in (inv.; Hukari Cw pəpəç'in?) Ck sç'ə́pəq Nk "seːts.pak" CV Sm pəpəc'in Sn pəpəç'iŋ ~ Sh sc'ipəq.

*c'apaʔx̌ *cedar root*. Be c'ap'ax̌ *bough tips of red or yellow cedar* Ld c'apx̌ *cedar root* Ok c'ápaʔx̌ *western red cedar (presumably a Cb word for cedar root)* Cb c'ápaʔ *cedar root*.

*c'ip' *to squeeze (shut), pinch*. Cx c'ə́yp'at *to pinch*, c'ip'ənxʷ *close one's eyes* Se c'ip'níxʷ *id*., p'əc'at (inv.) *pin together*, c'lp'at *to pinch* Sq c'íp'usm *close one's eyes* Cw ç'ə́p'nəxʷ *id*. Ck ç'ə́p'ləxʷ *id*. Ld c'íp'lil *id*. Tw ?asc'íp' *it's between (as fish in forked roasting stick)*, c'ip'áyasəb *to wink* ~ Li nc'ip'az'úsm *close eyes* Th c'ip'etés *pinch*, nc'ip'sm *blink, shut eyes* Sh xcəpcip'sm *shut eyes tightly* Cb c'ip'n *pinch*, nạc'íp'sn *wink*, nạc'íp'c'ip'sm *shut eyes* Cv c'ip'm *pinch*, nc'ip'c'p's *shut eyes* (Ok *hold eyes shut tight*), nc'ʕap'sm *wink* [Ka c'ip *pinch*, cap *blink w. the eyes*] Sp c'ip'n *pinch*, nc'ip'sn *blink, wink* Cr c'ip' *pinch fine*, [cap' *girls "snap" eyes to show contempt*]. – The item may be an inversion of *p'ic' treated under *p'əy.

31

*c'əq', *cəq' *to hit,* *c'/cəq'-min *throw away, discard.* [Be cq' *grab, pull, tear at st.*] Cx Se c'əq't *throw at, hit* Sl ç'əq'm *throw overhand, pitch* Sq c'aq' *get hit,* c'áq'an *hit* [Cl c'x̌ṇin *secondhand* Ld c'q'á(hə)b *pole a canoe* Ch c'áq'p- *pole up a river, punt*] Ti cq'əwin- *throw (away), discard* ~ Li c'əq'n *to pound,* c'q'álqʷmin *bump into (a tree),* c'aq'n *hit w. st. thrown* Th c'q'əm *throw and hit st.,* c'aq't *be hit, struck,* c'əq'min *hammer,* c'əq'mins *throw st. (in a particular direction)* Sh cq'em *to throw, hit,* cəq'méke? *pounding rock, arrow of Thunderbird,* cq'elnm *to shoot,* cəq'mins *throw away, discard* Cb c'q'aḷn *to shoot, bullet* Cv cq'am *hit by throwing,* cq'minm *throw (a rock),* c'q'c'q'am' *thunderstorm* Ka ʔescq'ém *be hit by lightning,* cq'am *to throw* Sp c'q'min *id.,* c'íq'- *poke/jab at* [Cr c'aq' *be bunched, clumped,* č̌čmin *throw (sg. obj.)*].

*c'uqʷ *to suck,* *c'qʷu?-(c-)tn *pipe.* Cx c'úqʷut *nibble on st.* [vs. Cx Sl Se t'úqʷut *suck,* Cx also t'úmut] Sq c'úqʷun?, snc'qʷu?ctn Cw Ms ç'aqʷət Ck ç'a:qʷət Sn ç'aqʷət Sg c'akʷət (poss. qʷ) [Cl c'uqʷt] Ld c'úqʷ/kʷud Ch c'úqʷi- ~ Li nc'(a)qʷú?ctn *pipe* Th nc'a?qʷú?ectn, nc'ə/aqʷu?éctn *id.* Sh c'qʷu?tn *id.* – Cf. *c'u/am.

*c'qʷay see *c'yaqʷ.

*c'əs *to rattle, hit,* IS *s-c'əs-l-us-a? *hail.* [Be c's *loud, noisy* Cx c'əc'əw? *hail* Se c'əl'ušn *id.*] Sn ç'əs *hit (by throwing)* Cl c'sət *punch,* [c'siṇəɬ *ring a bell*] Ld c'əsəd *to peck, nail st.* Ch c'əsqʷəl'ɬ *woodpecker sp.* ~ Li c'əs *to bump* Th c'əṣtes/c'ə́ṣes *shake a rattle* Sh scəsc'əslól'se *hail (small stones)* Cb ṣc'ə̣ṣlusạ? *hail* Cv sc'c'slusnt/sc'c'ḷusnt *id.* Sp c'slúse? *id.* Cr sšc'əslúse? *id.* – The Se word must be a loan fr. IS (because of š), though for Li and Th no suffixed forms are known; for the loss of s in the Cx Se roots cf. the Cv forms. The Ld word *to nail* has an alternative c'ísid, and must be related to Sq c'ísin? *nail up,* which in turn is hard to separate from Sq c'istn *horn, antler; nail*; the latter shows an irregular correspondence with Cw Ms c'əystn Ck c'əystl *horn* (Sq c' č̌ = Hl ç' c'), cf. also Sm c'istn Sn sç'istn *antler,* ç'isət *to nail* Cl sc'istn *antler,* c'isn

nail, c̓ist *to nail;* the Hl initial corresponds to that of Cr č̓i?
antler, horn (Nicodemus č̓i?mn *id.*).

*c̓əw̓ *to cut off (esp. limb of animal).* Ch c̓əwə́č̓- Cz
c̓awə́k̓- (<*c̓əwə́k̓-) ~ Li sc̓uw̓q *thigh (human or animal)* Th
sc̓u?xə́n *upper leg, hind leg of animal,* c̓íw̓es *to butcher,*
?esc̓íw̓ *cut up in pieces* Sh sc̓wxen *thigh, hindquarter,* c̓iwm
cut meat Cb sc̓u?xn *leg, foot,* [c̓iqʷn *skin an animal*] Cv
sc̓u?xán *leg, foot* Ka Sp sc̓u?šín *foot* Cr sc̓u?šn *id. (of
slaughtered animal).*

*c̓aw see ***c̓aˤʷ.**

*c̓aw̓ *to pull out.* Sq c̓u? *come out (being pulled),*
c̓u?n *pull out* Cw Ck ç̓at *id. (nail)* ~ [Th c̓aqes *pluck, pull
out (plant, hair)*] Cv kc̓wqntim Cr c̓aw̓q *pull out solid object
(as nail out of board).*

*c̓wan *salmon sp.* [Cw θe?wn *coho/silver salmon*] Ld
(s)c̓əwad(xʷ)/sc̓uwád *sockeye salmon* [Ch c̓awł *spring
salmon*] ~ Li c̓wan *dried fish (esp. salmon),* sc̓wánamx
Okanagan Indian Th sc̓(u)wén *dried salmon,*
c̓(u)wené/áy̓tmx *Sasquatch* Sh scəc̓wen̓mx *Okanagan
people,* sc̓wney̓tmx *giant* Cb sc̓uw̓án̓ *sockeye or blueback
salmon,* sc̓wanáytəxʷ *Stick Indian* Cv sc̓uwín *early sockeye
salmon,* sc̓wanáytm(x) *Sasquatch* Ka sc̓uweːné *giant* [Sp
ncocwáne?/ncucawána? *bullhead*] Cr sc̓uweːní *giant.*

*c̓ixʷ-c̓ixʷ *osprey, fishhawk.* Cx c̓íxʷc̓ixʷ Se
sc̓íxʷc̓ixʷ Sq c̓ixʷc̓əxʷ Cw Ck ç̓ə́xʷç̓əxʷ Nk ç̓úxʷç̓exʷ
buzzard (osprey?) Sn ç̓ixʷç̓əxʷ Cl c̓ixʷc̓xʷ Ld c̓íxʷc̓ixʷ Tw
c̓ixʷ Ch c̓íxʷ(c̓ixʷ) *buzzard, chickenhawk* ~ Li c̓íxʷc̓i/əxʷ Th
c̓íxʷc̓e/əxʷ Sh cixʷc̓əxʷ Cb c̓íxʷc̓ixʷ Cv Sp c̓ixʷc̓xʷ Cr
c̓ixʷc̓əxʷ. – Cf. KUT c̓oːc̓oː *fishhawk* and poss. NOO
c̓ixʷat-, c̓ixʷatin *eagle.*

*c̓ix̌ *prickly, stinging; burn, fry; cold.* Be c̓ix̌ *scald* Sq
c̓əx̌c̓ix̌ *stinging nettle* Cw Ms Ck c̓ə́x̌c̓əx̌ *id.* Nk ç̓əx̌ç̓ix̌ *id.*
Sm c̓/ç̓ə́x̌c̓/ç̓əx̌ *id.* Sn ç̓əx̌ç̓əx̌ *id.* Sg c̓ə́x̌c̓əx̌ *id.* Ld c̓íx̌id *to
fry* Ch c̓íx̌- *cold,* c̓íx̌i- *to fry,* [c̓íx̌ap- *horsetail root*] Ti c̓íx̌in
to fry ~ Li c̓ə́x̌małp *stinging nettle* Th c̓ix̌m *sear, cook,*

c'i?c'i?x̌íłp *dragonweed,* c'íc'x̌c'ax̌t *juniper* Sh cəx̌c'ix̌ *prickly,* cicx̌c'əx̌ *a small thistle,* sc'əx̌mem'łp *type of juniper* Cb nac'íx̌m *to fry,* [çəx̌çəx̌n'w'ál'l'/çx̌çx̌ənw'al'n' *nettles*] Ok nc'ix̌ *to fry* Cv nc'ax̌ *id.,* [c'i?c'i?x̌íłp *wormwood*] Sp c'ix̌ *stinging, slapping sound,* [c'ic'ix̌éy'łp *wormwood*] Cr c'ax̌ *to fry.* – See *c'ayx̌.

*c'ay *to resound.* Cx c'əyc'ay? *loud* Sl ç'aya?na *frapper l'oreille (bruit)* [Ch c'íqi- *scream*] Ti c'ay- *call sb.* ~ Sh c'eyt *echo,* c'eyqn *have a ringing in one's ears.*

*c'yaq^w/*c'q^way/*c'k^{'w}əy *sapsucker, flicker, woodpecker.* Be c'yaax̌^w Sq c'k^{'w}i?qs Ld c'əʒáq^w Tw c'áyaq^w Ch sc'əyaq^w, sc'əyəq^{'w}, sc'ayáq^w ~ Li c'ək^{'w}yəqs/c'ák^{'w}zəqs Th c'ek^{'w}áz'aqs Sh c'q^wéq^wyəqs.

*c'a/uyx̌ *fireweed.* Be c'ayx̌; c'ayx̌nk *fireweed root* ~ Sh c'yx̌nełp *fireweed* Cb c'i?c'ay'x̌áłp *unid. plant* Cv c'i?c'i?x̌íłp *wormwood* Sp c'ic'ix̌éy'łp *id.* – Cf. HEI OOW c'a'ix̌- *rope made of nettles* HAI c'ax̌m *fireweed* (LR no. 853); HAI c'ax̌m is not listed in Lincoln and Rath 1986, it formally resembles Sq c'áx̌i? Cw ç'ex̌əy' Ck ç'éx̌i? *white/straw grass.* See comment under *p'u/an.

*c'a?yx̌ see *?a?yx̌.

*c'əʕ-tin *poison, rattlesnake.* Cx Pt c'əx̌tn CV *poison* [Se cəq'tn *rattlesnake*] Sq c'əx̌tn *poison, rattlesnake* Cw ç'əx̌tn? *poison* Ck c'əx̌tl *rattlesnake* Sm c'əx̌tn *poison,* c'/ç'əx̌tən'it *to poison* Sn ç'əx̌tn *poison* Sg cəx^wtənitŋ (prob. c'əx̌...) *be poisoned* Tw c'áx̌təd *poison* ~ Li c'əʕtin *rattlesnake* Th sc'aʕtán' *id.* Sh c'ʕtin *id.* Cv c'a?tán (poss. c'aʕtán) *rattle of snake.* – Kinkade 1995:37 regards the meaning *rattlesnake* as the original one (idem Kuipers 1982:79), the CS words being borrowed from IS via Sq and Ck. But the suffix -ti/an is rare in animal names, and the word is found in the whole CeS area, mostly with the meaning *poison.* A possible cognate is Sq Ld c'əx̌ Cw Ck Sn ç'əx̌ *be gone, consumed (burnt, worn out, etc.).*

*c'aʕ^w/w *to wash, clean.* [Be c'x̌^w *white*] Cx c'əx̌^wt *to wash* Se c'əx̌^w *to clean* Sq c'əx̌^w *to wash* Cw Ms ç'x̌^wat *id.* Ck ç'x̌^waːt *id.* Sm c'ek^wt *wash st.*, sc'/ç'ey'c'/ç'əw' *clean (person, clothes, etc.)* Sn ç'ək^w *clean,* ç'ək^wəlk^watŋ *wash clothes* Sg ce?k^wət (prob. c') *wash* Cl c'ak^wt *id.* Ld c'a?k^w *id.*, c'ág^wad *id.* Ch c'ə́x̌^w *id., be clean, washed* ~ Li c'aw'án *wash,* c'aw'ləx *wash one's body,* c'aw'ál'us/[c'u?x̌^wál'us] *color runs,* [c'u?x̌^w- *get washed away, erode*], c'əʕ^ws *get soaked* Th c'éw'es *wash* Sh c'ewm *id.* Cb c'aw'n *id.* Cv c'iw'nt *id.* Ka c'é?u- Sp c'ew'n *id,* [caʕ^w/wlš *bathe*] Cr c'aw. – Cf. NWAK c'wx̌^w- *wash, launder* (LR no. 822) NOO c'o-, c'oya: *to wash.* The bracketed Li form may be borr. fr. CS.

*c'uʕ^w *sore* Be c'uc'q^w *having sores,* c'uux̌lx *develop sores* Tw c'ə́?wi *venereal disease* Ch sc'awé? *sore, a genital disease* ~ Th c'oʕ^wt *have a scab* Sh c'uʕ^wt *a sore.*

h

*hil see ***yə̣l.**

*hənəw/y *humpback salmon.* Se hə́nun Cw haːn? Ms həwn? Ck hə́wːləye Sm Sn hánən' Cl hənən Ld hədú(?) Tw hədíq^w Li háni? Th héni? Sh sheny' *unid. fish* Cb ḥánuw'.

*haw *to yawn.* Se hahí?əw [Ld ?ag^wáləb/?ág^wələb/ ?á?əg^wàləb] ~ Li nshaw Th shew Sh hehw Cb həw'háw'ən'ct Cv hawhíwi?st Sp hewhéwnt.

*haw'it *rat.* Sq həw?ít Cw Ms Ck hewt Sn hewt Sg hewət' (prob. t) Ti he/a?gít Si hag^wít CV ~ [Li háwint] Th hew't [Sh hewnt *flying squirrel*] Cv hiw't Sp hew't Cr šiw't. – Cr š results from the occasional confusion of x and h in IS.

*hay *to quiet down.* Se hayawát *console* Sq hay?án *pacify (a child)* ~ Th ?eshéysk'i? *pausing in singing during treatment (of shaman),* [x̌?azstés *quieten*] Sh h?ey *quiet down, become calm, give up.* – Cf. ***huy.**

*huy, *wi? (<***hwəy'**) *to cease, finish.* Cx Sl huy Se huy *finished, ready,* huyt *finish doing st.,* húyucin *finish* *eating*, wi(ʔ) *let's...* Sq huy; húyut *prepare, make* Cw hay Ck haːy; haːyθl *finish eating* Sm Sn hay Sg hayʔ Cl huy Sn hačθn *finish eating*, hačət *stop working on st.* Ld huyəxʷ *finish(ed) now, stop doing st.* Tw ʔashúy *it's done* ~ Th Sh wiʔ; wcin *finish eating* Cb ʔacwíʔ *done, finished*, wiʔstúnn *finish* Ka hoy *quit doing*, wiʔ *finish* Sp hoy *stop, finish*, wiy' *finish.* – Cf. *hay, NOO hawił-/hawiː *finish* and QUI hayós *stop, finish.*

*həyl see *yǝl.

*həyqʷ see *yəqʷ.

*s-(h)ayas *to play.* Sn ʔiʔ yəyasŋ *id.* Sg hiyásŋ *play (as children)*, siyásŋ *play games* ~ Li say'səz' Th séy'siʔ Sh séyse. – Sn Li Th have created reduplicative formations. The double reflex of *y' in the Li reduplication is striking; a parallel example is Li múzmit *pitiful.*

k

*kal *to go after, follow, chase.* Be kał- (also kas-) *gather, pursue, hunt:* kałkaẋ *hunt rabbit* Sq čay *follow, pursue* Cw celt *follow* Ck caːlt *id.* Sn čečəs *follow, chase* (2nd č < y < l), čiʔésəs *run after* Cl čiʔás *chase, pursue* Ld čal *chase, follow* ~ Li kaln *chase sb.* Th kéyes *follow*, nkelépm *id.* Sh kelns *chase away*, kəlepm *follow* Cv kilnt *chase, pursue* Cr sčil *game trailed, quarry.*

*kalk *to delouse.* [Cx c'ayč't Se c'alč't] Sq čaʔčn ~ Li kaľkn Sh kelkns.

*kalax *hand.* Cx čáyaš/s Sl čayəš Se čálaš Cw celəš Ms celəx Ck céléx Nk čéleš Sm Sn seləs Sg seːləs Cl cay(ə)s NLd čaləs SLd čaləš, Tw čálaš Ch čáliš- Ti čeléš *arm* ~ Th keyx Sh kelx Cb kalx Cv kilx Ka Sp čelš.

*kəlaxʷ *muskrat.* Be klaxʷ ~ Li (kə)kľéxʷeʔ Th kəkľéxʷeʔ Sh səkléxʷeʔ Ka čičiľéxʷ [Sp č'č'lexʷ] Cr čélexʷ. – Cf. KWA kɛlákʷ (Boas 1947:223).

36

*kəɬ *to be detached, come off/apart, separate.* Be kɬ *to fall* [Ch kʷə́ɬ- *divide*] ~ Li kəɬn *take off/apart* Th kəɬ(e)tés *detach*, kɬekstm *let go of* Sh kɬntes *take off (as clothes), undo (as fence)*, kɬep *come off/out*, kɬekst *let go (of one's hold)*, kɬew'sm *divide, split up* Cb kəɬkɬaw's *divorce, separate, split up* Cv tkɬam *to part, separate, divide*, kɬiw'snt *split st. in two* Sp čɬmsten *put aside separately* Cr čeɬ *separate, divorce, part.*

*kaɬ *to give.* Ch čáɬ- Ti čaːls CV ~ Cr čiɬ.

*kaʔɬas *three.* Cx [čálas]; čáɬayi *three persons* [Sl čaləs] Se čàɬás; čaɬáli *three persons* Ch čáʔɬi/a ~ Li kaɬás Th keʔɬés Sh kəɬes Cb kaʔɬás Cv kaʔɬís Ka Sp čeʔɬés Cr číʔɬes. – See comment to ***x̌əc** and cf. PCS ***čan**.

*kəm' *to carry (CS on the back).* Sq čmʔaʔs; čə́mʔətn *packstrap* Cw cəmʔət; Cw Ms cə́mʔətn *id.* Ck čmaːt (borr.); cámətl *id.* Sn θəŋ'eʔ Cl cə́ŋat; cəŋʔatn *packstrap* Ld čəbaʔ ~ [Li nkam'n *pick st. up*] Cb kəm'n *carry, take somewhere (pl. obj.)* Cv km'am *take (away, out, back).*

*kən *to touch, hold, keep steady; hit.* Be kan- *be hit, bumped, hurt*, kannmaxʷ *bump into each other* Cx čáʔnit *lean st. against st.* Se čənt *id.* Sq čənʔt *to support, steady* Cw cə́nʔət *lean st. against st.* Sn čənsənŋ *take a step* Cl cənʔə́t *lean st. against st.* Ti kənəníčin (Haeberlin p. 241) *he holds his back* ~ Li kənn' *get bumped* Th ʔeskə́n' *touching, in contact*, kən'tes *touch*, kən'n'stes *bump st. (part of body), hit st. w. force* Sh kntes *touch*, kin' *id., itr.* Ka čənnten *catch, grab*, čənxʷ *touch w. fingers* Sp čn'xʷum *touch*, ččn'čnim *hold on to* Cr čen' *take hold of large object*, čen'xʷ *hit person w. slight touch, bump into.*

*ka(n) *to do; do what? do something; (be) where, how?* Be kaks *which is it?* (cf. stamks *what is it?*), kan- *unspecified location*, kanmcnuks *from which country are you?* Sl ča *where?*, čam? *how?* Se častxʷ *do what w. st.?* Sq čanm *do what?*, (txʷ)čanm *go where?*, čas *do what w. st.?*, čaʔt *make st.*, ʔə́nča *where?, which?* Cw cəstəxʷ *do what with?* Sm čéʔe *when, which?* Sn čečət *make, build, work on* Cl can *who? someone* Ld čan *where?*, čay *how?* Tw č- *make, build,* dəčat *where?* Ch čč- *build, make,* čá:- *where?*, čá:nm' *which way?* Ti (x̌)čenš *where?, somewhere,* (x̌)čes *why?, what?* ~ Li kanm *do what, how, why?*, skənkan *be of what size/amount?* Th (ʔ)kenm *what's the matter?*, c'kenm *how, why,* kests *cause st. to happen* Sh kenm *do what/st., be (some)where, why,* kests *do what w. st., put st. where?*, c'kenm *be how (many), how about ...?* Cb ʔac'kánm *how?*, sac'kámx *why?* Cv ki? *who, what, when, where, how, why?* Ka ʔesčén *do what?* Sp ʔeščén'm *what happened?*, lčen' *at where?* Cr ečin *do with, put, be the matter.* – The all-Salish clitic **k** to which personal subject-suffixes are added may go back to this root.

*kanax^w *salmon (species).* Sm Sg sče:nəx^w *fish (generic)* Sn sče:nəx^w *salmon,* čənenx^w *fish for salmon* Cl sčanənəx^w *salmon* Ld sčədadx^w *id.* Ch sčanánx^w *id.* ~ Li kəkn'i *Kokanee salmon* Th kekn'íy *id.* Sh kəknex^w *id.* Cv kəkn'i *id.* – The IS forms in -i may be borr. fr. Engl. Cf. PS ***-anax^w**.

*kap see ***k^wup-i/aʔ**.

*kasəw'/kəw's (inv.) *spring/silver salmon.* Sq k^wu?s ~ Sh kəkesw' Cb kásuw' Cv kísu? Sp čsu?. – The Sq Sh Sp words refer to the *spring s.*, Cb Cv to the *coho s.*

*s-kətux^w *berry sp.* Cx čə́tux^wn? *blackberry* Se sčətux^wn *trailing blackberry* ~ Th sketúx^w *blackberry* WSh səkətúx^we? *bog cranberry* ESh skətux^w *id.*

*kaw I *relative through marriage (mostly of, to or through female)* Be stakaw *sister-in-law* Se sčəwitáł *son/daughter-in law* Sq čuáš *wife* Cw Ms Ck scutéł (Galloway also sciwté:ł) *child's/man's sister's spouse* Nk ččweš *wife* Sn sčwte:ł *man's sister's husband* Sg ščotéłəł *son/daughter-in-law* Cl sčutáʔił *man's sister's husband* NLd čəg^was SLd čə́g^wəš *wife* Tw ču?wáš *id.* Ch sčaw *sister-in-law* Cz kawáłani *his wife* (k^wuł *wife*) Ti čəg^wáš *id., to marry* ~ Li skaw *woman's sister-in-law (both types),* [skiʕ^w *wife,* *girlfriend,* scutáł *son-in-law* borr. fr. CS)] Th Sh skew *woman's sister-in-law* [Th scutéł *son-in-law* borr. fr. CS] Cb nskaw *sister-in-law (of a woman)* Sp sčew *id.* Fl isčéu *woman's brother's wife.*

*kaw II *down, downhill area (beach, lakeshore).* Be tx^{w}ukawk *descend to riverbank* Se čaw *beach,* cu čaw *go down to the beach* Sq kaw *descend* (borr.), Cw Ms cécəw? *(be down on the) beach* Ck čečəw (borr.) *beach, shore* Sm Sn sesəw' *id.* Sg séso *id.* Sn k^{w}ł sew' *go down towards the water* Cl caw' *id.,* łcu *id.* cácu(?) *(be down on the) beach* Tw ?asčáw *come downhill,* łčaw *below, on the front side, toward the mouth of the water* Ch čáw- *down,* čáwani- *id., lying/go down* ~ Li kəwkaw *lakeshore,* Th kewcín *go down to the beach* (cf. k^{w}úce *descend (to river)*) Sh xkəkew *run downhill (towards the water).*

*kaw III *far (out on the water/prairie).* Cw Ms cak^w *far* Ck ca:k^w *id.* Sm čak^w *id.* Cl cu?cáw' *far off shore* Ti yičáw *(far out on the) ocean* ~ Sh kəkéw *far,* xtkewltk *far out in the water,* xkewlx/xkew'lx *go where the water is deep* Ka ču?é?u *they went far away* (√čeu *open space*) Cr čeg^w *extend,* čig^w *go out onto prairie.* – A connection with ***kaw II** *down* is quite possible.

*kíx(-a?) *mother, elder sister.* Sq čə́ša *mother* Tw čəš *older sister* ~ Li skíxza? *mother,* kə́xkəx *elder sister* Th kix *elder sister, female cousin,* skíxze? *mother* Sh kix *elder sister,* kí?xe *mother* Cb kəx *woman's older sister* Cv łkíkxa? *older sister (man's or woman's)* Ka Sp łčíčše? *id.* – Cf. ***kay(-a?)**.

*kay(-a?) *grandmother.* Be kikya Cx čá?ža Ld kayə(?), kiyá?, kayá?, káya? Tw kayə, [ka?ə *mommy*] Cz kay? Ti číya CV *mother's mother* ~ Li kíka? *respectful and affectionate address to woman* Th kz'e Sh kyé?e Cb kkíy'a? *mother's mother, woman's daughter's child* Ka čičiy'é? *mother's mother* Sp čč̓y'e? *id., id.'s sister, woman's daughter's children* Cr čč̓éy'e? *woman's mother's mother, daughter's child.* – Cf. ***kix(-a?)**.

k'

*k'əc' I *to cross, put across e.o.* [Sn č'əç'tal' *hug e.o.*, sčç'e:nə *inside corner of house* Cl č'c'ust *hug*] Tw č'əc'əd *crosswise,* č'əc'úsad *crossbeam* ~ Li nk'əc'n *put st. across st.* Sh kc'em *put two things crosswise,* stkc'nwexʷ *crossed (eg. sticks)* [Sp č'ic'(i) *long obj. lies* Cr č'ec' *id.*].

*k'əc' II *mosquito, gnat, bug.* Cx c'áč'us (inv.) *mosquito* Sl ç'áč'us *id.* Se c'əč'ús *id.* [Sq č'č'us *sand flies, no-see-um*] Ld č'ic'qs *mosquito* Tw č'ič'ic' *id.* Ch c'əčqs (inv.) *id., gnat* ~ Li c'kʷus *horsefly* (inv.; labialization automatic) Th k'ec'éyn' *woodtick* Sh kəckəcéc'wł *whirligig beetle,* ck'eln (inv.) *woodtick* Cv kəkc'ilxkən *id.* – Cf. ***ck'aln.**

*k'ih, k'i-t *near.* Sq č'it *be near,* č'ími *approach,* č'íč'it *be close second in race* Cw c'iml?; c'iməθət *close, get self close* Ck c'iml *approach* Ld Tw č'it *near* Ch č'í- *bring,* č'ís- *come* Ti č'it *soon* ~ Li k'ítxnam' *get close to st., go on a short trip,* k'ík'ta? *close by* Th k'ítes *put st. near to st.,* k'í?k'e?t *near* Sh kík'?et *close second in race,* kəkík'?et *near* Cb k'k'íta? *id.,* k'il'x *id.* Cv k'a?ítt *approach,* k'ík'a?t *near* Ka č'i/e?ít *id.,* č'í?č'e?t *id.* Sp č'ič't *id.,* č'č'?it *draw near* Cr č'ih *approach, get near,* č'íte? *be near.*

*k'əl *to cut (esp. skin), rip.* Ld č'əl *ripped through* ~ Li k'əln *make mark by scratching or cutting,* k'ə̓lk'ln *cut (leather) into pieces,* sk'ə̓l *buckskin* Th k'ləm *cut (hide, cloth),* k'ílm *id. into pieces* Sh k'lam *cut strips of skin* (Canim Lake), *cut anything w. shears, saw, etc.* (Deadman's Creek), ck'il/ck'el *board,* ck'al/ckị̓k'l *strip of skin* Cb k'ərn *cut thin material (buckskin, paper, cloth)* Cv k'ram *cut* Sp č'rim *cut w. scissors,* č'rč'er *all cut up* Cr č'ar *cut flimsy object w. shears.*

*s-n-k'əl(ap) *coyote.* Ck slək'iyép/sk'ək'iyép Ch snəč'ə́l' ~ Li nk'yep Th snk'y'ep Sh sək'lep Cv snk'l'ip Ka sənč'əle(p) Sp snč'le?/snč'lep Cr hnč'el'é?.

*k'əl(-ay') *treebark.* Be k'lay *bark of western birch,* ?lk'laytp *birch* Sn č'əley' *any bark* (this could also reflect

*p'alay') ~ Th k'əzey' *outer cedar bark / thin, fine bark* Cv k'ylilxʷ/k'i?lílxʷ Ka Sp č"i?lélxʷ Cr čéle?.

*k'al *to listen to, attend, wait.* Cx číyit *hear, listen to* Cw c'ełm? *hear* Ck c'łe:m *id.* ~ Li k'alm *wait*, k'alán' *listen* Th k'y'əm *wait*, k'éy'nime *listen* Sh ck'lem *wait*, ck'elnm/ck'əlen'm *listen, obey* Cv tk'lam *wait for, expext sb.*, k'níya? *listen* Cr tčl'elíne? *he has sharp hearing.*

*k'ət *to drip; rain, mud.* Cx Sl č'əł *rain* Se sč'əł *id.* [Ch č'əł- *drown, fall into the water*] ~ Li Th sk'əłt *mud, clay* Th k'əłt *muddy* Sh sk'ałt *a drop*, (kəł)k'ałt *to drip* [Cv k'ram *swim*].

*k'ału? (mostly red.) *maggot, mite.* Sq č'łá?lu? *mite* Cw c'łá?la? *birdlice* Ck k'ék'əłe *pill bug* (borr.; prob. *maggot*) Tw č'ač'áłu? *white/body lice* Ch č'ač'áłu? *tick, dog louse* ~ Li k'ák'ła? *bugs in dried salmon* [Sh ckék'łe? *spotted*, ckək'łə?us *freckled*, k'łnéqs(e) *horsefly*, k'łqíse *no-see-um*] Cb k'ák'łu? *moth* (ICNSL 34:34) Cv k'ík'łu? *maggot* Sp č'éč'łu? *id.* Fl č'éč'ełu *black maggot in meat.* – The Li word with -?a may be an older borrowing from Hl.

*k'əm *to grab a handful; squeeze, bite.* Be k'm(a) *bite*, k'm *squeeze, catch in trap* Sq č'əm' *bite* Cw c'əm?ət *id.* Sn ç'ən'sistn̩ *get pinched by crab* Sg c'ə́ŋət *bite* Cl c'ŋət *id.* Tw ?asč'ə́m *it's tight* ~ Li k'əm'n *wedge/plug in*, sk'əms *hold st. in a narrow crack or split* Th k'əm'tes *chew, crunch* Sh k'mekstm *get a handful (eg. of berries)* Cb k'əmakst *handful* (Kinkade 1975:9) Cr č'im (Nicodemus č'em') *grab some*, [čem' *take hold of pl. objects*]. – See comment to PIS *k'əm.

*k'i/aməl Ck c'iml *almost, near* ~ Th k'émeł *at last, only* Sh k'eməł *but, only*, kék'me?ł *almost.* – Cf. ***k'ih.**

*k'amu/a(ma?) *(cover of) conifer needles (on ground).* Sq č'amam *fir needles* Tw č'abúbə *conifer needles* Ch č'amúma? *id.* ~ Li k'áma? *id. on ground* Th k'ém'e *id.*, Sh k'éme *id.* Cb k'amáma? *pine needles* Cv k'áma? *id.* Sp č'éme? *id. on ground* Cr č'ímul *pine needle.* – Cf. KWA k'amu(ma) *hemlock needles*, k'ak'mw'a *go after id.* (LR no. 1387).

41

*s-k'ínk'ʷu *snake.* Sq č'ínk'ʷu *a mythical serpent* Cw Ms sc'ínk'ʷa *lightning monster* Ck c'ilə́k'ʷa *id.,* sç'in'k'ʷə? *dragon* Cl č'ínək'ʷi *id.* ~ Cb sk'ink'ʷ *rattlesnake.*

*k'ənp' *to clasp (together), encircle, squeeze.* Ch č'ə́np'- *put together,* č'əná́p'- *scissors, chisel for cutting trees* ~ [Th k'n'əp *encircled tightly*] Sh kənip' *hemmed in,* knp'ekst *fingerring,* knp'éne *earring* Cb skɫk'ənp'cənakst *bracelet,* sk'ən'p'qən'uskst *ring* Cv k'np'iw'stn *strap, round band, belt,* k'np'qinkstn *ring, band* Sp č'inp' *banded* Cr č'enp' *clasp, encircle.* – Cf. ***k'ip'** and QUI k'adá:p'a *pinch,* k'adá?ap'iɫ *firetongs.*

*k'əpxʷ *to break, crush, gouge out.* Be k'ip *erode,* [k'ixʷ *gnaw*] Cx č'ə́pxʷat *break (as cookies or bread)* [Sl č'ep'xʷm *(être) fragile*] ~ Li k'əpxʷan *make a hole in st.* Th k'əpxwetés *id., gouge out deep* Sh k'əpxʷntes *crack nits,* xk'əpxʷntes *make a hole in st.* [Cr č'ep'xʷ *clip, click*].

*k'ip' *to squeeze, pinch.* Be kip' *grasp, pinch* Sn č'ip'ət *squeeze,* č'p'aləsŋ *close eyes,* č'əp'itŋ *press button* Sg č'epət (prob. p') *squeeze* Cl č'ipt *squeeze* Tw ?asč'ip' *it's jammed,* č'ip'íd *squeezing, pinched* ~ Li k'íp'in' *hold st. w. tweezers, tongs* Th k'íp'es *pinch, squeeze* Sh kip'm *pinch together,* ckip'x̌n *carrying (clasped) under the arm* Cb k'ip'n *pinch, clamp, squeeze* Cv k'ip'p' *get pinched,* sk'ip'm *squeeze* [Ka č'ep *lock a door*] Sp č'ip'n *pinch, clamp* Cr č'ip' *pinch.* – Cf. ***c'ip'**, ***k'ənp'** and NWAK k'p- *hold by squeezing (w. tongs, clip, under the arm)* (LR 1378).

*k'is *bad.* [Sq č'ə́sp'i *ugly*] Ti č'is-/č'iš- *bad,* ha(n)ná́šč'is *rain* ~ Li nk'san'k *mean-spirited* (borr. fr. Sh) Th k'ist, k'ə̣st (in other derivatives also k'əs-, k'ə̣s-) Sh k'ist *bad,* k'sesq't *(heavy) rain* WSh k'sos *ugly* ESh k'sus *id.* Cb k'ə̣st *bad* Cv k'ast *id.* Ka č'es- *id.,* č'esús *ugly* Sp č'sesq't *bad day/weather,* č'sus *ugly,* hesčč'éslsi *he feels queasy* Cr č'est (Nicodemus also q'est in English-Cr dictionary). – Retraction in Th Sh Cr must be of the emotive kind.

*k'əspan *neck.* [Tw dəxʷsč'əsdúʔbat *greedy*] Ch č'əspn ~ Cb k'əspn Cv k'span *back of neck* [Sp čspin *id.*].

*(k'ə)st/t'an' *nits.* Be st'n Sq šəst'an? Cw šəšt'en? Ck šə́st'əl Ld šəst'ad Ch č'usn' ~ Th k'əstə́n' Sh k'əsten' Cb k'ə́sn' *louse* Cv k'ək'stána? Cr č'esn' *louse.* – The Sq Cw Ck Ld initial š- may be due to that in other CS words for *nit*: Cx šašəy? Se šašl Sm šəšakʷ Sn šəšəkʷ.

*k'aw I *old, decrepit.* [Be ʔawk'awał *blind*] Cx č'ə́włim *rickety (as table)* ~ [Li sk'iˤʷ *delicate, frail,* k'iʔiˤʷ *run-down, withered, have t.b.*] Th k'uʔk'éw' *sickly, decrepit* Sh k'ewlx *old (person)* Cv k'iwlx *id.* Sp č'éwlši *id.*

*k'i/aw II *to go up, ascend.* Sn č'ew'sət *brag, boast* (semantically cf. Sh wis-t *high,* wswəsncut *be proud of o.s.*) ~ Cb tk'iwlx *climb up* Cv k'iwlxst *take sb. up(stairs),* tk'iwlx *climb* Ka č'íwulš *id.* Sp č'iwlš *id.*

*k'ay *cold (season).* Be k'ay *snow,* [k'l- *freeze,* sk'l *cold, cool st. off* Cx č'əm *cold* (cf. Li) Se č'álat *cool st. off* Cw θímaʔt *freeze*] Sm sč'ay'm *north wind* Sn č'iʔxʷel's *freezing* Tw č'iš *cold* ~ Li sk'iməl'c *ice* (cf. Cx) Sh k'yey *be cold weather, freeze,* sk'éye *glacier,* k'iyt *be scared of the cold* Cb sk'áʔi? *autumn* Cv k'iy't *cold,* sk'ˤay *fall, cold comes* Ka č'ei *shade,* sč'eʔéi *the fall* Sp č'ey *shade, shadow,* sč'ʔey *autumn* Cr č'id *be shadowy,* č'ed *shade.* – Cf. QUI k'í:ʔi? *cold (weather).*

*k'ay' *to dry out, wither,* ***k'ay'-xʷ** *dry.* Se č'iyxʷ Sq č'áy?i *dry out (of living things), die (of tree),* sč'ay? *dead tree,* č'iʔxʷ *dry* Cw Ms c'ey?xʷ *id.* Ck c'e:yxʷ *id.* [Tw č'əʔwə́š *id.*] ~ Li k'az'húsa? *berries remained on bush through winter,* [k'ax *dry* Th k'əxk'ex *id.*] Sh sk'y?elqʷ *dry/dead tree,* tk'əyəʔúse? *berries remained on bush through winter,* [k'exm *to dry meat*] Cb k'áya *dead tree* [Ok sk'xəxʷum *consumption*] Cv k'íya? *dead tree,* [k'l'al' *dried up* Sp č'exʷ *to dry,* sč'xʷum *consumption*]. – Li Th Sh have a √xʷik' which occurs in Sh sxʷik' *dried salmon,* xʷik'm *prepare (clean and dry) salmon,* which could be an inversion of *k'ixʷ < *k'ay'xʷ, but the Li Th words refer specifically to butchering.

kʷ

*kʷac CS / *kʷast IS *(to) name.* Be skʷacta *name,* skʷakʷactimut *nickname* Ch kʷacíli- *be named, called,* skʷacł *name* ~ Li skʷácic *name,* kʷastáy' *nickname* Th kʷéstes *to name,* skʷest *name* Sh kʷestns *name sb., give sb. a name,* skʷest *name* Cv skʷist *id.,* nkʷistxt *be named after* Ka Sp skʷest *name* Cr kʷis(-t) *be named.* – A root ending in *x in Se kʷíšit *to name* Sq kʷəšámin *ancestral name* Ms skʷix *name* Ck skʷix *id.,* kʷixət *to name* Sm kʷšem'n' *nickname* Sn kʷšem'n *id.*

*kʷəl *warm.* Be kʷl Tw ʔaskʷə́l *sunshine* ~ Li skʷəl' *id.* Th nkʷəlkʷel *lukewarm,* nkʷikʷéy' *warm,* kʷiʔetés *expose to sun/fire* Sh kʷlem *bake,* ckʷel *warmed up (food, body),* skʷluləxʷ *(early) summer* ESh kʷelmt *to sweat* Cb kʷəl' *warm,* kʷal'ənct *warm o.s. up* Cv kʷal't *warm,* kʷl'al' *sunlight,* kskʷal't *sweat,* kʷil/l'stn *sweathouse* Ka skʷkul'íl' *sun,* čskʷil't *to sweat* Sp skʷkʷl'il' *heat,* sčskʷil't *sweat* Cr kʷel' *be hot, sunny, warm.*

*kʷəl *green, yellow.* Be qʷli [Cx kʷúł?ay' *alder* Se qʷə́l'ay *hemlock*] Sq kʷlúl?ay *alder* Cw kʷəlál?ałp *id.* (Hukari kʷəlala?ałp), kʷələla?aləs *orange colored* Sn sqʷalŋəłč *red alder* Tw sqʷəlá?ay *grass, hay* Ch "kʷəłoi'əa" *green* Ti cqʷa?ł *faded* ~ Li kʷli?; kʷəlkʷal' *(light) yellow,* kʷə́ln' *gall bladder,* kʷəlmakst *Yellow Tree Moss (Evernia vulpina),* skʷlal'st *jade* (lit. *green stone*), kʷəlúl?az' *red alder,* kʷa?lús *pale in the face* Th kʷəl'kʷal', ʔeskʷlí?; kʷ?al' *(turn) green,* kʷlo? *gall,* ʔeskʷló? *bile color,* t(ə)kʷl'it *bile,* ʔestəkʷl'ít *light green, yellow,* skʷəle/ayst *jade,* nkʷl'ank *green hill(side),* ʔeskʷə́ł *brown* Sh kʷalt; kʷ?al *spoiled (of food),* kʷlékʷle (WSh)/kʷlikʷla (ESh) *grass,* kʷlalst *gall, green stone,* kʷle?á/éłp *alder,* tkʷlóse? *choke cherry,* xkʷlank *sidehill becomes yellow* Cb kʷrayq *yellow,* kʷarn *apply yellow paint,* kʷrit *gold,* skʷra?kán *id.,* qʷə́li *gall* Cv kʷr/r'i? *yellow, gold,* *sorrel,* qʷəláʕl' *gall bladder* Ka kʷaːlíʔ *yellow* Sp kʷriʔ *id.,* qʷl'in' *gall.* – Exceptional are Li nqʷuḷuṇátkʷa *algae* and Cb qʷə̣li *gall,* where retraction has affected both root consonants and also remains in the vowel.

*kʷul *to borrow.* Be kʷult Cx kʷúɬəma Se kʷuɬtn; skʷúlic'a *borrowed piece of clothing* Sq kʷuɬn Cw cálaʔɬ (progressive yəcákʷəlaʔɬ) Ck cə́ɬte (continuative cákʷəɬte) Ld čul'álc Tw biqúlas *he borrowed it* Ch čóːyaʔ ~ Li kʷuɬn Sh kʷəɬen Cb Cv Ka Sp Cr kʷuɬn (Reichard gives kʷuɬ *borrow* vs. kʷul *lend,* Nicodemus gives kʷuɬ- for both). – Cf. HAI guλú *borrow* (LR 1300).

*kʷəlx *spirit power.* Be ɬukʷala *student of supernatural power, shaman-to-be* [Se syaykʷɬ *Indian doctor*] Ch suff. -ikʷlaši/-ikʷliši, -kʷlš *spirit power,* "ɬakwillix" *id.* ~ Sh t'əkʷilx *shaman* Cb Cv λ'aʔkʷílx *id.* Sp λ'eʔkʷílš *id.* Cr t'eʔkʷílš *id.* – Cf. HEI λúgʷálá *person with supernatural powers (as eg. a shaman)* (LR no. 953).

*kʷ/qʷəm *lump, heap.* Be kʷm *thick, bulky,* [tqʷm(a) *hang st. over st.*] Cx kʷə́mit *burl,* [kʷə́pit *lump on ground, hill*] Se skʷəmʔit *piled up in a lump, bulge (as sand),* skʷəmix̌ *with a lump,* kʷəmapšə́n *heel of shoe,* skʷəmx̌ʷiws *lump on tree,* skʷəmx̌ʷiqʷ *eagle-nosed,* qʷəmx̌ʷ *ankle* Sq skʷə́/úmʔkʷúmc' *lump,* skʷúmʔəčn *humpback,* qʷəmʔx̌ʷšn *ankle* Cw Ms qʷə́mʔx̌ʷcəs *wrist* Cw qʷə́mʔx̌ʷšn *ankle,* qʷəmx̌ʷəst *wind wool into balls,* cqʷəmʔx̌ʷ *skinny* Ms qʷə́mʔx̌ʷxn *ankle* Ck sqʷaːmxʷ/sqʷamç' *lump,* qʷə́mx̌ʷcəs *wrist,* qʷəmx̌ʷxl *ankle,* qʷəmqʷə́mx̌ʷcəs *knuckles* Sm sqʷəm'xʷes: *wristbone,* qʷə́məx̌ʷsn' *calf and ankle ("lump on leg/foot")* (xʷ vs. x̌ʷ in last two items *sic*), sqʷəqʷə́m'x̌ʷ *skinny* Sn qʷəmʔəx̌ʷšn *(lump of) ankle,* qʷəmʔx̌ʷesəs *wrist,* məqʷeyčt (inv.) *pile up,* sməlməkʷ (inv.) *lumpy,* sqʷəm'x̌ʷ *skinny* Cl ʔəsqʷə́mʔx̌ʷ *skinny* Ld sbəkʷ (inv.) *ball* Tw qubqubʔə́x̌ʷ *body joints,* sbəkʷ (inv.) *ball* ~ Li qʷəmn *pile up,* sqʷəm *mountain, pile,* múqʷun' (inv.) *put together, mound up* Th sqʷəm *mountain,* ʔesqʷə́m *humped,* [nkʷummn *sack, pocket*] Sh qʷmntes *put pl. obj., pile up,* cqʷum *piled up, hill,* stqʷmel'qʷ *lump on tree,* cqʷmenk *pregnant* Cv kʷum *store away,* mukʷ (inv.) *snow mounds* Sp sckʷum *a stash,* snkʷmlscutn *storage place.* – Cf. *məqʼʷ and *qʼʷəm.

*kʷum *to go up/ashore, inland.* Cx kʷúmšin *walk away fr. beach* Se kʷum *ascend* Sq kʷumʔ *go upward/ashore,* kʷumʔs *take up (fr. ground), take upward/ashore* Cw cam (progressive yəcakʷm) *uphill, go up fr. shore* Ms caːm (continuative cakʷm) *go inland* Sm saŋ *go up* Sn θaŋ *id.* Cl cu(ː)ŋ *go inland* Ld čubə *go up fr. shore* ~ Li nkʷukʷmʼ *upstream area* Th kʷúme *ascend, go up away fr. water / away fr. fire in winter house* Sh ckʷúme *come out of the water,* kʷmum *flee into the bush (when raid is expected)* Ka kumš *walk up fr. the river* Sp kʷumšlš *go fr. the shore,* čʼkʷum *be away fr. the water.* – Cf. PIS *kʷum *save.*

*kʷan *to take.* Be kʷn Cx kʷínat *hold/carry in hands/arms* Se kʷə́nat, kʷənnə́xʷ Cw Ms kʷənet (Cw Hukari kʷə́nət); skʷənkʷen *captive* Ck kʷəleːt; skʷəlkʷə́l *captive* Nk kʷneʔ Sm Sn Sg kʷənət Ld kʷəd(á) Tw kʷədab Ch kʷaná- Ti cgʷənkʷanʼə́ni *hold* (√kʷən *get, take, hold*) ~ Li kʷan *(tr.),* kʷam *(itr.)* Th Sh kʷens *(tr.),* kʷnem *(itr.)* Cb kʷann *take, carry sg. obj.,* ʔackʷánsn *hold sg. obj.,* ckʷnam *get st.* Cv kʷi(n)nt; kʷnim *grab, hold in the hand,* kʷist *hold* Ka kʷen *take sg. obj.,* kuném *id, itr.* Sp kʷen, kʷnem Cr kʷin. – The root may be ultimately related to IS *ʔukʷ *bring, deliver, haul, etc.,* see comment given there.

*kʷ/qʷup *to push together, stuff,* ***kʷ/qʷup-xan** *stuffing to keep feet warm, makeshift leggings.* Cx kʷə́pit *pile, hill* Se kʷə́pliqʷ *piled up, collected* Cz qʷupšn *stockings, socks* ~ Li nkʷup *mattress,* qʷuʔpəqʷ *hair is bushy/messy* Th kʷúpes *push,* nkʷ/qʷúpcʼeʔ *quilt* Sh kʷupm *push,* xkʷupns *to stuff,* xkʷupxn *rags wound around legs, stockings, socks.* – Cf. *λʼaqʼʷ/*qʼʷuλʼ and IS *qʼʷuλʼ.

*kʷup-i/aʔ *elder.* Be kukʷpi *grandfather,* kuukʷpi *great-grandfather* Cx kʷúpaʔ *grandfather,* [čaps *uncle, aunt* Se čapc *id.*] Sl kʷúkʷpa *grandfather* [čapθ *uncle, aunt*] Sq kʷúpic *elder sibling* [Cw šcepθ *parent's sibling's spouse* Ms Ck xcepθ *id.* Sn Sg sečs *id.* Cl cačc *id.* Ld scápa(ʔ) *grandfather, brother or male cousin of one's grandparent,* cápaʔ *grandfather (vocative)*] Tw kʷúpic *master* [Ch čúpʼa (Kinkade 1973 čupaʔ) *grandfather,* kʷúpʼa *eel: "old man",* cáʔpa *grandfather (address form)*] Cz kʷúpaʔ *grandfather* ~ Li kʷukʷpəyʼ *chief,* Th kʷúpiʔ *sir, maʼam,* kʷúkʷpiʔ *chief, noble,* skʷupzʼéyt *public favorite,* [képiʔ *my dear (fellow)*] Sh kʷupy *master (as of dog), son or daughter of the house,* kʷukʷpyʼ *chief,* wɬkʷupi/[wɬkéʔpe] *you, pl. (story form only).* – The bracketed forms pointing to ***kap** (see PCS I ***kapc**) reflect either an old delabialized form or ***ku/ap** with automatic labialization of k before u. Cf. also CJ chope (Zenk 1993 chup) *grandfather.*

*kʷas *dusk.* Cx kʷə́sim *color of evening or morning sky* Se kʷəsim *blue* ~ Li kʷas (also qʷas) *dusk* Th kʷsəp *get pitchdark,* kʷəstes *to darken,* kʷəskʷə́st *dim* Sh kʷəses *getting dark* ESh ʔəstkʷes *sunset* [Ka kukuʔéc *night falls,* skukuʔéc *night* Sp skʷkʷʔec *id.*].

*kʷusən *star.* Cx kʷusnʔ Sl kʷusn Se Sq kʷusn Cw Ms kʷasn Ck kʷasl Nk kʷúsen Sm Sn Sg kʷasn Ld čúsad Cz kásiʔ (Kinkade 1973) ~ Li nkakúsənt/...snət Th nkʷəkʷusnʼ Sh səkʷusnʼt (< ***skʷəkʷusnʼt**) Cv skʷkʷusnt [Ka ɬkʷkusmʼ Sp kʷkʷusmʼ].

*s-kʷast see ***s-kʷac**.

*kʷutwal/n *eel.* Ck kʷáte/əwi ~ Li kʷútwan Sh Cv kʷutwn Sp kʷútul Cr kʷútgʷul.

*s-kʷ/qʷəy (red.) *groundhog, marmot, whistler.* [Cx qʷíqʷumis *marten*] Se sqʷiyqʷ *whistler* Sq sqʷiqʷ *groundhog* Ck sqʷi(:)qʷ *id., hoary marmot* Ld sqʷiʔəqʷ/ skʷiyəqʷ *squirrel,* sqʷiqʷəd *marmot* Tw skʷúykʷi *id.* Ch skʷúykʷuy *id., pika* ~ Li sqʷiqʷənt *whistler* Th (s)qʷiqʷnt *id.* Sh sqʷíʔqʷe *id.* Cb sqʷiqʷəntk *id.* Cv skʷúykʷi *id.* Sp qʷqʷyenč *baby chipmunk, squirrel, groundhog.* – Cf. ***s-kʷayu**.

*s-kʷayu *squirrel.* Cx kʷákʷaʔǰu Se skʷáyu Ms skʷáye Ck skʷayə NLd sqəʒú? (Hess) / sqʷáyə? (Thompson) SLd sqǝ́ʒu? Ch skʷayóh- ~ Cb skʷiyú. – See Kinkade 1995:42f. and cf. *s-kʷ/qʷəy.

*s-kʷuy-aʔ *child, offspring.* Cx Sl čuy? ~ Li skʷúza? Th skʷú/ó/ə́ze? (vocative kʷúye?) Sh skʷúye?.

k'ʷ

*k'ʷaʔ *to chew,* SIS *to bite.* [Cx c'ə́ʔat Sl ç'aʔt Se c'ə?át Cw ç'eʔt Ck ç'em *itr.,* ç'et *tr.*] Ch k'ʷayá- (k'ʷaːymʼ) ~ Li k'ʷzaplʼ *cheek* Th k'ʷʔem *itr.,* k'ʷeʔtés *tr.,* k'ʷz'é/ápyʼe *cheek* WSh k'ʷeʔém; k'ʷyépne *jaw,* ESh (inv.) ʔek'ʷm *chew,* ʔek'ʷns *id., tr.* Cb k'ʷaʔn *bite* Cv k'ʷʔam *id.* Ka k'ʷiʔépe *jaw* Sp k'ʷʔem *bite,* k'ʷeʔk'ʷʔem *chew* (also q'ʷeʔq'ʷʔem, fr. q'ʷʔem *squeeze*) Cr k'ʷiʔ *bite, chew.* – The forms with c' ç' are characteristic of Straits; for a similar intrusion see *way.

*k'ʷuʔ see *q'ʷuʔ.

*k'ʷəc' see *k'ʷə(l)c'.

*k'ʷəlʼ *skin, feather, quill (porcupine).* Be sk'ʷult *porcupine quill* Sq k'ʷlawʔ *skin (human, animal, fish),* k'ʷik'ʷləc' *feathers* Cw Ms k'ʷə́ləwʔ *skin, hide* Ck k'ʷələ́w: *id.* Sm Sn k'ʷə́ləwʼ *id.* Sg qʷə́lo (prob. k'ʷ) *id.* Cl k'ʷə́wiʔ *id.* Ld k'ʷaltəd *fish skin,* k'ʷəluʔ *skin, hide* Tw qʷə́ltəd *skin (fish or human)* ~ Li skʷʼəlʼ *quill of porcupine,* sʔúkʷʼalʼ *feathers* Th skʷʼiʔ *quill* Sh skʷʼel *id.* Cb skʷʼəlʼ *porcupine* Cv skʷʼalt *quill* Ka Sp skʷʼilʼ *porcupine* Cr skʷʼkʷʼelʼ *id.*

*k'ʷal *stomach, belly.* Be k'ʷla *belly* Cx k'ʷáʔwa *id.* Se k'ʷə́la *id.* Sq k'ʷəlʼ *stomach* Cw Ms k'ʷə́lʔə *belly* Ck k'ʷə́lːe Sm k'ʷə́lʼə *id.* Cl k'ʷə́wʼiʔ [SLd k'ʷyəxʷ *id.*] ~ Cb ctk'ʷaltn *food* [Cv sqʷlcnink *stomach*].

*k'ʷəl(c'), *k'ʷəc' *to bend, twist.* [Cx k'ʷə́yič *twisted* (also c'ə́yič) Sl k'ə́ləθ Se sc'əlíč] Se k'ʷúc'ut *bend st.* Sq k'ʷúc'un *bend in several directions, make crooked* Cw k'ʷə́ləç't *fold st. over* Sm sk'ʷac'ə́l/sk'ʷaç'ł *crooked,* sk'ʷəlʼk'ʷə́ç'/c' *real* *crooked* Sn sk'ʷaç'əł *crooked* Sg sk'ʷac'əł *id.* [Cl sk'ʷacł *id.,* kʷc'ət *bend*] Tw ʔask'ʷə́l *bent* (an alternative √ k'ʷy is quoted by N. Thompson, without example) ~ Li k'ʷuc' *crooked,* sk'ʷu̱lc' *id.* Th ʔesk'ʷúc' *awry, crooked* Sh ck'ʷloc' *crooked* Cv ck'ʷarc' *id.*

*k'ʷan *to inspect (try out, aim at).* Be k'ʷn *point/aim at, show* Cx k'ʷət *look at* Sl k'ʷə́nət *voir, regarder, examiner* Se k'ʷən?m *look,* k'ʷə(n)t *look at,* k'ʷənaláł *expect* Sq k'ʷn?us *to aim* Sn Sg k'ʷə́nət *look at* Cl k'ʷə́n(ə)t *id., see,* k'ʷənit *watch, observe* Ld k'ʷədad *forecast the weather,* k'ʷədč *suspicious,* [k'ʷałá *examine, size up*] Tw k'ʷədwil *look out (eg. of window)* Ch k'ʷə́n- *pay attention, size up,* sk'ʷə́nk'ʷəncštn *he's getting suspicious* ~ Li k'ʷa?ən' *see? (used eg. at end of demonstration),* k'ʷan'xn *track game,* nk'ʷan'ústn *mirror* Th k'ʷen'm *look at,* k'ʷé/ánme *inspect, criticize,* sk'ʷen'm *choice* Sh k'ʷenm *try, taste, choose,* ck'ʷenm *check up, inspect,* xk'ʷen'xnm *look for tracks,* ck'ʷnk'ʷenmsts *aim at* Cb k'ʷann *try, taste,* k'ʷənk'ʷan'n *examine,* ni?k'ʷán'm *choose, select* Cv k'ʷinm *try,* nk'ʷin *pick st. out* Ka k'ʷen' *show for inspection, inspect, try out,* nk'ʷen' *pick out, choose* Sp nk'ʷen'm *choose,* k'ʷe?k'ʷn'm' *try a little bit* Cr k'ʷin' *try, choose, consider, examine.*

*k'ʷin *how many?; several.* [Cx k'ʷixʷ] Se Sq Cw k'ʷin Ms wək'ʷí?nal? *few* Ck k'ʷi:l Sm Sn Sg Cl k'ʷin Ld k'ʷid Ch k'ʷi, k'ʷin-; ʔik'ʷinál *several* Ti k'in *little, not much,* k'iná̌x *how much/many?* ~ Li k'ʷin Th k'ʷínex Sh Cb Cv k'ʷinx Ka Sp Cr k'ʷinš.

*k'ʷəp *straight.* Ch k'ʷəp- *straight, right, very* ~ Li k'ʷəpk'ʷep, k'ʷ?ep Th k'ʷá/épix *straighten o.s. out, lie down* [Cb k'ʷəpt *fish backbone* Cr k'ʷept *spine, backbone*].

*k'ʷup' *bar, rod.* Be k'ʷup' *to skewer, run stick through st.,* k'ʷup'sta *skewer* ~ Th k'ʷúp'es *fasten by running stick through* Sh k'ʷup's *stick along top of cradle over which mosquito net is hung* Sp č'łnk'ʷp'č'leptn *locking bar, door.*

*kʷaq'-t *scream, bellow, weep* Cx Se kʷaq't *scream* Sq kʷáq'am *bellow (as sea lion)* [Ld č'iq' *scream*] ~ Th kʷiq't *weep, pl.* Sh qʷeq't *cry, howl, pl.*

*kʷas *hot, to scorch.* Cx kʷas *warm, hot* Sl kʷəs *id.* Se kʷas *id.* Se kʷəsim *black,* kʷásulwił *"cure" a new canoe* Sq kʷas *be hot, singe* Cw Ms Ck kʷes *burn* Ms kʷakʷəs *warm (day)* Ch kʷaːkʷəs *id.* Nk kʷes *hot,* [qʷəs *burned (of animates)*] Sm kʷesn̥ *to fry* Sn kʷes *burn, scald, scorch* Sg qʷes (prob. kʷ) *be burned to death,* skʷes *sweat* Cl kʷas *get burned,* kʷə́ʔus *hot* Ld kʷás(a) *burn body, roast, barbecue* Tw kʷasád *scorch it!* ~ Li kʷásan' *heat st. up,* kʷəsn *singe* Th skʷákʷes *sun* Sh kʷesm *warm up (dried fish or meat) by holding it above fire,* kʷʔest *scorched,* skʷékʷʔes *sun* Cb kʷusm *id.* Cv kʷas *singe, scorch,* kʷsntim *id., tr.*

*kʷət' *flea.* Nk kʷút'ep Ld č'út'əp' [Ch t'ákʷi- (inv.?) *lice, fleas*] ~ [Li ƛ'úp/p'z'ac' prob. < kʷƛ'úp...] Th kʷəƛ'kʷiƛ'p' Sh kʷətkʷit'p; kʷit' *bedbug* Cb kʷət'akʷít'ps Cv Sp kʷt'kʷit'ps Cr skʷət'kʷít'ups.

*kʷat'an *mouse.* [Cx čáč'at'an? *mouse, rat* Sl k'át'an *rat,* čáč'at'an *mouse*] Se kʷát'an *(bush)rat, packrat* Sq kʷát'an Cw kʷet'n? Ck kʷet'l Sm kʷet'n' Sn kʷet'n Cl kʷat'n *rat* [Nk kʷét'en] Ld kʷát'ad Tw sqʷat'át *(pack)rat* (final -t *sic*; CV has "skwáːtak" *mouse*) Ch skʷat'án' ~ [Th kʷətn'iy WSh kʷékʷtne] Cb kʷkʷát'əna? Ka kʷékʷt'ene? Sp kʷékʷt'ne? [Fl kʷékʷt'ene] Cr kʷít'en. – The IS bracketed forms clearly belong to this etymon, but the Cx and Sl forms are problematic. Cf. ***kʷaxʷ** II.

*kʷaxʷ I *to hollow out; container.* Cx kʷáxʷa? *box, coffin* [kʷáw?is *bucket, pail* Sl kʷəw? *id.*] Se kʷáxʷa *box* Sq kʷxʷum *make a basket* Sq Ms kʷáxʷa? *box* Ck kʷá(ː)xʷa *id., coffin* Ch kʷáxʷu *wooden bucket* ~ Th kʷxʷəm *weave a basket,* kʷuxʷtés *id.,* skʷuxʷ *basket,* kʷáxʷe? *box* Sh kʷxʷum *make a basket,* xkʷxʷum *hollow out ground, make shallow pit.* – Cf. IS ***k'əxʷ.**

*k'ʷaxʷ II *rat, mouse.* Be sʔixk'ʷxʷ *bushtail rat* Se sk'ʷáʔxʷmin *mouse* ~ ESh k'ʷék'ʷxʷne *id.* Cv k'ʷík'ʷxʷnaʔ *id.* – Cf. ***k'ʷatʼan.** Ti sg'ʷák'ʷx̌ʷəw *rabbit* shows the same reduplication type but differs both formally (x̌ʷ) and semantically.

*k'ʷəy *frosty, grizzly.* Sq sk'ʷíačn *grizzly bear* Cw k'ʷeyʔəcn (Hukari k'ʷə́yəcn) *id.* Ck k'ʷiːcl *id.* Sm k'ʷeyəčn *id.* Sn Cl k'ʷəyečn *id.* ~ Th tk'ʷíyk'ʷit *silver grey*, ʔestk'ʷi-k'ʷyéytxʷ *silvertip grizzly* Sh ck'ʷey *hoarfrost*, stk'ʷey' *id. on trees*, stk'ʷyk'ʷey *silver-tipped grizzly bear* (Deadman's Creek: *any frost-colored animal*) Cv sk'ʷíylaʔxʷ *hoarfrost, frosty ground.*

*k'ʷay *to suffer.* Se k'ʷay *be hungry*, k'ʷayacút *be in pain* Sq k'ʷayʔ *hungry* Cw k'ʷeyʔ *id.* Ck k'ʷeːy *id.*, k'ʷək'ʷíyəθət *train o.s. to be an Indian doctor* Sm k'ʷéyʼk'ʷiyʼ *hungry* Sn k'ʷeyʼ *id.* Sg k'ʷék'ʷiʔ *id.* ~ Li k'ʷázan' *to train*, k'ʷazləx/k'ʷazánʼcut *train o.s.*, k'ʷzusm *to work*, nk'ʷzánwasm *to worry* Th k'ʷzusm *suffer, have a hard time*, k'ʷzncut *to train* Sh k'ʷyusm *suffer*, k'ʷyekstmns *to torture.*

*k'ʷuy *mother, aunt.* Ld Tw sk'ʷuy *mother* (in Tw also *pet name used between mother and daughter*) Ch k'ʷuy *mother*, k'ʷúyaʔ *mother, daughter (address form)* Ti čʼuyə *mother of male* ~ Th sk'ʷoz *aunt*, k'ʷuy *auntie (hypocoristic)* Sh k'ʷúyʼe *aunt (parent's brother's wife)* Cb Cv sk'ʷuy *(man's) mother* Cv sk'ʷúk'ʷiʔ *man's father's sister* (uncertain form) Ka sk'ui *(man's) mother* Sp sk'ʷuy *id.*, sk'ʷúk'ʷi *aunt (man's father's sister), nephew (woman's brother's son).*

l

*laʔ *good.* Be ya *good* Sn le(ʔ)t *repair, fix* ~ Th yʼe *good* Sh leʔ *id.* – Cf. PCS ***ʔayʼ.** Here both the l/y interchange (Intro 3C) and prothetic ʔV- (ibid. K) or inversion (ibid. A) may be involved.

*lu/acʼ, *yu/acʼ *tight, crowded.* [Cx x̌úsut *push* Sl x̌úθut *id.* Se yucut *id.*] Sq yúcʼunʔ *nudge, push aside w.*

elbow/shoulder, [yúcun? *push*] Sn sleç'əł *crowd together* Cl ?əsyac'ł *be full, crowded,* ~ Li luc' *tight* Th zuc't *id.* Sh luc't *id.* Cr yac' (Nicodemus yoc') *id.* – Cf. CeS *λ'u/ac'.

*lək' *to tie, bind.* Tw ləč-, lič-: ?asléč'á?lač *bundle,* ?asličús *hair is tied in front* ~ Sh lk'em *wind (string) around* Cb lək'n *tie up,* lək'm *arrest* Cv lk'ntim Ka Sp lč'ənten Cr leč.

*lək'ʷ *to pluck, pull out.* Tw ?asłík'ʷ *it's plucked,* yək'ʷə́d *pull/unplug it,* ?asyək'ʷənís *tooth is pulled out* ~ Cr luk'ʷ *pull, pick off strings, fuzz.* – If one starts from an original meaning *remove (by plucking or rubbing)* then here belong also Cx ǯək'ʷt *rub* Se yək'ʷt *id.* Sq ?iq'ʷ *id.* ~ Sh (t)lk'ʷntes *rub off dirt.* Cf. also Ld čə3q'ʷəd *rub about (as two pieces of cloth rubbed together),* see also ***yuλ'**.

*lul *to sing.* Sq lúlum ~ Sh lulm *sing a lullaby* Cr dul *sing warsong.*

*ləpəxʷ/x̌ʷ *(to make/go into) a hole.* Cx yə́pixʷ *hole* Se ləpxʷ *be punctured* Ch ləpə́xʷ- *hole* ~ Th ləpxʷetés *make hole(s) through st.,* ləpxʷuxʷ *riddled w. holes* Sh ləpx̌ʷum *make large hole,* ?əstləpux̌ʷ *id. w. one blow* Cv nlipx̌ʷm *enter into (an opening), go in,* nləpləpx̌ʷ *slip in,* [nləp'x̌ʷups *stuck in anus* Sp lep'éxʷ *sound of foot accidentally falling into hole* Cr lep'x̌ʷ *fit into (as ball and socket)*]. – Cf. ***pəlxʷ**.

*li/ap' *to bend down (esp. treebranch), bend over, cover; skew.* Be lip' *to fold, bend* Sq láp'ncut *be warped,* ?əslə́p'ləp' *all warped* Tw ?aslə́p' *he's covered,* ləp'átəbəš *cover me up!,* sləp' *blanket, cover,* lip'- *hang over, cover (without resting on covered object),* ?aslíp' *it's covered,* lilíp'ucəd *Quilcene River (named thusly because the stream is overhung with brush),* ?aslúp' *it's bowed (stick, tree, plant),* y-forms in ?asyáp' *it is down (as grass, flowers after rain),* yap'təd *slanted or curved stake* Cz yáp'a- *bend down (a branch)* ~ Li lap'n *cover w. blanket,* [lápan' *bend st. over,* líp'in' *squeeze*] Th láp'es *bend st. over (eg. bush, in order to pick berries)* Sh lep'ns *bend down (esp. branches),* [lip'ns *pinch*] Cb slap' *wood, stick* Cv Cr slip' *wood.* – Cf. ***łap'** and

PIS *-ú/ásləp'. The vowel of Tw ʔaslúp' stands out, as does a Li form under *ƛ'i/al; these may be instances of the common a/u interchange.

*liq' *to bury.* Tw ʔasliq' *buried* Ti liq'ín ~ Th yíq'm Sh líq'm Cb kalíq'ənaʔm; liq'łtəmənáy' *funeral* Cv líq'm Ka laq'm Sp láq'n Cr leq'.

*ləw/ʕʷ *to come off (as skin, bark).* Be lum *remove bark fr. tree,* luta *stick used for peeling bark,* law *loose* Cx łə́wšin *barefoot,* yíyʔgay *inner red cedar bark* Sq sláway? *cedarbark,* łuíc'aʔm *undress* Cw Ms sláwəy *(inner) cedar bark* (Hukari Cw sláwi?) Ck sləwə́y *id.* Cw ləwʔç'eʔm *undress* Ck ləwç'é:m *id.* Sm sláwə/iy' *cedarbark* Sn sləwiy' *id.* Cl syə́wi? *id.,* ʔəstuʔícə? (prob. c') *naked,* łuc'áʔŋ *take off clothing* Tw ʔasłáw *it's shelled, peeling* Ch łíw- *come off, out* ~ Li łáʕʷalqʷm/łʕʷálqʷm *peel off bark,* slúwaz' *inner cedar bark,* [líʕʷin *take apart*] Th sláwec' *treebark* Sh stłətew'lqʷm *strip off bark,* WSh clwləwʔekst *w. chapped hands,* clwxen' *w. chapped feet* Sp sliwt *chapped hands,* cluliwqstšn *chapped legs.* – Note that the derivative **sláway'* *(inner) cedar bark* is limited to CeS and Li Th.

With extensions -qʷ, -qʷ, -q', -q: Be łuq'lx *skin is peeling off,* łuq'ałt *inner red cedar bark* Se łəqʷt *strip off bark* Sq łuqʷ *come off (skin),* łəqʷ *id. (bark),* łáqʷan *peel bark* Cw słəqʷ *treebark,* łqʷat *bark a tree* Cw słəqʷ *barked or pulled off material* Ck łəqʷat *bark a tree,* łəqʷłə́qʷəqʷ *dandruff* Sm łəqʷ *peel/come off* Sn Sg łaqʷŋ *undress* Ld łúqʷud *peel st.,* łúqʷə/ač *bald head* Tw łuyáqʷib *undress* ~ Li ləqʷn *tear off,* łułqʷ *naked,* łúqʷun' *undress, take blanket off sb.,* łuqʷləx *undress,* lúqʷalqʷm *peel a log,* nłúqʷlaqin' *bald headed* Th łóqʷes *strip, pluck, remove cover fr. bed,* łoqʷqn *bald,* yíqʷes *peel off (bark, skin),* łiqʷetés *pry st. off* Sh luqʷm *pull out (feathers),* łweq *peel away,* łwqntes *pry loose,* cxłúqʷw'sqn *bald,* [(t)lkʷntes *rub off dirt*] Cb niʔləqʷ/sləqʷul'əxʷ *clearing (in timber),* nləqʷáw'asqn *bald,* [ləqʷn *break, smash* Cv lq'am *peel,* lqʷam *break off,* nt'l'qʷʕaw'sqn *bald*] Ka ʔesčłóqʷqn *bald* Sp loqʷ- *torn loose* *from, crack away,* [loq'ʷm *break st. up,* lqʷnten *id., tr.*] Cr łaqʷ *to skin, pull off,* łoqʷ *bald, bare,* [laq' *pare, peel,* laq *pull out plants,* lukʷ *pull, pick off strings, fuzz*]. – See also *ləkʷ.

With other extensions: Be łuc' *strip, undress* Cx łúp'ut *to peel* Se łúp'uw *peel off,* łup'íwst *skin an animal,* łup'áliqʷ/łup'iqʷán *bald head,* słuc' *a sore* Sq łuc' *be scabby* Cw łipət *strip off (slices, berries)* Ch ləp- *peel, strip off.* – Cf. NWAK ƛ'wqʷ- *bald, bare, barkless* (LR no. 1108) KWA ƛ'ukʷa *peel (bark) off w. a lever* (LR no. 1106) KWA ƛ'uskʷyu *bald in front* (LR no. 1101).

*law *to snare, catch.* Ti sləgə́qs CV *hang fr. nail* ~ Li lawúw'se *snare (a grouse),* law *be hanged, hung,* láwan' *hang st./sb. (on rope or string)* Th yéw'es *loop st. w. noose,* yéw'seʔtn *snare for small game* Sh lewt *get trapped, caught,* lewyn *to catch,* llew'sm *to snare (grouse, fool hen),* clew *hanging* Cr ligʷ *snare, catch in trap.*

*lix *slime, slimy.* Be lixm *to slip, slide,* łix *slimy,* ʔanulixmuc *drool,* nułi(ł)xmuc *id.* Cx ƛiš(im) *slime* Se słiš *id.,* słíšqin *saliva,* ʔəłšácut *clear one's throat* [Sq łixt *spittle*] [Cl stixʷm *slime*] Tw stələ́š *id.,* ʔastə́ləš *slimy* Ti sli(n)š (CV səliš) *saliva* ~ Li liʔx *slimy,* slíxil *slime* Th ləxlə́xt *slimy,* ləxlix *id.,* slʔix *fish slime,* łixt *have running sore,* [łʔix̌ *get smeared, slimy,* łíx̌es *paint w. thin layer,* ləx̌tes *smear*] Sh slex *fish slime* Cv snl'xíc'aʔ *scale of fish.*

*lax̣ʷ, *xʷal̥ *to shake, hurry.* Be ʔał̥ʔałxʷ *hurry* Ch yaxʷá- *shake* ~ Li xʷʔal̥ *be anxious to,* ləxʷ *become frenzied, "shook up" (as in spirit dance)* Th xʷʔal *hurried,* x̌ʷyekst *hurry,* Sh xʷʔal *hurry,* xʷəl'akst *id.* Cb xʷərp *shake,* xʷərrpm *nervous* Cv xʷrap *shake, tremble,* xʷrrapp *be in a hurry* Ka x̌ʷa:líp *tremble,* x̌ʷeʔłéčst *hurry doing st.* Sp xʷer *shake,* xʷrip *id.,* x̌ʷeʔłéčst *hurry* Cr xʷar *tremble, quiver,* x̌ʷił *hurry at st.* – The association *tremble - agitation, hurry* recurs in Li ƛ'əłp *shake, shiver (fr. cold/fright)* Sh t'łep *tremble, shiver* vs. Th ƛ'əłpstes *hurry sb.* and also in Wakashan, cf. KWA x̌ʷna *shake, shiver, tremble,* x̌ʷnta *be excited, agitated, nervous* (LR nos. 2090, 2092).

*ləxʷ see ***yəxʷ**.

*li/ax̌ *clear, bright, light; intelligence, mind.* Be nulax̌lx̌ *clear water,* nusx̌l (inv.) *smart, clever* Cx yax̌ *sober up,* ǰíx̌it *take apart, dismantle* Sl yi:x̌ *sober,* yi:x̌m *faire attention* Se ləx̌ləx̌ *fresh (water),* lax̌ *revive, sober (up),* lilx̌mít *watch, take care of,* yíx̌it *take apart, dismantle* Sq yəx̌ *far apart, w. large openings (eg. mesh)* Cw ləx̌ *spaced apart* Ck lax̌ət *give sb. light* Ld ləx̌ *be light,* lax̌ *remember,* ǰíx̌(i) *break down* Tw ləx̌ *light, far apart,* ʔasləx̌ *it's lit,* léx̌šəd *lamp,* bilix̌íd *inspect* Ch x̌ə́łlap- (inv.) *basket w. open weave* Ti nšłəx̌n *remember* ~ Li ləx̌ləx̌ *smart, intelligent,* ləx̌lax̌s *remember,* nləx̌lix̌ *clear water,* lax̌ *wide-mesh net* Th yəx̌yix̌ *smart, clear-thinking,* nyəx̌pus *sober up,* ʔesláx̌ *having spaces, in form of mesh,* yíx̌es *move apart, separate pl. objects (boards, planks)* [lax̌ləx̌ *female Thunder spirit*] Sh lx̌em *inform,* (c)lex̌ *clear, visible, known,* ləx̌lex̌ *smart, intelligent,* lx̌lix̌ *sober,* xləx̌lix̌ *clean, clear (of water)*; inv. in SIS Cb sx̌ə́lx̌əlt *day(light),* x̌ə̣lx̌ə̣lanxʷ *sober* Cv x̌al *clear, glittering,* x̌lap *tomorrow,* ksx̌lap *daylight,* nx̌ʕal *clear water,* tx̌lʕasqʼt *bright* Ka x̌al *daylight* Sp x̌al *light* Cr x̌el *be clear, bright, light,* x̌al *redhot,* lax̌ *lightning, be electric.* – Cf. KWA lax̌stu *clear (water)* HAI láx̌sda *id.* (LR no. 1243). Here prob. belong words for *finger* and *toe* which are derived, with somatic suffixes, from Se x̌əl- Sq nix̌- Cw Ms nəx̌- Ck ləx̌- Sn Sg nəx̌- Ld dəx̌- Ch łax̌- ~ Sh Cb lix̌-, via a notion *having spaces* (as in Th ʔesláx̌); Tw has derivations of səqʼ- *split,* Cb has for *finger* an alternative derived fr. PS ***caʕʷ** *fringe.*

*lax̌ʷ/x̌ʷay *to laugh.* Ch lax̌ʷá- ~ Sh x̌ʷyx̌ʷéye *(pl.)* Ka x̌ʷa:x̌ʷeʔéi *(pl.)* Sp x̌ʷaʔx̌ʷʔey *(pl.)* Cr x̌ʷad *be comical, be amused, laugh.*

*liʕʷ *loose, free.* Be law *loose* Sq yəx̌ʷ *untied, loose, free,* [x̌ʷilʼ *come out (nail, tooth, come off (lid)*] Ck yəx̌ʷ *loose, untied* [Sn x̌ʷəylʼ *lose, die*] Cl yəx̌ʷ *free, unbound* Tw ʔasyáw *loose,* yuʔún *untie it!* [Ch x̌ʷíl- *leave,* wałá- (inv.?) *come* *loose/untied, open*] ~ Li laˤʷləxʷ *make room for o.s.*, líˤʷin *dismantle, take apart*, líʔiˤʷ *fall apart*, [tiˤʷín *turn loose, set free*] Th líˤʷes *undo, take apart, loosen*, yíˤʷes *loosen (as screw)* Sh lˤʷliˤʷ *loose, leaving room* Sp nl'al'óˤʷeʔ *she wore a loose dress without a belt.*

    *li/aˤʷ (CS ***yax̌ʷ**) *to melt, thaw, open up (of ice).* Be x̌ʷay (inv.) *melt* Cx ȝ̌ax̌ʷ *id.* Se yax̌ʷ *id.* Sq Cw Ms Ck yax̌ʷ *id.* Sn čəx̌ʷn̩ *id.*, čax̌ʷn̩ *thaw* Cl čax̌ʷ *melt* [Tw ʔasyáx̌ *id.* Ch yə́xʷ- *id.*] ~ Li zaʔx̌ʷ *id., thaw*, záx̌ʷan' *melt st.* [Th zʔexʷ *melt, thaw*, zéxʷes *id. tr.*, zíx̌es *liquefy, melt, render (fat)*] Sh (x)lʔiˤʷ *to thaw, open up (of ice)*, xliˤʷt *id.*, łʔaˤʷ *melt, thaw (of snow only).*

ł

    *łaʔ *to touch; close by.* Sq łaʔ *touch*, łaʔí *approach* Sn łeʔə *like this* Ld łaʔ *arrive there* Tw łiʔə́ *right there, this* Ch łéʔ- *join in, among, be with* ~ Li łaʔn *put things close together*, słaʔ *be/go close*, łʔusn *lean st. against st.* Th łʔe *over there*, ʔesłéʔ *close by, near*, łeʔtés *lean st. agains st.* Sh tłʔem *id.* Cb Cv kłaʔqínm *lean against* Cv łaʔcnítkʷ *get to the shore*, łʔap *close to the end, dying* Cr łiʔ *be close to edge, be border.*

    *łi(-t, -c, -n, -t', -l) *to sprinkle, spray, splash.* Se łítit *besprinkle* Sq łitánʔ *sprinkle (a liquid)* Cw łəltəst *id.* Ck łəlt *sprinkle st. w. water* Sn łələt *splash*, łəltast *sprinkle st, spray*, łəlitn̩ *id.* Cl łitúst *sprinkle st.* Ld łə́ltəb *start raining* Tw ʔasłíc' *it's scattered* Ch łíc- *splash* ~ Li łílin' *sprinkle*, łə́lləc' *to splash (as car going through puddle)* Th łíƛ'es *id.*, łíyes *id.*, łáƛ'es *wet st., sprinkle, splash, spatter* Sh łnic'm *sprinkle*, łʔat' *wet*, łat'leʔxʷm *irrigate* Cv łilnt *sprinkle st.*, łit'pt *spill, spray out* Ka łin *sprinkle* Sp łilm *id., spray* Cr łil *id.*, łel *id,,* łetq' *splash, drop hits surface.*

    *łuʔ *to stab.* Nk łúmn *to spear st.* ~ Th ʔesłúʔ *stabbed*, łuʔ(e)tés *spear, stab, poke* Sh łʔum *stab, sting* Cv łw'am *pierce, stab* Ka łuʔ *sting, wound* Sp łuʔ *stab, pierce.*

*łək/q *worn out.* Sq Cw łčiws *tired* Ck łči:ws *id.* Sn Sg łčikʷəs *id.* Cl łiłčə́qi *id.* ~ Li łək *settle, deflate,* łək *conk out* Th ləkłek *sickly, tired,* łeʔkstés *wear sb. out* Sh łikt *worn out (material)* Sp łiqn *wear st. out.*

*łik' *to cut, sever.* Be łk' *pull off* Cx ləč't *give sb. a slight cut* Se łač'tn *knife* Sq łič *be cut,* łač'tn *knife* Cw Ms łic'ət *cut* Ck łi:c'ət *id.* Ms łec'tn *knife* Ck łe:c'tł *id.* Sn łiç'ət *cut meat,* ləç'el's *cut (as wood)* Sg łic' *cut* Cl łic't *cut meat* Ld łíč'id *cut* Tw ləč *sharp,* ləč'ilas *file* Ch ləč *sharp* ~ [Li łík'ala *flesh on rib-cage of fish*] Th łek't *cut open* Sh łik'm *break (as rope),* łk'ep *broken (as rope), dead,* łek't *scratched,* łi/i̯k'mt *get ripped, torn* Cr leč *string breaks.*

*łk'am *weasel.* Be łmk'mani Cw słc'em Ld łə́č'əb/łač'b Ti "La:'č'o:" CV ~ Cv łətk'am Sp Fl łč'im' [Cr sč'im' *woodchuck, marmot*].

*łu/akʷ/qʷ *to lap up, lick up; bail.* Cx łáqʷat *lick,* Cx Se łúkʷuł *to bail* [Sq łqʷí?wił *suck blood (mosquito)* Cw łəqʷ *wet*] Sn łəqʷłəqʷ *slurp while drinking (as dog)* łaqʷt *lick* Ld łaqʷad (stress?) *lick* Tw dəxʷłqʷú?lwiłbəd *canoe bailer,* [dəxʷλ'uqʷbəd *ladle*] Ch łə́qʷ- *lap (up)* ~ Li łúkʷun' *bail water,* (n)łúqʷun' *scoop up, serve,* nłuqʷmn *ladle,* nłaqʷctn *spoon for eating soapberries (whipped into foam)* Th łukʷn's *bail st. out,* łukʷtn' *bailer* Sh cxłuqʷm' *to dip water,* łuqʷtn *bailer,* łqʷétkʷe *lap up water (of dog)* Cv łkʷam *dog laps* Ka łkʷetkʷ *id.* – Cf. NWAK łwqʷ- *dish, bowl, basin* (LR no. 1187).

*łikʷ *to hook up, spike, string (beads), pierce.* Be nułkʷm *to knit, make a net,* nułkʷaqʷs *insert sticks into fish heads (prior to barbecuing),* [łkʷ *pick up by handle, gills, etc.*] Cx Sl łíkʷit *to sew,* Cx [łáqʷə?a?natn *earring*] Sq łikʷ *get hooked up,* łikʷšn *stumble* Cw Ms łəkʷtn *hook, gaff* Ck łəkʷtl *id.,* łi:kʷ *hooked, gaffed,* łikʷət *hook, gaff st.,* łək̓ʷxl *trip, stumble* Sm łəkʷšán'ətn̥ *he was tripped,* łikʷn *gaffhook* Sn łikʷ *get hooked, snagged,* łikʷšn *stumble* Cl łikʷiyúst *hang on nail,* łikʷt *hook up* Ld łíkʷid *hook, snag, catch* [Tw ?asťákʷ *pierced*] ~ Li łəkʷ *get poked, get an injection* Th

57

ʔestúkʷ *hooked,* ɬəkʷtes *hook st.,* ɬikʷ *prayer beads, rosary* Sh ɬkʷum *fork up* [Cb λ'əkʷpcin'tn *fork*] Cv ɬikʷ *bead, rosary,* ɬkʷntim *string beads,* [λ'kʷpam *pierce*] Sp hecɬíkʷ *it's strung (like bead),* ɬkʷnten *pierce,* nɬkʷpqin *hung up on end of nail or tree limb,* ɬekʷpcín'tn' *(eating) fork,* ɬekʷpm'ín' *pitchfork* Cr ɬekʷ *pierce w. fine-pointed object, fork, barb, spike.*

*ɬim *to detach.* Be ɬima *take st. away fr. sb.* Sq ɬəmn *pick berries,* ɬmimʔ *id.* Cw ɬəmc't *chip, erode; pick (fruit)* Ck ɬim *pick fruit/leaves,* ɬə́mət *id.* Sn ɬəŋes *detach, pull out (nail), skim off,* ɬəŋ *come off (as button),* ɬəŋiqʷŋ *decapitate* Cl ɬəŋ *come off (as button),* ɬŋas *detach* [Ch ɬími- *pick up, hook w. claws*] ~ Li nɬmákʔan *limb a tree,* məɬn (inv.) *tear off leaves/branches,* ɬímin *pick fruit* Th ɬímes *to trim, prune* Sh ɬimns *snap off/apart (as string, shoot fr. plant),* ɬɬim'ns *remove stems fr. berries,* ɬɬim'kns *limb a tree.*

*ɬum' *to eat soup,* ***s-ɬum'** *soup.* Be ɬum(a) *to sip,* sɬum *make soup* Sq ɬum', sɬum' Cw sɬap'; ɬəp'ç' *slurp up* Ck sɬap'/p Sm ɬap' *eat soup* Sn ɬap'n *spoon,* sɬap' *soup* Cl sɬup' *id.* Ld (s)ɬub *id.* Tw ɬuʔb, sɬuʔb Ch ɬumó:-; sɬoʔm *meat soup* Ti ɬuwətn *horn ladle spoon* ~ Li ɬum', sɬum' Th ɬum'm *eat w. spoon,* ɬúm'es *sip, slurp, eat soup* Sh sɬúmɬkʷe *soup* Cb sɬumkʷ *id.* Cv ɬum'n *spoon* Sp ɬuʔmn *id.*

*ɬap *to dwindle, go out (of fire); forget.* Tw ɬápad *forget* Ch ɬə́p- *fire gets low, goes out; die* Ti ɬa/əh(a)- *forget, go to sleep* ~ Li ɬapn *forget,* ɬapt *extinguished* Th ɬépes *extinguish, forget* Sh ɬepns *forget,* ɬept *gone out (of fire),* ɬepsm *extinguish* Cv ɬip *disappear,* nɬipt *forget* Ka ɬep *come to an end, dwindle,* nɬeptəmn *I forget it* Sp ɬeps *go out (light),* ɬepsnt *blow out (candle)!,* scnɬept *st. forgotten.*

*ɬip *to blink.* Cx ɬiptn *eyelashes* Se ɬəptn *id.* Sq ɬíɬipm *to blink (of lights),* ɬíɬipnáyus *blink one's eyes* Cw Ms ɬəptn *eyelash* Ck ɬəptl *id.,* ɬə́p(x̌)ləxʷ *blink one's eyes* Sm Sg Cl ɬəptn *eyelash* Sn ɬəptn' *id.,* ɬəphəlasŋ *blink* Ld ɬəp *id.,* ɬə́ptəd *eyelash, eyelid* Ch ɬipáliʔsm *blink, wink* ~ Li ɬipsm *blink,* ɬpal'sm *id.,* ɬpal's *eyelashes* Th ɬipəpíp *flutter eyelids, flirt,* łipsm *blink,* łpey'st *eyelashes, eyelid* Sh tłapsm (Bonaparte dial. tłipsm) *blink* Cv kłłpłpsam *id.* – Cf. *cəpł.

*łəp' *hang folded (as blanket on clothesline).* Cx łəp'c'im *flap, flutter (as clothes on line),* łə́p'q'ʷim *id. (as tail of fish in shallows)* Sq łəp' *hang st. (over rail, line, not on hook),* łap'n *id.* Ld łəp' *id.,* łp'ud *id.* Tw ʔasłəp' *hanging (over st.)* ~ Li łəp'n; łə́p'ləqs *turkey, elephant* Th ʔesłə́p' *hung over line,* łp'əm *hang st. over line* Sh słłep' *hanging over st.,* cłip' (Dog Creek dial.) *id.,* cłep' (Enderby dial.) *id.* Cv xʷiʔsnłp'ałc'aʔtn (geogr.) *Hellgate canyon, perhaps named for the many (xʷiʔ-) drying racks.* – Cf. *lap'.

*łəq see *łək.

*łaq *to (cause to) land somewhere,* ***łáq-ilx** *to sit down.* Cw łqet *attach, join together* Ck łəqtálə́stəxʷ *id.* Ti łéqil *sit down* ~ Li łəqp *float down and get stuck, run aground,* łəqpan *stick/slap st. onto st.* Th łəqpetés *id.,* łáqix *sit down, pl.* Sh łqem *paste/tack on, patch,* łeqlx *sit down, pl.* Cb łaqəlx *sit (up), sg.* [Cv łáq'ilx *lay down*] Ka łaʔqq *sit down, pl.,* łáqšilš *id., sg.* Sp łaqq *sit down, pl.,* łaq(š)lš *id, sg.,* nłqqeʔtkʷ *fall into the water, pl.* Cr łaq *mend, patch.* – Cf. KWA λaq *to patch* (LR no. 1040).

*łəq' I *wide, to spread, stretch.* Se łəq'nač̓əwił *flat-bottomed* Sq łəq' *wide* Cw łq'et *id.* Ck łəq'et *id.* Sm Sn Cl łq'ət *id.* Ld łəq't *id.* Tw łəq'dís *id.* Ch łə́q'- *id.* ~ Li łq'ulm'əxʷ *wide (flat) land* Th łaq't *wide* Sh łeq't *broad,* łeq'm *spread/stretch a hide* Cb łəq't *wide,* łq'il'x *lie down, sg.* Cv łaq't *wide,* łq'ilx *lie down* Ka łaq'ət *wide,* łq'ilš *lie down* Sp łaq't *wide,* łq'ilš *lie down* Cr łeq' *be wide,* łaq' *person lies on stomach, crouch.* – Cf. łəqʷ.

*łəq' II *instruction, knowledge.* Sq łq'iʔs *be acquainted with, know how to do* Ms łə́q'ələxʷ *know* Ck słə́q'ələxʷ/łəq'ə́l:əxʷ *id.* Nk łq'ílnuxʷ *id.* [Cl łq'iyən *spirit power*] ~ Sh łəq'mntés *instruct.*

*s-łiqʷ *flesh, meat.* Cx ƛiqʷ Sl ƛiʔqʷ Se Sq Cw Ms słiqʷ Ck słiyəqʷ Sm Sn Sg Cl słiqʷ Ti słiqʷ *fish* ~ Li Th słiqʷ ESh słiqʷ *flesh, skin* Cv słiqʷ *meat.*

*łəqʷ *to fall/duck to the ground, lie there.* Ch łaqʷx-*fall to the ground* ~ Li łqʷut/łáqʷut *brood, sit on eggs* Th łáqʷut *bend over, stoop down* Sh łqʷut *duck away, lie (face) down,* xłqʷətił't *brood, sit on eggs* Cb sn(ka)łqʷútn *bed* Cv nłqʷut *lie there* Sp łqʷut *id.*

*łəťʼ I *to jump, skip.* Be łťʼmtimut *grasshopper* Se łaťʼiqʷúyšn *to stumble* [Ld gʷəłtqʷád *fly up all at once*] Ch słuťʼm *grasshopper,* "słtłťʼuwan" *bounce up and down* Ti łťʼšə́nu *to stumble,* łťʼíx̌en *break wind* ~ Sh łəťʼpúyʼe *fillip on the forehead* Cb łəťʼp *bounce,* łťʼpəncut *jump,* łiťʼp *explode* Cv łťʼpmncut *id.,* łťʼłaʔťʼáp *bounce* Ka łťʼəp *jump* Sp łťʼpmncut *id.* Cr łeťʼ *one jumps.* – Cf. QUI łá:ťʼal *nodding, hanging down and springing up (eg. branch).*

*łəťʼ II *to catch fish w. hook and line.* Be łťʼ- *attach to or catch w. a hook* [Cx łəťʼəmin *herringrake,* Se łəťʼə́min *id.* Sq łəťʼm *rake herrings* Cw Ms łə́ťʼəmn *herringrake* Ck łeťʼm *id.* Sn Cl łəťʼm *rake herrings* Sg łə́ťʼəmn *herringrake*] Ch łə́ťʼ-*catch a fish* ~ Cb łəťʼpáyʼn Cv łłťʼam. – The bracketed words may belong here but could also contain a reduced form of the word *herring*: Cx łáʔgaťʼ Se słáwaťʼ Sq sławťʼ Sn słaŋʼət Sg słaʔŋət (prob. ťʼ); cf., however, Sm łeťʼ(ə)t *scattering (a fire; "raking it").*

*ław *matting,* ***ław-alqʷ** *raft.* Sq sławʔínʔ *a type of mat,* łáwliqʷ *big raft* Cw Ms słewn *bedmat* Ck słewl Sm s/šłewn *mat* Sn słə/ewn *wall mat, cattail mat* Ld słágʷin *pallet, mat(tress)* Tw słáwad *mattress* [Ch wałáł- (poss. inv.) *cattail*] Ti "sła:gín" CV *large rush mat* ~ Li sławʼinʼ *bedding, blanket,* słą́wlaqʷ *raft* Th słewyəqʷ *raft,* [ʔesłé/áw *loosely piled or pressed together*] Sh słewlqʷ *raft.* – The Li forms may well be borrowings from Sq (because of the close correspondence and of Li ą).

*ław(-al) *to leave behind, abandon.* Cx łáwaš (borr.), [gánim *orphan*] Se ławt, [wanwánim *orphan* Sq wanim *id.* Cw Ms wenm *id.* Ck wélə́m *id.* Sm kʷeṇn (inv.) *id.* Sn xʷskʷeṇn *id.*] Cl łuy(ə)s; [nəxʷskʷaṇn *orphan, abandoned person*] Ld łə́gʷ(ə)ł; təgʷəlígʷəd *orphan* Tw łuwał (stress?) *leave (eg. a trail),* łuwʔálbəd *inherit* Ch ławáł/ ławáli- [Ti cwánin *be left behind*] ~ Li łwaln; [łwaľctn *autumn*] Th łweys (also:) *get ahead of,* słwey'mt *widow(er),* [łwey'st *autumn*] Sh łwelns *abandon,* słweł *person left behind,* słwelmt *widow(er),* [(s)łwelstn *autumn*] Cb łwann *leave st.,* łəw'aľəmt *widow(er)* Cv łwinm *leave st.,* słwilmt *be in mourning, widowed,* słwiľmtx *widow(er).*

*łəxʷ *to draw on, wear,* ***łxʷ-ilx** *get foggy.* Be nułxʷ *shut window, close curtains,* łxʷilx *it is getting foggy* Se łúxʷači *gloves* ~ Li łə́xʷn *put on (clothes),* łúxʷun' *insert in st. hollow* Th łəxʷtes *put on (dress),* łełúxʷ *item of clothing (esp. those that go on over head)* Sh xłxʷilx *dress o.s.,* łxʷilx *be foggy,* cłxʷup *hung up,* xłəxʷqin'kst *thimble* Cb łəxʷ *hang up,* łxʷpáya *dress, shirt* Cv łəłaxʷ *dress,* kłixʷpnt *hang st. (eg. on peg),* łxʷpntim *slip on clothes,* nłxʷpaẋnt *loop st. over the shoulder* Cr łaxʷ *wear, draw on,* łexʷ *draw together, slip on,* słuxʷčt *glove.*

*łəẋʷ *to pass through a hole; escape, run away.* Be łẋʷm *flee, escape,* łẋʷt *pass through hole* [Ch łə́xʷ- *get/run away*] ~ Li łəẋʷp *escape alive,* łaẋʷ *recover* Th łẋʷup *escape,* łiẋʷp(mt) *id.,* [łúxʷpes *thread a needle*] Sh łẋʷum *pass st. through a hole, esp. put thread in eye of needle,* łẋʷup *escape,* łəẋʷpnwen's *pull sb. through, manage to keep him alive* Cv łẋʷam *bore a hole,* łẋʷap *escape,* kłłẋʷípla? *needle* Ka łẋʷənten *drill a hole,* estóẋ *a hole* Sp hecłóẋʷ *hole,* čłłẋʷéple? *needle,* łẋʷup' *escape, dash out* Cr łaẋʷp *escape,* [łexʷ *sew*]. – Cf. IS ***łaxʷ.** The meanings *pass through hole* and *escape, recover* are also combined in Sq qʷəh and in Ch pə́lxʷ-.

λ'

*λ'əʔ *to go after, look for st.* Cx λ'ə́ʔat *what one does,* λ'ə́ʔust *pick sb. up, call for sb.,* λ'ə́ʔuɬkʷum(?) *dig clams* Se λ'ə́ʔat *go and get* Sn λ'əl'et *look/search for,* λ'əl'elŋ *id.* Cl λ'iyát *id.* Ld λ'a *go to some place,* λ'áčup *fetch firewood* Tw λ'áčup *id.,* biλ'a?áčəd *I'm searching* Ch λ'a?ə́m/λ'a?m *look for,* λ'á?ičp *look for wood* Ti sλ'ə?n *looking for st. lost* ~ Sh t'?em *look for,* xt'?il't *look for eggs* Cb λ'a?λ'a?án'n Cv λ'?am *seek, fetch* Ka λ'e?ém *look around, look for* Sp λ'?em *look for.*

*λ'iʔ see ***λ'əy'.**

*λ'ak/q *to protrude, come (forth); long.* Be λ'q-*protrude:* λ'qalii(x)cm *stick one's tongue out,* λ'quɬ *hill, mound* Cx Sl Se Sq λ'aqt *long* [Se sɬəč'it *stick out*] Sq λ'iq *to come* Cw Ms λ'eqt *long* Ck λ'e:qt *id.* Nk λ'eqt *id.* Sm λ'i/eqt *long, tall (of tree)* Sn Sg λ'eqt *long* Cl λ'aqt *id.,* λ'iq *rise (sun)* Ld λ'íq(i) *emerge (in general),* λ'qil *come out of hibernation* [Ti sλ'kən *door*] ~ Li sλ'ak *fishing platform,* λ'əkz'us *to sprout, just come up (of plants)* Th λ'əkm'əm *protrude, stick out,* Sh st'ek *fishing platform,* st'eks *protrude, stick out,* [t'?ek *go,* st'?ek *come*] Cv λ'kiwt *stick out* Ka λ'eč *come forth, rise, stick out* Sp λ'eč *be visible,* λ'eččsm' *a sprout* Cr t'ič *protrude.* – Cf. KWA HEI λ'aq- *stretch linearly* (LR no. 1138).

*λ'əkʷ/qʷ *spotted.* Tw ?asλ'ələ́qʷ *spotted* ~ Sh st'uqʷ *spot,* stktəqʷtút'qʷ *spotted, fawn* Cb (λ')λ'ə́kʷλ'əkʷ *fawn (spotted)* Cv λ'əkʷλ'ákʷ *early fawn.* – Tw intrusive l as in Ck λ'ələ́qʷ under ***t'əkʷ/qʷ** *explode;* see also ***λ'ay'/λ'yaʔ.**

*λ'ikʷ *shelter.* Be nusλ'ikʷ [Sq tikʷ *find shelter,* λ'kʷə́ni *deaf*] ~ Li λ'ikʷm *take shelter fr. rain* Th λ'íkʷest *id.,* sλ'ikʷ *umbrella,* [sλ'ukʷ *round basket w. shoulder and lid*] Sh t'?ikʷ *stop raining,* t'?ikʷm *take shelter fr. rain,* [tut'kʷ *watertight basket made of roots* Cr t'ekʷ *watertight*]. – Cf. ***təkʷ.**

*λ'i/al *to stop, become motionless; dead, sick.* Cx λ'áyat *hold on to, hold steady* Se λ'álat *hold in hands,* λ'al *still, again* Sq λ'ay *be/act as previously, still,* ʔíλ'i *keep still, refrain fr. action,* λ'əyn *stop, tr.,* λ'ii? *id., itr.* λ'lλ'əlnəp *home settlement* Cw Ms Ck məλ'el *to faint* Cw sλ'əlnəp *ancient ground (settlement)* Ck λ'ələxʷ *to stop,* λ'əlexʷstəxʷ *hold st. steady* Sg məλ'el *to faint* Cl λ'áyuc'i *stop st.,* λ'aʔyac'ít *hold st. steady* Ld λ'əl *silent (esp. stillness of deep forest),* λ'al *located, stranded,* λ'al' *also, too, still* Tw ʔasλ'əl *it's dead (of small animal)* Ch λ'əl- *come to a stop,* λ'ən *stop* Ti sλ'ət *sick* ~ Li λ'əl *to stop,* λ'álan *id., tr.,* λ'il *keep still,* [λ'ulún *calm sb.*] Th λ'ey *stop,* λ'iλ'íyt *remain still,* λ'istés *hold st. still/steady,* λ'ipstés *cause to faint,* λ'al'- *awkward silence* Sh ʔəst'il *stop, quit,* ʔəst'lstes *stop st. (car, fight, etc)* Cv λ'lal *die, dead, motionless, lifeless, sg.,* λ'lmist *be still* Ka Sp λ'il *still, motionless, dead,* λ'lip *to stop.* – Cf. ***t'al'**, NWAK tl'- *dead, inactive, paralysed* (LR no. 1166). For Li λ'ulún see comment to ***li/ap'**.

*λ'ut *to grow, rise.* Cx Sl λ'ut *grow up* Se λ'útuw *be growing, pl.,* λ'útut *raise a child* ~ Li λ'utt *erection* Sh tkλ'utt *id.*

*λ'əm *to cut, chop; sharp.* Se λ'əmt *cut w. axe* Ch λ'əm- *chip, hew, chop* ~ Li λ'amín *axe* Th λ'əm'tes *chop* Sh t'mntes *id.,* t'mepm' *cut down (tree) w. axe,* t'ə(m)min *axe* Cb naλ'əms *sharp (point),* nλ'λ'əm's *a point* Cv nλ'mλ'imqs *sharp point* Sp λ'im *pointed, sharp.* – Cf. ***t'əm**; note that the Li Th Sh forms may reflect either ***t'** or ***λ'**.

*λ'apat *cedarbark basket.* Cx λ'ápat Se λ'əpatt Sq λ'pat Cw Ck λ'pet ~ Cb λ'pat *burlap sack.* – Cf. NOO λ'apat-, λ'apaːt *large storage basket made of cedar.*

*λ'aq see ***λ'ak**.

*λ'aqʷ/*qʷuλ' *(to smoke) tobacco.* Be λ'awqʷ/λ'aaqʷ *tobacco* [Sq λ'iqʷm *to smoke (as stove)* Cw sλ'eyəq'm' *id.*] ~ [Li λ'úqʷun' *suck*] Sh x̌qʷut'm *to smoke tobacco.* – This etymology is weak, because (1) it is based on Be and Sh only, and that with inversion; (2) the Sh word may well be a special semantic development of IS qʷuλ' *stick away, stuff, fill up (eg. chinks)* and (3) there is another PS root for *smoke tobacco*, see *manəxʷ/x. Cf. HEI λ'áwqʷ *tobacco* KWA λ'âqʷ *id.* (Boas 1947:224).

*λ'əxʷ I *to win, beat in game.* Cx Sl Se λ'əxʷ Sq Cw λ'xʷət, λ'xʷə́nəq Sn λ'xʷət Sg λ'xʷə́nəq ~ Li λ'xʷum Th λ'xʷəm Sh t'xʷum Cb Cv λ'xʷup Ka λ'exʷúp Sp λ'xʷup Cr t'uxʷúp.

*λ'əxʷ II *cold (object); numb.* Ld λ'uxʷ/x̌ʷ *cold (thing)* [Ch λ'ə́xʷ- *sting*] ~ Li λ'əxʷp *paralyzed* Th λ'xʷəm *paralyze*, λ'xʷəp *paralyzed* Sh t'uxʷ *be numb, have cramps* Cb λ'əxʷp *dead, pl.* Cv λ'xʷam *kill many*, λ'xʷntim *id.*, λ'xʷaxʷ *be frightened to death.*

*λ'əx̌ *fast, quick, swift.* Ch λ'ə́x̌- ~ Cb λ'əx̌t; λ'x̌atkʷ *rapids* Cv Ka Sp λ'ax̌t Cr t'ax̌. – Here may belong words for *hail*: Ch λ'áx̌ilqs Ti sλ'éx̌əw'; with secondary labialization due to the suffix Be sλ'x̌ʷusmał Sh stəx̌ʷt'əx̌ʷlúl'se (deviant forms in Ld λ'əbx̌ʷíla Tw λ'əbəw?iyax̌).

*λ'ax̌ *grown up, old.* Cx λ'áx̌ay? *old* Sl λ'áλ'x̌ay? *id.* Se λ'áx̌ax̌ *(getting) old* [Ld λ'ax̌ʷ *grow(th) (plant, animal, people)*] Tw sλ'x̌aλ'əx̌təd *parents,* [?asλ'ə́x̌ *sitting/standing straight,* ?asλ'ax̌ʷ *real old person*] ~ Th λ'ax̌t *tall* Sh t'ex̌t *id.*, st'əx̌?em *grownup person* Cb λ'əx̌p *grow up*, λ'əx̌λ'əx̌p *old man* Cv λ'x̌ap *grown*, λ'x̌λ'x̌ap *old man.*

*λ'ax̌-ilx *to go upstream.* Ti λ'ex̌-íl- ~ [Li λ'ax̌il *attack*] Sh xt'ex̌lx *run upstream (of salmon)*, [t'ex̌lxmns *charge at*].

*λ'əy' *to want, desire; dear, difficult.* Sq λ'i? *dear, difficult, dangerous, excessive*, λ'ínit *wish for* Cw λ'i? *difficult*, sλ'i? *want, desire, like* Ck λ'i:ls *like, love* Nk λ'i? *difficult,* nə λ'i *I like/love* Sm λ'i? *difficult*, sλ'i? *want, like*, λ'i?tn *expensive* Sn λ'i? *to like, difficult* Sg λ'i? *difficult* Cl λ'e? *id., liking, want* ~ Li λ'inúxʷn *admire, wish for* Th λ'i? *difficult,* sλ̓i?s *he likes it* Sh t'ynuxʷm *want, desire.* – For the semantic connection *dear, desired - difficult* see also *x̌aλ̓.

*λ̓ay'/*λ̓ya? *(river-)canoe.* Be ?aλ̓a *build a river canoe,* saλ̓a *river canoe* Ck λ̓əle:y *shovelnose river canoe* Nk λ̓ley? *id.* Ld λ̓əlay? *id.* Tw λ̓al?áy *id.*, λ̓ay?úlał *notched-bow canoe, traveling canoe, small trolling canoe,* stálaλ̓li *vessel, craft, canoe* ~ Li λ̓l̓az' Sh λ̓ye? Cb λ̓íya? *birchbark canoe,* Cv λ̓'?i? Ka λ̓iyé? Sp λ̓ye? Cr t'éde?. – The CeS and Li words point to ***λ̓lay'**, with an unexplained intrusive l, see comment under ***λ̓əkʷ/qʷ**.

*λ̓əʕʷ *hard (substance).* Be λ̓ax̌ʷ [Cx Sl Se λ̓əqʷ] Sq Cw Ms Ck Nk Sn Sg λ̓əx̌ʷ [Ld λ̓əqʷ *solid*] Ch λ̓əx̌ʷ ~ Li λ̓əʕʷλ̓ʕʷm Th λ̓oʕʷt, λ̓oʕʷλ̓óʕʷt Sh tʕʷt'uʕʷt. – Cf. NWAK λ̓ax̌- *stiff, rigid* (LR no. 1139) QUI λ̓i:x̌ *hard (as surface).* Cb st'əʕʷána? *flint* would fit semantically but has the wrong initial.

m

*mu? *fish weir.* Be mu ~ WSh mu? ESh mu?t/muy't; for the latter variant cf. Li nmúz'xal *set a trap* and poss. Th múc'es *bend into arc,* múc'cetn *rim of birch basket or boat* Sh (Deadman's Creek dial.) cm?oy *bent.*

*məckʷ *blackcap (Rubus leucodermis).* Cx məskʷ Tw məcə́kʷ ~ Th mə́cəkʷ Sh mcukʷ Cb məckʷ Ok mcakʷ Sp mcukʷ.

*məc' *to cheat, trick, lie.* Sq nəxʷməc'(t)nalqp *a lie* Cw him?ç'é?nt *disbelieve* Ck (xʷ)meç'əlqə́yləm *a lie,* məç'ə́ləxʷ *disbelieve* Tw ?asc'əmə́qʷ'ab (inv.; m *sic*) *liar* ~ Li məc'ussm *to cheat* Sh mc'usm *id.* Cv mc'am *trick, fool sb.* – A possible (l)x- extension in Th məc'x- *miss, fail to meet* Li mic'ləx *to dodge,* məc'xxn *step on st. which then slips* Sh mec'x *to dodge.*

*məç'(-u̜l) *pus, matter;* (w. suff. *-qin) *brain.* Be numc' *squeeze out sb.'s boil,* mnc'łta *pus* (for -n- see ***pət**) Cx mác'uł *id.* Sl máç'uwm Se məc'uł *id.,* məc'ulm *be abscessed,*

smac'alaqin (stress?) *brains* (-al- connective) Sq mác'uɫ *pus*,
smǝc'alqn *brains* Cw Ck (Hukari, Galloway) mǝ́ç'ǝɫ *pus* Ms
mǝ́c'ǝɫ *id.* (c' irreg. instead of ç'), Cw Ms Ck smǝç'qn *brain* Nk
smǝ́ç'qin *id.* Sn ŋǝ́ç'ǝɫ *pus*, smǝç'qn *brain* Sg ŋǝcǝɫ (prob. c')
suppurate Cl ŋǝc'ɫč *pus*, sŋǝc'ayǝtn *brains* Ld bǝc'ulǝb *pus*,
sc'ǝbqid *brain* ~ Li mác'uɫ *pus*, sc'ǝmqin *brains* (inv., as common in IS), sc'mank *guts*, c'úm'c'm' *boil, big pimple* Th mc'uɫt
pus, sc'ǝm'qin *brain*, c'ǝ́me *smelt or eulachon roe* Sh mc'uɫt
pus, sxc'mɫos *matter in eye*, sc'mqin *brain*, sc'menk *tripe,*
guts Cb mǝc'uɫt *pus*, c'ǝm'qǝnalxʷ *brains* Cv mc'ʕaɫt *pus*,
skmc'mʕac'ǝs *eye matter*, sc'mqin *brains*, [mc'min *oil*] Sp
mc'oɫt *pus*, čmc'mac's *he has sleep in his eyes*, sc'mqin *brain*
Cr mác'uɫt *pus*, smc'c'oɫtm *abscess*, sc'óm'c'om'ɫt *a boil*.

*mǝc'ǝp *bee, wasp.* Tw mác'ap *bee, yellowjacket* ~ Th
mǝ́c'e *wasp, bee, hornet* Sh mác'pe? *wasp, blackjacket* Cb
mǝc'p *bumblebee* Cr mac'p *bee, wasp.* – The Sh form contains
the suffix -(ú)pe? *tail,* so that an alternative reconstruction is
*mǝc'-up(-a?).

*mǝkʷ(u?) *to cover (with blanket), wrap.* Sq mǝ́kʷ(u?)
be wrapped, mǝkʷtn *blanket*, (naxʷ)mǝkʷúcin *kiss* Cw
xʷmǝkʷǝθǝt *id.* Ck xʷmǝ́kʷeθm *id.* Nk qʷǝ́mten (inv.) *blanket*
Cl naxʷmǝkʷuct *kiss* [mǝkʷ'e?tŋ *buried*, mǝqʷ'e?ǝt *bury a*
corpse] Tw bǝqʷúsad *kiss her!* Ch "mukʷá:p" CV *breech clout*
~ Th m(ǝ)kʷu?tés *wrap sb./st. up (eg. in blanket, cloth)*,
?esmúkʷ *wrapped up* Sh mkʷ?usn *cover sb.'s face w. blanket*,
tmǝkʷ?en'm *tuck in blanket.*

*mǝl *to erase.* Be mil, ml ~ Sh mlxncut *erase one's*
tracks with the feet.

*mǝl in name of *hemlock/balsam tree.* Ck mǝlǝmǝ́ɫp
western hemlock ~ Li mǝ̣líntǝp *balsam tree* Sh mlenɫp *id.*,
mlnɫpal'txʷ *balsam-tree bark* Cb mǝrímɫp *id.* Cv mǝríɫp *id.*
Ka (Carlson-Flett) manínɫp Sp mrinɫp.

*mal(-a?) *(fish)bait.* Sq mámi?n *bait a line* Cw me?lm
to bait Ck mé:le/ǝ *any bait* Sm Sn ŋel'ŋl' *fishbait* Cl ŋáy'ŋi?
id., ŋa?ŋá?t *bait a line for fish* Tw bá?bǝl?i *bait* ~ Li maml' *id.*

Sh tmləqin'tn *fishbait*, mlmélns *to lure (animal)* Cb məl'ay'n *(to) bait* Cv míla? *id.* Cr m'el'e *id.*

*maḷ *to cure (as shaman).* Ld báɫ(a) ~ Li məḷa(m)mn *medicine*, mayt *fix, repair, be in session (Indian doctor)*, maysn *fix, cure patient* (the latter two words borr. fr. Th) Th mlamn *medicine*, meyt *perform healing ritual*, méyses *treat (as shaman)* Sh mlámns *apply medicine, heal, baptize* (also *marry*, cf. CJ malieh *id.*), mla(m)mn *medicine* Cb mryam *id.* Cv mrím- *cure* Ka ma:liyé *medicine*, ma:liyémn *to doctor sb.* Sp mryemn *id.* Cr marím *treat for illness.* – See PIS ***məlin-ɫp.**

*s-m?al *father's brother.* Ti swə?aɫ CV ~ Cb sm?al Cv "sme'əɫ" CV Ka "smê'əl" CV Sp sme?ɫ.

*mul *to dip, sink, flood.* Be mulm *to dive* Se məl *sink* Sq muy *submerge, flood over*, məl *sink* Ld bə́ləwᵊb *bubbling up, spring of water, boiling*, bulq/qʷ *fill, overload, dunk, push under water* Tw búli *spring of water* Ch mól- *id.* ~ Li múlun *put st. into the water* Th nmúyes *dip in liquid* Sh xmulkʷm *id.* Cb muln *id.* Cv mulm *fish w. dipnet* Ka mul *fetch water*, məl' *to flood* Cr mul *dip up.* – Here may belong the retracted root in Sh malt *deerlick*, smlóle?xʷ *clay* Cv sml'áˤla?xʷ *id.*, mlˤam *smear*, nmlˤasnt *fill w. clay-like substance* Ka malt *mud, clay, earth* Cr ml'ol'mxʷ *soil.*

*məlkʷ/qʷ *to twist, tangle, sprain.* Tw ?asbul?úqʷ *tangled up, pinched*, bibúl?uqʷ *twist*, bul?úqʷšəd *his foot is caught on st.* ~ Li mḷukʷ *sprained, dislocated* Sh (c)mlokʷ *out of joint*, mlkʷ- *dislocate, sprain (w. retracted suff.)*: mlkʷpakst *dislocate one's wrist* Cb mər'kʷ *id.* – Deviating forms for *sprain* in Sq Cw Ld p'əɫq'ʷ- Ch p'ayə́q'ʷ- Cv mɫq'ʷ-.

*məlkʷ *to wrap up, collect into a whole; intact, complete.* Tw ?asbulúkʷ *it's round; a ball*, bibulúkʷad *winding twine or yarn into a ball* Ch mə́lkʷ- *wrap* ~ Li məlkʷán *make round, smoothen out lumps on a stick* Sh mlkʷum *collect into a whole, round up, gather one's forces*, [plukʷ *gather*] ESh mlkʷépe?st *stallion*, Cb məlkʷ *round*

67

(pole), məl'k'ʷaľqʷ *bracelet* Cv cmalkʷ *whole*, mlmlk'ʷápaʔst *testicles*, nmlk'ʷápaʔst *stallion* Sp milkʷ *solid, whole*, [milqʷ *balled*] Cr melkʷ *be whole, intact, complete.*

*mal(-q) *to be aimless, lost; be pacified (child); forget.* Be numilik *confuse sb.* Cx míymaʔyaw *be lost (as in fog)* Se malmálaw *be lost, wandering around* Sq may *forget*, miʔmáyʔ *get lost, lose one's way* Cw melʔq *forget* Ck málml *blunder, make a mistake*, melqləxʷ *forget*, mlqi:wsm *faint* Sn məľəqt *forget* Sg mǽlʔəq *id.* Cl miʔmǽyəq *id.*, smǽy'əq *id.* Ld báli *id.*, báluqʷ *mixed up, entangled* Ch mǽľq- *id.* ~ Sh mlmélns *pacify (child)*, ESh also mélqes *id.*, Sh tməlmelkst *be unable to control one's hands* Cb máľn *sing lullaby to* Cv milmlt *be slow*, millx *linger* Cr miľ *be aimless.*

*malxʷ/x̌ʷ *naked.* Ch mələ́x̌ʷ- *undress*, malə́x̌ʷ *naked* ~ Cb ktmalxʷ Cr milxʷ.

*mał *to rest.* Be mnł *to pause, interrupt*, mnłimut *to rest* (for -n- see under **pət*), mał- *slow* Tw bałáb Ti wał- ~ Li máłam Th métest Sh metłx Cb matm Cv mił(m) Ka meł Cr mił.

*s-mułac *woman.* Ti swiłéc, diminutive swuwí/útec ~ Li smútac. – See comment under **ʔimac*.

*s-mł(ik) *salmon; summer.* Be smłk *fish, salmon*, ʔamł *spring salmon, summer*, samł *sockeye salmon* Ch mətíč *summer* ~ Ka Sp Cr smłič *salmon*. – Cf. KWA OOW młik *sockeye salmon* (LR no. 156).

*maƛ' *to mix, stir.* [Be mal- Cx mát'at *smear st. on st., besmear st.* Se mát'aw *besmeared* Ck məmíləc' *mixed up*] Ch máƛ'a- *stir*, ƛ'ám'a- *stir thin liquid* ~ Li máƛ'an', [miʔƛ' *dirty, kind of greasy*] Th méƛ'es Sh mét'm Cb niʔmáƛ' Cv miƛ'nt *rub st.* Sp miƛ'm *smear, spread, churn* (borr. fr. an i-language) – Cf. NWAK mł- *to stir, mix by stirring* (LR no. 154).

*mnak *excrements.* Be mnk Cx mə́nač Ch mənáč- (manə́č'uw'ł geogr. *"lavatory"*) ~ Sh mnek Cb mənák Ok kmn'akmnqn geogr. "deriving its name from its convenience"

Cv mnik, -ma?ník- Ka mn'eč Sp mneč. – Cf. PS *-anak, NWAK mnk- KWA mnak (LR no. 142).

*manəxʷ/x *to smoke (tobacco),* *s-manəxʷ/x *tobacco.* Be milixʷ *kinnikinnick berry (leaves were dried and smoked)* Sn Sg smenəš Cl smanəš Ld sbadəš ~ Li sman'x *Indian tobacco* Th men'xm *to smoke,* smen'x *tobacco* Sh smanx Cb sman'xʷ Cv man'xʷ Ka men'xʷ Sp (s-)men'xʷ Cr (s-)mil'xʷ.

*məq' *to swallow, eat one's fill.* Cx Sl məq' Se sməq'ít Sq məq'; sm?iq' *full fr. eating* Cw məq' *id.* Cw Ck máq'ət *to swallow* Nk máq'n *id.* Sm məq' *satiated (w. food),* ŋ(ə)q'ət *swallow st.* Sn məq'; ŋəq'ət *to swallow* Cl ŋəq'ət *id.,* ?əsmaq'ł *satiated* Ld bəq' *put in mouth, swallow* [Ch máqʷ- *to swallow*] ~ Li Th Sh məq' Cb məq'ank Cv mq'ink Ka mq'enč. – Cf. q'əm *to swallow* and CJ muck-a-muck (Zenk 1993 mê'k(ê)mêk) *to eat, food.*

*məqʷ *to pile up, lump.* Cw məqʷəyi?yəsm *pile up* Nk múqʷenes *clenches fist* [Sn məqʷeyəčt *pile up*] Sg məqʷé (= éy) *id.,* məqʷeyéč't *id.* Cl məqʷəye?čt *id.* Tw ?asbáqʷab *piled up* ~ Cb ?acmáqʷ *mountain, hill* Cv Ka Sp mqʷ-*mountain, bump, lump* Cr maqʷ *pl. objects lie, pile.* – Cf. *kʷ/qʷum, *qʷum.

*s-məqʷ-a? *crane, heron.* Be maqʷanc Sq smáqʷa? Cw Ms Ck smáqʷa (Cw Hukari smáqʷa?) Sm sŋákʷa? Sn sŋəqʷə? Cl sŋáqʷu? Ld sbəqʷá? ~ Li smáqʷa? Th smúqʷe Cb smúqʷa? Ka səmóqʷe? Sp smóqʷe?. – Cf. KWA maqʷns *story name of Heron* (LR no. 237).

*mus I *four.* Be Sl Nk mus Sm Sn ŋas Sg ŋəs Cl ŋus Ld bus, buːs Tw búsas Ch mus Ti wus ~ Th Sh mus Cb musəs Cv Ka Sp Cr mus. – Cf. NWAK mw- (LR no. 190), NOO moː-, moy-, moː, QUI bá?yas.

*mus II *to feel about, touch.* Be mus ~ Th Sh Cb Ok mús- Cv mssikst *feel w. hand* Sp mús- Cr mus *fumble, feel about.*

*mut see *?amut.

*mət'uṣ *kidney.* Ch mət'ús- ~ Li məƛ'uṣanktn Th
məƛ'oṣ-/məƛ'us-éłc'i?tn Sh mtmət'us Cb mət'uṣ Cv mt'ʕas Sp
mt'os Cr mót'us (Nicodemus mát'us).

*mat'ay/*t'amay *horse clam* (IS > *snail*). Cx mát'ay Se
smət'ay Sn st'əmye:q Ld st'ə́bc/ʒə? Tw st'ə́bʒa Qn mit'áqs ~ Cb
(s)t'əm't'əm'l'úy'a? *slug, polliwogs* Cv t'mt'm'aʕł *snail* Cr
t'am't'am'yúye? *id.* – See Kinkade 1990:201. KWA mət'áni?
(Boas 1947:233), -ani? suff. in animal names (ibid. 243).

*miX̌ał *black bear.* Cx Sl Sq míX̌ał ~ Li Cb míX̌ał. – A
poss. connection is Cv mX̌- *to stoop,* smX̌ikn *grizzly bear* Ka
səmX̌é?ičn' *id.* Sp smX̌ey'čn *id.* Cr smaX̌í?čn' *id.* (semantically
cf. Sq (?ə)sqʷúqʷus *sneak, have head lowered between
shoulders* and qʷúqʷusam *porcupine).*

*s-mɣaw *a large feline or canine.* Sm
sməyaw/sməy'aw *fox* Ld sbiáw(?) *coyote* ~ Li səmɣaw' *lynx*
Th Sh smɣew' *id.* Cb smiyáw *coyote* Fl skʷtisəmiyé *cougar,
any big cat* Cr smiyíw *coyote.*

n

*s-na?m *shaman (power).* Sq sna?m Cw šné?em Ck
šxʷla:m Nk šxʷné?em Sm š(xʷ)né?em Sn Sg šne?m Cl
sxʷna?m Ld (d)xʷda?ᵇb ~ Li s(xʷ)na?m *spiritual power,*
[sxʷnamt *co-parent-in-law* (cf. the semantics of *X̌a? I **and
II**)] Th səxʷne?m *shaman,* sne?m *spirit power (song),*
[sxʷnemt *in-law of child or sibling*] Sh (Kamloops dial.)
sne?m *spiritual power,* [sxʷnemt *in-laws*]. – Uncertain connection w. *nəh, *na(?), see p. 222.

*nak', *nk'-u? (IS *nkʷu?) *one, another,* (in
derivatives:) *family, tribe;* *nak' (also:) *to change, differ.* Cx
nač- *one,* náča?gił *one canoe,* náčaxʷ *once* Sl nəčnəxʷi:gas
être différents náčaxʷ *once, first* Se nəčáli *one person,*
náčawtxʷ *one/other house/room,* načáxʷ *once,* snəčə́lnaq
spouse's sibling's spouse, snəčuwyəł *step-sibling,* [nəčt *put
sb. on one's side,* náča *to look like*] Sq nču? *one,* náčaw'txʷ
one/other house/room, náčan *to change,* nčáy?uw?am *family*

(all descendants of one head), snč̓ínaq *spouse's sibling's spouse,* snč̓áwił *half-sibling* Cw Ms náč̓a? *one* Ck láč̓à *id.* Cw Ms xʷnac̓álwm *family* Ck xʷlac̓álwm *id.* Cw Ms snac̓áłaq *spouse's sibling's spouse* Ck slac̓áłaq *id.* Cw Ms snac̓áwayał *half-sibling* Ck slac̓áwayał *id.* Sm náč̓a?/náč̓a *one,* neč̓ *different,* snac̓/č̓a *spouse, "other half" (slang)* Sn nač̓a? *id.,* neč̓ *different, strange,* snač̓iwał *half-sibling* Sg náč̓a *one,* neč̓ *be different, changed* Cl nác̓u? *one,* nác̓u? *one (person),* snič̓íwał *half-sibling* nác̓aw'txʷ *next-door neighbor* Nk nač̓ú(?) *one* Ld dač̓u? *id.* Tw dač̓úsad *once (more),* dač̓úl?waltxʷ *next/another house* Ch náč̓- *one,* nač̓aw- *id. (compounding form),* nač̓áwumš *tribe* Ti snač̓ák̓ʷc *one basket,* na/ač̓ás/š *once, "snač̓ltx̌"* CV *son-in-law, wife's father* ~ Li snúk̓ʷa? *friend, relative* Th núk̓ʷe?me *befriend,* sné?ekʷ *wife's sister's husband,* nék̓es *change* Sh nkʷu? *one,* nkʷusm *party, family,* nek̓m *to change,* snek̓łxʷ *son-in-law* Cb nkʷu?qín *a hundred,* nak̓ʷspantk *year,* snak̓łxʷ *son-in-law* Cv nkʷspintk *one year,* nkʷcwixtn *one living group, tribe,* snak̓ʷł/s- *partner* Ka nk̓u? *one,* nkʷełxʷ *one house,* sankʷélixʷ *guests, family(?)* Sp nkʷu? *one,* snkʷpentč̓ *one year,* hisnkʷélixʷ *my people/tribe,* sneč̓txʷ *son-in-law* Cr nékʷe? *one,* nikʷ *tribe,* sničłxʷ *son-in-law.* – See comments under *x̌ac.

nik̓ *to cut.* Be nik̓ Tw dič̓- ~ Li ník̓in̓ Th Sh nik̓m Cb nnik̓mn̓ *knife* Cv nik̓m Ka Sp nič̓m Cr nič̓.

naqas *one.* Tw dáqas; dáqanaqs *alone* ~ Cb Cv naqs *one.*

nis *blow one's nose.* Se nast Tw dísad ~ Li nísqsam̓; nusas *breathing loud through nose* Sh x̌ʷnism; sx̌ʷnis *snot* Cb nism; snis *snot* Cv nʕasm; snʕas *snot* Ka nos *be snotty,* sanos *snot* Sp Cr snos *id.* – May ultimately belong to *nu̓/a̓s, or have been contaminated with it.

nu̓/a̓s *marrow, fat, oil; wet.* Sq snasqn *hair oil,* nsqinm *rub oil in one's hair* Cw Ms snas *fat* Ck la(:)s *id.* Cw snasšn *marrow* Ms snasxn *id.* Ck slasxl *id.* Sm nas *fat,* *grease*, snas *oil* Sn snas *fat, grease* Sg nas *be fat*, snas *fat, grease, oil* Ch núsi- *damp, wet*, snus *moisture* ~ Li nəsnus *damp*, núsun' *make damp* Th ʔesnús *damp*, nusm *dampen, soak* Sh sansn (inv.) *matter, pus* Ka Sp Cr nas *wet.* – Cf. *nis.

naw-ilx *to run.* Ti nenégil (√neg) ~ Sh newlx Cb naw'əlx. – Here probably belongs IS **naw** *wind blows.*

p

paci/aʔ *digging stick.* Tw paci Ti nhaci ~ Li pácaʔ Sh péce Cb pácaʔ Cv pícaʔ [Sp péc'eʔ] Cr píceʔ.

packl *leaf.* [Tw (Haeberlin) "pəcčlo:lx" *barn*, lit. *hay house*] Cz pəckł TCh "pîʔcəkł" [Ti iháči CV Si čéło CV] ~ Li pəckł Th pcəkł Sh pcekł Cb pəckl Ok packł Cv pickł Ka Sp picčł Cr peccle (Nicodemus adds pécceleʔ *blade, broccoli, etc.*, lit. *leaf, cabbage*).

puh see *paw.

pik' see p'ik'.

pək^w/q^w *to spill, pour.* Se pəq^{w}s *fall overboard* Tw spáq^{w}ał *waterfall* Ch páq^w- *spill* ~ Li pák^{w}ən *id.*, [p'úk^{w}un *pour solids into st.*] Th pək^{w}tés *dump out solids* Sh pk^{w}um *pour dry substances, scatter* Cv pk^{w}min *pour solids*, Ka pk^{w}ənten *shake off, throw down pl. obj.*, Sp pk^{w}nten *pile up*, yecpk^{w}úm *scatter.* – Cf. *pəq'^{w}.

pal *thin, flat.* Be lplii *thin* Se spáłxan *tideflats, prairie* Sq spałx̌n *flats, flatland* Cw Ms spáłx̌n *id.* Ck spətx̌l Sm spe/ałx̌n *field, grassy clearing* Sn Cl spətx̌n *id., valley, prairie* Ld spáłx̌ad *tide/marsh flats* Tw spəłx̌ad *marsh, swamp* Ch páłx̌n *swamp, valley* ~ Li spáləm *prairie, flat land*, Sh spelm *prairie* Cb pəl *flat* Cv pil *flat*, spilm *flat country* Sp pil *thin* Cr spílem *level land.* – Cf. *p'i/al and QUI pałá: *flat*.

pi/al *to scatter, smudge.* Cx páyit *scatter* Se pílit *id.*, pətq'^{w}ús *have dusty face* Sq pił *be smudged*, piłánʔ *scatter (ordered things)* [Tw ʔasp'ił *it's scattered/spread*, ʔasp'úł *it's powdered*] ~ Li pálan *spread out berries to dry* Th péy'es *scatter* Sh pilns *scatter*, xpillx *disperse (itr., of persons)*, pálns *to smear, smudge* [Cb ʔaçpáɫ *puddle*, kpạɫə̣tṣ *tears*] Cv pɫiwt *scattered about*, ppiɫ *be scattered*, kɫpiɫltm *spread berries to dry* [Ka pilš *to go in, pl. (disperse to homes?* AK*)*] Cr piɫ *be scattered*, [par *be white w. powder*].

*pul *to tip over.* Cx pəlm *fall down* Sq pəym *fall overboard* Tw púlal; ʔaspúl *tipped over* Ti √hul: chúʔli *I tip over* ~ Li pəl/lʼpuł *fall overboard* Th púyes *overturn* Sh pulm *put upside down*, xpúlkʷe *capsize* Cb napúlkʷn *turn st. upside down*, napúlʼlkʷ *capsize*.

*s-pl-ucin *mouth, edge.* Tw spəlúcad *edge of canoe or tub* Ti shəlucín *mouth* ~ [Th splimcn] Sh splucn *id.* [Cv Ka Sp splimʼcn *id.*].

*s-paḷ-mn *calf of leg, muscle.* Ld spálbəd *calf of leg* ~ Li spaḷʼmn *id.* Th Sh spalʼmn *id.* Cr sparmn *muscle.*

*pəlʼkʷ/*pətkʷ *to pierce.* [Ld pətq] Ch pálkʷ *have holes* Cz pəlʼə́kʷ- ~ Li pətkʷ *boil bursts open*, pátkʷa *needle* Th pétkʷe *id.*, ptukʷ *ooze out*, [pəlʼxʷə́m *pierce*, pl'uxʷ *id.*, puʔxʷstés *id.*] Sh pətkʷum *pierce*, pétkʷətn *needle* Cb patkʷcínʼtn *fork* Ok sptkʷam *nail* Ka esptkʷéneʔ *his ear is pierced* Sp ptkʷum Cr párʼkʷ *pierce*, perʼkʷ (Nicodemus pérkʷ-) *to nail.* – The forms with t may be due to a special development, cf. Sh mítkʼye *blood* Cb mɫkʼáyaʔ *id.* Cv mɫkʼíyaʔ *id.* (Vogt 1940b mlkʼíʔæʔ *id.*) Cv mlʼalʼ *to bleed* Sp mlʼlʼaqs *nosebleed*, mlʼilʼ *it flowed* Cr mítʼčʼede *blood.* Cf. ***pəlxʷ**, PIS ***mitʼkʼayaʔ**. See comment to ***ʕʷəlqʷ**.

*s-pəlan *skunk.* Ti shəlen ~ Li s/sp̣ḷaṇt Th s(pə)plant Sh splant Ok splant.

*s-pəlq *penis.* Tw spələ́q Ch spəlq (suff. -aq *sexual organ*) ~ Li spəlʼq Th spéyeq, pəlqeʔ (in myths) Sh spelq ESh plqecút *masturbate* Cb spəlq Ok Sp spalq.

*pəlxʷ *pierce, pop out* Ch pálxʷ- *put, force through, get well*, [pələ́wa- *pass through, pierce*] ~ Li pəlxʷán *stick out* *from st.,* pləx̌ʷ *pop out (as potatoes fr. ground)* Th pəl'x̌ʷetés *make hole right through.* – Cf. **pəl'k̓ʷ, *ləpəx̌ʷ/x̌̌ʷ.

*pəlax̌ *to put a spell on; to tell.* Ld pəɬáx̌ *what is put on a person's possessions (esp. clothing) to gain power over him* Ch pɬəx̌ *(love)charm,* spəɬáx̌itn *to dope* ~ Th píləx̌m *tell, inform, bring news,* pɬax̌ *sorcery* Ok pɬax̌nt *put spell on sb.* – Semantically cf. Gothic spill *tale,* Engl. spell (incantation).

*pəɬ, *pɬ-u/aɬ *thick (layer).* Be pɬuɬ Cx Sl Se pəɬt Sq pɬuɬ, pəɬ- Cw Ms pɬet Ck pɬe:t Sm Sn Sg Cl čɬət Ld pəɬt Tw pəɬ-: pəɬəqs *thick nose* Ch páɬ-; [pilúctnɬ *thick lips*] Ti hɬuɬ ~ Li pɬuɬ, pəɬ- Th pɬəɬt, pɬ- Sh pɬeɬt Cb páɬəɬt Cv pɬaɬt Ka Sp pɬiɬt Cr peɬ-, peɬt.

*puƛ̓ *to come, come to an end, come out (of the bush).* Be puƛ̓ *come* ~ Th puƛ̓m *exit* Sh puƛ̓m *come out of the bush, come to end* Cv puƛ̓m *end* (possibly p̓uƛ̓) Ka puƛ̓m *arrive at the end of st. (eg. of the wood, where the prairie begins)* [Sp p̓up̓ƛ̓m *go out of the woods* Cr p̓uƛ̓ *come to the end (as river, road, woods)*].

*pan I *time, period.* Se spánw̓uɬ *last year* [pəʔíya *spring* (ʔiy *good*)] Sq tpánu *next year,* k̓ʷi tpánu *last year* Sn čən'-: čən'teŋ *when?* Cl čənʔtaŋ *id.* Ld pəd-: pə(d)tab *when?* Tw pəd-: pədt̓áqaʔ *time when salalberries ripen* Ch pən- Ti han- ~ Th spən'pán'ze *a year removed* [piʔstéʔ *when*] Sh k pətpénye *next year,* l pətpénye *last year,* pnhéʔe *when,* etc. Cb pantk *always,* pan'káʔ *when* Cv pintk *always,* pnkin *when, sometime, at the time* Ka pen(tə)č *year* Sp pentč *always,* spentč *a year,* [pistém *when,* spiʔsc'éʔ *yesterday*] Cr pintč *always,* spintč *year,* pinč'eʔ *(stress?) when.*

*pan II see **ʔupan.

*pu/an *to find, get.* Be pun- *accept, receive* Nk pun *see* ~ Li pun *be found,* pan'c *have a meal with others,* pan'cs *share a meal with obj.* Th punm *find,* spúneʔ *dead animal found and used as food,* pens *meet unexpectedly* Sh pəpen, pnmins *find,* tpúneʔqm *pick up dead animal or fish for use as food,* also *take sexual advantage of s.o. inebriated,* x̌lpnews *go* *and meet, intercept* Sp mipn(n)ún *I found out* Cr pon'én'tses *he took advantage of me* (Nicodemus).

*pəq *white.* Cx páqpəq Sl pəq Se pəqím Tw pəq Ch páqin *bloom,* spaqáln *bald eagle* Ti chaʔq *white,* chaʔqéw's *bloom, blossom* ~ Li pəq; pəqpaq *light of color,* paʔq *red-hot* Th páqes *bleach,* ʔestpíq *white* Sh piq; peqm *get mouldy,* xpəqcin *dawn* Cb paʔq *faded,* [payq *white*] Cv piq (sometimes heard as payq); npaʔqcín *dawn* Ka piq Sp piq; paqmqn *grey hair* (vs. čpiqqn *white hair*) Cr peq *white, bleached, silver,* paq *be made white.* – Cf. PS ***p'əq'** and IS ***paʕ.**

*pəqʷ see ***pəkʷ/qʷ.**

*pəqʷ/kʷ (CS), ***p'əqʷ** (IS) *to scatter; powder.* Be pqʷ *fine, powdery (snow)* Cx púwqʷim *dust is flying* Sq páqʷan *scatter (as feathers, seeds),* páqʷusm *powder one's face,* pəkʷn *scatter in clouds,* spəkʷm *dust* Sm pəkʷn̓ *dust/smoke is spreading* Sn pəqʷn̓ *powder, flour* Sg pəkʷn̓ *to smoke, be dusty,* spəkʷ *flour, powder* ~ Li np'əqʷmintn *black (gun)powder* Th np'ə/oqʷmín *gunpowder,* p'íqʷes *crumble up st.* Sh xpqʷum *load a gun,* (n)pəqʷmin *gunpowder* Cb nap'əqʷn *pour dry substances,* np'əqʷmin *gunpowder* Sp p'oqʷ *powder is spilled,* np'qʷmin *gunpowder* Cr p'aqʷ *powder.* – Cf. ***pəkʷ.**

*pisaʔ *small animal (bird, bug, worm).* Ch péːsaʔ *bug, insect, worm,* "peᵉsa" *little birds,* psayqs *mosquito,* pósaʔ *monster* (Boas *evil spirit, gnat*) ~ [Sh pəp'íʔse *snake,* pəpíp'ʔese *worm, caterpillar*] Cv pəpʕaspəs *baby chicks.*

*pət *to boil, bubble.* Be nupapnt *boil* ~ Li pətat̓ət *make bubbling, gurgling noise* Sh pətət̓it Ka ***pat-:** nptap *it boils in the kettle* Sp ptntan. – For n in the Be root see Nater 1977:5 (cf. also ***mac̓uɬ, *maɬ).** The Sh form is a reduplication type with i/i̧, see Kuipers 1989 sect. 22.

*pat *to arrange, line up, splice, spread.* Tw ʔaspát *it's all in a row,* ʔasptpát *it's all spread out (eg. hay/clothes in a field),* patáyasbəčəd *I looked at it,* patíyəʔiqʷ *gr. gr.*

grandparent/child, ʔaspə́t *it's all wrapped up* Ch pətákʷ *cover, wrap*, pə́t- *stick on* ~ Li pátan' *add to, extend, inherit*, pátalqʷn *look like, take after* Th petm's *take after*, petn's *inherit (a quality)* Sh ptem *spread out (as blanket)*, pétns *splice (rope), take after (parent)*.

*pit *to notice, think.* Cw pitət *recognize* [ptem? *ask*] Ck pə́tləxʷ *recognize* [pətem/pteːm *ask*] Sn pitnəxʷ *recognize* [Cl čtaŋ *ask, inquire*] Ld pitəb *notice, pay attention to, understand*, ptidəgʷasəb *think, memory, mind* Tw pipiʔíptədwəsəb *she's thinking*, ʔaspítasbətəbs *he's paying attention* ~ Li ptínusm *think (of)* Th ptínusm *id.* Sh ptin(ə)sm *id.* [Cv sk'ɫpitm *announcer at Indian ceremonies* (uncertain form)].

*put *right, sufficient, exact, very.* Ld put *very, very likely, much, often, soon* [Ch putínp *middle of the floor* -inp] ~ Li Th Sh Cb Cv Ka Sp put.

*pətkʷ see ***pəl'kʷ**.

*pə(tə)x̌ʷ *to spit.* Se pəx̌ʷt *spit out* Sq pəx̌ʷn *spit at (esp. w. medicine)* Sm čx̌ʷaɫs Sn čx̌ʷət Sg čx̌ʷətsə Cl čx̌ʷaɫc [Tw ɫpixʷab *spittle*] ~ Li ptix̌ʷn; pəx̌ʷn *squirt (esp. of shaman squirting water on patient)* Th pəx̌ʷ *spray w. mouth* Th Sh Cb ptix̌ʷm Th Sh Cv sptix̌ʷ *saliva*, Cv px̌ʷncut *spray o.s. with a mouthful of water* Ka pitáx̌ʷ, pitx̌ʷ- Sp ptax̌ʷ- Cr təpex̌ʷ; stépax̌ʷ *spittle.* – Cf. CS ***ɫəx̌ʷ**.

*paw, *puh, *pu/axʷ *to blow, breathe, swell.* Be pucut *swell, rise (of water)*, pus(m) *grow, swell, float*, puɫm *it (dough) is rising* Cx puhʔm, púhʔim *wind*, púsum *rise (of dough)*, pə́xʷim *steam* Sl púhut *blow*, puhʔm *wind* Se put *blow on, inflate*, pəxʷə́m/pəxʷim *steam* Sq puht/pəh- *blow*, pum? *swell*, spəhim? *wind*, spúxʷam *steam* Cw Ms Ck paːt *blow* Cw Ms spəhels *wind* Ck spəheːls *id.* [Cw p'aːm *swell*], pxʷat *blow spit in spray, whale blows* Ck paxʷət *blow on patient (to cure him)* Nk puhn *blow*, spuss *wind* puhúmtm *swell* Sm sčaŋ *wind* Sm Sn Sg paxʷət *blow w. mouth* Sn pxʷəlaʔ *blow* Sm Sn spxʷəlaʔ *wind* Sg spxʷələ *id.* Sn speʔxʷn̓' *misty* Sg spe?xʷ *fog* [Sm pʼaŋ *swell* Sn Sg pʼaːŋ *id.*] Cl sčuŋ *wind,* spusŋ *abscess,* puxʷt *blow w. mouth,* pxʷə́yu *blow (wind)* pa?xʷŋ *fog* Ld pu?(u) *blow, wind* Tw puhúd *blow through lips,* spuhúb *breeze,* [sppaháb *mist*], spus *a boil,* spúsəb *suds, foam,* spusáləč *inflated bag, stomach of large animal,* spxʷəb *smoke* puxʷúd *blow* Ch pusú- *swell,* [pʼól- *id.*], póxʷi- *blow* Ti húšin CV *blow (up a fire)* ~ Li paw *swell,* spə́wʼpəwʼ *lungs,* phaʼsm *winnow,* púxʷunʼ *blow on st.* Th pewt *swell up, swollen,* pú?pu? *lungs,* púxʷes *blow on st.,* pəxʷtés *id.* Sh pewt *swollen,* spuwʼpw *lungs,* puxʷm *blow at,* pxʷntem *snowdrift* Cb púxʷn *blow on st.,* spáwʼpawʼ *lungs,* spapúwʼa? *air sack in salmon* Cv snpiwtn *balloon,* púxʷm *blow* Ka péw *breathe, pant,* pe?éxʷ *swell* Sp pupéwlš *breathe,* púxʷm *blow* Cr pigʷ *swell,* pu?us *swell, bubble, foment,* pexʷ *wind-blown.* – Cf. NWAK pws- *swell through soaking,* pwƛ- *satiated, full,* pwxʷ- *inflate, blow w. mouth* (LR nos. 76-78), NOO poːtq-, poːtqa: *blow horn, breathe upon (in doctoring),* poːxʷ-, poːxʷa: *blow, breathe,* QUI poxʷ- *blow.*

*pwan see *cip(wn).

*pəx/*xəp *to comb (out).* Be px/xp *run wet string between thumb and forefinger to squeeze the water out* Ld špac/špaʒ *a comb* Tw pšəd *id.* Ch šápayi- *comb hair* ~ Sh píxm *unravel* Cv pixm *wool combing.*

*pax *to air* Cx pəš-t ~ Sh pexm *break wind noiselessly.*

*pəxʷ *faded, stale.* Sq pəxʷ [Sm pʼéxʷəŋ *stale, boring*] Sn nəpəxʷ *brown, blond, gold* ~ Li pa?xʷ *give up, be fed up* Th p?exʷ *get tired of st., get tasteless,* pe?xʷmíns *get tired of st.,* puxʷt *tasteless* Sh p?exʷ *stale, having lost interest,* pexʷt *tasteless,* p(ə)xʷelʼqʷ *faded.*

*pu/axʷ see *paw.

*pəy *happy, joyful.* Cx pípis *feel good because of liquor (not really drunk)* ~ Sh pyey *happy,* spyey *joy, happiness* Cb npiyls *happy, glad* Cv npyils *id.* Ka Sp pi(y)- *id.* Cr piy *id.*

*s-pyu/aʔ *bird.* Be spyu *auklet* Se spípyiws
unidentified duck Sq piis *murrelet* Sn čiy'əʔ *jay* [Ld p'iw *bat?*
hawk? Ch p'iw'/p'íaʔ *nighthawk*] ~ Li spzúzaʔ *bird,* spzuʔ
(big) wild animal, grizzly bear, (s)pạzísnak *young bird of any*
kind, spzə́ʕʷə́ʕʷ *unidentified large bird* Th spzuʔ *animal,*
(large) bird Sh spyuʔ *bird* Cb piyá *chickenhawk* Ok pyaʕ
red-tailed hawk Sp spyaʔ *id., snake hawk.*

*pəʕʷ/w *to prod, knock, drum.* Be puš *poke, prod* Ck
pəwmil *a drum* Tw cpawád *pierce,* cpáwʔad *pierce, stab* ~ Li
pəʕʷxál *bump, knock on, peck at, itr.,* pə́ʕʷn *id., tr.* pumákaʔ
a drum (also puláka?) Th poʕʷtés *knock, rap,* pwup *make*
drumming, pounding noise, pumín *a drum* Sh pʕʷpeʕʷm
knock, rap, pwum *to drum,* pwmin *drum* Cb puwmín(tn) *id.*
Ok pwmin *id.* Cv pwpwʕalx *make noise* Ka Sp pu:m *to beat*
the drum, pu:mín(tn) *drum* Cr paw' *drum on drum,* pew' *drum*
on tin.

p'

*p'uʔ *to fart.* Be sp'uʔ Cx p'utn *buttocks,* p'əcx̌ *fart* [Sl
pa:c *id.* Se puʔ Sq puʔq *id.* (prob. to *puh w. suff. -q *behind,*
bottom) Cl spuʔ *excrement*] Tw sp'uʔ *fart* ~ Li p'uʔ *id.,*
(n)p'uʔtn *anus* Th p'uʔ *fart,* np'uʔtn *anus* Sh sp'uʔ *fart,*
xp'uʔtn *anus* Cb sp'uʔ *fart,* p'uʔm *id.* Cv p'wam, sp'aw *id.,*
snp'uwtn *anus* Sp p'ʔum *fart.*

*p'əc' *to spit* [Cx p'ác'ət *tin can* poss. 'spittoon'] Se
p'əc't *spit out* ~ Li p'c'íqʷn *spit on* Sh pcíqʷm *spit out w.*
force.

*p'ac' *hemp, string, fix with string, sew.* Be pac' *pierce*
Cx Se p'əc'át *pin together,* pác'at *sew* Sq p'ác'an *id.,* p'ác'iʔn
repair net Cw Ms p'eç' *sew* Ck p'e:ç' *id.* Sm Sn Sg č'eç'ət *id.*
Sm č'eyc'/ç'ŋ *needle* Sn č'eç'n' *id.* Cl č'ac' *sew,* č'c'iŋəɬ *id.,*
č'əc't *join together, stitch up* Ld p'ác'ad *sew* Tw p'ac'ád *id.,*
imp. ~ Li sp'ac'n *hemp, fishing net* Th sp'ec'n *twine* Sh spec'n
Indian hemp, twine, string, Cv sp'ic'n *id.* Ka Sp sp'ec'n *id.*

*p'ic' see *p'əy.

*p'ik' *glitter, shine* Be pik' *bright, shining, sparkling* Cx píč'im *to spark* Se pič'ím *id.* Sq pič'm *id.* ~ Th p'ek'm *shine up* Cb p'ik' *bright, sparkle* Cv p'ik'st *shine up,* p'ik'míst *reflect, shine* Sp Cr p'ič'. – See Intro 3J.

*p'ək'm *bobcat.* Sq p'lač'm (-la- unclear) Ld p'óč'əb Tw p'əčab (stress?) also pč'əb Ch p'ač'ám Ti hč'əw' ~ Cb pək'm/m' Ok pk'am [Sp pičn' Cr p'eč'n (Nicodemus n') *lynx*].

*p'alan'/y' *treebark.* Cx Sl p'á?yan Se p'əl/l'an Sq p'óli? *thin bark* Cw p'óləy? *fir bark* Sm č'ólə/ey' Sn č'əley' Sn č'əle? Cl č'óyi? (the last four could also reflect *k'əlay') Tw p'əl?ád Ch p'alán- Ti həlílə *cascara-bark* ~ Th p'e?yén *rough bark* Sh p'əlen' Cb p'alán.

*p'il *to overflow.* Sq p'ip'iám Cw p'ilm; p'i:lt *fill to the brim* Ck p'i:ltm Sn p'ilŋ Cl p'a?yíx̌ʷŋ Ld p'iləb Tw p'il- *spread (of water only):* ?asp'íl *it's full of water, pond, puddle, marsh* ~ Li p'əł, p'əlíx̌ʷəx̌ʷ Th p'ə/əł-: p'əltés *he floods, overfills it* Sh p'ilt Cb p'ə́rmənct *spread of water* Cv p'ir't Cr p'er. – Cf. NWAK pał- *rise, flood, overflow* (LR no. 90).

*p'i/al *flat; to lie down, pl.* Cx p'ílit *flat,* p'íp'əy? *thin (layer)* Sl p'ip'əy *thin* Se sp'itít *flat,* p'ip'l *thin (layer)* Ck p'iłət *flatten,* sp'ip'əł *flattened* Nk p'ilekʷs *flat-nosed* Ld p'ílid *flatten* [Tw ?asp'ił *scattered, spread* Ch p'íλ'i- *flat*] ~ Li p'ił- *flat, low:* np'iłłəqs *have a very flat nose,* np'ał *people lying around* Sh cp'éł *lying, pl.,* p'ełlx *to lie, pl.* ESh cp'ał *flat* [ESh has alternative forms with p; Cb pəl *flat*] Ka p'ə/ełé?ut *lie down, pl.* Sp p'łew't *they're lying around (like on the grass)* Cr p'ił *sit, pl.* p'ıp'ıl *smashed flat.* – Cf. *pal.

*p'əlk'/q' *to turn (around, over).* Be tplq' *turn inside out,* [plik *tip/turn over*] Cx p'íyč'at *turn over,* [pəlkʷ *roll down,* pəwkʷ *cylindrical*] Se p'əlč *be turned over or inside out,* [sp'əlíqʷ *twisted,* sp'əlikʷ *ball-shaped*] Sq p'lač'm (snəx̌ʷił) *(canoe) with heart of cedar at bottom, "turnover canoe",* [p'əłqʷ- *sprain* Sn mələč't *roll st. over*] Ld p'alq' *turned out of shape, bent out of line, shape, position,* [p'əłqʷ *sprained, out of joint, twisted*] Tw p'əlóč *turn over, capsize* Ch p'əláč'- *turn over/around, roll over* [p'ayə́q^w *sprain* Cz pele:č'əm' *inside out*] ~ Li p'əlk'án *turn st. over* Th p'éyq'es *overturn, upset,* p'ik'etés *roll st.,* p'i(y)q'etés *turn over, around, inside out* Sh plk'em *roll st. over,* plq'em *return st.* Cb lcp'əlk'úsm *return (from),* [p'úlk^w- *fold*] Cv plk'-: p'lk'usm *turn around,* p'rq'-: cp'rq'us *be turned inside out,* [pl'pl'k^{w}iw's *break one's spine*] Ka p'əlč'usm *turn back without going to the goal* Sp p'lč'- *id.* (also p'lc'-), [p'úlk^w-, p'lk^w- *roll up, wrap,* p'rq^w- *bent/turned back*] Cr p'elč' *turn flat things over,* p'ilč' *turn round objects,* [parq' *be curved,* pulk^w *fold sheetlike object*]. – The SIS r-languages have r < l̦ before uvular, l before velar C$_3$ in this root.

*p'u/aλ' *smoke, fog, steam.* Se p'aλ'm *to smoke (tobacco),* sp'aλ'm *Indian tobacco* Sq p'úλ'am *to smoke (of fire)* Cw sp'aλ'm *tobacco* Ms sp'aλ'm? *smoke* Ck sp'a:λ'm *id.* Sm Sn Sg sp'aλ'n̦ *id.* Ti "s'ho:Le:'L" CV *tobacco,* [huł *smoke tobacco*] ~ Li p'uλ' *smoke, dust whirling up, form clouds,* sp'uλ't *fog, cloud* Th p'uλ'- *haze, smoke,* p'uλ't *foggy* Sh sp'?ut' *fog, steam* (Deadman's Creek and ES sput'nt) Ok sp'uλ'nt *fog* [puľnt *smoke s.o. (as cure)* sp'?uľ *smoke from a fire,* spa?lísľp *id. from housefire*]. – For occasional interchange λ' - l/l' cf. ***maλ', *məl.**

*p'um *to darken by smoking; smoke color.* Sq p'am?án? *to darken (a paddle) by holding it in smoke* (poss. borr. fr. Hl; otherwise root w. u/a) ~ Li p'úmun *smoke skins, fish,* [p'amm *make fire*] Th p'úmes *smudge st. dark brown, smoke fish* Sh p'úm' *smoke a hide,* stp'umltx^w *palamino-color horse* Cb p'um *brown, buckskin* Cv p'um *brown, buckskin-colored, smoked* Ka p'um *brown* Sp p'úm *tan (color)* Cr p'um *be mouse-colored,* Nicodemus also *smoke (a hide).*

*p'ən *besides, parallel, straight.* Se p'ənqát *put parallel* Sn č'ənesət *straight,* č'ən'e?sət *steer (car, boat)* Ch p'ə́n- *near, beside* ~ Sp p'in- *long objects lying on the ground,* henp'néw's *planked bridge* Cr p'en *pl. long objects lie.*

80

*p'u/an in Be p'aniɬp *green/mountain alder* Sn p'e/iynəʔeɬp *vine maple* Ch p'ánin'ɬ *id.* ~ Li p'uníɬaz' *wormwood*, Th p'uʔn'éɬp *id.* Sh p'neɬp *id.* [punɬp *juniper* Cb c'ək'c'ek'púnɬp *rosebush*]. – This is one of a number of plant names that cause semantic difficulties, see also ***ʔi/alk**, ***c'ayx̌**, ***p'uq^w**, ***q^wən**, ***t'unx^w**. The present item is also formally doubtful because CS has a vs. IS u.

*p'əq' *white, bright*, ***p'aq'-m** *to bloom, flower.* [Sl p'əq' *smoke*] Sq p'əq' *white*, [spáq'am *flower*] Cw Ms Ck p'əq' *white* Cw Ms sp'eq'mʔ *flower* Ck sp'e:q'm *id.* Sm p'q'əl'qn *mountain goat ("white wool"),* [pəq' *white* Sg pəq' *id.* Sn pəq' *id.*, pəq'əlqn *mountain sheep*, speq'ņ *flower* Cl pəq' *white*, paq'ņ *to bloom* Tw sp'əqəb/spq'əb *flower* Ch páqin- *bloom*] ~ Li Th p'aq'm *to bloom*, sp'aq'm *flower* Ka Sp p'aq' *flash, shine brightly* Sp sp'ʔaq' *a light.* – Cf. ***pəq**.

*p'uq^way *a shrub* (CS *a type of currant*). Ld p'uq^w (also p'uq) *wild currant* Tw p'úq^way *trailing currant* Ch p'úq^waʔ (also p'úqaʔ) *red-flowering currant (Ribes sanguineum)* ~ Sh sp'úq^wy' *unidentified shrub (silvery, small white berries),* pəq^wp'q^wey' *unidentified bush similar to rosebush, grows around Lake La Hache.* – See comment to ***p'u/an-**.

*p'əq'^w see ***pəq'^w**.

*p'əs *flat.* Tw ʔasp'ás *it's flat, the swelling has gone*, p'ásas *id.* ~ Sh cp'es *flat*, p'əsés *id.* [Cb pəs *flat, low*].

*p'us *lungs, heart.* Be ʔusp'ús *lungs* Ch sp'us *id.* ~ Sh p'usmn *heart* (possible inversion in sup' *breath*, see ***sup'**) [Cb scpuʔs *heart*] Ok p'up'smn *salmon heart* Cv p'úp'saʔ *fish heart* [Ka spuʔús *heart, mind* Sp spʔus *heart* Cr hiycpúʔs *id.*].

*p'əsq'^w/k'^w *to crush, squeeze.* Se p'əsq'^wát *crush* Sq p'əsk'^wan *squeeze*, [p'əɬq'^w-/p'alq'^w- *sprain*] [Ld p'əsq'^w/k'^w- *joint*, p'əɬq'^w- *sprain*] Ch p'əsq'^w- *sprain* Ch p'əsq'^w- *sprain* ~ Cr p'usq'^w *crumple, collapse*, p'əsaq'^w *bone breaks.*

*p'əy, *p'əh; *p'i-c' *to squeeze, press (grasp, push), squirt.* Be ip' *grab, squeeze* Cx Se p'íc'it *squeeze* Sl p'íç'it *id.* Se p'ə́ʔat *crush w. tongue (as soft fruit),* [p'əc'át *pin together* prob. to *p'ac'] Sq p'ˀiˀʔ-, p'əh-, p'aʔ- *grab:* p'íʔt *id.,* p'aʔáči?n *grab sb. by the hand,* np'əhač *palm of hand,* p'íc' *get squeezed, trapped* Cw Ms Ck p'iç'ət *squeeze* Cw p'ç'əlməxʷ *milk a cow* Sn č'ç'əŋ' *catch (animal in trap),* č'əç'el'ŋəxʷ *milk (a cow),* č'iç'ət *wring st. out* Cl č'c'- *squeeze,* č'aʔc'áyŋəxʷ *milk a cow* Ld Tw p'əc' *defecate, excrement* Tw p'ic'álbəs *to milk* Ch p'íc'- *squirt, spray,* [p'icí- *id.,* míc'i- *squeeze, pinch*] ~ Li p'íʔn *squeeze out,* p'íc'in' *press down,* [p'ácan' *trample down (grass)*] Th p'iʔtés *wring (out),* p'íc'es *press, push,* p'əlc'etés *crush, squeeze* Sh [p'yusm *frown* (more probably to IS *p'uy *wrinkle*)], xp'ém'xʷm *to milk,* píc'ns *squeeze* Cb p'iy'n *id.* sp'əc' *soft excrement* Cv p'ic'm *squeeze,* p'c'ntˁas *squirt,* sp'ˁac' *soft excrement,* Ka p'eʔ *press, milk* Sp p'ʔim *squeeze,* p'ʔintén *I squeezed it,* p'ep'eʔmín- *to milk,* p'c'ntas *let bowels go,* sp'(ˁ)ac' *diarrhea* Cr p'iy *squeeze,* p'eʔ *id.* p'iʔ *crush by pressing,* p'ey' *press, milk,* p'ic' *push,* p'ac' *squirt, defecate.* – Cf. *c'ip'.

*p'ayaq, *ready, ripe, cooked.* Sq p'áyaq *recover, get well,* p'áyaqn *fix, get ready, cure,* sp'áyaqimʔ *bread* Ld p'ayəq *hew/carve out* ~ Cb p'iʔq *ripe* Cv p'y/y'aq *ready to eat, cooked* Ka p'iy'áq *ripe, cooked.*

q

*qal *spring (salmon).* Ti qe(ʔ)ĺə́w' *Chinook salmon* ~ Th sqeyéytn *salmon sp.* Sh sqleltn *salmon (gen.),* sx̌qeľqltmx *summer,* pəsx̌qéľqltmx *June.* – Cf. *s-mł(ik), *-anaxʷ.

*qu/al see *qʷuʔ, ʔuqʷ.

*qal-mixʷ *person.* Cx Sl qáymixʷ Se sqálmixʷ ~ Li sqəlməxʷul'xʷ *ghost, ghost-like people,* [sqayxʷ *man,* sqəlqal'xʷ *rooster* Th sqayxʷ *man,* sqal'xʷ *elf,* ƛ'əlsqal'xʷ *person,* ƛ'uʔsqál'xʷtn *soul, shadow,* ƛ'u/iʔsqáyxʷ *person*] Sh qlmuxʷ; sqelmxʷ *man,* sqələlelmxʷ *male (animal),* x̌qlməxʷul̉əxʷ *mythical beings* Cb sqəl̉tmixʷ *man, husband* [Cv sqilxʷ Ka sqélixʷ/sqalíxʷ Sp sqélixʷ *Indian, man*], sqltmixʷ *Indian* Cr qil̉təmxʷ *man, husband.* – For the Cb Sp Cr forms with t- in the suffix cf. ***tmixʷ** and comment to PS -mixʷ/x).

*s-qəlaw' *beaver.* Sq sqlaw? Cw Ms sqlew? (Cw Hukari sqəl?ew?) Ck sqəlaw (Suttles-Elmendorf), sqəle:w (Galloway) Nk sqəlé?wiye Sm Sg sqəl̉ew' Sn sqəlew' ~ Li sqlaw' Sh sqlew' Cb sqəlaw' Cv sqlaw' Ka sqalé?u Sp sqlew' Fl sqelé?u.

*qa?ł/qahł *offspring.* Ti √qehał: isqéhał *your (adult) children* ~ [Sh qətmín *parent*] Cv qa?ł- *children of*: qa?łilmíxʷm *children of the chief.*

*qił *to wake up, be awake.* Ld qəł *wake up, come to,* qə́łəd *wake up, tr.* ~ Th qiłt *wake up,* qíłes *id., tr.,* qəłtes *cheer sb. up* Sh qiłt *wake up,* qiłm *awaken sb.,* q?ił *waking up,* cqił *awake,* qəłqełt *(feeling) better, cheered up* Cv qiłm *wake sb. up,* Ka Sp qiłn *awaken* Cr qeł *be awake,* qił *wake up.* – A semantic connection *awake - cheerful* is common; more doubtful is a further connection with Li qil̉qəl̉t *have fun,* Sh qilqlt *nice, funny* and with Cv qłnunt *be able to do st.* Cr qeł *overcome great resistance, lift, succeed at what seems impossible.*

*qəm I *soft, lukewarm, calm, gentle.* Be qmqmi(i) *soft* Ck sqəm *quieter water, died down a little,* sqeqm *calm, quiet water,* qem *be calm (water, wind)* Nk ?əsqéqem *quiet water* [Sn qeqṇ' *back eddy*] Tw ?asqə́b *calm* Ch qə́m- *become calm, no wind* ~ Li qəmp *hot, warm (weather, object)* Th qəmqə́mt *warm,* qməp *get warm* Sh qmqemt *lukewarm, cooled off (as hot tea), gentle (person)* Cv qmap *give up, quiet/settle down,* qmscut *go slowly, take one's time* Sp qmqemt *calm, serene, indifferent,* čqmqims *his eyes are untroubled* Cr qem *be unconcerned, pay no attention.*

*qəm II *to ask for st. (esp. to get st. back).* Be ?usqam *remind sb. of a debt, tell him how much he owes* Sn qəm'eṇ' *beg* Cl qəm'aŋ *id.* ~ Sh qmcney'm *supplicate, beg (to get st. back)*.

*qam *to nurse,* ***s-qam** *woman's breast, milk.* Be sqma *chest* Cx qáqam? *take mother's milk* Se sqam *woman's breast,* qamstx^w *nurse a baby* Sq skim? *woman's breast* (nursery language), kim? *take the breast* (idem) Cw Ms sqə́mə? *breast* (Cw Hukari sqəma?; qəma? *nurse, feed on the bottle*) Ck sqə́má *breast, nipple, milk* Sm Sn sqəma? *breast* Sn qəma?stx^w *nurse a baby* Sg qə́mə? *breast,* sqə́mə? *milk* Cl sqəmu? *breast,* qəmustx^w *nurse a baby* Ld sqəbu? *breast, milk* [Ch qáma- *work the mouth to swallow*] ~ Li q?am *be nursed, breastfed,* sq?am *woman's breast* Th q?emstés *to nurse,* qe?méyt *nurse a baby,* sq?em *woman's breast, nipple* Sh q?em *take the breast,* sq?em *woman's breast, milk* Cv sq?im *milk,* sqaq?ím *woman's breasts,* qa?mílt *nurse a baby* Ka sqe?ém *milk* Sp sq?em *id., breast* Fl sqe?ém *woman's breast.*

*qəmx̌^{w} *a lump, ball, cluster.* Tw qubqub?ə́x̌^{w} *body joints* Ch qəmúx̌^{w}šn *ankle* ~ Li qamx̌^{w}n *coil st. up,* [q'əm'x̌^{w}an *roll st. into a ball,* qəm'q^{w}an' *wind/spool st. up* Th q'əmx̌^{w}etés *make st. round, spherical*] Sh stqmx̌^{w}éke? *lump on tree.* – Cf. ***k^w/q^{w}um** and ***q^{w}um** II.

*qan *to hear.* Se qanám ~ Li qan'ím, qan'ímns *tr.* Th qe?ním, qe?nímes *tr.* Sh qənim, qəqnim, qəqnimns *tr.* [Cb cqána?, cqána?mn *tr.* Cr tcaqíne?, tcaqíne?mn *tr.*]. – The Cb Cr forms contain PS *-ana? *ear.*

*qana? *father's mother, woman's son's child.* Ti qáni CV *father's mother* ~ Sh qné?e *great-grandmother* Cb qqán'a? *father's mother, woman's son's child* Cv qáqna? *grandmother* Ka qéne? *father's mother* Fl qéne? *id., sister's grandchild* Sp qéne? *id., woman's son's child* Cr qíne? *father's mother.*

*qənu/a(x^w) *throat, gullet.* Se qənx^w Sq qə́nax^w *throat, (front part of) neck* Cw Ms šqənx^{w}eylə (Cw Hukari šqənx^{w}élə; sqə́nəx^w *glutton* (semantically cf. the Sh item under ***q'əm**)) Ck qəlx^{w}elə Sm šqənx^{w}elə Sn qənəx^w *greedy* Sg čɬqən?x^w *to* *starve* Cl ʔəsqə́nəxʷ *greedy* Ld qədxʷ *mouth* Ch qənúš- *id.* Cz qənx *id.* ~ Li qáqnaʔ *front part of neck,* qə́qnəkʷ *uvula, salmon heart* Sh qnuʔ *uvula,* qəqnew' *fish gullet* Cb qənuxʷ *throat,* tqənuxʷ *hungry.*

*s-qəp-min *breast, brisket* Tw sqəpbíd *human chest* ~ WSh spəqmín' (inv.) ESh sqəpmín' *brisket* Cb sqəpmin *id.*

*(s-)qap(-c/s) *spring, summer, spring salmon.* Be sqapc *old spring salmon* Tw pədqə́p *summer* Ti hənqeʔhə́w̓š *summer,* cqehəw *get warm (as near fire)* ~ Li Th sqapc *spring* Sh sqepc *id.,* qepcm *become spring* Cb sqip/panʔítqps *spring* (cf. panʔístkʷ *winter*) Cv qipc *spring* Cr sétqaps *April* (Nicodemus). − Cf. HEI qáps, HAI qaabs (Lincoln-Rath 1986 qabs) *spring salmon,* OOW qaqabm *small id.* (LR no. 2249).

*qəs *to scratch, tickle.* Tw qəsə́d *scratch it!* Ti cqsə́ni *I scratch st.* ~ Sh qəsqísm *tickle,* qəsqsép *itch* Cb qəsn *scratch (an itch)* Cr qes *scratch with nails.*

*qasa/iʔ *uncle.* Ld qsiʔ Tw qási Ch qásiʔ Ti "käse:" CV ~ Sh méqseʔ *woman's father's brother* Cb qásaʔ *mother's brother.*

*s-qawc *(Indian) potato.* Cx qaws Sl qawəθ Se Sq sqawc Cw Ms Ck sqewθ Sm sqews Sn sqewθ Sg sqewəs Cl Ld sqawc [Tw qaʔwəb Ch qa:wim'-] Ti sqagəc CV ~ Li sqawc Cv sqáqaw'cn Sp sqaqwcn Cr sqigʷc. − Cf. QUI NOO qá:wac *potatoes.*

*s-qaǂaʔ *dog.* Se sqáǂi *male id.* Sn sqeǂəʔ Sg sqéǂeʔ Cl sqə́ǂəʔ Ld sqíǂa(ʔ) Ch qáǂaʔ Ti sqéǂe(ʔ) ~ Li Th sqáǂaʔ Sh sqéǂeʔ Cv suff. -sqáǂaʔ Sp suff. -sqáǂeʔ *domestic animal.*

*qayǂ *to err, fancy, be drunk, crazy.* Sl qíǂiganm *tell a lie* Se qiqǂiwánm *id.* Sm qeyəǂqən *to lie, tell a made-up story* Cl qayyáǂct *tell a lie* ~ Sh qyeǂ *drunk,* cqyǂqin *crazy,* qyey'ǂ *make a mistake.*

q'

*q'aʔ *to remain stuck in st., be wedged into st.* Sq q'əh/q'aʔ *get caught,, remain stuck (as arrow in tree)* [Sn q'aʔət *let join* (prob. reflects *qʷʷuʔ)] Ld sq'aʔšəd *moccasins,* q'aʔq'áʔšənm *put on moccasins* ~ Li q'aʔn *hang st. on hook/branch,* q'aʔxn *get caught on st. w. foot,* nq'ʔákʔan *hand over* Th q'eʔtés *wedge in,* q'ʔeʔ *stuck, lodged* Sh q'ʔem *put/stick into, add,* q'ʔépse *choke* Cb q'aʔm *put away,* sq'aʔxn *shoe,* q'aʔálpsaʔ *choke* Cv q'ʔaʔ *get stuck,* q'aʔxán *shoes,* nq'aʔíkst *put in sb.'s hand* Ka q'eʔ *put, stick* Sp q'eʔéps *choke on food,* č'łnq'ʔepn *I stoppered/corked it,* q'aʔq'eʔšín *shoes* Cr q'iʔ *stick to, wedge into.*

*q'ac' *to intertwine, braid, weave, (embrace, strangle).* Cx q'ác'at *to put together* Se q'ác'aw *get together* Sq q'ac'- *be enfolded, embraced*: q'ac'čánʔ *hold arm around sb.'s body,* q'ac'úsn *id. around sb.'s neck/head* Tw ʔasq'əc' *it's woven,* q'əc'átəwəl *hug e.o.* Ch q'áyac'i- *braid/make rope,* q'áyc'ł's *braid of hair* [Ti qʷc'- *weave*] ~ Li q'əc'n *knit, weave, make nets,* q'ac' *make headstraps* Th q'c'əm *weave,* nq'əc'min *needle for weaving nets* Sh qc'em *weave,* x̌qc'usm' *to darn,* x̌qc'epsm *strangle (w. a rope)* [Cv qc'am *to braid*] Sp q'ic' *braided,* q'c'im *to weave* Cr q'ec' *braid, intertwine, weave, knit.*

*q'əl *to spin, curl, wind/tie around.* Be q'alm *to twist, spiral, zigzag (eg. fish in water),* ʔalq'almaał *drill,* q'lsxʷ *spun, braided* [Cx q'əys *anchor* Se q'əls *id.*], sq'əlnač *skirt* Sq q'lq'an *wind around,* q'is *be tied, knotted* Cw q'əlq' *get tangled* Ck sq'elq' *tangled* Sm sq'əlp'iʔqʷ *curly hair* Sn q'əlisət *turn around bend,* q'ələq' *tangled* Cl q'əyəxʷ/q'ixʷ *tie up* Ti q'ələ́ʔn *tying st.,* q'alanétn (Haeberlin 239) *ear ornament* ~ Li q'əl'q'al'ps *kerchief* (suff. *neck*, not productive in Li) Th q'i(y)q'etés *make st. round,* q'əlxʷám *curl st.,* ntəq'leptn *diaper* Sh təq'lntes *wrap around,* x̌qlq'el'ps *bandana,* təq'lqin'tn *headband* Cv sq'ł'ips *(hand)kerchief, locket, medallion* Cr sq'el'éps *horse collar, necklace* [Nicodemus sqel'éps]. – Very doubtful is a connection with Li q'áł- Sh q'éł- *to braid* (cf.

NWAK q'aɬ- *id., plait* LR 2358) and with Cv q'liw'snt *match st., put things together.*

*q'al/y (CS *l, IS *y) to build a structure, raise a tent; to camp. Cx q'a?ym/q'á?yim *to camp* Se q'əlm *id.* Sq q'əym *id.* Cw Ms q'əl?mn *camp* Cw q'ələm *to camp* Ck q'əlám *make camp,* q'əlml *camp* Sn q'əlŋn *make camp* Sg q'əl? *be camping* Cl q'əyŋ *make camp* Ld q'əl(ə)b *camp out* Ch q'əl- *id.* ~ Li q'əq'áya *shed, lean-to,* q'ázam *make roof over st.* Th q'iym *camp out,* q'i?mín' *camping place,* q'áyɬx^wes *make a shelter for st., put the roof on a structure* Sh q'eym *set up a structure (eg. poles for tent, drying rack, etc.),* cqeq'y *small lodging, lean-to,* x̌qəq'ey'tn *tipi,* q'eyɬx^wm *place sticks w. tops together as frame for lodging,* q'eyɬx^wtn *tent,* Ka q'ei *build a lodge, raise a tent,* sq'eyəmən *tipi-pole* Sp hecq'é?i *they lived (somewhere),* hccq'iq'é?i *they were camped,* sq'ey'mntn *tipi poles.* – Possible cognates are PIS **q'əy'* Sq q'is *be tied* Sh q'éyx̌m *tie up solidly,* sq'yex̌ *drying rack for salmon,* cf. also the words for *barrel*: Cx qəq'i?yas Se qəq'yas Sq q'əq'i?ás Ck q'əyas Li q'yaṣ Th q'yaṣ.

*q'əl to steam-cook, *q'əl-ya take a sweatbath, *s-q'əl-ya sweatbath. Be q'lst *steam-cook,* q'lstcut *take a sweatbath* Sq q'əlya *id.* Ld q'l *steam-cook,* q'əld/q'əls *id., tr.* Ti gəlq'els *cook in pit* ~ Li q'al'st *heat rocks for cooking,* q'əlza? *sweatbath* Th q'iyst/q'əstəm *steam-cook,* q'əstes *id., tr.,* ?esq'ás *steam-cooked* (q'əs in the last three forms prob. reduction of **q'əys*), q'əlze? *take a sweatbath* Sh q'lstem *steam-cook,* q'ilye *take a sweatbath,* sq'ilye *sweatbath* Cb sq'əlstáɬc'a? *barbecue (fish, meat),* snaq'álsn *roast underground* Ka səláq'i(st) (inv.) *sweatbath,* činesəláq'i *I am being buried, I am in the sweathouse* Sp sláq'ist *sweathouse* Cr hnléq'ncutn *id.* – The Ka Sp Cr inverted forms seem to have been contaminated with **liq' bury* (Ka Sp laq'-). Cf. **q^wəl'.*

*q'ilt, *q'iyt day(light), sky. Se q'ilt *there is daylight,* sq'ilt *day* Sq q'it *morning, first daylight* Cw q'ilt *mid-morning* Sn t'x^wq'ilət *noontime* Cl q'eyət *id.* Tw sɬq'it *day, (early) daylight* Cz q'it *tomorrow* Ch q'ít- *day(light),* "x̌iyq't" *dawn* Si

87

sck'e:t (Haeberlin 295) *today* Ti q'it *now* ~ Li sq'it *day* Th siƛ'q't *id.* Sh sitq't *id.* Cv sq'it *rain,* sasq'tm *id.* – Cf. IS *-asq'it *day, sky, atmosphere.*

*q'əlaqa see ***qʷəlaqaʔ.**

*q'əlx̌, *q'lax̌ *round; fence, stockade, corral.* Be q'lax̌ *fence* Sq sq'yáx̌atkʷúʔm *whirlpool* q'iáx̌n *stockade* Cw q'elex̌əctn *stockade* Ms q'ə́ləx̌n *id.* Ck q'ə́ləx̌l *id.,* q'əyə́x̌m *whirlpool* Sm q'əlex̌n *fence* Sn q'ələx̌n *id.* Cl q'əyax̌n *id.* Ld q'əlax̌əd *id.* Tw q'əlá x̌ad *fence, stockade* [Ti q'elə́x̌n *tighten*] ~ Li q'lá x̌an *fence* [Th q'lax̌/q'əlx̌- *move into gap*] Sh q'lx̌em *make a circle, arrange things in a circle,* c(ql)q'lex̌ *round,* q'lex̌n *fortress,* cx̌q'lx̌étkʷe *round lake (unconnected w. river)* Cb q'alá x̌ *corral, fence,* q'əlax̌mn *id.* [Cv kɬq'l'x̌kn'iɬt *brood, sit on eggs*]. – Cf. CJ k'/q'alá x̌ *fence(-rails), corral, field,* probably a Salish element in CJ. Cf. also ***q'əl.**

*q'iƛ' *to heal up,* ***s-q'iƛ'** *scar.* Se sq'əyiƛ' Sq q'iƛ', sq'iƛ' Cw Ck sq'iƛ' Sn sq'əyƛ' Cl sq'áʔiƛ' Ld q'iƛ' *a wound* ~ Li q'iƛ', sq'iƛ' [Th qʔiƛ' *heal over, leaving scar* (borr. fr. Sh), ʔesqíƛ' *healed over, scarred*] Sh cqit' *scar* [Cb sk'ət'm *id.* Ka Sp sqt'im' *id.*]. – The Li Th Sh forms can reflect *t' as well as *ƛ'; the CS forms point to *ƛ', the SIS ones to *t'.

*q'aƛ'an see ***q'(y)aƛ'an.**

*q'əm *to swallow.* Sq q'əmn; ɬlq'əm *inhale (smoke)* Sn ŋəq'ət (inv.) Ld bəq' (inv.) Tw k'əbə́dasdəxʷ *swallow it!* [Ch mə́qʷ-] ~ Li q'əmxal; q'maltn *greedy* Th q'məm; q'meytn *glutton,* sq'meytn *throat* Sh q'mem; q'meltn *glutton,* sq'meltn *throat, gullet* Cv q'mam; q'mílaʔ *greedy,* sq'miltn *hunger* Ka q'am; sq'améltn *throat,* sčsq'améltn *hunger* Sp q'mim; q'máleʔ *glutton,* čsq'meltn *hungry* Cr q'em. – Cf. ***məq'.**

*q'im *to be joined together, repaired, healed.* Be q'im *filled up, complete, whole, closed, etc.,* sq'im *scar* ~ Li q'amán *join together* Sh qmq'im *repair, join together* Cb q'am't *to heal.* – Cf. ***q'iƛ'.**

*q'əp *firewood.* Cx ʔitq'əp *gather firewood* Se ʔit'q'p *id.* Ch ʔitč̓ *id.* Ti sq'ə/eh *(fire)wood* ~ Li ʔiƛ'q'əp *gather firewood* Sh tq'epm *id.* – See PCS *ʔitq'əp.

*q'ap'x̌ʷ/x̌ʷ (SIS *x̌ʷ) *(hazel)nut.* [Cx q'əpx̌ʷayʔ *unid. tree w. strong wood,* q'ə́px̌ʷim (poss. q'ə́p'x̌ʷim/q'ə́p'k̓ʷim) *make crunching noise* (cf. Ka below), q'ə́px̌ʷiʔq̓ʷ (poss. q'ə́px̌ʷiʔq̓ʷ) *edible cartilage in salmon's nose*] Se q'əp'ax̌ʷ Sq q'p'ax̌ʷ Cw p'q'ʷax̌ʷ (inv.) Nk q'p'uxʷ Sn q̓ʷp'ax̌ʷ Ld q'áp'ux̌ʷ/q'p'ux̌ʷ Tw q'áp'ux̌ʷ Ch k'ap'úx̌ʷ ~ Li q'ap'x̌ʷ Th q'apúxʷ Sh qep'x̌ʷ Cb q'áp'x̌ʷaʔ Cv q'íp'x̌ʷaʔ [Ka q'e:p'éxʷ *sound of st. hard that cracks when you unexpectedly bite on it, eg. stone in bread* (cf. Cx above)] Sp q'ép'x̌ʷeʔ Cr q'íp'x̌ʷeʔ.

*q'əs *to be of (too) long duration.* [Be q's *tight, firm, do thoroughly, be very, be violent*] Cx q'əsənač *be tired of sitting* Se q'ə́sq'əs *id.,* q'əsƛ'ač *be tired of talking/ crying/laughing* Sq q'siws *get tired of waiting, get impatient* Cw Ck q'səm *tired of waiting* ~ Li q'əsp *wait a long time, wait too long,* q'aʔsálqʷ (?) *old tree (still green)* Th k'ʔes *get homesick,* q'əsq'sə́p *feel stiff (after long sitting)* Sh q̓ʷʔes *take a long time, be of long duration, long ago,* q'əsnwens *long for,* q'əsnweɫn *get tired waiting, get impatient* Cb q'əsp *long ago, old (object), past* Ka q'asíp *late* Sp q'sípiʔ *long time (ago), old (object)* Cr q'esp *be long time, long ago.*

*q'i/at' *to hoist up; fishhook; (deriv.) swing(-cradle).* [Be q'aat *small baited hook*] Cx q'át'aʔ/q'át'ustn *stick for hanging fish in smokehouse,* [q'at'm *heavy*] Se q'it' *belt,* q'ít'it *to bandage, tie* [Sq kítuʔ (borr. or nursery language) *a swing*] Cw q'ít'a(?) *id.* Ck q'éyt'a *id.* Sn q'it'ə *id.* Ld q'ít'id *hang st. up* Tw ʔasq'ít' *it's hanging on st. (as string on tree limb)* Ch q'ít'-*fish w. hook and line; fishing tackle* ~ [Li qiƛ'(tn) *fishline w. many hooks,* q'aƛ'q'ʷtn *strings on cover of basket serving as hinges or lock*] Th nq'iƛ'éx̌n *carry st. over the shoulder* Sh qet'm *hoist up,* cqét'ye *(baby) is in swing-cradle,* qit'm *to angle,* qít'e *fishhook* Cb q'aq'ít'aʔ *id.,* q'aq'ít'aʔm *catch fish w. hook and line* Cv q'it'mn *fishhook* Sp q'it'm *a hook.*

*q'aw see *q'ʷuʔ.

*q'awał (red.) *bone.* Se q'aq'áwał *bone (stuck in throat)*
~ Th q'ʷəq'ʷuʔł *(large) bone* Sh q'ʷəq'ʷuʔł *bone* (labialization
as in Sh xʷəxʷweł, see ***xəwal**). – Poss. borr. by Se, in which
case we have a NIS root *q'ʷuʔł.

*q'axʷ *stiffen, harden, freeze* Sq q'axʷ *be callous* [Sn
Cl q'ixʷ *knot*] Ld q'áxʷ(a) *freeze* Tw ʔasq'áxʷ *frozen,* sq'axʷ
ice Ch q'axʷá- *freeze* ~ [Li Th q'ixʷ *fit, convulsion* Th
q'íxʷuxʷ *id.*] Sh q'ʷəxʷúxʷ *stiff (as fr. cold), paralysed*
(labialization in q'ʷ automatic).

*q'əy *to doubt sb.'s power or words.* Sq q'iát *consider
too small or weak* ~ Li q'iyn *doubt that sb. can do st.* Sh
tq'yem/n *doubt, disbelieve sb.* Cv q'əyiw'snt *dispute sb.'s
word* Sp q'éyuʔsntm *express doubt, argue with* [Cr q'edm
refuse, be balky, stubborn].

*q'ay see q'al/y.

*q'əyiʔək *an ungulate.* Cx q'íʔič *elk* Se q'éyič *moose,
elk, reindeer* Sq q'iíʔč *moose, elk* Ms q'eyʔíʔəc *elk* Ck
q'əyéy:əc (Elmendorf-Suttles), q'ayí:c (Galloway) *id.* Sm
q'ayé:č *id.* Sn q'əyəʔəč *id.* Sg q'ayéʔeč *id.* Tw sqq'əli *elk,
animal,* [sq'əliʔ (stress?) *bogeyman,* cf. Ld sq'əliʔ (stress?)
name of Basket Ogress] ~ Li q'y'əy'y'ək *colt* Sh q'yíʔek *id.* Cb
q'əq'aʔík *id.* Cv q'q'ʔik *id.* Ka łqq'əʔi *colt, fawn.* – Cf. PIS
*q'əy' and CJ q'ayík *colt.*

*q'(y)aλ'an *snail, slug.* Be λ'aq'an (inv.) Se λ'iyáq'an
(inv.) Sq q'iáλ'an Cw q'əyáλ'nʔ Ck q'ayéλ'iye/ə Sm Sn
q'əyaλ'ən' Sg q'eyáλ'n Cl q'əyúλ'n Ld q'iyáλ'əd Tw sq'áλ'ad Ti
słeq'én ~ Li λ'ayáq'an'/λáq'an' (inv.) Th q'(ə)λéniy Cr
[q'eły'ílumxʷ *earthworm*].

*q'ə *to stir, move.* Ch x̌ə́q'- (inv.) *move away (a little
way, from sitting)* ~ Li q'əp *move (as clock),* q'ʕilx *glide (as
flying squirrel)* Sh q'ʕem *set in motion,* q'ʕeʕ *move, keep
going* (Deadman's Creek *move slowly and heavily*), q'ʕep *id.,*
q'ʕilx *move (away)* Cv q'ʕap *move.*

q^w

*q^wu?, *?uq^w, *qu/al *water, to drink*. Be qla *water*, qaašla *to drink*, smqla *thirsty*, suff. -aašla *water* Cx Sl q^wú?q^wu *to drink*, qá?ya *water* Cx qíy?awus *tears* Se q^wu *fetch water*, q^wúq^wu *to drink*, qə́lus *tears* Sq tisq^wú?q^wu *be thirsty*, (sn)q^wú?us *tears*, q^wult *to dip up*, sq^wuq^wl? *small quantity of collected water, pond, bucket of water, etc.*, q^wúlačí?m *scoop up water w. hands*, q^wúlay?us *high tide* (cf. also taq^w *to drink*, staq^w *water*) Cw Ms qa? *water*, qá?qa? *to drink* Cw šqa?əs *tears*, qa?lm *fetch water*, cqə́l?qəl?a *thirsty*, šqaql? *puddle, pool* Ck qa: *water*, qa:m *dip/fetch water*, qa:qə *to drink*, qə?a:ləs *a tear* Sm Sn Sg q^wa? *water* Sm q^wáq^{w}aq^{w}ə?/q^waq^{w}ə *to drink* Sn q^wa?q^wə? *id.* Sg q^wá?q^wa? *id.* Sm šqá?as *a tear* Sn Sg šqa?əs *id.* Cl q^wu? *water*, q^wú?q^wə? *drink* Ld q^wu? *(fresh) water*, q^wú?q^wa? *to drink*, ?əstáq^{w}u? *be thirsty*, q^wu?álus *tears* Tw q^wu? *water*, sq^wu? *a drink*, q^wu?áyas *tears* Ch q^wo:? *to drink*, qa:? *water, river* Cz qal? *water* Ti qəw' *water (as drink)*, sqə/ew' *the water (you can fall into)*, stéqew' *sb. is thirsty*, steqə́wi *I get thirsty* ~ Li q^wu? *water*, q^wúq^wu? *pool, puddle*, nq^wu?c *spittle*, ?úq^wa? *to drink* Th q^wu? *water*, nq^wu?tn *bucket* Cr oq^{w}s *drink*. – Cf. PS ***-q^wa, *-k^{w}a**.

*q^wəc see ***cəq^w/*q^wəc.**

*q^wəl' *to boil (food), cook*. Se q^wəlsat *boil, steam-cook* Sq q^wi?san *boil (food)* Cw q^wəl?s *boil* Ck q^wəls *boil (as water)*, q^wa:ls *boiling*, q^wəlst *boil st. (food)* Sm q^wəl'əst *to cook* Sn q^wəl'əs *id.* Sg q^wələst *to boil* Cl q^wəy?əs *boil st.*, šx^wq^way's *pot for cooking* ~ Ka q^wəl' *cook the camas or other food by fire underground* Sp q^wl'epm *bake in the ground*, snq^wl'apmn *fire pit*.

*q^wal *to speak, think*, ***q^wil** *to cheat*. Cx Sl q^way *speak*, q^wáygan *think, feel, opinion* Se q^wal *speak*, sq^wal'm *reveal, announce*, q^wə́lq^{w}əl *gossip* Sq q^wlq^{w}álwan *think, plan*, sq^wálwan *mind, heart (spiritual), speak*, q^wəlq^{w}l *talk* *excessively*, nqʷəltn *voice*, qʷíʔqʷi *to talk*, qʷíʔqʷis *talk to*, sqʷíʔqʷi *talk, conversation, discussion*, nəxʷsqʷíʔqʷi *talkative* Cw qʷal *say, speak* Ms qʷəyl *id.* Ck qʷeːl *id*, Cw Ms šqʷəltn *voice* Ck šqʷəltl *id.* Cw šqʷaləwən *mind* Ms šqʷeləwən *id.* Ck šqʷeləwəl *id.* Nk šqʷəltn *language*, sqʷuqʷél *speech*, šqʷeʔləs *his words* Sm qʷel *talk* Sn Sg qʷelʼ *id.* Sn qʷəlʼqʷəlʼ *talkative*, kʷilm *cheat* Cl qʷay *say*, sqʷay *language* Ld qʷilb *cheat at bone game* Tw biqʷiʔə́b *he's telling lies*, sqʷiyə́b *a lie* Ch qʷə́lam- *think;* sqʷəlm *heart* [Ti qʷay- *lie, prevaricate*] ~ Li qʷalʼút *speak, talk*, sqʷəqʷʼlʼ *story (realistic)*, sqʷalʼn *report to sb.* Th qʷincút *talk*, qʷintés *speak to*, qʷiyqʷéy *talkative, easy to talk with, unreserved*, qʷilm *cheat* Sh qʷəqʷlut *speak*, x̌qʷəqʷlut(t)n/x̌qʷlten *language*, qʷʔel *discuss*, qʷilns *deceive* Cb qʷilm *cheat* Cv qʷlqʷilt *talk*, qʷlqʷilst *id. to sb.* qʷilm *cheat* Ka qʷel *speak, talk (mostly sg.)*, qʷelm *song, tale*, qʷilm *cheat* Sp qʷlqʷelt *talk*, qʷelm *song* qʷiln *cheat* Cr qʷáʔqʷeʔl *speak, talk*, qʷil *cheat*.

*qʷalc *conifer bough.* Be qʷals *needle of conifer* Cw qʷəlʔəcəs *fir bough* Ck qʷə́lə/ecəs *id.* ~ Li qʷalʼc *fir/cedar branch* Sh qʷelcn *pine bough* Cv qʷilcn *bough(s)* Sp qʷelcn *grand fir.* – For -cn in Sh and SIS cf. Cb kʷʼuxʷkʷʼuxʷcínʼ *pine.*

*qʷlawl *edible tuber, bulb.* Sq qʷláwa CV *edible root (allium?)* Lm qʷtóʔl(?) *camas* Sm qʷtal/qʷtáʔal *id.* Sn qʷtaʔl *id.* Sg kʷtaʔ(əlʔ) (prob. qʷ) *id.* Cl qʷtúʔiʔ *id.* [Ch qiwátqs *onion*] ~ Li qʷláwaʔ *onions* Th qʷléwe(ʔ) *id.* Sh qʷléwe *id.* [Cb tʼəlíwaʔ/pʼəlíwaʔ *wild onions* Cv x̌líwaʔ *onion*] Sp qʷléwi *id.* Cr qʷliwlʼs *id.*

*s-qʷuł *wasp (esp. yellowjacket), bee.* Be sqʷuł *bee, wasp* [Nk "skwêʼət" CV *wasp*] ~ Sh sqʷuʔtt *wasp (yellowjacket)* Cv sqʷuʔł *wasp, bee* Ka sqʷúʔuł *wasp, yellowjacket* Sp sqʷuʔł *wasp, bee.*

*qʷətin *birch.* Sq qʷə́tiʔn; [qʷtiʔšn *shoe*] ~ Li qʷə́tʔin *birchbark*, qʷətʔináz' *birch*, qʷətalín *birchbark basket*, [qʷtiʔxn *white man's shoes*] Th qʷtinʼétp *birch*, sqʷətnetmx

92

birchbark basket, qʷłiyt *cradle* Sh qʷłin *birch* (WSh), birchbark (ESh, qʷəqʷłin'łp *birch*), x̌qʷłin't *cradle* Cb qʷəqʷłin' *birch* Cv qʷəqʷłin/n' *alder, birch,* qʷłniłp *alder* Sp qʷqʷłin' *waterbirch.*

*qʷum see ***kʷ/qʷum.**

*qʷən in name of *a plant (unid.)* Se qʷənałp *Indian hellebore* Sq qʷnałp (borr.) *id.* Cw qʷənəłp *pine* Sn qʷənəłp *Indian hellebore* Ch qʷə́nqʷn *nettles* ~ Li qʷnałp (borr.) *Indian hellebore* Sh qʷunłp *waterlily* Cv qʷaqʷaqʷníłp *unid. plant.* – See comment under ***p'n-ałp.**

*qʷan(im) *mosquito.* Sq qʷan?ímač Cw Ms qʷé?en Ck qʷê:l Sm qʷé?en Sn Cl qʷa?n Sg kʷé?en (prob. qʷ) [Ti gʷuqʷunč'íwa *fly, insect*] ~ Li qʷa?límak Sh qʷəníməqł.

*qʷəs *(younger) sibling, nephew, niece; son.* [Be suux̌i/susqʷi(i) *younger sibling*] Cw Ms sá?səqʷt (inv.) *junior sibling, cousin of junior line* Ck sa(:)səqʷt *id.* ~ Li sqʷsa?/sqʷsə́sa? *nephew* Th sqʷse? *id.* Sh qʷse? *id., niece (husband's brother's child),* sqʷse? *son* Cb sqʷə́sa? *nephew, niece (woman's sister's child),* ?ásqʷsa? *son,* sqʷəsqʷə́sa? *baby* Cv sqʷsi? *son,* sqʷsqʷsi? *boy child,* ta?xʷsqʷsqʷsí? *have a child* Ka sqʷse? *son (after puberty)* Sp sqʷse? *son,* sqʷs?elʼt *nephew (woman's sister's son),* sqʷqʷs?elʼt *younger son* Cr asqʷ *son* (inv.), sqʷásqʷə/ase? *child.* – The Be words could formally belong here, but more probably reflect ***?uqʷ'ay.**

*qʷisp/t *bovine.* SLd Tw qʷist ~ Li Th Sh qʷisp *buffalo* Cb qʷisp *buffalo, cow* Cv qʷəspíc'a? *buffalo, buffalo robe.* – This word must be a borrowing into the CS languages; the change in the final consonant is unexplained.

*qʷtał *animal fat, grease.* Tw qʷtał *deer or elk fat* [Ti qʷə́qʷtin *fat, grease*] ~ Sh qʷteł *id.*

*qʷətíx̌a? *louse, lice.* Tw qʷatíx̌ə Ch qʷatíx̌a? ~ Th qʷtíx̌a? Sh qʷtíx̌e? Cv qʷtíx̌ʷa? Ka Sp qʷtáx̌ʷe?. – Note that the Tw Ch forms are closer to NIS than to SIS.

*s-qʷəy see ***s-kʷ/qʷəy.**

*q^{w}ay *blue, green; bruise.* Be q^{w}it *sky blue,* [q^{w}ilac *crush, bruise*] Cx q^{w}a?čm *moss* Se q^{w}aym *id.,* q^{w}əyim *grassy place up the mountain* Cw Ms cq^{w}ay *green* (Cw Hukari also *blue*) Ck cq^{w}a:y *green* Sm nəq^{w}áy/y' *green (as grass), yellow, pale, dark navy blue* Sn q^{w}ey'l' *green (bluish), greenish yellow* Sg nəq^{w}é (= éy) *green, yellow* Cl ?ənəq^{w}ay *yellow, pale* Tw ?asq^{w}áy *light blue* [Ti cq^{w}ał *grey*] ~ Li q^{w}əzq^{w}az *blue* Th tq^{w}ázq^{w}əzt *blue,* q^{w}?e/az *turn phosphorescent, turn (black and) blue,* q^{w}?ezstés *bruise* Sh q^{w}yq^{w}iyt *blue, purple,* q^{w}yíkne *bluebird,* cẋq^{w}eys *having a black eye* Cb q^{w}iy *blue,* q^{w}iyq^{w}íy *bruise (black and blue),* [q^{w}in *green*] Cv q^{w}ʕay *blue,* [q^{w}in *green, blue*] Ka Sp q^{w}ay *id.* [Sp q^{w}in *green, purple*] Cr q^{w}el *be livid, bluish, angry,* [q^{w}in *blue*]. – Cf. ***q$^{'w}$al/y.** Here may belong words for *copper:* Sq q^{w}áyq^{w}i Se q^{w}áyq^{w}iy (borr.) Cx [q^{w}á?is] Th sq^{w}li? [also sq$^{'w}$iy].

q$^{'w}$

*q$^{'w}$a? *to burp, belch.* Be nuq$^{'w}$aat [Cx q^{w}ač't Sl q^{w}ač Se q^{w}ač't] Ld q$^{'w}$aač Ch q$^{'w}$uyq' ~ Sh q$^{'w}$e? (onomatopoeia), ?stq$^{'w}$e?k [Cb q'awm] Cv q$^{'w}$a?q$^{'w}$?ímt Cr (Nicodemus) q$^{'w}$i?nt (poss. q$^{'w}$in't).

*q$^{'w}$u? (prob. a contraction of ***q'aw;** IS mostly w. suff. -t, **SIS *k$^{'w}$ut**) *(other) side, half, companion.* [Cx q'áx^{w}šin *one-legged* (also q'áƛ'šin)] Sq sq'aw?čq *hip, side of body,* (?ə)sq'áw?/(?ə)sq$^{'w}$u? *companion,* q$^{'w}$u?t *include* Cw q'a? *together,* sq'a? *companion* Ck q'əq'atl *to meet* Sn q$^{'w}$a? *join a group,* sq$^{'w}$a? *companion,* sq$^{'w}$a?s *part of it* Cl q$^{'w}$u? *join a group* Ld ?əsq$^{'w}$u? *together with,* sq$^{'w}$u? *girlfriend, wife, mate,* q$^{'w}$ú?axəd *neighbor* ~ Li sq$^{'w}$ut *one side of st.,* q$^{'w}$utána? *the other ear,* nq$^{'w}$tána?s *the other side of the road,* sáq$^{'w}$uł *half, halfbreed* Th sq$^{'w}$u? *one/other side,* sq$^{'w}$əteyq^w *(international) border* Sh s(ə)q$^{'w}$ut *half, side,* sq$^{'w}$teqs *other side, far end,* sq$^{'w}$tew's *half, halfbreed* Cb sk$^{'w}$ut *half* Cv sk$^{'w}$ut *one side, across, half,* sək$^{'w}$taqs *one side,* ksk$^{'w}$tus *one/other eye* Ka ?esč'ut *half* Sp sč'utm *id.,* čsk$^{'w}$utšn *one foot,* čsk$^{'w}$tus *one eye.*

*q'ʷuc *fat, stout.* Sq q'ʷuc [Ti q'əwc, q'ewc-, q'ec-, q'c-]
~ Li q'ʷuq'ʷc Th Sh Cb Cv Sp Cr q'ʷuct Ka q'ʷuc Cb Cv Ka Sp
Cr sq'ʷuct *fat, grease, lard* [Cr q'ʷec *pl. are enduring, solid,
firm*].

*q'ʷəc' I *to wash, launder.* Be qʷuc' *to wash (car, feet,
floor)* ~ Li Th qʷic'm *launder* Sh qʷic'm *id.,* sqʷic'm *laundry.*
– This etymology is not strong; in Li there is a homophonous
√qʷíc' *squeeze st. through st., strain* and a √qʷí? *squeeze or
wring out water (fr. clothes), squeeze out fruit,* so that the NIS
root could contain a reduction of the PS suff. *-ic'a?.

*q'ʷəc' II *chipmunk.* Ld sqʷəc'ł/sqʷəcł Tw sqʷác'ał
squirrel Ch q'ʷəc'əł- ~ Sh q/qʷəc'wéw'ye Cb q'ʷəc'əw'áy'a? Cv
q'ʷq'ʷc'w'íy'a? Ka q'ʷq'ʷc'uw'é Sp q'ʷq'ʷc'w'éy'e?.

*q'ʷac' *full* (CS *of water).* Cx q'ʷuc' *waterlogged wood*
Sl q'ʷəç' *id.* Sq q'ʷac' *rise (of tide),* q'ʷəc' *wet* [Tw biqʷác' *he's
vomiting*] Ti qʷəc'- *wet* ~ Th c'áqʷes (inv.) *dampen,* c'əqʷc'aqʷ
(inv.) *thoroughly wet,* qʷec't *full,* qʷác'es *fill st.* Sh qʷec't *full*
Cb q'ʷac'sn *fill,* q'ʷac't *full* Ok qʷic't *id.* Cv nqʷic't *id.* Ka
q'ʷec'n *fill,* q'ʷec'ət *full* Sp qʷec't *id.* Cr qʷic' *id.* – The
semantics in part parallel those of IE *pel- in English *full* and
flood (Pokorny 798, 835; a meaning *wet* also in Greek πλαναν
be wet).

*q'ʷal/y *to scorch, (burn to) ashes, black; roast,
ripe(n); berry.* Be q'ʷay- *ashes, charred, black(ened):* ?ałq'ʷay
smeared w. ashes, q'ʷayusm *apply charcoal to one's face,*
sq'ʷałkʷ/sq'ʷayx̌łł *ashes,* q'ʷalmuuł *roast potatoes under
sand,* [sq'ʷalm *edible fern root*] Cx q'ʷáygas *charcoal* Se
sq'ʷáywas *id.,* q'ʷayičúp *soot,* q'ʷəl *ripe, cooked, done,*
q'ʷəlust *barbecue fish,* q'ʷəliwst *id. meat,* sq'ʷəlus *barbecued
salmon,* q'ʷiqʷl *salmonberry,* sq'ʷəlúma *berry (generic)* Sq
q'ʷáyat *"fire" a canoe,* q'ʷayčp *soot,* q'ʷəl *ripe, cooked, done,*
sq'ʷlam *berry (generic),* sq'ʷəlm?xʷ *blackberry* Cw q'ʷəl *ripe,
cooked* Cw Ms q'ʷəlm *cook, roast,* skʷi:lməxʷ (Hukari Cw
sq'ʷil?məxʷ) *blackberry* Cw sq'ʷa?əyčəp *soot* Ck
skʷəw:lməxʷ *id.,* q'ʷələm *to roast* Nk q'ʷəl? *cooked* Sm q'ʷəlŋ

barbecue qʼʷéyʼečəp/qʼʷéʔečp *ashes*, qʼʷəl/qʼʷalʼ(ə)ł *ripe, cooked*, skʼʷəlelŋəxʷ *blackberry* Sn qʼʷəlŋ *barbecue*, qʼʷayʼəč *ashes*, qʼʷayčəp *soot, cinders*, qʼʷəl *ripe* Sg qʼʷélət *grill, roast* Cl qʼʷəy *ripe, cooked, done*, qʼʷəy(ə)t *roast st.*, sqʼʷəyayəŋəxʷ *(wild) blackberry* Ld qʼʷəl *burn, warm, bake, cook, ripe*, sqʼʷəlátəd *berry, fruit*, qʼʷəlastəb *(stress?) service-/saskatoonberry*, qʼʷəqʼʷél' *huckleberry* Tw qʼʷal *cooked, baked, done, ripe*, sqʼʷálap *ashes*, qʼʷalástab *serviceberry*, qʼʷəlʔílas *cooking stone* Ch qʼʷəlí- *cook, roast, ripe(n)*, qʼʷalčp *cinders, ashes*, qʼʷə́lpaʔs *tinder made of pounded cedar bark*, qʼʷəlastm *serviceberry*, [qʼʷalí- *smoke (tobacco)*] ~ Li qʼʷəl *ripe, cooked, done*, nqʼʷəltn *barbecuing stick*, qʼʷəln *roast*, sqʼʷəl *ripe, cooked, done, berry*, sqʼʷlap *strawberry*, qʼʷəłn *scald*, sqʼʷútucʼ *ashes*, sqʼʷzuck *charcoal*, qʼʷázan *blacken* Th qʼʷyəm *barbecue, roast*, sqʼʷyʼep *strawberry*, qʼʷyewʼm *pick berries*, sqʼʷułcʼk *soot, fine ashes* Sh qʼʷlem *to roast*, qʼʷłem *to burn, scorch*, qʼʷilns *warm up*, qʼʷyqʼʷiyt *black*, sqʼʷuł(ł)cʼm *cinders*, sqʼʷyi/uck *charcoal*, [qʼʷl- *dust, powder, ashes*: sqʼʷleslʼpʼ *ashes*], qʼʷlewm *pick berries* Cb qʼʷəlm *roast over fire*, qʼʷiy *black* Cv qʼʷlam *barbecue, roast meat*, [qʼəlmin *ashes*], qʼʷlʼiwm *pick berries* Ka qʼʷay *black*, qʼʷaléʔu *pick berries* Sp qʼʷay *black*, qʼʷlim *barbecue*, [qʼʷlʼmin *ashes*], qʼʷlewm *pick berries* Cr qʼʷal *be black fr. burning*, qʼʷed *be black*, qʼʷid *blacken*, qʼʷelíwʼ *bear eats berries*. – Cf. *qʼʷəl, *qʼʷay, *kʼʷ/qʼʷəl.

*qʼʷlaq/qʼʼa *crow, raven*. Sq qʼlʔáqʼa *crow* ~ Cb qʼʷuláqaʔ *raven*. – Though the phonetics are not regular, the overall similarity of the words is striking. Poss. to *qʼʷal/y.

*qʼʷam *to shorten, pull/reel in*. Cw qʼʷəm *uprooted*, qʼʷə́mət *uproot, pull out (as hair)* Ck qʼʷəmə́t *pull up by the roots* Sn qʼʷəqʼʷmels *casting, fishing near shore*, [qʼʷəməlaʔ *chop wood*] ~ Li qʼʷmilx *squat down, curl up*, qʼʷəmqʼʷamímlʼəx *curl up (caterpillar, when going along)*, [qʼʷə́mqʼʷməλʼ *all have departed*, nqʼʷə́mλʼəqtn *last child of mother*] Th ʔesqʼʷə́m *curled/hunched up*, qʼʷəmλʼetés *shorten st. string-shaped* Sh qʼʷemns *pull close, reel in*, qʼʷmntes *shorten*, q'ʷmpep *be exhausted, all gone* [Cv nq'ʷimp *withdraw/withhold one's due fr. sb.*]. – Some cases of q'ʷ(ə)m-may belong under *q'ʷum II.

*q'ʷum I *(hair on) head; skull.* Be q'ʷumniq'ʷ *skull* Sq sq'ʷúmay? *hair on head* Sm Sn Sg sq'ʷáṇi? *head,* Sn q'ʷaṇət *fall out (as hair)* Cl sq'ʷúṇi(?) *head* Tw sq'ʷúbay *brain* ~ Li q'ʷumqn *head* Th q'ʷumqn *id., skull* Cb q'ʷumqn *head* Ka Sp q'omqn *hair on head.* – Cf. *q'ʷum II.

*q'ʷum II *top, high, pile, lump.* Be q'ʷum *high, large* Cw q'ʷəmx̌ʷəst *wind wool into balls* Sn q'ʷaṇət *bring up a child* Ld q'ʷəbx̌áči? *knuckle (?),* [q'ʷəpx̌(šád) *ankle*] Ch q'ʷə́mx̌ʷ *lumped, humped; scar* ~ Li sq'ʷum'c *ball,* [q'əmx̌ʷan *roll st. into a ball* Th sq'mox̌ʷ *ball*] Sh q'ʷumkst *knuckles,* q'ʷm- *higher ground*: tq'ʷmut *climb/be on top,* q'ʷmcin *shore,* q'ʷmus *reach plateau beyond top edge of mountains* Cv snq'ʷmxan *calf of leg,* sq'ʷmikst *arm muscle,* q'ʷmqin *horns, antlers* Sp hecq'ʷúm *it's a pile,* sq'ʷumšn/snq'ʷmšin *calf of leg.* – Cf. *q'ʷum I, *məq'ʷ, *kʷ/q'ʷum, *qəmx̌ʷ.

*(s-)q'ʷsu? *bundle.* Ld q'ʷsu? *gathered at waist* ~ Sh sq'ʷsu? *bundle* [Cv q'ʷəsq'ʷás *meadow hay (gathered in sheaves? AK)*] Sp q'ʷus *bunched, gathered, puckered* Cr q'ʷus *be gathered, wrinkled,* q'ʷesu *bunch.*

*q'ʷax̌ʷ *skinny.* Ti cq'ʷax̌ʷ ~ Li sq'ʷax̌ʷ Sh q'ʷex̌ʷt.

*q'ʷax̌/x̌ʷ I *to smoke (of fire), smoke color.* Ld x̌ʷi/əq'ʷix̌- *navy blue, dark green* Ch q'ʷix̌- Ti q'ʷá?əx̌ʷus *he got his face smoked up* ~ Li q'ʷəx̌q'ʷix̌ *black* Sh q'ʷex̌m *to smoke skins,* sq'ʷ?ex̌ *smoke.*

*q'ʷax̌/x̌ʷ II *claw, leg, foot, nail.* [Be sq'ʷx̌ʷlun *kneecap*] Sq q'ʷx̌ʷúy?q'ʷuy?ač *fingernail,* q'ʷx̌ʷúy?q'ʷuy?šn *toenail* Cw q'ʷx̌ʷál?wəcəs *claw,* q'ʷx̌ʷəlšn (Hukari q'ʷá?ləw?šn) *toenail,* Ms q'ʷx̌ʷəl?cəs *claw,* q'ʷx̌ʷəlxn *toenail* Ck q'ʷx̌ʷal:cəs *claw,* q'ʷx̌ʷálcəs *fingernail,* q'ʷx̌ʷəlxl *toenail* Nk q'ʷhúlšin *id.* Sg q'ʷx̌ʷá?lu?čəs *fingernail* Ld q'/q'ʷəx̌ʷqsáči? *id.,* q'/q'ʷəx̌ʷq(s)šad/ q'ʷax̌šəd *toenail* Tw kʷáx̌ʷači *fingernail,* kʷax̌ʷšəd *toenail, claw,* kʷax̌ʷ?útšəd *deerhoof* Ti qʷəx̌ʷáči *fingernail*, qʷəx̌ʷšn *toenail* ~ Li Th sqʷax̌t *leg, foot* Li qʷəx̌ʷqín-aka?, -xn *finger-, toenail* Th qʷox̌ʷqín'-kst, -xn *id.* Sh sqʷex̌t *leg, foot*, qʷəx̌ʷqin-kst, -xn *nail* Cv qʷəx̌/x̌ʷqinkstn *(finger)nail*, qʷəx̌/x̌ʷqinxn *toenail, claw* (in Ok both with -qin'-) Ka q'ox̌qí(n'čt) *fingernail* Sp q'x̌ʷqin'-čst, -šn *nail* Cr k'ʷax̌ *be claw.*

*qʷəy *to rock, shake, sway,* ***qʷəy-ilx** *to dance.* Sq qʷiílš *dance* Cw qʷəy?íleš (Hukari qʷəyə́l?əš) *id.* Ms qʷəy?iləx Ck qʷəy?ílix *id.* Nk k'ʷyíliš *id.* Sn qʷi:ləš Sg qʷeyél?əš *id.* Cl qʷəyiyəš *id.* ~ Li (s)qʷəz' *keep in time w. music,* qʷz'ilx *dance* Th qʷi?cút *dance* Sh qʷyem *shake, rock, ring (bell),* qʷyilx *dance* Ka qʷəy'əməncut *id.* Sp qʷyim/qʷuym *shake,* qʷimncút *dance* Cr qʷey' *bounce, dance.*

*qʷay see ***qʷal/y. *qʷəy-pa?** (red.) *(young or female) deer.* Sq sqʷə́qʷipa *yearling deer* ~ Li stqʷáqʷipa? (also c'qʷá...) *doe* Th stx̌ʷáqʷi?pe *id.* Sh stqʷəqʷí?pe *id.* – Almost certainly contains the suff. ***-upa?** *tail;* cf. further either ***qʷal/y** or ***qʷəy.** The Th form must go back to a reduplication.

s

*sukʷ *to be blown along, float with current.* Be ?asuk' *wind* ~ Sh sukʷt *get blown away* Cb sukʷt *drift downstream* Cr sukʷ *float w. current.*

*sukʷam *cedar (bark).* [Be sk'ʷ(a) *undo, untie,* sisk'ʷuuɬ *peel a fruit* Cx sə́wk'ʷat *cover st.*] Se Sq súk'ʷam *cedar bark* Ck sák'ʷm *outer bark of red cedar,* [sə́k'ʷəmiy *western white birch,* sík'ʷət *pull skin off st.*] Ld suk'ʷəb *cedar bark still on tree, remove cedar bark* [Ch súk'ʷt- *ninebark,* suk'ʷú- *butcher*] ~ Th sə/ik'ʷém *inner bark of red cedar,* si/usək'ʷ *id.* Cb sək'ʷm *cedar.* – Cf. ***suqʷ.**

*sal(i/a) see ***?əsal(i/a).**

*səl(-p) *to spin, twist.* Cx səlt (borr.) *to spin,* síyawus *get drunk* Sl səsyews *be drunk* Se səlt *spin wool,* sásalp *be*

98

going in circles (around st.) Sq nsə́lus *spin thread,* sə́l?sltn *spindle* Cw səl?ət *spin wool,* sál?ləs *tipsy* Cw Ms sə́l?səl?tn *spindle* Ck sə́lsəltl *id.,* sə́ləs *getting dizzy/drunk* Sm sə́l'səl'tn *spindle* Sn sə́l'səltn *id.* Sg sal?ləs *tipsy,* səlq'tŋ *dizzy* Cl nəxʷsáyic' *whirlpool* Ld səlp *spin, whirl* Tw ?assə́l *it's rolled,* bisəlsál *staggering around* Ti séluhs *thread* ~ Li səl *string,* səlm *make string,* səlpan *spin st. around,* nsə́l'us *desperate,* səl'k/sl'ək *dizzy,* səl'kpus *drunk* Th syəm (*tr.* si(ye)tés) *to twist, twine,* səl(ke)tés *turn/whirl sb./st. around* Sh slem *to twine,* slep *be excited, hurry,* slpus *be startled* Cb səl *round, circle,* snsələncut *whirlpool,* səl'l' *crazy, drunk* Cv sələm *spin wool,* slal *forget,* salp' *twisted* Ka selp *somersault* Sp sil/l' *wrong, confused,* slpqin *dizzy, confused* Cr sil *turn, cause dizziness,* sel *turn, spin,* sɪlup *id.* – Cf. NWAK sl- *drill* (w. extensions -t, -p, -qʷ; LR no. 873).

*sum' *to smell, sniff.* Sq sum? Cl su?ŋət *sniff,* suŋ'naxʷ *smell* Ld súbud Sn sap'ət *sniff, suck, draw in w, breath* Tw ?assúb *it smells,* sub?údas *smell it!* Ti su?úwi *I breathe* ~ Li sum'ún *sniff at* Sh sum Cb sum'm Ka sú?um Sp Cr sum'.

*sapn *daughter-in-law.* Tw sápad Ch sápan- Ti sáhan CV ~ Li sapn Th Sh sepn Cb sapn Cv sipn Sp sepn Cr sipn (Nicodemus; Reichard's sipəm may be a misprint).

*səp' *to hit, club, whip.* Be sp' Cx Sl səp't Se səp't, sáp'at Sn šč'ət (š < s by assimilation) Tw ?assə́p' *whipped,* bisəp'ə́n *he's hitting* Ti dənsáhtn CV *whip* ~ Sh sp'em Cb ssəp'qin' *wheat,* [sap'i?áx̌n *bat*] Cv sp'am *hit,* sp'qin *thresh (wheat),* ssp'qin *wheat* Ka Sp sp'nten Sp ssp'qin' *wheat.*

*sup' *to breathe.* Se xʷə́səp' *get out of breath* (cf. Sh nxʷətpsup' *id.,* to IS *xʷət *come to end*) Sn sap'ət *suck in, draw in breath* [Cl šup't *id.,* sac'ŋ *breathe*] ~ Li súp'um Th sup' *breath, air,* sup'm *breathe* Sh sup' *breath.*

*səq' *to split, crack.* Be sq' *tear, cut open* Cx səq' *cracked,* sasq'/sə́?asq' *to yawn* Se səq' *broken, cut, torn in half,* [šaq'ám *have the mouth open* (borr. fr. Li)] Sq səq' *split, crack, itr.; middle, half,* sáq'an *split, tr.* Cw Ms Ck sq'et *split,*

99

łsəq' *half* Sm séq'ət *cracked* Nk ʔełsáq' *half*, sisq' *kindling* Sn sq'ət *break, tear, rip*, se/əq'ət *cracked, ripped*, łsəq' *half* [Cl šaq'ŋ *open one's mouth*] Tw ʔassáq' *it's split* Cz sək'- *split* [Ti sq'ʔəh *wood*, c'qeʔ- *split*, łq'- *id. (of tree)*] ~ Li səq'n/səq'xal *crack tr./itr.*, [səqn/səqxal *split wood tr./itr.*], saq'm *open one's mouth wide*, sək' *to crack (of ice)* Th səq'/qpstes *cause to crack*, ʔe(s)sáq'/q *cracked, split*, ʔe(s)sák' *id. (small cracks)*, siq'/q- *id. (augmentative form)* Sh sq'ewłm *break a glass/cup*, siq'm *break, crack* Cb səq'm/səq'p *split*, səq'sn/nsq'aw's *split wood*, ksiq'n *chop wood* Cv nsq'iw's *forked, split in half*, siq'm *split wood* Ka saq' *to split*, saq'cənm *open one's mouth* Sp sq'em *to split*, hecsáq' *it's a crack/gully* Cr saq' *gape, split in two*.

*saqʷ *to fly, jump; a gallinaceous bird.* Be sqʷ *fly, jump* Se səqʷ *to fly* Ld saqʷ *id.*, sə́səqʷ *quail* Ti saqʷ- *to jump* ~ Li saqʷ *to fly* Sh səsuqʷ *blue grouse*, sqʷúmqe *prairiechicken* Cb səsə́qʷ *blue grouse* Cv sqʷaqʷləlqʷ *prairiechicken.*

*suqʷ *to strip off (skin or treebark).* Be suq' *to peel, skin, strip off bark* Ck siqʷm *peel cedar bark* Tw ʔassú/íqʷ *it's peeled*, ʔassə́qʷ *it's chipped* Ch súqʷi- *strip (cedar bark)* ~ Li suqʷm *skin an animal*, [suqʷ *thick middle part of deer* (cf. Ka below)] Th soqʷm *butcher*, sukʷm *id.* Sh xsuqʷm *skin a small furry animal* Cv sksaqʷm *skin large animals* [Ka soq'om'é *rump* (cf. Li above)] Sp soqʷn *to clean, get skin off.* – Cf. KWA saqʷa *peel off bark* (LR no. 929) and *sukʷam.

*sutik *winter, cold wind.* Be sutk *winter* Cx Se sútič *id.* Sq sútič *cold north wind* Cw Ms sasətəc *id.* (Cw Hukari satəc) Ck saːtəc *id.* Sn Sg satəč *id.* Cl sutč *cold northeast wind* Ch "Sut'k" *September* Ti hənsútič *(beginning of) winter*, sitíč *year* ~ Li sútik *winter*, sʔistkn *underground winter dwelling* Th sʔistk *winter*, sʔistkn *pit house* Sh sʔistk *winter*, ʔistkm *become winter*, xʔistktn *pit house* Cv sʔistkʷ *winter*, panʔístkʷ *id.* Ka ʔistč *id.* Sp sʔistč *id.* Cr sitkʷ *id.*

*si/ət' *to sniff.* Ld sit'qsəb ~ Sh sat'ns.

100

*səw I *to whisper.* Sn sək^{w}əqsə, səw'qəŋ' Ld səg^{w}q-
[Ch sak^{w}á-] ~ Cb suw'suw'ilx Cv sw'ncut Sp su?su?ntém *they whispered..*

*səw II see ***səΩ^w**.

*saw *to ask.* [Sq síwi *become attentive,* səsəw?it *try to draw sb.'s attention* Cw siwəl *notice (sb.'s presence)*] Ch sáwla- *ask* ~ Li sawn *ask sb.,* sawɬn *ask a question* Th séwes *ask sb.,* sewɬn *ask a question* Sh sewns *ask (in any sense),* swsewcnm *ask indirectly, hint that one would like to be given st.,* tswɬtimx *enquire* Cb sawn *ask* Cv siwm *id.,* swɬtiɬn *ask information,* nswcnmist *propose* Ka séun *ask sb.,* su:ɬtú(mš) *ask for information* Sp sewn *ask sb. st.,* sewɬtn *ask sb. about st.* Cr sig^w *ask for.*

*six^w *to pour, spill.* Be sx^w *to leak* [Ch sə́x^w- *(get) wet,* sáx^{w}iyin'- *otter*] ~ [Li sax^{w}m *take a bath* Th sex^{w}m *id.*] Sh six^{w}m *spill,* [sex^{w}m *bathe*] Cb six^{w}n *scatter,* nasíx^{w}n *fill w. solid,* səx^{w}p *drip* Ka six^w *pour, spill liquid* Sp six^{w}n *pour* Cr six^w *pour solid objects or liquids,* [sux^{w}lš *fish dives/jumps*].
– See also ***səΩ^w**.

*sux^w *to recognize, identify, understand, know.* Se sux^{w}t/sux^{w}nəx^w *see, find, discover* Sq sux^{w}t *identify* Ld sux^{w}t *recognize* [Ti síš- *know, recognize*] ~ Li sux^{w}tn *recognize* Th súx^{w}tes *id.* Sh sux^{w}m *id.* Cb sux^{w}ɬn *id.* Cv sux^w *id., know* Ka sux^w *understand,* sux̌^{w} *know, recognize* (poss. misrecording for sux^w) Sp sux^w *know, understand, recognize* Cr sux^w *be acquainted with, know.* – Cf. **yux^w**.

*saX̌ *to scrape.* Be sX̌(a) *to plane, scrape st.* Sq sáX̌an? Ld sáX̌ad Tw bəsáX̌atəb *scraping a canoe* Ch sáX̌a- *get scraped* Ti seX̌- *scratch* ~ Th séX̌es *whittle* Sh seX̌m *scrape* Cr saX̌ *hew, whittle.* – A labialized final in Cx sáX̌^{w}at *scrape, shave* Se sáX̌^{w}at *scrape (as hide)* Sq sáX̌^{w}an? *rub* Th séX̌^{w}es *strip bark off*; here only the Cx and Se words are clearly related to each other.

*siX̌ *to move (from one place to another).* Ck síX̌ət Cl siX̌t [Ch səyX̌- *replace*] ~ Sh síX̌m Cv síX̌lx.

*səy *friend, relative,* *si? *parent's sibling,* *si-l(a?)
grandparent. Be sissi *uncle,* Se síla *grandparent,* Sq sísi?
uncle (parent's brother), si?á? *sweetheart,* si?l *grandparent,*
sí?la *granny* Cw Ms sí?lə *gr.parent* Ck si:lə *id.* Sm síl(:)a? *id.*
Sn si?sət *parent,* silə? *gr.parent* Cl siyə? *id.,* Tw silə
gr.father, silə?íč *brother, sister, cousin* Ti "se:'el" CV *mother's
father* ~ Li sísqa? *uncle* Th sísqe? *id.,* ṣəṣiym *(commit)
adultery* Sh si *friend,* səs(y)i *sweetheart, buddy,* síse? *uncle,
mother's brother* (in the Deadman's Creek dial. *in relation to
female,* sí?se *id. to male),* slé?(e) *grandfather* Ka Sp síle?
mother's father Fl si? *maternal uncle/aunt while connecting
relative is alive* Cr síle? *mother's father.* – In a continuous
NCS area there are words beginning with *(s)y- where s- is the
nominalizer: Cx ǰá?ǯa *friend, relative* Se syáya *id.* Sq syay?
friend Cw Ms syé?ye? *friend, relative* Ck syé:ye *id.* Cw Ms
s?áy?e? *sweetheart, lover* Ck s?ey:é *id.* Cw Ms yáy?ytl?
blood-relative Ck yaytl *id.* Sm Sg sčé?če? *friend* Sn sče?čə?
id. Cl sča?čə? *id.* Sn s?əy'ə? *sweetheart* Cl sə́yu? *id.*

  *say *sound of voice(s).* [Se sáyiš *show st.*] Sq sáy?i?n
be audible, voice an opinion, say ~ Sp say *sound of voices,*
sa?s?aycán *the diminishing voices and sounds of people as
they wander away.*

  *səʕʷ, *səw *to flow; wetness, dew.* Cx sa?sx̌ʷ *dew,*
sə́x̌ʷa? *urine, urinate* Se sasx̌ʷúlmixʷ *damp ground* Sq sasx̌ʷ
damp, sə́x̌ʷa? *urinate* Cw Ms Ck sə́x̌ʷa *id.* Nk sə́x̌ʷ/x̌ʷeten
bladder Sm Sn sa?sx̌ʷ *dew* [Cl six̌ʷ *wade*] Ld s(?ə)x̌ʷa?
urinate (male), [síx̌ʷid *make a noise w. the water (eg. when
wading)*] Tw sə́x̌ʷu *urine (male)* [Ch sə́xʷ- *(get) wet,*
sáxʷiyin'- *otter*] ~ Li səwsuwt *dew, wetness of vegetation
after rain* Th susúwt *wet, dewy,* su?s?éw *get wet fr. dew* Sh
tswsuw't *dew,* séwɬkʷe *water* Cb sa?x̌ʷ *melt,* sawɬkʷ *water*
Cv siw'st *drink,* siwɬkʷ *water* Ka séuɬkʷ *id.* Sp nsewɬkʷm *be
in the water* Cr saʕʷ *flow.* – See also *six̌ʷ. For the
development *flow* > *dew* cf. Skt dhávate *flow* and Engl. *dew.*
The Ch words are formally closer to *six̌ʷ, semantically closer
to the present item.

t

*tac *to pet, stroke.* [Be ťc *knock on, strike and break*] Cx tásat Se tácat Sq tácan' [Ld ť'ác'ad *shape it*] ~ [Cb kť'ac'ləxʷn *pet, stroke*] Ka tec *pat, touch gently.* – The reconstruction is based on the Cx Se Sq and Ka roots. Via the Cb word a further connection is possible with Sh tíc'- *to press, iron* Cv ť'íc'- *stroke, iron* Sp ť'éc'- *to smooth, straighten, iron* Cr ť'ic' *smooth by rubbing.*

*təkʷ *to be blocked, choked off.* Cx təkʷanʔa *deaf* Se təkʷə́na *id.* [Sq ƛ'kʷə́ni *id.* Ck ƛ'ə́kʷəle *id.*] Ck stəkʷtekʷ *in a daze, day-dreaming* Ld t(ə)kʷádi *deaf* Ti nəštkʷays *one eye is out* (-ays *eye*) ~ Li təkʷ *stop crying,* n(təkʷ)tkʷánaʔ *deaf,* stə́kʷc *mute, dumb* Th təkʷtes *to shelter,* ʔestəkʷpcín *dumb, mute,* ʔesntəkʷtkʷén'i *deaf,* təkʷtukʷt *sheltered* Sh cxtəkʷtkʷéne *deaf,* stəkʷcin *dumb,* tkʷup *stop talking/crying* Cb təkʷ *no wind,* təkʷp *choke,* ntəkʷtkʷánaʔ *deaf* [Ka ť'kʷus *blind*] Sp ntkʷpaqs *he smothered,* tukʷ *close-knit, stifling, muggy.* – Cf. ***ƛ'ikʷ.**

*takʷ I *perceive.* Sq tkʷáyʔaʔn *hear* (suff. *ear*) ~ Sh tekʷxʷ *smell proximity of animal or man* Cr tikʷ *suspect, smell out,* tekʷeːníʔ (Nicodemus) *hear.*

*takʷ II *willow/ruffed grouse* Be takʷs ~ Li tákʷxʷaʔ (təkʷ *sound of the bird*) Th tékʷxʷe Sh təkʷtəkʷəlí *sound of the blue grouse* Ok ".tstukʷám" CV. – See Kinkade 1990:205).

*tu̠/a̠l *to extend, stretch, untie; fathom.* Cx təɬt *spread out* Se təɬt *to open fan-wise,* táɬat *measure w. arms,* tə́ʔaɬ *harpoon,* túlukʷ *unraveled* Sq taʔlm *lengthwise, parallel,* taɬ *fathom* Cl ʔəstaʔyúx̌ʷsn *hold legs straight out* Ld taɬ *stretch (unit of measure),* staʔɬ *two-prong harpoon,* [təɬ *true,* tə́ɬət *arrive safely*] Tw staɬ *armspan, fathom,* taɬád *measure armspan,* taʔɬšəd *accompany* Ch táɬ- *flat,* túɬi- *stretch* ~ Li tə̠ln *spin string fr. ball,* tətn *put string/net across,* təɬmn *clothesline,* taɬləx *stand up,* stɬayn *stationary net* Th tə̠/áles *unravel, unwind, string out, stretch (rope, line),* tə́ɬtes *string st. up, hang a line,* téɬes *id.,* tə̠ɬtés *straighten,* tə́ɬxn'me *sit w. legs* *stretched out*, ntɬuym'xʷtn *chain for measuring ground*, ntəɬtɬuym'xʷ *Lathyrus sp.*, téɬix *stand up*, ntəɬmin *clothesline* Sh talm *stretch, extend*, stal *clothesline*, stltalləxʷ *unid. plant ("stretched on ground")*, xtálkʷetn *net stretched across creek*, téɬns *stretch, spread*, teɬlx *(go and) stand*, stɬteɬxn' *sitting w. legs stretched out* Cb təɬ *straight* Cv tram *unravel*, statár' *string, twine*, taɬt *straight, sure*, tíɬ *straight*, tiɬm' *lie flat* Ka taál *untie, unwrap* Sp trntexʷ *you unraveled it*, ctúrrsi *he motioned to sb. to come over*, túrrsm'nc *he set me free fr. my debt to him* Cr tar *untie*, tor *stretch out, extend (as hand)*, teɬ *straight*.

　　　*tam *close relation (friend, husband, relative).* Be kʷtmc *husband*, smatmx/smatix (inv.) *friend* Sq kʷtams *husband* Cw smetəxʷtn (inv.) *spouse's sibling, sibling's spouse* Ck smetəxʷtl *id.* Sn Sg sŋeʔtxʷn *id.* Tw kʷətábac *husband*, stibʔát *man* Ti stiw'át *person, friend* ~ Li kʷtamc *husband*, təmitáqs *friendly* Th stiʔmét *distant relative*, sʔiʔtm' *parents*, ʔiʔeʔistətm' *cross-sex sibling-in-law, man's friend's wife, woman's friend's husband* Sh stəmet *friend*, stmtem'ətn *in-laws*, [smeʔstm *sibling of opposite sex*] Cb sktamqn *relative(s)*, natámtn *co-parent-in-law*, (təm)tamstúl *friendly*, saʔstm *cross-sex brother-in-law*, [məʔastm *woman's father*] Cv tmiw's *be relatives*, titmtn *daughter's mother-in-law*, stmtímaʔ *grandmother* [Ka mestm' *woman's father*] Sp tetm'tn *one's children's in-laws*, čtammqn *distant relative*, seʔstém *cross-sex brother/sister-in-law*, [m'estm' *woman's father*] Cr stemílgʷes *relative.* – Cf. PIS ***maʔstm**.

　　　*s-tam *what? something.* Be stamks *what is it?*, tistam *something* Cx Sl tam Se stam Sq stam, təm- Cw Ms Ck Nk stem Sm Sn Sg steŋ Sn staŋət *do what?* Cl staŋ; stáŋənu? *things* Ld Tw stab Ch tam Ti taw; stuʔtíw'at *slave* ~ Li stam' Th stem', steʔ Sh stem, stem'y; stmtetm' *stuff, belongings*, stmstitm't *id.* Cb stam' Cv stim' Ka stem' Sp tem' *thing* Cr stim'.

*ti/am *to exert o.s.* Sq tímit *perform w. all one's might* Cw Ck timət *id.* Sn stitm' *go very fast* ~ WSh stetm' *hurry* ESh stétme? *id.*

*tum see ***t'um.**

*tum-a? *mother, aunt.* Ti dúwə *mother (of female;* CV túwa*)* ~ Sh túm'e, tətúm *aunt (mother's sister)* Cb Cv Ka Sp tum' *mother (of female).*

*tumn *dead; sleep, dream.* Be ?atma/?atmn- *to die, be dead,* cituma/citumn- *to sleep* Ld Tw ?atəbəd *die (*Ld *of people, not animals)* Ch ?átmin- *die* ~ Sh tumn *get a dream-vision,* stmtumn *a dream* Cb təmtəmnay' *corpse* Cv tmtmni? *id.* Ka təmtəmné?i *id.* Sp tmtmney' *id.* Cr tmtmni *id.*

*s-tu/amix *man, warrior.* Cx túmiš *man* Se stúmiš *id.* Sq stamš *warrior,* Cw staməš *id.,* Ms staməx *id.* Ck stáməx *id., leader of raiding party* Sn staməš *hero* Ld stubš *id.* Tw stúbəš *strong* ~ Th y'eneɫtúm'x *sense* (y'en-) *the presence of an enemy* Cr stum'š *friend (used by Coyote and Fox only).* – Cf. PS *-mix^w/*mix.

*tmix^w *world, nature, earth, river, animal, spirit.* Be tmx^w *river,* ?ask'tmax^{w}tum *he is torn between two places, cannot decide where to settle* Se təmix^w *(big) waves, wind (?)* Sq tmix^w *earth, land* Cw Ms táməx^w *id.* Ck tám:əx^w *id.* Nk təmix^w *id.* Sm Sn Sg təŋəx^w *id.* Cl sčtəŋx^{w}n Tw təbix^w *earth, land, dirt,* təbtábax^w *earth dwarfs* [Ch təmíš- *earth,* suff. -am(i)š *river*] Ti "to:wi'x̌" CV *earth, land* ~ Li Th Sh tmix^w *earth, land* Cv tmix^w *soul, spirit, power; any animal* Cr ttm'ix^w *animal.* – See PS suff. *-mix^w/*-mix.

*s-tinəws *cedar-root rope used for sewing up baskets.* Tw stídəwəs ~ Sh stínəstn.

*tinx *sinew, muscle.* Se tinš *vein, poss. muscle, sinew* [Ld ti𝌆] Ch tinš Cz tinx ~ Th tinx Sh titn'x Cb Cv tinx Ka Sp tinš Cr tinč.

*tup *to pound.* Sn tčət Nk túpun *hit* Ld tup Ch táp-
hit, strike, hammer Ti təh- *stab* ~ Li túpun' *punch, hit w. fist,*
tápn *sting* Th túpes *smash* Sh túpm. – Cf. NWAK tp- *crush*
(LR no. 343).

*tupl' *spider.* Ld túpl', təplúla? Ch túpa? Ti tóhəl CV ~
Cb túpla? Cv tupl/l' Ka tupl' Sp tupl/l' Cr túpen'.

*təq *to pin down, touch; obstruct.* Be tqan *deaf* Cx Se
təqt *close (as door, road)* Sq təq *be pinned down* Cw stəq *log
jam,* xʷtqet *close (door), turn off (water)* Ck tqet *close (door),*
stə́qtəq *log jam* Sm s/štəq *dam across river* Sn tqep *fishtrap,*
təqəstn *aerial duck net* Cl tqət *close,* tqapn *trap fish* Ld tqad
close, block, tə́qʷus *blind* Tw təqə́d *close it!,* stəq *log jam,*
təqustəd *salmon weir* Ch tə́q- *close, be stuck,* təqan' *deaf* Ti
nštqesč'i *choke* ~ Li təqn *touch,* stəq *log jam,* stqap *(beaver)
dam* Th təqstes *cover w. hand, touch, close,* ʔestáq *close
together (of fingers, boards),* ntəqcintn *door* Sh tqem *touch w.
hand, hold in place w. hand,* təqtqem *cross o.s.,* stəqqin *dam,*
cxtqew's *stuttering,* təqpqin *log jam* Cb təqn *touch w. hands,*
stqap *dam,* ntqaw's *id.,* təqtqəncut *cross o.s.* Cv tqntim
touch w. hand, tqipm *put in a dam* Ka tqem *touch (w. palm of
hand)* Sp tqem *touch,* tqepn *dam up* Cr taq *touch, cover w.
hand.* – See also CS *tqači?.

*taw I *to buy, sell.* [Cx tə́gaš *take revenge on, "pay
back"*] Se táwiš Sg tekʷəs Cl takʷs (actual tə?a?wəs) Ld tagʷ
Tw bitawáɬət *buy groceries* Ch tə́w- *pay for,* tawákʷsi- *sell,*
[táxʷiway *id.*] ~ Li tawn *sell st. to sb.,* táwmin *sell st.,* [təxʷp
buy] Th tewm *sell,* ntewmn *store* Sh tewm *buy,* [txʷum *add
to store*] Cb tawn *buy* Cv tíwm *id.* Ka téu *buy, sell* Sp
tumístmn *sell,* tewcn *buy groceries.* Cr tagʷ, tegʷ *buy, sell,*
[texʷ *add to store*]. – For the bracketed Ch Li Cr forms cf.
*tixʷ.

*taw II *(small and) growing up, child, young person.*
Cx tə́giwaɬ *children, descendants,* Se tə́wixʷal *children of one
family* Sq staw?xʷɬ *child* Ms sté?exʷəɬ *id.* Ck ste:xʷəɬ Sm
stéwixʷəɬ *id.,* sté:xʷəɬ *id.* Ld stáwixʷə/a?ɬ *id., pl.,* stáwigʷəɬ

id. ~ Li twit *good hunter/trapper,* twiw't *boy (over 13), young man,* twə́ww'ət *young boy* Th twit *grow,* twiw't *young man,* t?u?t *pre-teen boy,* stuytéke?/stwitéke? *shoots* Sh twit *grow up,* twwiwt *child, young man* Cb tw'it *boy,* staw'tqən'ús-kst/-xn *little finger/toe* Cv ttw/w'it *boy* Ka ɬtətəw'it *young, unmarried man,* tw'tíwa?nt *spoil (a child)* Sp ttw'it *boy* Cr ttw'it *youth, young boy,* tíwe? *indulge,* Nicodemus tíwe?nc *coddle, baby sb.*

*tiw see ***tuy.**

*təx *to comb one's hair.* Cw tši?qʷm; tšet *comb out* Ck təxqə́ylm Sm (s)təšel'qn' *wool carder* Sn tšiqʷn̩ Sg tši?qʷn̩; tšəl?qn *to card wool* Cl tše?qʷn̩; tše?qʷn *comb,* tšayəqn *wool carder* ~ Th stəxmin *comb,* təxqinm *brush one's hair* WSh txncut Sh stxmin *comb* Cv txam; stxmin *comb.*

*tixʷ *to obtain, add to a store,* ***tixʷ-c'i?** *kill game.* Be tix *catch* (for delabialization see Nater 1977:5 and cf. Be tixca under ***tixʷcaɬ**) Ch tíxʷni- *kill,* tíxʷc'i *kill a deer/elk/bear* ~ Li təxʷn *give more of st.* Th tíxʷc'i? *kill, murder,* txʷəm *add to, increase,* təxʷpxíc *buy (st.) for sb.* Sh tíxʷc'e *kill game,* təxʷc'esqéx̌e? *slaughter,* txʷum *add to* Cv tíxʷm *obtain, gather, harvest* [Ka tix̌ʷ *get, obtain* (poss. recording error)] Sp tíxʷ *id.,* čtxʷum *add more* Cr tixʷ *collect, gather, secure,* texʷ *add to store..* – Cf. ***taw** I.

*tixʷc *tongue.* Be tixca (see comment to Be tix under ***tixʷ**) Cx tíxʷsaɬ Sl tixʷθəɬ Se tíxʷcaɬ Cw Ms Ck tə́xʷθəɬ Sm tixʷs(ə)ɬ Nk tíxʷceɬ Sn tixʷθəɬ Cl tixʷɬc [Tw sdəxʷcáč] Ch tíxʷcaɬ- ~ Li təxʷc̣ą́ɬ (also tą́ɬą?) Sh tíxʷe?ck Cv tixʷck Ka Sp Cr tixʷcč. – For Sh (orig. also the Th suffix) inserted -a?- cf. Cv -isa?xn *rocks* vs. Sh -esxn *id.* – See PS ***-xʷc-**

*tax̌ *wrong, bitter.* Sn Sg stex̌əl *wrong,* [Cw t'əx̌ *make a mistake* Sn t'əx̌ *do/say st. wrong,* t'əx̌naxʷ *disagree*] ~ Li təx̌ *bitter* Th tax̌t *id.* Sh t?ex̌ *ill-disposed,* təx̌mins *be inimical to* Cb təx̌ *bitter* Cv tax̌t *id.* Sp tax̌ *id., sour* Cr tax̌ *bitter, sharp to taste.* – The bracketed forms may belong under ***t'əx̌.**

*təx̌ʷ *straight, just, settled.* [Be tiix̌ʷ *hit, guess right*]
Cx tə́x̌ʷənix̌ʷ *know*, [tutx̌ʷłał *kerchief, necklace*] Sl tə́x̌ʷnix̌ʷ
know Se stəx̌ʷit *certain, real, right, correct, very*, təx̌ʷnə́x̌ʷ
find out, realize, tú́x̌ʷut *stretch (as line)* Sq təx̌ʷ *settled*,
tx̌ʷaya?ní?m *make sure, get correct(ed) information*, tə́x̌ʷa?č
bow (for shooting) Cw tə́x̌ʷa(?)č *id.* Ck tə́x̌ʷəc *id.*, tá́x̌ʷəsm
pull canoe w. rope Sm təx̌ʷq'elət *noon*, tax̌ʷnét *midnight* Sn
tətax̌ʷsn *hold legs straight out* Sg təx̌ʷac' *bow and arrow* Ld
tú́x̌ʷəb *stretch (a net)*, tux̌ʷud (stress?) *stretch* Tw ?astú́x̌ʷ
strung out Ti tux̌en'i?- *hear, understand*, tux̌ecin- *taste*,
tùx̌el'g'ʷás- *be sensible, thoughtful, good to remember people* ~
Li təx̌ʷn *straighten out*, təx̌ʷps *get st. straight, find out the
truth*, tə́x̌ʷ?ač *bow (for shooting)*, [stax̌ʷ *dangle, hang down*,
tax̌ʷləx *id.*] Sh təx̌ʷtux̌ʷt *straight, right*, tx̌ʷum *straighten*,
xtx̌ʷéne *receive correct(ed) information*, [tex̌ʷm *hang st.
straight down* Cv tax̌ʷnt *dangle st. down*], tá́x̌ʷmist *stretch,
reach over to hang* Ka tx̌ʷomstén *straighten* Sp tox̌ʷ *straight*,
ntx̌ʷtox̌ʷs *sober.*

*tax̌ʷac *chest.* Ch tax̌ʷc ~ Li tá́x̌ʷac, suff. -ax̌ʷac Cv
-ax̌ʷck Ka Sp -ax̌ʷcč.   (Haeberlin 277 quotes Sh tk'mex̌ʷck
collarbone, tk'meləs *breastbone;* for the former I recorded
c'éwe, for *chest, breast* only suff. -(é)ləs). – Cf. PS ***-ax̌ʷac**.

*tuy, *tiw (inv.) *to stoop, to go across.* [Se t'úyut *bend
st. down*] Sq tuy *go across (water)*, túy?un *incline, lean*, [tuyn
leave, abandon], tltiwət *west wind* Cw təw?e?nə *sloped (eg.
land)* Ck təwelə *be tilted* Sm təw'in' *tilted*, stiwət *warm (east)
wind* Sn stiwət *northwest wind* Cl tuyəs *go across* Ld tú́ȝil
bend over (forward), [túlil *cross water*], tíg'ʷil *hide fr. raid* Ch
tíwat- *cross a river*, txʷtiw *get across, disappear* [Ti tiyu-
go] ~ Th túzix *to stoop, bend over*, (n)pstewt *across the
river/lake* Sh tuylx *stoop, bend over*, pəstewt *area beyond
river* Cb pəstawt *across water* Sp čtoyqnm *lower the head* Cr
tewš *go across*, téw'še(čt) *six* (cf. ***t'aq'**), tuy'mncut
(Nicodemus; stress?) *bow, bend down.*

t'

*t'ək *to prop up, support.* Sq t'čač *walking staff* ~ Li λ'ək?an *lean st. to st.*, λ'əka?mn *prop*, λ'ək?úsn *prop up branches of fruit tree* Th λ'ékes *prop up*, λ'ək?em *id.* Sh t'ək?em *id.*, [tək'lekstn *cane*] Cb kłt'əkcinn; t'kaksn *cane* Cv t'k-: t'kikst(t)n *cane*, nt'kiw's *crosspiece.*

*t'ək^w *to bleed.* Be t'k^w ~ Cr t'ək^ws.

*t'ək^w/q^w *to explode, burst open; slap, strike.* [Be tk^wi-*chipped*, t'ksn *to shoot*, t'ksn(i)mta *arrow* Cx t'ək^wt *to crush*] Se t'ək^w *burst (as boil)*, t'ək^ws *go off, explode* Sq t'ək^ws *id.*, t'ək^w *burst (as boil)* [Ck λ'əláq^w *explode* Tw biλ'áq^wab *crackle, spark (of fire)* Ti tq^w- *break*] ~ Li λ'ək^wn *burst st. open (as boil, pimple, louse)*, λ'ək^wp *explode*, λ'iq^wt *crackle, explode (in fire)*, λ'ək^wp *explode*, λ'əq^wn *slap* Th λ'ək^wtcs *cause to burst*, [λ'k^wəp *balloon/egg bursts*, λ'əq^w- *crack open, explode*], λ'əq^wtes *slap* Sh t'k^wupt *burst (as egg)*, t'q^wupt *id. (as tire)*, t'q^wum *strike, whip, kill (as chicken)* Cb t'ək^wp *burst, blow up*, t'əq^wn *slap* Cv t'uk^w *pop out*, nt'k^wpus *eye bursts*, t'q^wam *slap*, t'iq^wt *burst, explode* Ka t'q^w *to pat, slap* Sp t'ik^w *to pop, burst*, t'iq^w *small bursting sound* Cr t'eq^w *go off, explode.* – Cf. ***t'aq^w.**

*t'ik^w/q^w *muddy (water).* [Cw t'ək^wt'ək^w *muddy, swampy*] Tw ?ast'ík^w *id.*, bit'íyək^w *(water) gets dirty* ~ [Th tiq^w-] Sh xtiq^wns *make muddy*, xtəq^wtíq^w *dirty, muddy (of water)* Cv nt'iq^w *muddy water.*

*t'əl *to slice, split, rip.* Sq st'əl *spring salmon cut in half* Cw Ck st'el *split and dried salmon* Ld t'al *to slice, split open* Tw ?ast'ál/y *sliced*, t'áyad/t'aládəx^w *slice it!* Ch t'ál- *slice off, dress meat* ~ Li λ'əl *cut*, λ'úl'ax^w *to plough*, λ'əlq'an *tear*, λ'əl'q^w *to break (rope, line)* Th λ'lúle?x^wm *to plough* (loan fr. Ok) Sh t'lúle?x^wm *id.*, t'ilx^wm *rip at seam*, t'lux^w *(get) ripped*, t'lq^w- *break off a chunk*, t'luq^w *come apart* Cb t'əl'n *rip, tear*, t'íl'x̌^wn *cut up, cut to pieces* Cv t'lam *tear open*, t'iłc'a?m *carve fish*, t'lúla?x^wm *to plough* Ka est'il *torn*, t'əlim

109

tear Sp t'il' *sound of ripping* Cr t'el' *rip, tear.* – Cf. HEI, HAI t'ał- KWA t'ls- *slice fish/meat.* (LR no. 473).

*t'al *numb, tired.* Sn t'əlt'əlel'sŋ *numb* ~ Th λ'yəp *faint, swoon* Sh t'lel *tired.* – Cf. ***λ'il**.

*t'ul *charm, medicine* (CS), *spirit* (IS). Se st'əlmixʷ *medicine* Sq t'uyʔt *id.* Cw Ms Ck st'əlməxʷ *id., charm* Sn st'elŋəxʷ *medicine,* st'lmeyɫ *sung spell* Sg stelŋəxʷ (prob. t') *medicine, supernatural healing power* Cl st'ayŋ(ə)xʷ *medicine,* st'eʔwiʔəλáw'txʷ *church* Ld st'əlǰixʷ *medicine* ~ Li λ'əl/l'sqal'xʷ *spirit, soul* Th λ'əlsqal'xʷ *person* Sh t'úlns *work magic on sb. (as done by shaman),* st'lsqeləxʷ *soul* Cv t'lsqilxʷ *come to life,* t'lsqilxʷm *revive a person.*

*s-t'ul *a type of deer.* Sq st'əl' *newborn deer* Cw st'ít'leʔ *fawn* Ck st'it'ələ *id.* Ti dəlt'əléstu *deer, elk* ~ Th sλ'úleʔ *mule deer* Cb st'úlc'aʔ *id.* Cv st'úlɫc'aʔ *id.* Sp st'úlc'eʔ *female id.* Cr st'únɫc'eʔ *mule deer, ass.* – See Kinkade 1991:235 and 1995:38f.

*t'əls *highbush cranberry.* Be st'ls Cx t'əys Se t'əls ~ Li λ'əlc [Sh t'nis]. – See Kinkade 1995:33. Cf. NWAK t'lc/s-*viburnum edule* (LR no. 428).

*t'əm *to cut.* [Cx t'əmqʷat *break (as bread, chocolate bar)*] Sq t'əm- *be cut, wounded, hurt* Cw t'əmʔət *pound, beat,* št'ət'əməlʔs *adze* Ck t'əmáls/t'əmáls *to adze, chop* [Sn t'əm' *get hit*] ~ Cb t'əm'n *cut (meat, etc)* Cr t'em *cut w. scissors,* t'em' *cut cloth by sliding scissors through.* – Cf. ***λ'əm**.

*t'am (in name of) *gooseberry.* Cx t'amʔxʷ Se st'amxʷ Sq st'amʔxʷ Cw Ms t'emʔxʷ Ck t'eməxʷ [Cl tám'əqʷ] Ld t'əbxʷ Tw t'əbʔə́xʷ Ch t'əmáxʷ ~ Cv nt'it'mlps (-lps *neck*) Sp nt'ey'mlps.

*t'um/*tum *to suck.* Be t'um, t'uma, tums Cx t'úmut [also t'úqʷut (Sn has ç'aqʷət)] Tw but'- (inv.) Ch mút'i- (inv.) ~ Li nλ'úλ'm'ək' *straw (to drink through)* Th λ'umk' *drinking tube* Sh t'um *eat soapberries or other foamy food,* t'umntm *get leeches* Cb (Krueger) t'uməm *teats, milk* Cv tum Ka t'əm

Sp tum Cr t'um *smirk, mouth in sucking position,* st'úmum *breast, milk,* tum *pump, suck through tube.* – Cf. *c'ṷ/ạm.

*t'amin *fur, animal hair (feathers).* Sq t'ámin *animal hair* Ld t'ábid *id., fur* Ch t'amín *id., hair (in general)* ~ Li ƛ'ámin *wool, fur* Th ƛ'emn *body covering, hair, fur, feathers* Sh t'emn.

*t'amay see ***mat'ay.**

*t'ani/a? *ear.* Ti t'əní ~ Li ƛ'ə́na? Th ƛ'én'i Sh t'éne Cb t'ána? Cv t'ína? Ka Sp t'éne? Cr t'íne?. – Cf. PS *-ana?.

*t'unxʷ see ***t'uxʷn.**

*t'əp I *dark* Ti st'hšən *it's dark!* (√t'əh, vs. √ƛ'əh *under, below*) ~ Li ƛ'əpƛ'əpmál'us *dark color* Th ƛ'əpƛ'ə́pt *id., pitch dark* Sh t'ept *dark.*

*t'əp II *to tip over, fall.* Tw ?ast'əp *it's upside down,* ?axʷ t'ə́pəs *laying down on stomach, face down, upside down,* [t'əpəd/tp'əd *sleep*] ~ Cv t'ppúsnt *fall on one's face,* nt'pqsam *tip one's head* [Cr t'əp *jump aside*].

*t'aqa? *berry sp.* (CS *salalberry*). Cx t'áqa? Se t'áqa Sq t'áqa? Cw t'éqe(?) Ms t'éqe Ck t'eqə Sm t'éqe? Sn st'eqə? *bruise* Sg t'éqe *id., purple, bruise* Cl t'áqa? Ld Tw t'áqa Cz t'áqa? ~ [Th t'áqe? (borr. fr. Hl)] Sh sət'éqe? (ultimately < *st'ət'áqa?) *highbush blueberry.* – See Kinkade 1995:37.

*t'aq' *to cross over;* (in derivatives:) *six.* Cx t'əq'št *return (st. borrowed)* Sq t'áq'nəw?ásn *to cross (two things, eg. one's legs),* t'áq'ač *six* [Ck t'ekʷl] ~ Li ƛ'aq' *to cross, go over,* ƛ'aq'əmkst *six* Th ƛ'a/eq'm *transport across,* ƛ'q'əmcin *crossing place,* ƛ'áq'mekst *six* Sh teq'm *cross river,* təq'mekst *six* Cv t'aq'm *cross a stream,* t'aq'mkst *six* Ka Sp t'aq'n *id.* – Cf. *t'əx̌.

*t'əqʷ *to bathe, swim.* Be (Kimsquit dial.) nut'ax̌ʷm *bathe* ~ Sh t'əqʷesxnm *tread water, swim.*

*t̓əqʷaʔ *to interweave.* Cl t̓qʷeʔt *splice* ~ Li ƛ̓əqʷʔum *sew* Th ƛ̓qʷuʔtés *id.* Sh t̓əqʷʔum *id.* Cv t̓qʷam *id.* Ka Sp t̓qʷum *id.*

*t̓aqʷ *to lick.* Be t̓aax̌ Tw t̓aqʷáʔdas Ch t̓aqʷá- Ti t̓aqʷ- ~ Li [ƛ̓úqʷun̓]; ƛ̓áqʷamaz̓ *bunchgrass (on strands of which soapberries were stored)* Th ƛ̓aqʷm̓; ƛ̓áqʷeɫp *timbergrass, pinegrass* Sh t̓eqʷm; t̓eqʷnɫp *timbergrass* Cb t̓aqʷn; [t̓aqənɫp *pine grass*] Cv Sp t̓aqʷm.

*t̓iqʷ see ***yəqʷ**.

*t̓aqʼ́ʷ *to break.* Se t̓əqʼ́ʷt *break (a rope)* Sq t̓áqʼ́ʷan *break, bruise, cut in two (rope)* Ld t̓əqʼ́ʷ *(flexible object) snaps in two,* t̓qʼ́ʷud *break (pl. obj.)* ~ Th ƛ̓əqʼ́ʷ- *crack open, explode,* Cr t̓aqʼ́ʷ *egg or eye bursts.* – Cf. ***t̓əkʷ/qʷ**.

*t̓iqʼ́ʷ see ***t̓ikʼ́ʷ/qʼ́ʷ**.

*t̓uqʼ́ʷ *down feathers.* Ld st̓uʔqʼ́ʷ Ch st̓uqʼ́ʷ ~ Sh stuqʼ́ʷ.

*s-t̓aqʼ́ʷm *thimbleberry.* [Cx t̓əqʷm Se st̓əqʷə́m] Sq st̓áqʼ́ʷam [Ck t̓qʷəm Sg t̓əqʷm Sm t̓əqʷm̓] ~ Li sƛ̓aqʼ́ʷm Sh (Palmer) steqʼ́ʷm. – The forms w. plain qʷ may result from contamination with PS ***t̓aqʷ** *lick.*

*s-t̓əwin *skin.* Be st̓win *animal hide,* st̓winlic̓ *any treebark* [Se st̓únač *feather(s)*] Ti st̓égi ~ Th sƛ̓enwn *buckskin skirt* WSh t̓en̓wn *fish skin* ESh st̓wiʔ *skin,* esp. *fish skin.* – See PIS ***t̓ənw-ayaʔ**.

*t̓ax, *xat̓ (inv.) *to ladle.* Sq šát̓an, šat̓tn *a ladle* ~ Li (s)ƛ̓axímn *spoon,* xáƛ̓an̓ *take st. out of st.* Th sƛ̓eʔxímn *ladle, spoon,* xeƛ̓m *skim off, remove fr. stove/basket* Sh t̓exm *take food out of container,* sət̓ximn *a ladle* Cv st̓xitkʷ *soup,* nt̓ixlnt *dip out, serve* [Cr t̓eȝ̌ *pour liquid*].

*t̓uxʷn, *t̓unxʷ (inv.) *a plant (cattails, scouring rush).* Cx t̓úʔnaxʷ *cattails* ~ Li ƛ̓úʔl̓axʷ *roots of cattail* Th ƛ̓uxʷn̓ *scouring rush* Sh t̓uxʷn̓ *id.* Sp t̓uxʷn *id., horsetail* Cr t̓uxʷen *jointgrass.* – Except for the l/n interchange, the Li word agrees formally and semantically with the Cx one. See further comments to *p'uqᵂ.

*t'əx̌ *to open up, branch out; six.* Be t'x̌ᵂuɬ *six* (labialization automatic) Cx Sl t'əx̌m *id.* Se t'əx̌əm *id.* Sq st'əx̌ *branch or prong of antler,* st'x̌i *fork in stream/road,* st'x̌ačxᵂ *limb of tree,* t'əx̌cam? *open one's mouth,* t'ax̌maɬšá? *sixty* Cw Ck t'x̌əθət *forks in stream* Ms st'əx̌əθət *id.* Cw Ms t'x̌əm *six* Ck t'x̌əm: *id.,* st'əx̌ *forks (in river /tree/ road)* Sm t'x̌əŋ *six* Sn t'x̌ət *deviate, turn into other path,* st'əx̌qn *fork in river,* Sn Sg Cl t'x̌əŋ *six* Cl t'əx̌naxᵂ *disagree,* t'x̌əct *go the wrong way* Ch t'əx̌əm- *six* ~ Li λ'ix̌əx̌ *become wide, spread out,* Th λ'íx̌es *spread, unfold* Cv t'ix̌ *spread open, umbrella-like* Ka Sp t'íx̌- *open up, spread out.* – See comment under *tax̌.

w

*wa(?) *to cry, holler.* Sl wə́wəm *chanter d'une voix forte,* Ld wə?a *sound of a baby crying* ~ Sh wewm *holler* [Cb wwawəlx *speak, talk*] Ka Sp we? *holler* Cr wi? *cry out, shout.*

*s-wa? (mostly red.) *cougar.* Cx gíy?giy Sq (n)swú?wu Ck šxᵂə́wə Nk šwúwe Ld swəwá?/swéwə? ~ Li swúw'a Th Sh smúwe? Cb sˁʷáˁʷa? Cv sw'aˁ Cr sw'a. – Cf. KUT swa? *panther.*

*wi? see *huy.

*wac' *to pry loose, pick out; tease.* Cx gáwc'at *tease* Se wác'at *id.* Sq wác'at *pry loose, lever up,* wəwc'at *tease* Cw weç'ət *knit* Ck wəç'et *tease* Sn kᵂeç'ət *pry up, lever up,* kᵂəw'ç'en'əq *tease* Cl kᵂac't *lever up, pry out* Ti cgᵂác'iw *be digging,* cgᵂac'i(w)w'íni *I dug it up* ~ Li nwawc'aná?m *clean one's ear w. finger* Sh wec'm *extract marrow* Cv wic'm *dig, pick (a sliver, root)* Sp wec'm *pick/pry out* Cr gᵂic' *pick out w. stick.* – Sq x̌ᵂúc'un? *lever up* points to a PS doublet with *ˁʷ-. Cf. *wat'k.

*wu/ah *to bark (at).* Cx gúhut Se wum, wəwum, wəwut Sl guhm Sq wu?n Cw wəwa?əs [Sn wəsəla? Cl wa?wə?sə́y's] Ld gʷuhəb Tw biwəhúb *it's barking* Ti "wowo'han" CV ~ [Li wáz'am Th wéc'eme Sh xweym] Cb wahm Cv wahám, wahntím Ka uhentés *he barks at him* Cr wih.

*wəl, *ʕʷəl *to burn, shiny, bright,* ***wəlim** *iron, metal.* Be wiłwił *mica* Cx x̌ʷəłímuł *suitcase ("because the first ons used to be shiny"),* x̌ʷáx̌ʷatičinm *fish show back above water while going upstream,* [gə́c'gəc' *shiny*] Sl gəyc'm *briller* Se x̌ʷalám *to glow,* [x̌ʷáyuls *id.*], sx̌ʷal *spark,* swil *sunshine* Cw x̌ʷay *red hot (rocks)* Ld gʷílič'əb *shine (as fur), luster,* wíłwił *a small snipe* Tw x̌ʷələ́qʷ *it's burnt* Ch x̌ʷalá:? *hot,* wələ́č'- *glitter, shine, sparkle,* wə́lq'- *polish* Ti cgʷə́luw *feel warm,* nšgʷələ́wn *make st. hot,* gəlgə́ləw CV *iron* ~ Li ʕʷəln *burn, set fire to,* ʕʷəyʕʷəy'ə́p *northern lights,* wəlwəlqʷ"usm/ ʕʷəlʕʷəlqʷ"usm *lightning,* wə̣lwə̣lm *shiny,* swalálm *iron* Th ʕʷyəm *make/set a fire,* ʕʷyəp *catch fire,* ʕʷłəp *get scalded,* tʕʷəlstés *make st. greenish and shiny,* w?al *get worn smooth, shiny,* w?ał *shiny,* wəlwlim *metal* Sh xwlnte/as *light a kindling fire,* x̌ʕʷlan'ktn *kindling,* wlwalt *shiny,* ʕʷ?eł *to shine, glitter, sparkle,* ʕʷəłʕʷełt *shining, glittering,* swəłweł *mica,* wiwłwəł *snipe,* swlwəle/i̧lm *iron* Cb ʕʷəl' *bright, shiny, glisten,* swərusm *fishing torch,* wəlwəlim *iron* Cv wr'am *build a fire,* wr'usm *fish w. torch,* wlam *burn, scorch,* wlwlim *iron* Ka (?)o:l'-/o:l-/u:l- *burn,* u:lu:lím *iron, money* Sp ?urntén *burn st.,* ?ur'ús *a burning fire, he has a fire burning* Ka (Carlson-Flett) ?ol'ús *id.* Cr gʷel *burn, blaze,* gʷar' *be silvery, clear,* wəlwəlim *money, valuables,* w'əl'w'əl'im' *iron, knife.* – Cf. PIS ***s-wal, *s-wəlm-in'k..**

*wal *to tilt.* Se wəl *capsize* Ld gʷal *capsize* [Ch wałá- *come loose/untied, open* (may belong under ***liʕʷ**)] ~ Li wal'án; swal' *tilted* Th nwéy'es *turn st. on its side,* nwéy?i? *tipped over* Sh xwelns; cwel *tilted* Cb wal'n Cv wil'l' *be leaning,* cwil' *tilted* Sp wel'n *tip st. over* Cr gʷel'.

*wil *canoe* (independent word in Ts only). Ch wił (Lower Ch gwí:ł Haeberlin 264). – See PS ***-wil**.

*wətqʷ see *ʕʷətqʷ.

*wa/ina?w *horn, antler.* Se swəná?əw Nk wénew Ld gʷáda?kʷ Tw wədá?w Ch wináw' (also *wedge*) Ti Si ganáw CV ~ Th Sh Ok wənaw CV *chisel.*

*wənaxʷ *real, true.* Cx gənaxʷ; [ginm *parent/child-in-law*] Sl gə́nəxʷ Se wənaxʷ; [swinm *parent-in-law*; swəniš *unid. relative*] Sq wanáxʷ Ck wəl *real(ly)* Ch náxʷɬ- ~ Li wənaxʷ; wənaxʷc *(speak) loud(ly),* wín'axʷ *similar, same* Th nexʷ(m) *very much so, exceedingly,* [wənwíne?xʷ *in-laws*] Sh wnexʷ; nxʷmi? *forever,* nexʷm *"ain't it?"* Cb wənaxʷ Cv wnixʷ Sp ?unexʷ Cr gʷənixʷ. – The words for *in-laws* may well belong here, cf. Dutch 'echt' 1. *real,* 2. *marriage,* originally perhaps *according to law or ritual,* cf. also *x̌a? I and II.

*wəna?x̌ *berry sp.* Ld (s)wəda?x̌ *mountain blueberry* Tw wəd?ax̌ *id.* Cz wənay'x̌ *huckleberry* ~ Sh wnex̌ *id.* Cb sw'ə́n/n'a?x̌ *id. (highbush).*

*wiq' *to undo, remove, take apart, open.* Be wiiq-/wiix̌- *to (pry) open* Cx gəq't *to open* Se wəq't *id.* Sq wiq'cn?/wiq'cán? *pull/force open* Cw wəq'els *dig hole* [Cw Ck wiqəs *yawn*] Ld gʷəq'-/gəq'- *opening* Tw ?aswíq' *lying with legs spread out,* wiq'íd *spread your legs!,* ?aswə́q' *it's open,* wəq'ə́d *open it!* Ch waq'á- *to open* Ti "ge:k'" CV *id.* [gʷəq-*untie, loosen*] ~ Li nwaq' *hole,* wíq'ʷus (labialization automatic) *come loose (as button)* Th wəq'ə́p *open up,* nwəq'pew's *unfold,* wəq'puym'xʷ *rift, ground cracked open* Sh wiq'm *undo, wreck* Sp soq'éw'snt (√wq'(e) *cut, split*) *cut (playing cards)* Cr gʷaq' *spread apart as to part hair, remove layers.*

*was *both of a pair, mutual; two.* Be ɬnus/ɬwaas- *two* Se wasakʷə́na *both cheeks,* wasšə́n *both legs* Sq ?án?us *two* ~ Li ?án'was *two,* tíwasq *both legs/ shoes,* tiwasáka *both hands.* – Cf. PS *-was and *x̌əmanwas.

115

*wis *high, above.* Tw (ʔ)wis *high* Ti gis *up, above* ~ Sh wist *high* Cb wísxən *long* Cv wist *high, stand* Ka wis *long* Sp wis/š- *stand up,* nwist *it's up high* Cr gʷis *be high.*

*(s-)wat *who?, someone.* Be wa-ks *who is it?* (cf. stam-ks *what is it?*) Cx Sl gat Se wat Sq swat Cw Ms Ck Nk Sm wet Ld gʷat Tw ʔwatči *who is it?,* sʔwat *someone* Ch wa: *who,* ʔiwát *someone,* swátaɬ *whose* Ti gʷátu (CV gata) ~ Li swat Th swet Sh swet(iʔ) Cb swat Cv swit Ka suwét Sp swet Cr ségʷet.

*watʼk/*watkʼ/*watʼkʼ *to pry/lever up; vomit.* Be ʔutʼak *vomit* Cx gátʼat *pry, lock* Sl gatʼət *pry* Se wátʼat *lever up* ~ Li waƛʼk *vomit* Th weƛʼkʼ *id.,* wəƛʼkʼetés *pry st. up* Sh wetkʼx *vomit,* wetkʼxtn *vomiting stick,* wtkʼelm *pry up* Cb nawátkʼəlx *vomit,* nawə́tkʼm *dip* Cv witkʼx *vomit,* kʼɬwatkʼ *pry up* Sp ʔutčʼélʼn *to pin, fasten (as brooch)* Cr gʷetʼčʼ *prong, gore.* – Nater 1994 compares Eyak wətʼ *vomit,* PALG *-wəʔtʼ *belly,* but the meanings *vomit* and *pry up* are closely associated in Salish, as the Indians habitually induced vomiting before going hunting, with special "vomiting sticks" (this may also explain the semantic shift to *prong, etc.*). – Cf. ***wacʼ**.

*way *to be visible, revealed, public.* Be twinm *emerge, show up (fr. behind st.),* twinmuc *reveal* Se swayníxʷ *to notice,* [ʔə tkʷayl *today*] Sq wáyat *reveal, make public,* [skʷayl *day(light), sky,* kʷayləs *tomorrow*] Cw weyl *become day,* [skʷeyl *day,* [wilʔ *appear, come into view*] Ms wəweyələs *tomorrow* Ck we:y *be found out,* weyl *become day,* sweyl *day* Sn kʷey *reveal, announce* Cl kʷiʔ *show up* Ld wíʔə/ad *holler,* [wəliʔ *appear, be visible*] Tw wayʔád *show it!,* waysəb *appear* ~ Th wazm *to show,* ʔeswáz *visible,* [wəl- *clearing,* wəlp- *clear up (of weather)*] Sh weym *reveal.* – Forms w. initial kʷ, regular in Straits, have spread northward along the coast, cf. comment to ***kʼʷaʔ**.

116

X

*xəl see *xʷul.

*xa̱l, *xal *to hang spread out; steep.* Se šálat *hang up (as flag, sail)* Ck x̌ə́ylós *very steep slope, steep shore/dropoff* Sn šəlŋ *climb (a tree, ladder, etc.),* šəlŋistxʷ *bring/hoist st. up* ~ Li xa̱ln *hoist up flag,* sxal *edge, rim (of hill or table),* ka xál-a *get to or hang over an edge,* sx̌əl' *steep,* x̌əl'x̌l'm *id.* Th xéyes *put st. on the edge,* ʔesxéy *close to the edge,* ʔestxéye *hanging over the edge,* nx̌yəm *erect partition in house,* xé/ázes *raise flag,* xəztes *hang st., show off st.,* ʔe stxáze *just right on edge,* x̌iʔx̌áy't *steep,* x̌iʔptéw's/x̌i(y)ptéw's *take shortcut through mountains* Sh xalm *partition off by hanging up a mat/curtain,* xlxalt *steep,* xlapt *shortcut,* txlptaw's *(trail) runs over mountain* Cb xə́r'xər't/xə́l'xəl't *steep (bank)* Cv xrxart *steep,* nxarnt *hang a curtain in front,* nxrinktn *wall mat,* txirp *run uphill,* txrutm *id.,* cxilsm *edge* Ka šə́lšált *steep,* ša:l'ú(tiʔ) *go uphill* Sp hečšrew's *it's hanging,* šrutm *climb a hill* Cr šar *one hangs,* šáršart *steep.*

*xil *to bite, gnaw, chop, cut.* Be xil *nibble, gnaw at* Cx xə́ltat *(borr.) cut w. saw* ~ Sh xlem *to bite* Cv xlam *to chop (wood),* nxlxlusnt *cut off (head)* Ka šilím *chop, cut w. axe* Sp šlim *chop* Cr šel *chop, split.*

*xəƛ' *to scorch, bake.* Ld šəƛ' *scorch* ~ Sh xəťcin'm *bake bread in open fire* Cv xəƛ'cin *basket to cook in.*

*xəm *both (sides),* ***xəm-an(-was)** *other side, alter ego, enemy.* Be xmanwas *guardian spirit* Cx Sl šə́man *enemy* Se šəmán *id.* Sq šman *id.* Cw šəmen *id.* Ms sxəmen *id.* Ck sxəmel *id.* Sm Sn šəmen *id.* Sg šəme:n *id.* Cl šəman *id.* Ld šəbad *id.* Tw ɬšəbad *other side of the waterway* Ch šə́m- *both* [Ti šaʔwán *awfully, very*] ~ Li xman' *enemy* Th xmen' *id.,* xəmn'un's *opponent* Sh xmen *enemy,* xmnun's *id., opponent,* xm'nəsews *be enemies,* txmnews *on both sides,* txmnwsus *double-bladed* Cb xəman' *enemy* Cv xmin' *id.,* stxmniw's *both sides* Ka šəmen' *enemy* Sp šmen' *id.* Cr šemen' *(stress?) id.*

117

*x/x̌am *dry.* Cw šemət *dry st.* Ld šáb(a) [Ch x̌əpí-] ~ Ka x̌am'. – Cf. *x/x̌aw.

*xən *to lie flat.* Ch šaná?s- *lie on one's back* ~ Th xn'ikn'tn *any cover for structure,* xnéyeptn *floor covering* Sh cxen *lying spread out,* txnén'e *to cover,* xnekst *mat made of rushes,* xnekstm *spread out a mat (for dinner, gambling, etc.),* nxneləstn *floor covering,* xnqin's *put st. over st.* Cb katxən'qínn *cover, put a lid on* Cv xnqin *close a box,* xnikn'm *carry on one's back* Ka šən'qin *id.* Sp hecšín' *a flat object is lying there,* šn'nten *to close,* šn'qin *put cover on* Cr šen' *one flat object lies.*

*s-xanx *rock, stone.* Ti šenš ~ Th Sh sxenx Ka Sp sšen'š.

*xəp see *pəx/*xəp.

*xit see *xəyt.

*xit' *to be stretched out, project.* Cx xít'alšin (borr.) *to tiptoe* Se šət' *be stretched out* ~ Li xíxiƛ'xn' *stand on one's toes* Th nxíƛ'nekxənme (Lytton) *stand on one's toes, tiptoe* Ka Sp šit' *to stand (one long object)* Cr šet' *one long object projects.*

*xat' see *t'ax.

*xaw *to grow.* Sq šə́way Cl šə́wi *grow (as child),* š(ə)wə́yət *grow* Ld šəgʷa?əc *salmonberry sprout* Ch šəwál-*grow, raise* ~ Sh (xə)xexw'tm *young girl* Cv xixwtm *girl* Ka (ł)šešú?təm' *little girl* Cr šiw'tm *adolescent girl (13-21).* – Semantically cf. *taw II.

*xəwal *trail.* Se šawł Sq šuáł Cw šeł Ms xeł Ck xe:ł Nk šeł Sm Sn Sg sał Cl suł Ld šəgʷł Tw šuw?áł/šu?wáł Ch šəwł, šə́wil-, suff. -ušwał- Cz xʷuł; xawáli *his road* (cf. *kaw I) Ti šəgʷáł ~ Li xʷwał Th xw/w'eł, suff. -xwey/y' Sh xʷəxʷweł Cb xəwal Cv xwił Ka šu?šuw'éł Sp šu?šw'éł Cr hnšégʷel (CV gives final n instead of l).

*xəyt *fore, front, first.* Se šəyt *bow of boat* Ld šə3t *id., front* ~ Th x?it *scout, spy* Sh xəx?ít *id.,* sx?itmx *elder sibling* Cb scx?it *first,* xi?tús *ahead, forward, lead, be in charge,* sxə?ítəx^w *oldest* Cv x?it *first, best, top,* sxx?íta?x *be the oldest,* xa?x?ít *man's grandmother,* xa?tús *leader* Ka ši?ít *be first,* sši?íti *the oldest of siblings,* [šiy'- *proceed, continue going, pass*] Sp ši?tús *bow of boat,* sx^{w}š?it *forbears,* š?it *first, ahead, before* Cr ši?t *be first, oldest.*

x^w

*x^{w}a *light of weight.* Be x^{w}aax^{w}i Cx Se x^{w}íx^{w}x^{w}a Sq ?á?x^{w}a Cw x^{w}ə?é:x^{w}e? Ck x^{w}áx^{w}e Sm x^{w}əx^{w}ew'x^{w}ə Sn x^{w}əx^{w}ewə?x^{w}ə? Cl x^{w}a?wáwə Ld x^{w}ə?á?x^{w}ə? Tw sx^{w}ak^{w}k^w *breath,* nisx^{w}ak^{w}k^w *lungs* (x^w *corrected fr.* k$^{'w}$) Ch x^{w}e?k$^{'w}$ ($\sqrt{}$x^{w}ík$^{'w}$) Ti cx^{w}ə?x^{w}ə́? ~ Li sx^{w}ák^{w}ək^w *heart, feelings, mind* Sh x^{w}ək^{w}x^{w}ék^w *light(weight),* sx^{w}ék^{w}ək^w *lungs.* – Cf. QUI x^{w}o?w *light(weight).*

*x^{w}i/ak$^{'w}$, *x^{w}ik^w *to wipe, brush, smooth, clean, bathe.* Be x^{w}uk' *bathe sb.,* x^{w}uk'm *take a bath* Se x^{w}ák$^{'w}$at *to smooth, sandpaper* Sq x^{w}ík^{w}in? *to brush,* šúk$^{'w}$um *to bathe* (vs. ƛ'íčim *swim*) Cw šəšk$^{'w}$ə́m (Hukari šk$^{'w}$am?) *swim* Ms xəxk$^{'w}$ə́m *id.* (elicited as translation of *swim*) Ck xak$^{'w}$m *bathe,* xixk$^{'w}$ám *swim* (also ƛ'icm) Sm s/šak$^{'w}$ņ *bathe,* šišk$^{'w}$ám' *swim* Sn sak$^{'w}$ņ *bathe,* šk$^{'w}$am' *swim,* šq$^{'w}$m'alk^{w}ət *bathing suit* (prob. šk$^{'w}$...), [x^{w}əčsəntn *doormat*] Sg šəšk$^{'w}$ə́m? *swim* Cl x^{w}ik^{w}u?áčn *diaper,* suk$^{'w}$ņ *bathe* Ld x^{w}ík^{w}id *scrape, rub hard* Ch x^{w}ík^{w}i-*wipe, rub,* [x̌^{w}áq^{w}a- *scrape*] ~ Li x^{w}ík^{w}in' *polish, rub sb. w. medicine* ESh x^{w}ik$^{'w}$w (<x^{w}ik$^{'w}$m) *rub off (as skin),* x^{w}ik^{w}w (<x^{w}ik^{w}m) *rub against st. smooth,* x^{w}ik^{w}lx *rub the body against st. (of animals)* Cb x^{w}uk$^{'w}$n *to clean, wipe,* x^{w}úk^{w}x^{w}uk$^{'w}$t *clean* Cv x^{w}k$^{'w}$am *to clean,* kx^{w}ik$^{'w}$nt *id. st.,* x^{w}úk$^{'w}$la?x^w *clean soil* Sp x^{w}uk$^{'w}$ *clean, clear,* x^{w}k$^{'w}$um *to clean,* x^{w}ik^w- *scrape,* [x̌^{w}aq$^{'w}$ *grind*] Cr x^{w}ek^w *clean, sweep.* – Cf. QUI x^{w}í:č'il *scratch, clean by scratching, scrape.*

*x^{w}uk$^{'w}$, *x^{w}uk^w *to pull (out).* Sq x^{w}uk$^{'w}$m Cw x^{w}k$^{'w}$at Ms k$^{'w}$xem (inv.) Sm x^{w}əx^{w}ək$^{'w}$a:t *play tug-of-war* Sn x^{w}k$^{'w}$at

Cl xʷəkʷ ~ Li xʷukʷⁿn; xʷúkʷcan' *remove cork, open bottle* Sh txʷukʷⁿm *pull out (nail, feather)*, xʷukʷm *pull st. out of a pile* Cb xʷukʷm *pull out (nails, teeth)* Ka nxuqʷn *pull out.*

*xʷəl *to dig out, make a hollow, divert water.* Se x̌ʷəlt *dig out,* x̌ʷəlaqʷt *dig a ditch in,* tr. Sq x̌ʷəlt *make small channel w. stick,* sx̌ʷlayšn *rill,* x̌ʷəlʔšm *to flow* ~ Li x̌ʷlə́lʔik *small slough draining into larger body of water* Th x̌ʷy'əm *make an opening through st.,* x̌ʷiʔtés *id.,* x̌ʷiʔpéw's *water runs through gap in dike* Sh xʷelm *open a ditch, divert water,* xʷelemt/xʷlap *there is a break or side trench in the ditch* ESh xʷílat (<xʷiḷmt) *bursting along the seams* Cv sxʷr'cin (geogr.) *"area torn out of riverbank",* nxʷr'us (geogr.) *"having a narrow gully".*

*xʷal see ***xʷay/l.**

*xʷaḷ see ***ḷaxʷ.**

*xʷul (often delabialized to ***xəl**) *to turn, spin, drill, wrap around, round,* ***xʷul- (i-)kʷup** *firedrill.* Be xʷulta *drill,* xʷulxʷulm *drill frire,* ʔałxʷulxʷuluuł *biscuit, pilot bread* Sq šúyuy'n *make holes w. awl,* šíši?č *round,* ši?úkʷ *id.,* šə́yčəp *firedrill* Cw šə́lcəp *id.* šəlakʷ *round* Ms sxə́lcəp *firedrill,* xəlakʷ *round* Ck xa:lt *bore hole,* sxə́lcəs *firedrill,* xəla:kʷ *round,* xʷəlkʷ *to eddy* Sm šə́ləč' *to circle* Sn šəlčəp *firedrill* Sn Sg šəlakʷ *round* Sn xʷələkʷt *wrap up* Sg xʷə́ləqʷt (prob. kʷ) *id.* Cl xʷə́yəkʷt *wrap up, bandage* Ld šulá?kʷčup *firedrill* Ch xʷúlup- *hoop, round, circle* Ti šultn CV *drill,* "šó:leu:" (Haeberlin 273) *he drills a hole,* "šole:'to:" CV *firedrill* ~ Li xʷúlun' *bore hole in st.,* xʷuḷún *drill fire,* sxʷu?ľ *firedrill, match,* xʷəlp *spin around* Th xʷuym *to drill,* xʷuymn *firedrill* Sh xʷulm *to rub fire,* xʷúľke *firedrill,* xʷuləkp *match,* xʷlem *turn st. around,* xʷlep *spin around,* Cb xʷulmn *drill,* txəlk'íc'a?n *wrap up,* Cv xʷulnt *drill st.,* xʷulkʷp *firedrill,* sxʷułxʷ *tipi,* xlak *whirl* Ka čšəlčim *go around st.* (also forms w. səlč-) Sp šlšlčm'n'cut *circle dance,* yecšlčmím *I'm turning it around* Cr xul *bore hole,* xʷel *set to spinning,* šelč *move in a circle.* – Cf. PIS ***xʷlakʷ** *whirlwind.*

*xʷəm *to be lonesome, pining (for).* Cl xʷam'xʷm' Ch xʷimí- ~ Li xʷəmxʷam, xʷəmp Th xʷəmxʷə́mt; xʷəmxʷem *lonely (place)* Sh xʷmxʷem(t); ESh xʷwxʷumt (<*xʷmxʷumt) *deserted, empty (place)* Cv nxʷm'ałqʷltm Ka xum'm'ín Sp xʷm'm'in Cr xum'.

*xʷəp see ***ʔapxʷ**.

*xʷap *to unfold, spread out (as blanket, arms).* Ti "xue:'xhan" CV *fathom* ~ Li xʷápan' Th xʷépes; sxʷepkstm *arm-span, fathom* Sh xʷepns; sxʷəpup *fathom* Cb snkłxʷpaw'stn *clothesline* Cv xʷipm Ka esxʷép *it is spread* Sp xʷepn; sxʷepčst *arms-length measurement* Cr xʷep *spread, flatten out blanket.*

*xʷup *a night bird.* Sn šapšəp *night bird power, nightingale* Cl šupšp *night bird power* Ld xʷupšəd *saw-whet owl* ~ Sh sxʷupxʷəp *screech owl* [Cb Sp sxʷúpxʷup *flying squirrel*]. – Cf. ***xʷiw** and KWA xupxup *owl* (LR no. 1530).

*xʷp' *unhook.* Be xʷp' *unhook, untangle* ~ Th xʷp'əm *rip out (as cedar roots)* Sh xʷp'ist *snap loose (as safety pin).*

*xʷət *to come to an end, be exhausted, all gone.* Ch xʷə́tm- *finish work, all gone* ~ Li nxʷətp *go around (full circle),* sxʷətpaszánuxʷ *year* Th xʷtəp *to end, finish, come to end* Sh xʷtep *reach end, come to end,* nxʷətpepł'qs *end of story,* t/nxʷətpił't *to stop having children* Cv xʷtmscut *lose st. that can't be replaced,* [xʷtxʷatt *ungrateful*] Cr xʷet *be exhausted, come to end.*

*xʷiw *to whistle.* Cx xʷupt Se xʷúpum; xʷúqin *swan* Sq šupn; sxʷuxʷlm *a whistle,* sxʷəwqn *whistling swan* Cw Ms šxʷəw?qn *id.* Ck xa:pm; šxʷəwql *whistling swan* Sn šapt; sxʷəwqn *whistling swan* Sg sxʷoqn *id.* Cl šupt *whistle* Ld x̌ʷiw'əd Tw xʷíwad; šaw?qəd *white swan* Ch xʷípaq- ~ Li xʷitn; xʷúxʷlam *make music,* xʷúxʷlatn *flute, whistle,* Th xʷúxʷle *play a musical instrument* Sh xʷiwm; xʷíw'ke *a whistle,* ʔstxʷwxʷiw *wind howls,* xʷúxʷletn *mouth organ* Cb xʷiwm; xʷiwmn *a whistle,* tx̌ʷʕʷx̌ʷʕʷalqʷ *flute* Cv xʷiwm, xʷaxʷʕála. – Cf. KWA xʷipa HEI xʷíqʷa HAI xʷìkʷa (LR no. 1783). Cf. also PIS *xʷəlaʔ *meadowlark*.

*xʷəy *to appear*. Sq xʷəy ~ Sh sxʷyeyləsm *new sprouts come out*.

*xʷay/l *alive, allright, alert*. Cw xʷəy *wake up* Ck xʷiy *id*. Sm sxʷay'əɬ *awake*, sxʷə́y'xʷəy' *lively, diligent* Sn xʷəy *wake up*, sxʷəy'əɬ *awake* Cl sxʷəy'xʷiʔ *ambitious* (stress?) ~ Sh xʷlxʷelt *allright, well* Cv xʷlxʷalt *live, alive, safe* Ka xulxʷíl *live, be alive*, xʷi(ʔ) *id*. Sp xʷlxʷil *alive* Cr xʷel *live, be alive*.

*xʷ/x̌ʷay-aʔ *fly, maggot, worm, ant*. Be x̌ʷax̌ʷi *eggs of housefly* Cx x̌ʷáx̌ʷaʔǯumʔ *fly* Se x̌ʷax̌ʷayúʔ *black fly*, sx̌ʷax̌ʷc'ús *tiny biting mosquito*, sxʷíxʷnam *worm* Sq ʔáx̌ʷayʔ *housefly*, ʔíx̌ʷic' *maggots* Cw x̌ʷəx̌ʷəyáʔye (Hukari x̌ʷəyx̌ʷəyáʔyə) *fly*, xʷəxʷiyémʔ *sandfleas*, xʷəxʷiyím *leech*, šáyaʔ (<*xʷúyaʔ) *maggot* Ms x̌ʷəx̌ʷəyíʔye *fly* Ck x̌ʷəx̌ʷəyá:ye *id.*, x̌ʷəx̌ʷé:yə *big fly, blowfly*, xʷəxʷíye *salmonberry worm* Sm šáyeʔ *maggots* Sn xʷəxʷəyem *sand flea*, šayəʔ *maggots* Cl sxʷaʔxʷənám' *small insect/bug* Ld šuʒəʔ *maggot* Tw x̌ʷayə́x̌ʷx̌ʷayəx̌ʷ *fly* Ch məx̌ʷx̌ʷíyx̌ʷiy *salmonberry bug*, x̌ʷíc' *hornet* Cz x̌ʷay'ə́x̌ʷay'əxʷ *fly* ~ Li x̌ʷəyx̌ʷyaqs *maggots on head of deer*, nax̌ʷít *snake*, nax̌ʷə́x̌ʷt *worm*, sxʷuxʷəz' *ant* Th x̌ʷəc'x̌ʷác'e *maggots*, sxʷúxʷec'e *ant* Sh x̌ʷyx̌ʷéye *maggots*, sxʷyxʷéye *ant*, səxʷyenst *woodworm* Cb sxʷiyáľqʷ *worm sp.* Cv sxʷúxʷyaʔ *ant*, sxʷyalqʷ *woodworm* Ka sxúxʷiye *ant* Sp sxʷúxʷy'eʔ *id.*, sxʷyalqʷ *worm* Cr suxʷenéy' *ant, rice*, xʷádalqʷ *woodworm*. – Note the forms with c' < y' in Se Sq Ch, a development regular in Th only.

x̌

*x̌aʔ I *sacred, taboo, forbidden, impressive, smart, violent, etc.* Cx x̌ə́x̌əʔat *respect a dead person and his relatives*, x̌áx̌əgiɬ *have magic power, Indian doctor*, x̌áx̌iya *different, exceptional*, (Sl *bizarre*) Se x̌áx̌a *holy, sacred*, x̌əx̌ʔátm *be forbidden to have contact w. sb.* Sq x̌əx̌əʔə́naq

122

mythical creator Cw Ms x̌éʔx̌e *holy* Ck x̌éːx̌e *id.* Sn x̌eʔx̌əłnet
Sunday Sg x̌éʔx̌e skʷečl *good Friday* (skʷečl *day*) Ld
x̌á(ʔ)x̌aʔ *great, sacred, taboo, mighty,* x̌ax̌áʔ *forbid* Tw x̌ax̌áʔ
taboo, holy Ch x̌ax̌áːʔi- *sacred, taboo, forbidden, holy* Ti
x̌əx̌áʔəw *menstruate* ~ Li ʔáʔx̌aʔ *sacred, supernatural,*
endowed w. spiritual power Th x̌aʔx̌áʔ *supernatural,*
powerful, spooky, taboo, x̌aʔx̌aʔstés *prevent, restrain* Sh
x̌əx̌eʔ *impressive, powerful, smart, difficult, violent* Cb x̌áx̌a
smart, intelligent Cv x̌aʔx̌áʔ *great, powerful, important* Cr
x̌aʔm *monster.*

Without extension also in SIS words for *rattlesnake* Cv
x̌aʔx̌ʔúlaʔxʷ Ka x̌eʔúleʔxʷ Sp x̌ʔúleʔxʷ Cr x̌eʔúl'mxʷ.

With extension -l: Se wáx̌als *mythical being, prob.*
Transformer Sq x̌ayʔs *Transformer* Cw Ms x̌eːls *id.* Ck
x̌əx̌eːls *id.* Sm x̌éʔel's *id.* Sn x̌eʔəl's *supreme being* Sg x̌éʔels
id. Cl x̌aʔyəs *id., Transformer.*

With extension -y/-i-: Be sx̌ayax̌ʷ *taboo* Cx x̌ígit *stop*
child fr. bringing itself in danger Se x̌íwit *stop sb. fr. doing st.,*
tell sb. to quit. Sq x̌əyn *restrain,* x̌iáyʔłm *discipline one's*
children Tw x̌əyʔ *stop sb.* (Drachman 274) Ch x̌íp'i- *stop fr.*
st., forbid.

With extension -n: Li x̌ʔann *forbid, prevent, stop fr.*
doing Sh x̌ʔens *forbid, scold,* x̌ʔenílm *discipline one's*
children Cv x̌ʔnam *stop st.,* stx̌aʔníplaʔ *taboo* Ka x̌eʔn *forbid*
Sp x̌eʔntém *be told, warned,* x̌eʔnéltm *warn one's children,*
sčx̌eʔnépleʔ *taboo.*

– Note that the first two extensions are found in CS, the
third in IS. The root may well be identical with *x̌aʔ II (cf.
comment under *wənaxʷ).

*x̌aʔ II *parent/child-in-law.* Sq saʔx̌ Ld sx̌áx̌aʔ
parents-in-law Tw sx̌ax̌áʔ *father/son-in-law* ~ Li sáʔx̌aʔ *id.*
Sh səx̌éx̌ʔe *father-in-law (of man or woman)* Cb ʔasx̌áʔx̌aʔ *id.*
Cv sx̌áx̌a *id.* Ka Sp sx̌aʔx̌éʔ *id.* (Ka *of man*) Cr nasx̌áʔx̌ *id.*
(of man). – Cf. *x̌aʔ I.

*x̌əc *ready, completed,* *x̌əʔuc *complete count: four.*
Sq x̌aʔúcn *four* Cw Ms x̌aʔáθn Ck x̌aʔáθl *id.* ~ Li x̌ʷʔúcin *id.*

(borr. fr. CS; x̌ʷ labialized by ú), x̌əcpqíqin'kst *a hundred,* x̌əcpasq'ət *week, Sunday* Th x̌cəp *(become) complete, round out,* x̌əcpqiqn'kst *a hundred* Sh x̌cep *all kinds, everything,* x̌əcpqiqnkst *a hundred,* sx̌əcpesq't *Sunday* Cb x̌əccakst *a hundred* Cv x̌cmstim *get things ready,* x̌əccikst *a hundred* Ka Sp x̌cmncut *get ready, dressed* Cr x̌ec *be/get ready, clothed.* – This item is doubtful; an argument in favor is KUT -x̌a:ca- *four,* cf. KUT -o:kʷe:- *one,* -as- *two,* -qałsa- *three* and PS *nk'(ʷ)uʔ, *(ʔə)sal(i/a), *kaʔłas.

*x̌ic' *wrinkle* Tw ʔasx̌ic'usəb *she can wrinkle her face* Ch x̌íc'- *wrinkled,* ʔacx̌íc'usm *face and nose wrinkled, teeth show,* ʔacx̌íc'qsm *wrinkled nose* ~ Th ʔesx̌ic' *wrinkled,* ʔesx̌íc'qs *wrinkle one's nose* Sh x̌ic'qsm *bare the fangs,* x̌ic'sm *id.*

*x̌əc'(-ay') *log, stick, wood.* Be x̌c'a (also qc'a) *log, stick, wood* Sq x̌c'ayʔ *unfinished canoe hull* Cw Ms x̌əc'eyʔ *id.* Ld x̌əc' *tally sticks for slahal game* Tw sx̌əc''ʔay *fish roasting stick* Ch x̌əc' *tally sticks for slahal* ~ Th s/ṣx̌c'ec' *slahal stick* Sh səx̌c'ey *wood, stick* [Cb x̌əc'm *to chop,* sx̌cay' *sticks in slahal game* (poss. influenced by IS *x̌əc *to bet*)] Cv sx̌x̌c'iʔ *stick, sprig* Sp sx̌x̌c'ey' *tipi poles.* – Cf. HEI x̌c'a'í *canoe* OOW x̌c'a'i *id.* HAI x̌c'e *id.* (LR no. 2382).

*x̌ək *to think, remember, teach.* Se x̌əčt *consider* Sq x̌əčx̌əč *remember* Cw Sm x̌cət *figure out* Sm Sn Sg x̌čit *know* Sn x̌čṇin *mind, thought* Cl x̌čət *figure out,* x̌čit *know,* čx̌čṇin *smart,* Ld x̌əč *mind, thought,* sx̌əč *teachings, lessons* ~ Li x̌ək *instruct, order,* x̌əkn *count st., correct sb.,* nx̌ək-mn/-tn *law, custom,* x̌əkamsút *guess, imagine* Th x̌kəm *to mark, count, know* Sh x̌qem *learn, predict, guess* (q < k by assimilation).

*x̌ikʷ *to scratch, crunch.* Cw x̌ikʷət *gnaw* Ch x̌ikʷí- *to scratch* ~ Sh x̌ikʷt *sound made by snow when stepped on.*

*x̌əl *to cover w. planks; board covering.* Ld x̌alšəd *bridge* Tw x̌alšəd *id., ladder* Ch x̌əlšn *bridge, boardwalk* ~ Li x̌əln *build a wall,* x̌əltn *wall,* x̌lílap *floor,* nx̌law's *boardwalk,* x̌lákaʔ *bucket* Th x̌əltes *form cribwork (as in* *making floor),* x̌léw'ses *lay boards for bed platform,* nx̌liw's (borr. fr. Ok) *bridge,* x̌yéke? *bucket* Sh x̌lem *build a log cabin,* sx̌lem *wall,* nx̌lew's(tn) *bridge,* tx̌lew'sns *place logs/boards across beams to form a surface (as boardwalk)* ESh cx̌lewł *(wooden) barrel* Cb sx̌əllup *floor,* nx̌law's *bridge,* tx̌almnáw's *log cabin* Cv x̌lstim *board st.,* x̌lína? *shed,* nx̌liw's *bridge* Ka x̌al *cover w. planks, rugs:* čłx̌alélp *a rug on the floor,* esənx̌alé?us *bridge* Sp x̌lnten *lay logs next to e.o.,* sx̌laqs *storage scaffold in tree,* čłx̌el *roof, floor, shelf, ledge made of long objects,* nx̌lew's *log bridge* Cr x̌el *lay evenly (as lumber),* hnx̌elíw'es *bridge.*

*x̌al-u-mix *puberty, menses.* Ch sx̌aló:mš *menstruate,* Tenino dial. x̌alamx ~ Sh łx̌ʷuməx (inv.) *puberty (either sex)* Sp łłx̌ʷún?ey *puberty,* hecłx̌ʷéw'si *first menstruation.* – The comparison is doubtful but possible: besides inversion, Sh Sp would have devoiced l, the labialization of x̌ʷ being automatic (and analogical in the second Sp word).

*x̌il, *?ax̌il *thus, like, similar.* Be x̌ił *be frequent, be/do st. often* Sl x̌ət *avoir la possibilité, encore* Ld x̌ət *as if, like, seem* ~ Li x̌ilm/x̌ił(c) *act thus* Th x̌eym *act,* x̌ił *act thus* Sh x̌ilm *id.,* x̌iłt *do st. thus* Cb ?acx̌ílx̌il *same, similar* Cv ?x̌ilm *do like, do as,* ?ax̌lásq't *every day,* c?x̌ił *like, same* Ka ?ax̌ilm *behave in this/that way,* ec'ax̌í(ł) *id., like, similarly* Sp ?ax̌ílm *be/do in a certain way,* ?ax̌lásq't *every day,* c'x̌íli/c'x̌ił *seem like, be the same* Cr ax̌il *do thus,* (Nicodemus:) aac'áx̌l *similar,* ax̌əlsq'it *every day.*

*x̌ələq'/k' *to turn, whirl, roll.* Be x̌lq'iix̌ʷ *turn st. around* Se sx̌lq'alús *crosseyed,* (s)q'łx̌iwán (inv.) *puzzled, worried* Sq x̌əlq'm *roll/fall down* Cw Ms Ck x̌əlc't *turn st.* [Ck x̌elqm *roll, turn around in circles*] Sm Sn sx̌éləč' *whirlpool* (Sm adds qʷa? *water*) Sg x̌éləč't *to twist, turn* Cl x̌éyəč't *wring st. out* [Ti cx̌ʷəlaqʷ *round*] ~ Li x̌əlq' *roll down* Sh x̌lq'em *roll st.* – Cf. **x̌ʷələqʷ* and **q'əlx̌.*

*x̌aλ' *to want; difficult.* Cx Sl x̌aλ' *to want,* x̌áλ'it *difficult* Se sx̌aλ' *what one wants,* sx̌aλ'ít *difficult,* x̌aλ'nə́x̌ʷ *love sb.*, [x̌ax̌’x̌ax̌’ *wild (animal), unsociable, shy,* x̌ax̌’ə́nmut *stingy*] Cw Ms x̌ex̌’ *blow hard (wind)* Ck x̌e:x̌’ *id.* Sn x̌ex̌’ *rough (water)* Cl x̌ax̌’ *rough, windy, stormy* Ld x̌ax̌’ *want, like* Tw sx̌ax̌’ *liked, wanted,* sx̌ax̌əx̌’ *friend, sweetheart* Ch x̌ax̌’ *brushy place, place hard to cross (woods, river, etc.),* x̌ax̌’í- *force, compel, use roughly; difficult* ~ Li x̌ax̌’ *difficult,* x̌ax̌’m *climb hill/ladder* Th x̌ax̌’m *go uphill,* ʔesx̌əx̌’stés *to pity* Sh x̌ət’mins *be hungry for st. one hasn't had for a long time* Cv x̌ix̌’m *go uphill.* – For the association *want, like* ~ *difficult* cf. *x̌’əy’; cf. also the Th Cb Cr forms under *x̌əm I.

*x̌ix̌’ *to cut, bite, gnaw.* Se x̌əx̌’t *bite* Sq x̌íx̌’in *chop, cut* Ld x̌áx̌’əd *bite,* ʔux̌íx̌’id *fell a tree* Tw x̌əx̌’ən *bite it!* Ch x̌ə́x̌’- *break* Ti x̌íx̌’in *gnaw* ~ Li x̌ə́x̌’n *chew on st. (mainly grass, of horses),* [ʕíx̌’in’ *take a bite*] Th x̌x̌’əm *chew, gnaw, bite* Sh x̌it’ns *gnaw,* x̌t’usm *eat of the deer head* ESh (t)x̌t’úseʔ (< -usm’) *take a bite (as of apple)* [Cb ʔacḥax̌’stús *gnaw,* sḥḥəx̌’mix *id.* Cv ʕax̌’ám *id.*] Sp x̌x̌’im *chew, eat* Cr x̌et’ *gnaw, eat close, graze.* – The bracketed Li Cb Cv forms point to IS *ʕix̌’ q.v. Cf. KWA x̌iʌa *nibble, gnaw* (LR 2401), QUI x̌ix̌’í:las *bite.*

*x̌əm I *heavy,* *x̌i/am *weigh down, grab to hold.* Be x̌amlx *be stuck, not moving away fr. st.* Cx x̌ámat *rake towards one (as loose objects, eg. beads)* Se x̌əm *heavy,* x̌ámat *pull towards one,* x̌ímit *to claw (as bird catching fish), pull sb.'s hair* Sq x̌əm *heavy,* x̌ámi *grab and hold,* x̌amanʔcut *back up, withdraw,* x̌ímʔx̌imnáčtn *kidney ("weighing down"),* x̌íminʔ *pull sb.'s hair* Cw x̌imət *grab hold of, claw* Nk x̌im- *grab* Sm Sn x̌əm *heavy* Ld x̌əb *heavy,* x̌íbid *grab, claw st.* Cl x̌iŋət *grab a handful* Tw bəsx̌əbib *black pigeon hawk ("grabber"),* x̌ibúsatəb *pull sb.'s hair* Ch x̌əm *heavy,* x̌ími- *grab a bunch (pl. obj.)* Ti x̌əw/w’ *heavy* ~ Li x̌mank *heavy,* x̌ə́man’tn *dragnet pulled by two canoes,* x̌ímxal *get a handful of st.* Th x̌menk *heavy,* x̌mekn’ *(have) heavy pack,* x̌mink (loan fr. Ok) *to like* Sh x̌menk *heavy* Cb x̌mank *like, love,* *want* Cv x̌mink *id.* Ka Sp x̌emt *heavy* Cr x̌em *id.*, x̌emínč *like, love.* – See comment under **x̌aƛ'*.

*X̌əm II *bite* Be x̌m ~ Cr x̌em *(id. of animal).*

*X̌apaʔ *(paternal) grandfather.* Ti "xa:ʔha" CV *father's father/mother, child of son* ~ Sh x̌péʔe *grandfather* Cb sx̌x̌ápaʔ *father's father, son's child* Cv sx̌áx̌paʔ *man's father's father, brother or cousin* Ka sx̌épeʔ *uncle* Sp sx̌épeʔ *grandfather, granduncle, man's son's child, man's grandniece or grandnephew* Cr x̌ípeʔ *man's father's father, man's son's child.*

*X̌əq *to envelop, wedge in.* Ld x̌ə́qəd *wrap string/cloth around st.* ~ Li x̌əqn *put st. in between* Th x̌qəp *become stuck, wedged*, x̌əqtes *wedge in* Sh x̌qem *put in between, wedge in* Cv cx̌aq *be empty*, k'łx̌qntim *make room for st.* Sp x̌aqn *id.*

*X̌it see **x/x̌it.*

*X̌aw *dry.* Sq sx̌əwʔ *dried salmon backbone* Cw Ms sx̌ə́ʔwə *fish backbone* Ck sx̌ə́wə *id.* [Ch x̌əpí- *dry* Ti šagʷ *dried (preserved) food*] ~ Sh x̌ewt *dry*, sx̌wum *dried meat* Cv x̌w'ntim *to dry*, x̌w'x̌aw't *dry.*

*X̌əyl *(to make) war.* Cx x̌íyiq Sc x̌ílix̌ Sq x̌əyx̌/x̌iʔx̌ Cw Ms x̌ə́yləx̌ Ck x̌ə́yləx̌ Sm x̌eləx̌ Sn x̌iləx̌ Sg x̌eləx̌ Cl x̌eyəx̌ Ld x̌ílix̌ ~ Sp x̌yilš *he went and showed himself in battle*, sx̌ʷx̌yilš *warrior*, x̌ix̌ilšúł *id.*

X̌ʷ

*X̌ʷuʔ see **ʔəx̌ʷuʔ.*

*X̌ʷəc' *to break (as stick).* Cx x̌ʷəc't *break (as handful of cornstalks)* Se x̌ʷəc'; x̌ʷə́c'x̌ʷəc'qʷ *joints* Sq x̌ʷəc'qʷan *cut off*, sx̌ʷəc'qʷ *joint*, sx̌ʷəc'qʷač *wrist* ~ Th x̌ʷc'əp *snap, break in two*, [x̌ʷíces *break, snap into strips* Sh x̌ʷit'm *to crack (branches, wood)*] ESh x̌ʷic'ys (< x̌ʷic'ns) *to cut (as grass), cut up (as lettuce)* Cv x̌ʷc'am *break (as stick)*, x̌ʷíc'laʔx̌ʷm *cut grain*, nx̌ʷc'ap *broken rib* [Sp x̌ʷícleʔx̌ʷ *mow hay*, Cr x̌ʷic

127

crop hair, (Nicodemus also: *short*), x̌ʷat *cut in two*]. – Cf. *x̌ʷu/ic' and *x̌ʷəƛ'.

  *x̌ʷu/ic' *defecate* Ti sx̌ʷuc' *excrement, defecate* ~ Th x̌ʷic'm *defecate*. – Prob. related to ***x̌ʷəc'**, cf. the development of IE *skeid-.

  *x̌ʷəc'qʷ *dipper (bird)*. Ld sx̌ʷəx̌ʷc'qʷ *river snipe* ~ Li x̌ʷəc'qʷ Cb x̌ʷx̌ʷəc'qʷ.

  *x̌ʷal see *xʷạl.

  *x̌ʷələqʷ *round, to roll*. Ti cx̌ʷəlaqʷ *round* ~ Ka x̌olqʷ *roll*, scx̌olqʷšn *wheel* Sp x̌ʷolqʷm *roll* Cr x̌olqʷ *wind string evenly*. – Cf. *x̌ələq'.

  *x̌ʷəƛ' *to break, cut*. Cx x̌ʷəƛ't *to cut off (as branches)*, x̌ʷuʔx̌ʷəƛ' *cedar shakes*, [x̌ʷáƛ'igan *half full*] Se x̌ʷux̌ʷəƛ' *plank, shake*, [x̌ʷaƛ'íwan *half* Sq x̌ʷíƛ'wiɬ *be half full*] Ld x̌ʷəƛ' *break rigid object in two*, x̌ʷúƛ'ud *chew up* ~ Sh x̌ʷit'm *to crack (branches, wood)*, [xʷit'ns *to cut up, cut out (eg. pattern)*, sxʷət'min' *hide, buckskin*, cxʷətxʷit' *cut up, wounded* Cb xʷƛ'xʷaƛ'ákstm *to whittle*] Cv x̌ʷiƛ'n *break* [Ka Sp xʷƛ'im *to whittle*] Sp čɬx̌ʷíƛ'is *he broke sticks for counters in stick game*.

  *s-x̌ʷiƛ'ay *mountain goat*. Cx x̌ʷíƛ'ay? Se Ld Tw sx̌ʷíƛ'ay (Tw *sheep, goat*) [Ch ƛ'á:xʷltam- (inv.?) *sheep*] ~ Li sx̌ʷiƛ'áz' Th sx̌ʷiƛ'éc' Sh sx̌ʷət'ey Ka sxʷƛ'éʔi (Carlson sxʷƛ'ey') Sp sx̌ʷƛ'ey'/[sx̌ʷɬx̌'a] Cr sxʷut'i? (stress?) *goat*, [x̌ʷɬx̌ʷáɬ *Rocky Mt. sheep* (Nicodemus *billy goat*)]. – Forms with xʷ are limited to Ka Cr and possibly Ch.

  *x̌ʷən *to buzz, hum*, (red.) *hummingbird*. Be x̌ʷnx̌ʷnm *hummingbird*, [ʔax̌ʷni *a small bird (thrush?)*] Ch x̌ʷə́n- *buzz, hum* ~ Sh x̌ʷéx̌ʷne *hummingbird* Cv x̌ʷnámx̌ʷnam *id.* Sp x̌ʷnímx̌ʷnim *id.* – Cf. HEI ʔax̌ʷʔax̌ʷní/hax̌ʷhax̌ʷní *thrush* (LR nos. 2620, 2507), especially for the bracketed Be word.

  *x̌ʷu/aqʷ *to grind, rasp; snore*. Be x̌ʷuq' *scratch, rasp, file* Cx Se x̌ʷuqʷt *snore* Se x̌ʷáqʷat *cut w. saw* Sq x̌ʷuqʷn *snore* Ck x̌ʷi:qʷm *id.* Cl x̌ʷaʔyúqʷŋ *snore* Tw bix̌ʷuqʷúb *he's snoring* Ch x̌ʷáqʷ- *scrape,* [x̌ʷúqʷ- *Adam's apple, windpipe*] Ti x̌ʷqʷ- *scratch (an itch, or as cat)* ~ Li x̌ʷuqʷləqs *snore* Th x̌ʷóqʷyəqs *id.* Sh x̌ʷuqʷləqs *id.* Cb x̌ʷuqʷm *id.,* x̌ʷaqʷsn *shave/scrape sb.'s face* Cv x̌ʷaqʷm *grind,* x̌ʷaqʷlqsm *snore* Ka Sp x̌ʷaqʷn *grind, sharpen* Cr x̌ʷeqʷ *grind meal.*

*x̌ʷus *to foam,* ***s-x̌ʷus-m** *soapberry.* Be nux̌ʷski *soapberries* Cx x̌ʷasm *id.,* [qʷə́sim *foam*] Se sx̌ʷúšum (borr. fr. Li) *id.,* [sqʷəs *foam*] Sq sx̌ʷusm *soapberry,* x̌ʷúsum *prepare soapberries,* x̌ʷux̌ʷsə́l'qn *mountain goat* (cf. Cw p'q'əl?qn *id.* and Cw p'əq' *white*) Cw Ms sx̌ʷesm *soapberry* Ck sx̌ʷəwsm *id.* Sm sx̌ʷesŋ/sx̌ʷesm/sx̌ʷəysm *id.* Sn Sg sx̌ʷesm *id.* Cl sx̌ʷasm *id.* Ld sx̌ʷu/asəb *id.* Tw sx̌ʷasəb *id.* ~ Li x̌ʷusəs *to foam,* sx̌ʷúsum *soapberry* Th Sh Cb Cv Sp Cr sx̌ʷusm *id.* Th x̌ʷusm *make st. foam* Sh stx̌ʷəsétkʷe *foaming water,* x̌ʷəx̌ʷ?u?s *beer* Cb sx̌ʷust *foam,* nax̌ʷúskʷ/kat(x̌ʷəs)x̌ʷúskʷ *beer* Cv sx̌ʷust *bubble up, foam* Sp sčɬx̌ʷu?sétkʷ *foam* Cr x̌ʷus *id.*

*x̌ʷay *to perish pl., disappear.* Cx Sl x̌ʷay *perish, pl.* x̌ʷáǯat *kill* Sl x̌ʷaǯm *être massacré* Se x̌ʷay *perish* Cx x̌ʷay *die, pl* Ck x̌ʷe:y *id.* Nk x̌ʷey *die* Sn x̌ʷəy *id.* Cl x̌ʷə/ay/y' *id. perish* Ld x̌ʷáʒad *wipe out a village, annihilate the whole populace* Ch x̌ʷáya- *disappear* ~ Li x̌ʷayt *many people die,* [x̌ʷaz' *disappear for good, pass away,* x̌ʷáy'nun' *miss, feel the loss of*] Th x̌ʷayt *pl. persons die,* ?esx̌ʷáy *dead,* nx̌ʷáykʷu *drown, pl.,* nx̌ʷazxn *starve to death, pl.* Sh x̌ʷeyt *perish, pl.,* sx̌ʷyx̌ʷeytmx *the dead, people long since dead,* nx̌ʷéykʷe *drown, pl.,* nx̌ʷey'cn *be out of grub* [Cb x̌ʷay'm *escape, run away*].

*x̌ʷay-a? see ***xʷ/x̌ʷay-a?**.

y

*yə- (Prefix or stem for derivation with somatic suffixes, see PCS *yə-nis, *yə-xən, Cv syups under PS *s-up-s, Cl yə́nəwəs Ld yədwas Ti yingas Si "ye:nega:'s" Tw yadwás

under PS *-was (2) and the Cx Sl Se Th and Sh forms under PS
*-anaxʷ.)

*yac *to rub, soften by rubbing.* Be ʔic *rub, scrub* ~ Li
zácan' *crumble up, soften paper by rubbing it between one's
hands* Th zecm *rub to soften* Sh yecm *rub as when washing
laundry, rub material against itself (as when removing dry
mud).*

*yu/ac' see ***lu/ac'**.

*yik *fall (as tree).* Be ʔasikaax̌ *timber* ~ Li Th zikt;
szik *log, fallen tree* Sh yíkt; syik *fallen tree.*

*yukʷ see ***yəw'kʷ**.

*yəḷ, *yul, *həyl *to roll, turn over; round.* Be ʔilayx
go around, ʔillx̌s *go around a point,* nuʔiliił *to coil a rope,*
yalx̌ *to be round,* yalquuł *ball, sphere,* yul *stir, rub, stroke,*
yulm *walk in a circle, around st.* yulmta *firedrill* Cx hílit *roll
st. over* Se hílit *roll st. down,* yəḷšin *return,* yalwát *circle
around st.,* yəlkʷú *back eddy,* yúlut *stir* Sq hílit *roll,* syilíq'
top for spinning, silʔánm *year* Cw Ms syilʔánm *id.* Ck
syilá:lm *id.,* čəḷə́wt (borr.) *turn over/inside out* Sn čəl'əs *turn
around o.s.,* čələqsn *go to other side of point* Cl sči?ánŋ *year*
Ld ʒálalcut *turn o.s. around,* ʒalqəd *turn over/around,*
ʒúlə/aq' *hand spinning wheel* NLd sʒəlč̓ (Snohomish sǯəlc')
year, NLd yəlaʔc (stress?) *six* SLd ʒəlači? (stress?) *id.* Tw
biyalád *twisting (eg. twine),* yalbáyaqs *around the point,*
biyálqisəb *he's whirling around,* yaláqʷ *return, turn around,*
ʔasyulʔúlxʷiʔas/ ʔasyúlʔuxʷiʔas *round, curled* Ch yəḷə́kʷ-
roll Cz yal'ə́mn *go around,* yəlwič *go clear around* Ti
cyəlháʔwin *turn st. over,* cyəl'yəl'ə́wi(n) *crooked,* tyaláhan
CV *apron* ~ Li zálan *twist (esp. branches),* zə́lkʷaʔ *whirlpool,*
zalkʷʷn *wrap up,* syalməc (borr.) *ring* Th ʔeszə́l *(persons)
gathered in a circle,* ʔestzə́lzəlt *round,* ziqínm *to roll, coil,
spool,* zəlpqins *string things on (circular) string* Sh ye/alm
put (rope) around st., xylap *end of round trip or trip around
(eg. checking traps),* sxylap *hour, o'clock* (Canim Lake), tylap
turn full circle, go all around, ylqinm *coil st. up* ylpi̧/elx

change direction, turn back, cylok^w *coiled up,* cxyi̯/elk^w *horseshoe-shaped* Cb yər *round, spherical,* nyəlqin *coil up,* ʔacyárk^w *crooked,* kɫyərk^wcənakst *bracelet* Cv yir *round,* cyark^w *curved* Cr dar *sun, clock, month,* yar *hooplike object rolls,* yark^w *curved, crooked,* yarp' (Nicodemus) *arc, hoop, tire.* – Cf. KWA ylsa *twirl a firedrill, rub w. palm of hand* (LR no. 1560). In IS n-forms are found: Th zenm *go around,* zənkə́m *coil st.* Sh xyenm *go around,* ynep' *wound around* Cb syanmúsm *lightning* Sp yanp' *slither like worm/snake,* nyánq^we? *eddy, whirlpool* Cr yanuq^w *snake is coiled,* yenp' *clamp screw.*

*yu̯/a̯l *to burn.* Sq yuɫ Sn sča̓ɫ *(fire)wood* Cw Ck syaɫ *firewood* Sg sčəɫ *id.* Cl sču̓ɫ *id.* ~ Cr yar *be torch.*

*s-ya̯lt *watertight basket, woven dish.* [Be ʔilt *put cover over st.*] Ld syalt *cedar-root basket* ~ Th szelt *dish, plate,* szeltʔúy *aboriginal dish for food, cattail mat* Sh syelt *plate,* yeltm *put plates on table* Cr dar *objects stand w. curved surface up,* darents *he set the table* (lit. *he set vessels upright*).

*yaƛ' *to descend, go home from stay in mountains.* Be ʔiƛ'(a) *to shift, move st.* [Cx Sl ǰəƛ' *run* Se yəƛ' *id.*] Nk tx^wyeƛ' *return* Ch yaƛ'á- *go home* ~ Li zɔƛ'q' *topple, come down (as rock- or woodpile)* Th zeƛ'm *take down (things hung up),* zeƛ't *drop down (things hung up)* Sh yeƛ'lx *descend, pl.,* yƛ'lxeɫx^w *move down fr. highland to river, pl.*

*yuƛ' *to rub.* Sq yəƛ'q'án *rub, paint* Cw yaƛ'ət *rub* Cw Ms Ck yiƛ'q't *id.* Nk yúƛ'un *id.* ~ Sh yƛ̓em *rub, scrub,* yúƛ̓m *make smooth* ESh xyƛ̓eləstn *a brush* Cb yəƛ̓úsn *sharpen (blade).* – CS has also forms with l/y as C_2: Sq yulk^w- Ld čə3q^w- (3<*y) Ch yə́l̓č-, cf. NWAK ylx̌- *rub, smear (body part)* (LR no. 1562).

*yman *bird's nest.* Be ʔimanta Se yəmánuɫtx^w ~ Li zəmán *eagle's nest, aerie* Th zmen' Cr dmíne?.

*yan(u)c *driftwood.* Be yanc Ch yanc; c'əlyáns *drifting leaves, etc. between logs in water,* sč̓əlyánc *snag,* *drifting bushes and rubbish,* xʷəlá:yans *log drifted ashore* ~ Li zánuc Th zens Sh yens.

*yəq', ***ʔiq'** *to file, whet.* Be ʔiq'uc(a) *to rasp, file,* ʔiq'ucta *file, grindstone* Cx ʔə́yq'at *to shine, polish* Se yəq't *to file,* yəq'ə́min *a file* Sq yáq'an *sharpen by filing* Cw yəq'əst *to file* Ck yáq'ət *id.* Sn čəq'n̓ *to sharpen,* čq'ən' *a file* Ld ӡəq' *to grind, sharpen* Tw ʔasyə́q' *sharp, filed,* biyəq'úsačəd *I'm filing it* ~ Li zəq'n *sharpen,* ʔíq'in' *scrape a hide* Th Sh ʔiq'm *id.* Cb yəq'n *to file* Cv yq'min *a file* Sp ʔaq' *scrape* Cr yaq' *file, whet.* – Cf. **ʔi/aqʷ.*

*yəqʷ, ***həyqʷ** *fire(wood);* ***t'iqʷ** *spark.* Be iix̌ʷ/iiqʷ- *burn,* niix̌ʷ/niiqʷ- *fire* Cx ӡ́əqʷӡ̌əqʷ *lukewarm* Se hiʔqʷíʔn *lamp,* yáqʷat *warm o.s. w. blanket,* syayqʷ *sun,* ƛ'íqʷit (borr.) *throw sparks on st.* Sq hiʔqʷín *light, lamp, torch,* xʷiʔqʷls *steamship,* yəqʷlčp *put wood on the fire,* t'iʔqʷm *throw off large sparks,* st'iʔqʷm *large spark* Cw Ms hayʔqʷ (Hukari Cw həyʔqʷ) *fire,* šxʷhəyʔqʷelə *ashes* Cw Ck yəqʷ *burn,* yəqʷt *id., tr.,* heyəqʷ(t) *burning,* šxʷhè:yəqʷélə *ashes* Ms syaqʷm *sun* Ck sya:qʷm *id.* Sm Sn Sg čəqʷ *be afire* Sm Sn čaqʷɫ *fire,* sya(lə)qʷm *sun* Cl čəqʷ *burn,* čaqʷɫ *id.* [Ti shuqʷ *fire*] ~ Li hiʔqʷín *candle,* zə/uqʷát *sagebrush kindling,* ƛ'iqʷt *snap, pop, spark* Th t'ʔikʷ *still smoldering,* tikʷm *transfer fire,* tíkʷes *tend a fire,* tekʷɫp *burn tree at root,* [metkʷ *transport fire*] Sh yeqʷns *to light, burn, add wood to fire,* cyeqʷ *firewood,* stəqʷtit'qʷt *spark.* – Cf. NWAK lqʷila *make a fire, set fire to st.* (LR no. 1234), also PIS **ti/akʷ*, p. 220 **nəqʷ.*

*yəqʷ *rotten (wood).* Cx ӡ̌əqʷ/q' *rust,* [pə́qʷay *dry rotten wood*] Se syə́qʷay *dead tree, starting to rot inside* [Sq p'əyqʷ *rotten wood* Cw Ms Ck ç'aqʷm *rotten,* Cw pqʷayʔ *rotten wood* Ck pqʷa:y *id.* Sn ç'aqʷn̓ *rotten,* pqʷey' *rotten wood* Ld č'qʷil *become rotten decay*] Tw yuqʷʔáy *fungus,* ʔasyuqʷʔáyab *rotted tree without leaves* [Ti tiyuq'éy *rotten,* syéq'i *rotten wood*] ~ Li zuʔqʷ *to rot (as wood, bone)* Sh yʔuqʷ *rotten,* s/cyʔuqʷ *rotten wood,* yuqʷy *rotten log,* xyqʷen's *have a rotten tooth* Cv yakʷiʔ *rotten wood* Sp

132

yóqʷⁱi? *id.*, niqʷétc'e? *heart of tree is rotten* Cr doqʷ *wood is rotten.* – Cf. QUI paːqʷ *rotten wood.*

*yaw, *yəw *to be fed up,* ***?uy** II (inv.) *to be slow.* Cx ǯə́wigan *be fed up w. what one does* Sl ǯə́wt *faire avec effort* Sq ?úyum *slow* Cw ?ayəm Ck ?áyə́m *id.* Sn ?a?čŋ̩ *slowpoke,* ?a?čəníkʷəs *delay sb.* ~ Li zaw't *fed up,* za?w' *id.* Th zéw'zu?t *tiresome,* zew't *fed up,* zwəm *cause delay,* zuzúwt *slow* Sh yewt *fed up,* ywum *delay, slow down.*

*yəw'kʷ, *yukʷ, *?awkʷ *property, stingy.* [Cx ?əwkʷ *all, every*] Se ?awkʷ *clothing and blankets (collectively),* [?u(w)kʷ *all, every*] Sq ?əsyu?kʷ *stingy* Cw Ms ?ewkʷ *wealth, property* Ck eːwkʷ *id.* Sm ?ewkʷ *stuff, belongings* Sn čkʷe? *own st.,* čakʷəs *use st.,* ?ewkʷ *stuff, belongings,* ?aw'kʷ *used up, all gone* Sg ?eyəwkʷ *wealth* Cl ?awkʷ *belongings* ~ Cb yu?yu?kʷúl *stingy* Ka yeyúkʷe? *id.* Sp y'ey'úkʷe? *miser* Cr du?kʷ *stingy,* du?du?kʷúl *id.*

*yəxʷ, *ləxʷ *to descend, drop.* Se yə́yuxʷ *rockslide,* [yaxʷ *come loose*] Sq lixʷ *fall down,* t'ixʷ *descend (as fr. hill, reach level country)* [Ck syəx̌ʷ *rockslide (result)*] Ch lixʷí-*walk downward, descend, come down* ~ Li nzəxʷ *fall into st.,* slə́xʷəlxʷm *rockslide (result)* [Th zəxctɛ́s *lower st.,* zix *go lower (by stages)*] Sh yuxʷt *move downstream, (lake) empties into river; to be born,* yuxʷe *waterfall,* yxʷup *fall down* Cb nayə́xʷm *go downstream* Cv yaxʷt *dropped,* cyxʷitkʷ *waterfall,* yxʷmncut *dismount* Cr dexʷ *lower, descend, dismount.* – Sq t'ixʷ *has a parallel in* *t'iqʷ, *see* *yəqʷ.

*yuxʷ *to be acquainted with, used to.* [Be yutlx *get used to st.* Cx čə́?əyxʷ *id.* Se čə?íyxʷ *id.* Sq čá?ixʷ *id.* Sn kʷɬ čəw'etsət *id.*] Ch yúxʷi- *know (a person), recognize,* yaxʷt'-*understand (words)* ~ Li zu?xʷ *get used to st.* Th zu?xʷmíns *id.,* z?uxʷ *id.* Sh yxʷmins *id.,* y?uxʷ *id.* – Cf. *suxʷ.

*yəʕ, *?iʕ *to grind, scratch, scrape.* Be ?ix̌ *grind, apply friction* Cx ?íx̌it *sharpen (as pencil)* Se ?íx̌it *make thinner, smooth w. knife,* ?əx̌t *scratch* Sq ?ix̌ *id.* Ck ?ix̌ət *id., scrape* Sn ?ix̌ət *scrape* Cl ?ix̌t *id.* Tw ?ix̌íd *scrape it!* Ti yix̌-

scratch, yəx̌- *id.* ~ Th ʔíx̌es (borr.) *scratch, make stripe on* Sh yʕem *to grind.* – See comments under *ʔi/aqʷ.

*yaʕʷ see *li/aʕʷ.

ʕ

*ʕəl *to lose (ability, object, contest).* Sq x̌əx̌iʔ *be lost (of special ability)* ~ Li ʕəʔiʔlʼ *lose in game* Th ʕalʼmíns *id.* Sh ʕʔiʔl *id.* Cb ḥəlp *lose, broke* Cv ʕaláp *lose (in gambling)* Ka aál *id.* [Sp ʔalíp *lose,* ʔalpícʼeʔ *lose one's blanket (in gambling)*] Cr ʕelpmínc *lose as a forfeit, fine.*

*ʕi/al *to cut (as hair).* Sq x̌ax̌lqʷn *cut sb.'s hair* ~ Li x̌áx̌əlʼqʷanʼ (borr.) *id.* Cb tḥilaʔstm *cut hair* Cv kʕilsxnm *id.* Ka aíl *cut w. scissors,* sxʷčaílqənm *barber* Sp ča(y)lqnm *cut hair* Cr syatʕélqn *barber.*

*ʕin see *ʕəy.

*ʕ/ɣap *to stand upright; tree.* Cx Sl x̌əpayʔ *cedar (log), stick* Se x̌əpáy *wood of red cedar, stick* Sq x̌payʔ *cedar* Cw Ms x̌pey *red cedar* Ck x̌paːy *id. (as material)* Sm Sn x̌peyʼ *red cedar* Sg x̌pe (= ey) *id.* Cl x̌payʔ *id.* Ld x̌pusəb *lift head up, straighten up* ~ Li syɣəp *upright, standing up,* syap *tree,* ɣípinʼ *to raise, grow* Th ɣépes *erect (pole),* syep *tree* Sh ɣepm *put up (as pole),* cyep *tree* Ok cɣip *id.,* snyipwɬ *mast* Cv cyip *standing (a single long object).*

*ʕis *to shrink.* Cx x̌ísicut *have cramps, shrink* Se x̌ísitcut *shrink,* x̌ísiwat *to curl,* x̌ix̌isiwláx̌an *have a cramp in the arms* Sq x̌ísinʔtm *shrink,* x̌isačíʔntm *have a cramp in the arm,* x̌isqsm *turn up one's nose* ~ Li ʕis *shrink* Th ʕism *id.* Sh ʕʔis *id.,* x̌ʕsʕissm *arch one's eyebrows.*

*ʕəy, *ʕi-n *hot, angry, growl.* Cx x̌ínit *growl* Se x̌iním *id.* Sq Cw x̌iʔnm *id.* Ck x̌əylm/x̌əylə́m *id.* Sn x̌iʔənŋ *id.* Cl x̌aʔníti *id. (as dog)* Ld x̌ídib *growl,* x̌ícil *angry* Ch x̌ayí- *growl, snarl* ~ Li zə́ʕn (inv.) *id. at sb.,* ʕənʼ *angry, getting tough* Th ʕzəm *growl at,* ʕəzmins *get angry at (of animal)* Sh ʕeyt/ʕyep *angry,* ʕnem *to growl* Cb ḥáʔi *hot,* ḥiym *growl,* ḥimt *get angry,* sḥaḥím'a *detest, dislike* Cv ʕayám *growl,* ʕimt *angry* Ka aímt *get angry* Sp ʕaymt/[ʔaymt] *id.,* [hayím *growl*] Cr ʕid *glow, become redhot,* ʕey' *angry.* – Cf. QUI x̌íːda *growl,* x̌ilá:(ʔ) *angry.*

ʕʷ

*ʕʷəl see *wəl.

*ʕʷal' *to become weak, tired, faint, sleep.* Sq x̌ʷay *become senseless, paralyzed, faint* Ld x̌ʷal' *lack control* Ch x̌ʷál- *lose control, give up,* x̌ʷíl- *fail in health* ~ Li ʕʷuy't *to sleep* Th ʕʷoy't *id.* Sh ʕʷuyt *withered, tired* [Cv ʕayt *tired*] Cr ʕʷuy *waste,* ʕʷuyčt *mistreat old or helpless.* – Cf. PCS *x̌ʷal.

*ʕʷəɬqʷ, *wəɬqʷ *to boil, cook.* [Se məɬqʷat *boil until tender*] Sq wəɬqʷm *boil,* wəɬqʷan *id., tr.* ~ Li t(ə)ʕʷɬqʷán'ak *salmon stew* Th nʕʷoɬqʷm *boil liquid,* nʕʷɬoqʷ *boiling* WSh wɬqʷum ESh ʕʷ/wɬqʷum *to cook* [Cb sʕʷət'qʷ *steam*]. – If the Cb word belongs here, it shows a development similar to that mentioned under *pəl'kʷ.

*ʕʷəy *to play, joke, make fun, laugh.* Be sx̌ʷis *game,* x̌ʷism *to play, joke,* x̌ʷiicana *active, playful, cheerful* [Ld x̌ʷísid *make a lot of noise,* gʷəx̌ʷisəd *spontaneous, be thrilled*] ~ Li ʕʷicám' *joke about st., make teasing comments* Sh ʕʷyem' *make fun; do a sloppy job,* cʕʷey *to joke* Cv ʕʷyncut *laugh* Ka oy'incút *id.* Sp hoy'ncút *id.*

135

PROTO-COAST-SALISH (PCS) ROOTS

This list gives roots attested for minimally (1) Bella Coola down to Lushootseed and (2) from Squamish down to Tsamosan.

ʔ

*ʔiləq see *ləq.

*ʔalix *sibling/cousin of opposite sex.* Se ʔáliš *bro., si., first cousin* Sq ʔáyiš *sibl./cous. of opp. sex* Cw ʔeləš *sibling* (Hukari *sibl./cous. of opp. sex*) Ms Ck ʔeləx Cw šxʷʔeləš *woman's sister-in-law* Ms šxʷʔeləx *id.* Ck šxʷʔéləx *id.* Sm Sn šxʷʔeləs *id.* [Sg šxʷʔelət *sibling-in-law of same sex*] Cl ʔáy(ə)s *sibling* Ld ʔalš *sibl./cous. of opp. sex* Tw ʔališ *younger sibl. of opp. sex* Ti ʔéliš *man's sister.* – Cf. QUI ʔá:lis *"cousin" (term used by women for all relatives).*

*ʔałx̌an *wind or stream direction.* Be ʔaax̌ł *upstream area,* cf. ʔulx̌ł *go upriver* Sq ʔałx̌án *downstream area* Ld ʔáłx̌ad *id.* Tw ʔałx̌ád *id.* [Ti ʔełx̌én/ʔéłx̌n *Garibaldi, north,* ʔełx̌n *good wind, blowing to the south from Columbia river*]. – Cf. PS *-ax̌an.

*ʔupal *to eat.* Tw biʔúpałčəd *I'm eating* Ch ʔupál- Ti ʔəhaləw *the eating,* sʔəhaləw *food,* hałʔə́win *eat st.,* sʔuhálu? *any small fish,* hał *eat.* – IS only Th ʔúpis *eat st.,* ʔupəp *edible.* The extension *-al is CS.

*ʔu/as-txʷ *to go/be inside.* Be ʔastxʷ *be inside,* ʔustxʷ *go inside* Nk sʔustxʷ *inside* Ti wacústxʷ *go back inside.* – Cf. PS *ʔu/acq, *ʔuł-txʷ.

*ʔasxʷ *seal.* Be Cx Se Sq ʔasxʷ Cw Ms ʔešxʷ Ck ʔe:sxʷ Nk ʔešxʷ Sm Sn Sg ʔesxʷ Cl ʔasxʷ Ld ʔas/šxʷ. – IS only Li ʔasxʷ Th ʔesxʷ.

*ʔitqʼ/kʼəp *to gather firewood.* – See PS *qʼəp. Initial ʔi- is CS, in IS only in Li ʔiƛʼqʼəp.

*ʔax̌ic *to lie down.* Be ʔax̌cm *be lying down,* sx̌icta *bed* Cx ʔáx̌is Sl ʔáx̌iθ Se ʔáx̌ic Sq ʔəx̌íc Cw Ms ʔex̌əθ Ck ʔeːx̌əθ Tw ʔax̌ícnəxʷ *(imp.),* ʔáx̌acəd *bed* – IS only Li ʔəx̌ic.

*ʔayʼ *good.* Be ya Cx Sl ʔəyʔ Se ʔiy Sq Cw Ms ʔayʔ Ck ʔey: Sm ʔə/ayʼ Sn Cl ʔəyʼ Sg ʔayʔ Ld ʔiʔáb *wealth* Tw ʔay Ch ʔəy Ti ʔiyə́ʔiyə *all right.* Also in words for *right hand/side:* Sq syəhiws *r. side* Cw Ms sʔeyʔíwʔs *id.* Ck sʔeyːíws *id.* Ld ʒəh- *id.* Tw yayyáči *r. hand,* yáyalwəd *r. side of body.* – Cf. PS *laʔ. IS only Li ʔaz- *good* Th ʔəys- *to like,* siʔhékst *right hand.*

c

*cu *to go.* Cx su Se cu Ti cukʷ-, cuye-.

*cucin *mouth.* Be cuca, cucn- Cx súsin Sl θúθin Se Sq cúcin Cw Ms θaθn Ck θaθl Nk cúcen Sm sasn/θaθn Sn θaθn Sg sasn Cl cucn Tw cucíd Ch -ucin. – IS only Li cúcin. See PS *-cin.

*cəkʷ *to put, place.* Cx sə́kʷənačəm *sit down* Se cəkʷšə́nəm *go and stand on st. high* Ch cəkʷí- *lie down,* also in derivatives for *dish, pan, cradle, cupboard.*

*caʔaɬ *lake.* Be caɬ Cx sáʔyaɬ Sl θáʔyaɬ Se cəlʼaɬ Cl cayʔəɬ SLd caləɬ (cəlaɬ *Big Lake*) Ch cálaʔɬ Ti céʔlə/eɬ-. – Cf. KWA ʒəʔláːɬ (? √ʒɬ *spread out.* LR no. 594). IS only Li cəlʼaɬ, cf. also Cb cəlʼan *Chelan Lake.*

*cam *twice, second.* Cx sáma *twice* Se camá *id.,* cámícʼa *two (animals, pieces of cloth)* Sq camʔá *twice,* cámyas *two days,* cámʔič *two hundred* Cx Ck θəme *twice,* sθəmə́lts *Tuesday* Sm səŋe *twice* Cl cəŋəɬnat *Tuesday* Ld cəb- Tw cab- Ch cam- Ti cuw-/cəw-; cuwxʷ *twice.*

*cum *eyebrow.* Cx súman Se cacúman Sq cumn Cw Ms θamn Ck θaːml Sm saṇn Sn θaṇn Sg saṇn Ld cubəd Ch cúmay'is.

*ciqʷ *to dig.* Sq ciqʷ-: ciqʷálč *dig up potatoes,* cəqʷíuɬ *dig up bones of dead* Cw Ms Ck θiqʷéls (Hukari Cw θəyqʷ, Galloway Ck θiy(ə)qʷt) Sn θəy'əqʷt *dig (a pit),* θiʔqʷel's *dig (roots)* Sg seʔqʷiṇəɬ Cl cə́yʔəqʷt Ld ciqʷ Tw ʔascíqʷ *dug up* Ch cíqʷi-. – Cf. PS *ciq; forms with q are found in Be Cx Se and in Sq ciq *stab.*

*cataw *red cedar.* Be cactawɬp Ch catáwi [Ti datági]. – IS only Li cátawaz' Th cétwiʔ.

*cəxʷ *to poke.* Cx səxʷt *stab* Se cəxʷ *poke, stab* Sq cəxʷ *get hit* Ch cíxʷi-. ~ Cf. NWAK c'əxʷ- *stab, stick into* (LR no. 806).

*s-(c)x̌al-m *sword fern.* Be x̌ala Sq cx̌alm Cw Ms Ck sθx̌elm Sm sx̌elm' Sn sθx̌elm Sg sx̌elm Cl scx̌ayəm' Ld sx̌a/əx̌əlč Ch sax̌lm' Ti sx̌elíwi. – IS only Th sx̌áʔy'eq.

<h2 style="text-align:center">c'</h2>

*c'uʔ (in words for) *seven* (poss. *to point).* Cx c'úʔčis (cf. c'əmalə/c'əmálə *index finger)* Sl ç'úʔčis Se c'účis Cw Sn ç'áʔkʷəs Ck ça:kʷs Cl c'uʔkʷs Ld c'uʔkʷs Ch c'úps-. – Cf. PIS *c'uqʷ.

*c'ikʷ/c'iwq' *elderberry.* Cx c'iwq' Se sc'iwq' Sq sc'iwʔq' Cw ç'íwəq' *red elderb.,* ç'íkʷəkʷ *blue e.* [Ck θiːkʷəkʷ/θiːqʷəqʷ *red e.*] Sn ç'íwəq' *id.* Cl c'iw(ə)q' *id.* Ld c'íkʷikʷ *blue e.* Tw c'iqʷíqʷ *id.* Ch c'kʷikʷ *id.* – Phonetically cf. PS *c'ikʷ-aʔ *left side,* where only Ch has c'íwq'-. Cf. QUI c'iwóːkʷ *elderberry.*

*c'əkʷaʔ *an edible root.* Sq c'ə́kʷaʔ *root stocks of sword fern* Ck ç'ə́kʷe *spiny wood fern* Ch c'aqʷéʔ *tiger lily root.* – IS only Th c'úkʷe/iʔ *bracken fern roots.*

*c'əl *to twist, spin.* Cx c'əyič' Se c'əlč'át Tw bic'ələpiʔas *dizzy* Ch c'ələ́p.

*c'ap/p' *to insult, derange, interrupt.* Be c'p *stuck, blocked* Sq c'áp'an *derange, interrupt* Cl (Thompson) c'əpt *bother,* [(Montler) caʔpáʔt *id.*] Ld c'áp'(a) *ill-bred, insulting* Ch c'áp'a- *disgrace, disgust, hurt feelings, etc.*

*c'q'ap *pole, spear.* Se c'əq'p *long spear for cod* Ld c'q'ap *canoe pole* Tw c'əq'ap *fish spear, harpoon shaft* Ch c'əq'p *canoe pole.*

*c'ixʷ *five.* Be c'ixʷ Tw Ti c'xʷəs.

*c'iX̌ *sand, gravel(beach).* Be sc'iX̌ *sand, gravel,* [sqc' *id.*] Sq c'əX̌t *gravel beach* Cw ç'X̌ət *id.* Ms ç'ə́X̌ət *id.* Cw ç'əX̌ə́t *id.* Nk c'ə́X̌ət *id.* Sm c'/ç'X̌et *gravel, pebbles* Sn ç'X̌it *id., beach,* ç'əç'X̌it *beads* Sg cX̌et (prob. c') *be stony, covered w. pebbels, beach* Tw c'əX̌at *sand* Ch c'aX̌éʔs *id.* – Cf. PIS *c'əX̌ʷ II.

č

*čiľuɫ *to steal.* Cx čə́wʔuɫ Sl čəwt Se čəľút Tw číləʔuɫ, bičíčəlud *breaking into the house* Ti [də sč'ələ́ʔəɫ *he stole it*], "sčəláoɫ" CV.

*čəm' *to cover, fold, close (mouth).* Sq čə́mʔus *come together, meet; double* Sn xʷčəm'snəkʷəl *meet* Tw ʔascəbús *folded,* čəbúsad *fold/double it* Ch čə́mš(it)n *cover,* čəm'ɫnalm *close mouth.*

*čan(at) *three.* Cx Se čànáxʷšá *thirty* Sq čánat Tw Ch čan-: čánštumš *thirty* Ti čenét.

*čit *older close relative.* Se čičt *older sibling* Sq čiʔčt *father, parent's sibling* [Ch číťu- *older brother*].

č'

*č'sayʔ *fir/cedar wood, log, stick.* Sq č'sayʔ *Douglas fir* Cw Ms c'seyʔ *fir, log, wood* Ck c'sa:y *id.* Sm Sn č'sey'

Douglas fir Ld č̓say? *spearpole, stick of firewood* Tw č̓əsč̓si *cedar wood* Ti yə́sč̓si *fir tree*.

h

*haqʷ *to smell.* Cx həqʷt Sl hə́qʷit Se haqʷnə́x̌ʷ Sq haqʷ Cw Ms haqʷət Ck ha:qʷət Sm Sn Sg Ld haqʷ Tw saqʷ Ti ta?qʷ- *stink*.

k

*kapc *uncle, aunt.* Cx čaps Se čapc Ck xcapθ Sm Sn sečs Cl cačc Tw čap Ti čec *aunt.* – See PS ***kʷup-i/a?** and comment under PS ***?imac.**

*s-kətxʷn *black bear.* Se sčətxʷn Ld sčə́txʷəd Ch sčətxʷn'.

*kəwaš *wife.* Sq čuáš Nk č̓čweš *seek a wife* Ld čəgʷas/š Tw ču?wáš Ti čəgʷáš. – The root ***kaw** is all-Salish but the extension ***-aš** and the meaning *wife* are CS. Poss. the same extension in *brother-in-law* Cx Se č̓ə́maš Sq č̓maš Ld č̓əbás.

k̓

*k̓am *beaver.* Be k̓manwas/k̓amwas *young beaver* Se sk̓amƛ̓ (borr.) Ch č̓əmáq *beaver castorium.* – Cf. KWA k̓mw̓a/k̓miwa *young land otter* (LR no. 1380).

*k̓ən *shake, tremble, shiver.* Be k̓nm Cw c̓e?nm? Ld č̓ə́dəb Tw č̓əd- Ch č̓ə́n-.

*k̓ipt *red elderberry.* Be k̓ipt Cz č̓ipt. – Cf. NWAK k̓ip- *elderberry* (LR no. 1432), more doubtfully QUI c̓ibá:? *id.* (b < *m).

*k̓əyuya *twins.* Se sč̓iyč̓iyúya Sq (s)č̓iúy Cw Ms sc̓iyáyə Ck sc̓iyílm Sn sč̓əyayə? Sg sčiyáyiyə (prob. č̓) Cl č̓iyúwi Ld sč̓íyuya? Tw č̓í?uyəb Ch č̓iyúya? [Ti č̓iyúc *son, male offspring*]. – IS only Li k̓zuz *have twins,* sk̓zuz *twins.*

kʷ

*kʷac *name.* Be skʷac- *(to) name,* skʷacta *name* Ch kʷacíli- *be named, called,* skʷacɬ *name.* – See PIS ***kʷac**, ***kʷast**; the form with c is typical of CS (IS only Li skʷácic, but kʷastáy' *nickname*).

*kʷəɬ *to divide, split.* Be kʷɬ *crack, split* Sq kʷəɬč *split open* Ld skʷəɬt *fishtail* Ch kʷə́ɬ- *divide.*

*kʷim *blood, red.* Be mukʷ (inv.) *red* Cx kʷə́miws *red cod/snapper* Se kʷəmím *red* Sq kʷəmkʷím *id.* Cw ckʷim *id.* Ck ckʷiːm *id.* Sn nəkʷim *id.* Sg nəkʷim *reddish brown* Ti gukíw (red.) *blood.*

*kʷ-tam-c *husband.* Be kʷtmc Sq kʷtams Tw kʷətábac. – Cf. PIS ***tam**. IS only Li kʷtamc (PIS ***s-x̌alwi/a**). See comment under PS ʔimac.

*kʷutx̌ *halibut.* Se sčutx̌ Sq sča?tx̌ Cw sca?tx̌ Sn θatx̌ Sm sa(?)tx̌ Ld sčutx̌ Tw sčútax̌ Tenino Ch "sk otxa".

k'ʷ

*k'ʷuk'ʷ *skunk cabbage.* Be ʔuk'ʷuk' Sq č'úk'ʷa Cw Ms c'ák'ʷa? Ck c'ák'ʷa Sm (s)c'ák'ʷiy'/ç'ák'ʷiy' Sn ç'ə́k'ʷi? Ld č'u(?)k'ʷ Tw č'uk'ʷáy. – Cf. HEI k'ʷk'ʷuk'ʷ HAI k'k'uk'ʷ (LR no. 1453). IS only Th c'úk'ʷe/i?, borr. fr. Ck.

*k'ʷəl *to spill.* Be Cx Se Sq Cw Ck k'ʷəɬ Cl k'ʷa?nə́t *pour* Ld k'ʷəɬ Tw ʔask'ʷə́ɬ Ch k'ʷə́l-. – Cf. PCS ***wal**. IS only Li Th k'ʷəɬ.

*(s-)k'ʷuɬ-a?/-wi *leaf of tree.* Sq sč'úta? Cw sc'áte? Ck sc'áːɬe Sn sç'aç'ɬə? Sg sc'atə Cl sc'úc'ɬa? Ld sč'uɬəy, č'ú?ɬac *maple leaf* Tw q'ʷiɬu?áy Ch k'ʷɬoy', k'ʷúɬwi?- *maple tree* Ti č'iɬə́w', č'iɬə́?əs.

*k'ʷəx *to count.* Cx Sl Se k'ʷə́št Sq k'ʷšat Cw k'ʷšem Ck k'ʷxe(ː)m Sn k'ʷsəŋ Cl k'ʷəs Ld k'ʷəš Tw k'ʷəš- [Ch k'ʷən-] Ti ck'ʷx'ʷə́ni *I count st.*

*k'ʷuxʷaniʔ *clam sp.* Be kʷuxani *butter clam* Ld
k'ʷúxʷdiʔ/k'ʷúhədiʔ *littleneck clam* Tw k'ʷáxʷadi *id.* Ch
k'ʷə́x̌ʷni *id.*

l

*lək' *full, to fill.* Be ʔałlik' Cx Sl yə́č' Se ləč'/lač' Sq
yə́č'/yič'- Cw ləc' Ck ləc'-/lic'- Nk nə́č' Sm Sn ləç/leç'- Sg lec-
(prob. c') Cl yic'ət *fill,* ʔəsyaç'ł *full* Ld lə́č' Ch ləč'/lač'- (*pl.*
lič'-). ***ləm** *to thump, kick.* Cx yəmt *kick* Se ləmt *id.* Sq
lə́miʔn *make bumping noise* Cw ləmeʔt *kick* Ck ləme:t *id.* Ch
ləmə́kʷ- *hum, rumble, thump.*

*ləq, *ʔiləq *to buy.* Cx yəqt Se sliq *what one buys* Sq
liq *receive at potlatch* Cw ʔəlqəls, ʔiləqəls; ləq *sold* Ck
ʔelqéls, ʔilə́qət Sn ləq *sell,* ʔiləqət *buy* Tw ʔaslə́q *bought* Ch
lə́q-.

*liq *easy.* Cx yíyqit *cheap* Se lilíq *easy, cheap* Sq lilʔq
id. Ck líləq Sm lil'əq *easy, cheap* Sn liləq Cl ye'yəq / ʔiʔíqtŋ
cheap Tw liq Ch líq-. – IS only Li líqaʔ, lil'q.

*liqʷ *calm, no wind.* Se líqʷil [Sq yaq'ʷ] Cw liqʷ, slíqʷl'
Ck liqʷl Sn sliqʷl Ld líqʷil Ch líqʷ-.

ł

*łik' *to cut, sharp.* [Se lac'-] Sq łič' *be cut,* łač'tn *knife*
Cw Ck łic' *be cut* Sm łic'n *knife* Sn łiç'ət *cut meat* Cl łic' *get
cut* Ld łič'(i) *cut w. knife* Tw łə́č' *cut* Ch łə́č' *sharp.* – IS only
Th łek'- *cut open.*

*s-łan-ayʔ *woman.* [Cx łə́nʔəm *weave*] Se słánay,
[łən'- *weave*] Sq słánayʔ, [łən'ʔt *weave*] Cw Ms słénəyʔ Ck
słé:li [łi:lt *weave*] Sm Sn słeniʔ [łən'ət *weave*] Sg słéni Cl
słáni(ʔ) Ld słádəy' Tw słáday Ch łánay'-, suff. -łn'. – IS only
Th słénec' *maiden.*

*łəx̌ʷ *to spit.* Be łx̌ʷta Cx λə́x̌ʷt *spit out* Se łəx̌ʷt *spit
on/out,* łáx̌ʷat *stick out tongue* Sq łəx̌ʷn *spit at,* łx̌ʷut *spit out*

Cw Ms ɫx̌ʷat Ck ɫx̌ʷaːt Sn ɫax̌ʷət *remove from mouth* Cl ɫax̌ʷt *id.* Ch ɫax̌ʷá- *vomit.* – IS only Li Th ɫax̌ʷ- *spit out.*

λ'

*λ'ak *belly.* Sl -λ'ač Sn λ'es Ld Tw λ'ač Ch λ'áč, -λ'ači- TCh (Tenino dial.) -λ'k, -λ'č.

*λ'ukʷ *high.* Be λ'uk' Ch λ'úkʷ.

*λ'əl *1. to crackle, pop, 2. a plant providing berries or seeds.* Sq λ'ikʷnʔ *bearberry* Cw λ'ikʷnʔ *(wild) pea, Indian tobacco* Ck sλ'əɬəqʷ *chocolate lily,* λ'ik'l *kinnikinnick berry,* also *pea, bean* Sn λ'liqʷəɬp *yarrow* Ld λ'alx̌ *pop, crack,* λ'əlx̌ulč *cranberry (called so because they pop)* Tw λ'əlx̌- *pop, crack,* sλ'əlx̌úləs *cranberry,* sλ'əlx̌uʔálsi *id., Labrador tea plant* Ch λ'ələqʷ- *crackle, pop, burst,* λ'əlx̌in *red elderberry.*

*s-λ'luʔm *cockle.* [Cx λiyʔm] Se sλ'əl'um Sq st'luʔm (poss. misrecording for sλ'luʔm) Cw sλ'laʔm Sm sλ'(ə)laʔm Sn sλ'əlaʔm' Cl sλ'(ə)yúʔm Ch λ'óːlim-: nsλ'óːlm' Cz sλ'uʔəlm'.

*λ'aɫ *bitter, salt.* Cx Sl Se Sq λ'aɫm Cw Ms λ'eɫm Ck λ'cːɫm Nk λ'éɫem Sm λ'eɫŋ' Sn Sg λ'eɫŋ Cl λ'aɫŋ Ld λátəb Ch λ'əɫ *bitter, sour, salt* Ti λ'əʔ(ə)ɫ *bitter.*

*λ'ʔimin *muscle, sinew* Be λ'ima Sq λ'əʔímin Cw Ms λ'ímən Ck λ'əʔíməl Sm λ'íʔiŋən Sn λ'iŋ'ən Cl λ'ɫeʔŋn Tw λ'iʔíbad. – IS only Li λ'ímin (IS has PS *tinx).

*λ'əməq' *yew.* Sq λ'əmq'áyʔ *red hardwood* Sn λ'əŋ'q'ilč Cl λ'əŋ'q'aɫč Tw λ'əbáqay (q *sic*) Ch λ'amq'ɫ. – Cf. NWAK λ'mq-, OOW HAI HEI KWA λ'mq'- (LR no. 1050).

*λ'əp *deep, under.* Cx Sl Se λ'əp Sq λ'p-, λ'ápat *lower st.* Cw Ms sλ'páʔiθn *lower lip* Ck sλ'payθl *id.* [Nk ɫep *low*] Sm λ'ečɫ *bottom of water,* λ'iλ'əč *at the bottom* Sm Sn λ'əč Sg ɫəč (poss. λ'); λ'ečəɫ *below,* λ'əčiləŋ *sink to the bottom* Cl λ'əč *deep,* λ'ačɫ *bottom of water* Ld Tw Ch λ'əp Ti λ'əh. – IS only Li Th λ'əp.

*λ̓əq *to go outside.* Se λ̓əq Ch λ̓əqí-.

*λ̓əq̓al *wing, feather.* Ck sλ̓əq̓e:l *wing* Sn sλ̓q̓e?n *long feather* Tw sλ̓əq̓ɫ Ch sλ̓əq̓ɫ (λ̓əq̓ali-).

*λ̓aq̓an see *q̓(y)aλ̓an.

m

*makn *testicle.* Be maka Sq mačn Cw mecn? Ck mecl (and suff. -écl) Sm ŋesn Ld Tw bačəd Ch máčini-. – Cf. Sh mek̓p *id.*

*mak^w *to eat.* Cx mək^wt [Sl muk^{ʷw}t *avaler*] Cl ŋak^wt *put into mouth, chew* Ch mák^wa- *id.*

*mak^{ʷw} *corpse.* Cx mák^{ʷw}a *grave* Se smák^{ʷw}a Sq smək^{ʷw}ə?ál *graveyard* Cw šmək^{ʷw}élə *id.*, cmémək^{ʷw}e (Hukari cmek^{ʷw}e?) *funeral* [Sn ŋəq^{ʷw} *bury*] Cl mák^{ʷw}ə? *grave,* [məq^{ʷw}e?ɫ *bury a corpse*] Ch mák^{ʷw}t; sə?ák^{ʷw}t *funeral,* suff. -ak^{ʷw}ti- *corpse, ghost, grave.*

*mik^{ʷw}əɫ *salalberry.* Be mik^{ʷw}ɫ Ti wič̓úɫ.

*ma/ulq^w *to mix.* Be maliix̌ Cx míq^wənx^wigast *mix up* Sq malq^w, [mlmilč̓ *get mixed up* Ck məmiləc̓ *be mixed up, confused*] Sn malək^wət, [mileč̓ət Cl məyč̓t] Ld báluq^w(u) *mixed/messed up, entangled* Tw bul?úq^wšəd *foot is tangled in st.* Ch múluk^wi- *go crazy, get drunk, etc.*

*məl(al)us *raccoon.* Be mayas Cx máyus Se Sq məlalus Ms máləs Ck máɫás Ld bəlups Tw bál?ayas Ti wəláx^ws or wəluhs (cf. the Ld form), nənšwuláys CV. – IS only Li máḷalus/málalus Th "mî'lls" CV. Cf. HEI máyás.

*man *father,* *məna *child (offspring).* Be man, mna Cx man, má?na Se man, mə́na Sq man, mən? Cw Ms men, mə́n?ə Ck me:l, mə́lə Nk men Sm Sn men, ŋənə? Sg men, ŋə́nə Cl ŋə́nə? *offspring,* ŋa?ŋá?nə *baby* Ld bad, bədá/bə́də?, Tw bad, bə́də Ch man'/mən' (both:) *offspring* Ti wúwə *father of female,* múman *boy between 2 and 14.*

*s-man(i) *stone, mountain.* Be smt *mountain* Se smánit *id.* Sq smánit *id.*, smant *stone* Cw Ms sment *id.* Ck sme:lt *id.* Sn sŋenət *id.*, *mountain* Cl sŋant *stone* Ld sbádil/t *mountain* Tw sbádid *id.* Ch mániči- *id.*

*maqin *hair (on head).* Cx Sl Se máqin Ms méqən Ck meql Ti wa/eqín. – IS only Li máqin.

*məqsn *nose.* Be maax̌sa Cx Sl máqsn Se məqsə́n Sq Cw məqsn Ck məqsl Nk məqsn Sn Cl ŋəqsn Ld bə́qsəd Tw bəqsə́d Ch máqsin Ti wəqsə́n. – IS only Cb məqsn, while the rest of IS points to *s-p'saqs. Cf. PS *-qs.

*muʔqʷ *waterfowl.* Cw Ms Ch ma:qʷ (Cw Hukari maʔəqʷ) *duck (generic)* Nk múʔ(u)qʷ *id.* Sm máʔaqʷ *id.* Sn maʔəqʷ *id.* Sg máʔəqʷ *bird* Cl múʔəqʷ *duck* Ld buʔqʷ Tw buʔqʷ, buqʷúlə *Dixon white-winged scoter* Ti nəšwuʔqʷ *a sea duck (not eaten)* (the latter not to the etymon *loon* Kinkade 1995:32).

*maqʷam NCS *swamp,* SCS *field, meadow, prairie.* Se máqʷam *swamp* Sq máqʷam *id.*, *moss* Cw Ms máqʷm *id.* Ck ma:qʷm *id.* (for *moss* cf. PCS *qʷaym) Sn maqʷəŋ *swamp* Ld xʷbáqʷus *prairie, field,* xʷbáqʷabus *meadow* Tw báqʷab *prairie, field* Ch máqʷam- *prairie.* – Ch has a suffix -aqʷa- *prairie.* IS only Li máqʷam Th maqʷm *swamp* (meaning as in NCS).

*məqʷ *to swallow.* Cx məqʷt Se məqʷt, məqʷə́m Ch məqʷ. – For *swallow* the all-Salish root *q'əm/məq' is used in Sq Hl Sn Ld.

*mʔus *face, head.* Be musa *face* Cx Sl mə́ʔus Se məʔús *head,* məʔústn *face* Sq smʔus *face* Tw bus *id.* Ch cmus, (Tenino dial.) samús *id.* Ti wus. *id.* – Cf. PS *-us I.

*məskum' *mink.* Cx mámsčum' Cl mə́ščuʔ NLd bə́ščəb Ch məsčm', (Tenino dial.) məskm Cz meʔščm'.

*məsən *gall.* Cx Sl mə́sn *gall-bladder* Se məsə́n Sq Cw Ms məsn Ck məsl Ch masə́ntn.

*muʔt/mutʼ/hum' *blue grouse.* [Be muxʷmukʷt] Se húmhum Sq mumʔtm Cw Ms Ck miːtʼ Sm ŋíʔitʼ Sn ŋiʔətʼ Sg ŋíʔet Cl hə́mhəm [Ld Tw sbə́kʷᵂbəkʷᵂ] Ch moʔm. – Cf. QUI híbhib *grouse.* IS only Li Th smum'tm'. This sound-imitative name has various forms in CS; the reduplication type is no reason to regard the Sq word as a borrowing from Li (thus Ki 1995:34) as this type is found in CS as well (Sq tʼutʼɬm *flea,* skʷᵂukʷᵂc *tail* Sn sçʼaçʼɬə *leaf,* etc.); for the IS name of the bird see PS ***suqʷ** (see also Ki 1995:39f.).

*məxkʼ/kn *(head)louse.* Cx mačn Sl maːčᵊn Se məčʼə́n Sq məčn Cw məšcʼn? Ms mexcʼn? Ck mexcʼl (also *chickadee*) Sm ŋəsn/n' Sn ŋəsn' Sg ŋəsn Cl ŋə́scən Ld b(ə)ščʼad Tw bəsčə́d Ch mə́̌ščin'- Ti swəščʼə́n/n'. – IS only Li məkn' (IS has PS ***qʷtiẋaʔ**).

*(s-)mayac *meat.* Cx mə́ȝas Sl mə́ȝəθ Sq smic Cw smayəθ (Hukari sməyəθ *deer meat, deer*) Ck smeyəθ *id.* Sm sma/əyis/θ *id.* Sn sməyəθ *id.* Sg smeyəs *deer* Cl smayəc; (Montler) smə́yəc *elk* Ld báyac/biác Tw báyac, suff. -abac *body, skin* Ti wiyéc *belly.* – Cf. HEI miás *meat, flesh.* IS only Li məzac *body* Th smiyc *meat,* mzec *small amount of meat left on fishbone.*

*miy'ak *harpoon.* Sq miáč QUI bíʔyak. – Though Sq is the only Salish source, the word must have been more widespread in CS.

n

*nam *to throw.* Cx náʔmaš *throw away* Se nəmʔáš *id.* Ch nam- *throw(?).*

p

*s-pəču? *watertight basket.* Cx pə́ču? Se spə́ču? Sm Sn spča? Sg spča Cl spču? Ld spəču? Tw spə́ču Ch spə́ču? *cooking basket.* – Cf. QUI pikʷó? *watertight basket,* KWA pku? *id.,* pku?sɢm *cedar root hat* (-sɢm *round obj.*) (LR 69).

*pk'/p'k *mosquito*. Be pk'm Ch p'ačé:wqs.

*pal *crane*. Cx pal? Ch pəlwé:-. – The comparison is doubtful; cf. also Cw Ms spa:l Ck spâ:l *raven*.

*ptak^w *bracken fern*. Sq ptak^wm Cw Ms Ck ptek^wm Ch (Oakville) paták^wn'ł.

*pax̌ *to be split, come apart*. Cx pəx̌ *to tear* Se pəx̌ *burst*, páx̌at *tear up* Sq ?əspx̌átm *tight, not reaching (around)* Cl čx̌a?yíwc *split wood* Ld pax̌ *spread apart (of things untied)* Ch pəx̌č *split*, Lower Ch páx̌čn *id*. [Ch pə́x̌- *pierce, go through*]. – Cf. PIS *pax̌.

p'

*p'ak^w *to float*. Cx p'ək^ws *float up* Sl p'ə́k^wəs *id*. Se p'ək^wtn *floater* Sq p'ak^wm? *rise to surface of water*, p'ək^wtin *float on net, cork* Cw sp'əp'ek^w Cw Ms p'ɔk^wten *wood float* Cw p'k^wət *let st. float* Ck p'ək^wtel *wood float* Sm p'ek^wŋ Sn sp'ak^wəł Cl p'ak^wŋ [Ch p'úk'^w-]. – IS only Li p'ak^w Th p'ek^w-.

*p'al *conscious, sober*. Be p'alx (< p'al-lx) *come to, wake up* Sq p'əł *sober(ed up)* Cw Ck p'əł *be conscious, come to, sober up* Sm sp'ał *sober*, p'əł *be sober* Sn p'ɬəsət *sober up* Cl ?əsp'ałł *sober*, p'łəct *sober up*, p'ɬnax^w*bring to, revive* Tw p'alil *regain consciousness*, p'álildəx^w *he's sober now*, ?asp'ə́ł *smart, wise* Ch p'ála- *wake up*, p'alúx^w *come back to life, come to*. – Here may belong Sm Sn p'əł *hatch, come out of egg* Ld p'łúsəb *fix/comb hair*.

*p'an (w. suff. *tree*) *vine maple (?)*. Be p'aniłp *green/mountain alder* Sn p'e/iynə?ełp (borr.) *vine maple* Ch p'ánin'ł *id*.

*p'a/uq^w *gray (not of hair), faded*. [Cx p'uq'^w] Se p'uq^wúm Tw ?asp'áq^w *faded, pale color, light brown (horse)* Ch p'áq^w- *gray, light color*. – IS only Li p'əq^wp'uq^w *greyish brown*.

*p'əway' *flounder, (halibut).* Be p'wi *halibut.* Cx p'ə́gay? *id.* Sl p'a?gəy Sq p'uáy? *black-dotted flounder* Cw p'əwi? *flounder* Ck p'əwi *flounder, halibut* Sn p'ə́wi? *flounder* Sg p'áwe? (=i?) *id.* Cl p'ə́wi? *id.* Ld p'uáy? /p'úwəy? *id.* Tw p'əway *id.* Ch p'awáy *id.. –* Cf. KWA p'o:?i/p'wi? OOW p'ùi *halibut* (LR no. 116), NOO p'oxʷ-, p'o:?i *id.*

q

*qəl *bad.* [Cx qəy? *die*] Se qəlqəlmút *weak,* qəlatílm *be sick* Sq qəy; qlim *weak* Cw Ms Ck qəl Sm Sg qəqəl'em *weak* Sn qəqəl'em' *id. (of person, board),* qəla?θ *blunt-edged* Sg qəla?s *id.* Sn Sg qəli:mə *untidy* Ld Tw qələ́b; qəlíba *poor, pitiable, orphan* Ch qələ́m. – IS only Li qəl̥ *bad,* qiql' *weak* [Th qlil *get angry*].

*qal *water.* Be qla, smqla *be thirsty* Cx qíy?awus *tears* Sl qa?yə Se qə́lus *id.* [Sq sqʷúqʷl? *small quantity of water (pond, bucket),* qʷúlačí?m *scoop up water w. hands*] Cw c/ɬqá:lə *be thirsty* Ck ɬqa:le/ə *id.* Ch qá:?, Cz qal?. – Cf. PS ***qʷu?, *?uqʷ.**

*qəlx̌ *fish roe.* Cx "qe:'ix̌" CV Se qəlx̌ Ck qə́l:ə́x̌, [qawx̌] Sn qələx Cl qə́yəx̌ Ld qəlx̌ *dried salmon eggs* Tw dəxʷqəláx̌ *fish w. eggs in it* Ti qəlx̌ CV.

*qalx̌ *digging stick.* Be qalx̌m *dig fern roots* Cx qay?x̌ Se sqaləx̌ Sq sqalx̌ Cw Ms Ck Sm Sn sqeləx̌ Ld sqaləx̌. – IS only Th qálèx̌. See PS ***paci/a?.**

*qəm *to fold, pack.* [Be qm *cover, wrap, shelter it*] Cx qəmsát *store away* Se qə́msat *id.* Sq qmsan *pack together* Tw qəbə́cad *fold it* Ch qəmə́kʷ- *bend, fold.* – IS only Li qəmsan *put things away, tidy them up.*

*qəp' *cover, lid, to close.* Cx qáp'iqʷu?ǯa *nail (anat.)* Se qəp'iqʷúyatn *fingernail,* qəp'íqʷɬatn *kneecap* Sq qəp' *close, shut* Cw qp'ət *stick st. to st.,* qp'e?le?ct *cover (container)* Ck qp'e:qət *close (as box),* qəp'télə́m/(s)q'əp'taləqʷtəlxl *kneecap* Sm q'pəlíčn *cover* Sn qəp'əličt *close (box),* q'p'əličn *cover, lid*

Ld qp'úcid *id.* Ch qə́pc'- *close.* – IS only Li q'əp'qʷtn *cover, lid* (IS uses PS *xən). Cf. PIS *qəp. See Intro 3J, end.

*qiw'x̌ *steelhead.* Cx qiw?x̌ Se sqiwx̌ Sq sqiw?x̌ Ms qe?wx̌ Ld Ch qiw'x̌. – Cf. KWA gx̌ʷa, gyux̌ʷ (LR no. 1305), NOO qiw' aḥ. IS only Li qiw'x̌.

*qəx̌ *much, many.* Cx Sl Se Sq Cw Ck qəx̌ Tw qəx̌- Ch qə́x̌. – IS only in Li qx̌áslaq *many berries* (-aslaq *quantity of food;* IS has *xʷ?(it) *much*).

*qəyx̌ *to swish around, sway.* [Se qíx̌it *slide down, tr.*] Sq qíx̌it *sway, tr.* Ch qiyx̌- *swish around.*

*qayax̌n *shadow.* Sq qín?qn?x̌ni Cw qi?x̌əne?tn Ck qəyqəyx̌əlá Ch qaqáyax̌n. – Li sqn'íw'ał partially resembles the Sq word.

q'

*q'al *to believe, convince, fool sb.* Cx q'áq'iya?naq *fool sb.* Sl q'aymət *accept what is said* Se q'aq'lnáqt *id.,* sq'alít *believe* Sq q'al? *be convinced, agree,* nq'íq'ls *to fool sb.* Cw q'el? *believe* Ck q'a:l *id.,* q'əlstaxʷ *deceive, fool* Sm Sn Sg q'el' *believe* Ld q'al *convince, fool* Tw ?ask'ál *believe,* sk'al *faith,* biq'í?qlt *fool sb.* Ch q'al *get "hoodooed".*

*q'a/il *raise (and place somewhere)* Sq q'áyan? *put on top* [Sn q'əla?əŋ *put up (preserve food)*] Ld q'ílid *load (into conveyance)* Tw cq'il *climb* Ch q'íli- *lift, be raised.* – IS only Li q'il *lift up, put up.*

*q'ət *sweet.* Se q'ət Ch q'ə́ł.

*q'ała *carrying strap.* Se q'áła *headband of carrying strap* Ti "k!ä'Le:" CV *carrying strap.*

*q'aƛ' *cloud.* Sq sqaƛ' Ld sq'aƛ'əb Tw sqaƛ' Ch q'aƛ'-. – Sq and Tw have deglottalized C_1 before a glottalic C_2, see Intro 3J.

*q'a?may? *maiden.* Sq q'á?may Cw Ms q'eməy? Ck q'eməy Nk q'émey Sn q'e?ni? Cl q'á?ni? Ld q'abəy? Tw q'á?bi

149

Ch q'ámayał *girl.* – IS only Li q'ámaz' *teenage girl* (IS has *xaw'tm).

*q'ətx̌ *to rattle.* Cx q'ətx̌ím Se q'atix̌ím Sq q'ətx̌án? *rap, make clatter* Sn q'təx̌ *a rattle,* q'ətx̌t *shake a rattle* Ch q'ə́tx̌i- *hit w. projectile,* q'ə́tx̌mi- *bump,* [ƛ'ətx̌- *rattle*].

*q'yax̌ *guts.* Se q'əyáx̌ Sq q'iáx̌ Cw q'əq'éy? (Hukari q'əq'i?) Sn q'əq'i? Ld q'ə3ax̌ Tw q'əy?ə́x̌ Ch q'əyáx̌-.

qʷ

*qʷil *blood, to bleed.* Cx qʷił *blood* Se sqʷił *id.* [Tw s?áqʷil *a skin blemish*] Ch qʷilí(m)- *bleed,* sqʷił *blood.*

*qʷalił *pitch.* Cx qʷá?wił Se qʷəl'ił, qʷaqʷalítm *chew gum* Ld qʷálił Ch qʷal'íł. – IS only Li qʷal'íł (IS has *c'it'/*t'ic').

*qʷin *hair (on face, body).* Sq Cw Ms qʷin- Ck qʷil- Sm Sn Sg Cl qʷin- Ld Tw qʷid- Ti qʷunúcin *whiskers, beard.*

*qʷənis *whale.* Cx Se qʷə́nis Sq qʷənís Cw Ms qʷə́nəs Ck qʷə́l:ə́s So qʷə́nəs *killer whale* Sn qʷənəs NLd qʷədís SLd qʷə́dis [Ti qanís CV]. – IS only Li qʷn'is.

*qʷu/ax̌ʷ *gray, to fade.* Cx qʷux̌ʷ *fade* Se qʷux̌ʷúm *grey(ish)* Tw qʷax̌ʷ *grey(-headed)* Ch qʷáx̌ʷ *gray,* qʷúx̌ʷ- *white.*

*qʷaym *moss, lichen.* Cx Sl qʷá?ǰim Se qʷaym Ck qʷá:m Ld qʷə3áb Ch qʷí/ə́ym. – Cf. PCS *maqʷam.

q'ʷ

*q'ʷil(a) *salmonberry.* Se q'ʷiq'ʷl Qn q'ʷələ́ Lower Ch q'ʷəláh/sq'ʷəlil'ł.

*q'ʷəl-an'a *ear.* Cx q'ʷúwa?a?na Sl q'ʷúwa?an?a Se q'ʷəlána Sq q'ʷə́la?n Cw q'ʷi:n (Hukari q'ʷu:n?) Ck q'ʷə́wəl phonet. [q'ʷo:l] Nk k'ʷlen Sn q'ʷəln' Sg q'ʷə́ln Cl q'ʷayn? (Thompson), q'ʷəy?a?n (Montler) Ld q'ʷəládi? Tw q'ʷəládi Ch q'ʷalán'. – See PS *-ana?.

*q'ʷas-tan *mountain goat wool.* Be q'ʷasta Se q'ʷástan Sn q'ʷəq'ʷastən'álkʷət *paddle shirt* Ld q'ʷástədulic'a? *ceremonial blanket.* – IS only Li q'ʷastn.

*q'ʷan *pubic hair.* Be q'ʷna Sq q'ʷəq'ʷna?m Sg q'ʷəné?em *boy's puberty* Ch kʷáns, Tenino dial. q'ʷan-.

*q'ʷix̌ *dark color.* [Hl Sg Cl Ld q'ʷix̌ʷ-] Tw ?asq'ʷíx̌ *blue, green* Ch q'ʷíx̌- *blue.* – IS only Li q'ʷəx̌q'ʷix̌ *black.*

*q'ʷa/uy *to wilt, be sick, die.* Se q'ʷuy *die* Sq q'ʷuy *id.,* sq'ʷuy *sickness* Cw q'ay *weaken, die* Ck q'áq'əy *sick,* q'a:y *die* Sn q'ʷay *die* Cl q'ʷuy *die* Ch q'ʷáya- *wilt.*

s

*suli?č *(cattail wall-)mat.* Se súlič Sq súyi?č Cw sá:lec (Hukari salə?əc) Ck salé:c Sn salə?əč Sm sálec Ld s?úl(ə?)ič/súlič (?úlal *cattail*) Tw súl?əč Ch súlac' (also čəláš-).

*sin *large, huge; eldest offspring.* Cx Sl Se sínkʷu *ocean, sea* Sq sinƛ' *senior-line children* [Cw sine?əc *spring salmon after going upriver*] Ck sə́lƛ'a *eldest child* [Sn sine?č *big salmon going upstream*] Tw sisíd *big, large, huge,* sídakʷ *bay, salt water, sea,* síd?li *eldest brother* Ti sisín *old,* [sisiná?əq *blue-neck clam (a large clam)*], sə́nči CV *ocean.*

*sa?q *bracken fern (root).* Cw se?əq Ck se:q Sm Sn səqe:n Ld sa?q Ch s?ə́q. – IS only Li sa?qʷúpza? Th sé?aq.

š

*šəlkʷ *(a type of) clam.* Sq šəykʷ *clam, dig clams* [Ld šil(í) *come/dig out from under*] Ch šə́lkʷ *butter clam.*

*šam *dry (land).* Cx šəm? *dry* Se šam *run aground,* šəm?áš *hang st. to dry* Sq šam *low tide, be in shallow water, emerge/stick out from the water, run aground* Cw šemət *dry smoke st.* Sn Sm šem *low tide* Ld šáb(a) *dry* Ch šam'- *go inland.*

*šaw' *bone.* Se šaw Sq šaw? Ld šaw' Tw ša?w Ch šáw?.

t

*təčtəčni *hummingbird.* Sq təčtəčnís [Ld tətí?əd] Ch tə́čtəčni.

*tal-mixʷ/x *person, chief.* Be staltmx *chief* Sq stə́lməxʷ *person, Indian* Sg Sn ?əł-telŋəxʷ *id.* Cl ?əcłtayŋxʷ *person* Ld ?áciłtalbixʷ/[?áciłtəbixʷ] *person, Indian.* – See PS *-mixʷ/-mix.

*təmł *red paint (ochre, Indian paint fungus).* Be tłmas (inv.) Se Sq təmł Cw Ms tə́məł Ck təmə́ł Sn Sg tə́məł Cl tə́məł Ld təbł Tw tábał *ochre* Ch suff. -tumł *paint* Ti łə́wən (inv.) *paint/rub st.* – See *təmł-apsm p. 229.

*tan *mother.* Be stan Cx Sl Se tan Cw Ms ten Ck te:l Nk Sn Sg ten Cl tan Ld š/čəłtadəb *stepmother, uncle's wife* Ch tán'- Ti dənténə *parents.*

*tqači? *eight.* Sq tqač Ms tqéce? Ld t(ə)qači? Tw təqači Ti tqéči. – See PS *təq and *-ak(-ist).

*stiqiw *horse.* Se stəyqíw Sl ti:qiw Sq staqíw Ck Sn Sg stiqíw Cl stiqíw? Ld Tw stiqíw Ch stiqíw'. – Sn stiqiw is given without stress mark, implying stíqiw.

*tə́wixʷ *nine.* Cx tə́gixʷ Se tə́wixʷ Cw Ms Ck tu:xʷ Sn təkʷəxʷ Ch tə́wixʷ-.

t'

*t'akʷus *seven.* Sq t'akʷusáč (t'ákʷus *to point*) Tw təkʷús Ti tč'əws. – See Intro 3J.

*t'əlqay *to soak (dried food).* Sq t'í?qi Cw t'əlqi? [Ck łəlqi] Sn t'ələqit Ld t'əlqay Ch t'íqi-.

*t'am *in words for* *clam.* Be t'amas *cockle* Sn st'əmye:q *horse clam w. white neck,* t'əŋ'səweč *stick shoes* Cl t'əŋ'suʔéʔč̌ *id.* Ld st'ə́bcəʔ/st'ə́bʒəʔ *a kind of horse clam* Tw st'ə́bʒa *id.* (borr. fr. Ld).

*t'əmuc *wild rhubarb.* Ck t'əmáse Sn t'əm'asə Ld t'əbása Tw st'əbuc Ch t'ə́mc-.

*t'əm(x) *to braid.* Se ʔúmt'at; t'mš̌in *two* Sq t'əmš̌ Cw t'ə́mš̌ənəm? Ck t'eməx Sn t'əŋsen'ət Sg t'əŋsə́nət Cl t'ə́ŋəst *weave*, st'əŋ'sn' *braided hair*, t'əŋ'saʔnŋ *to braid* Ld t'əbš̌ Tw t'abʔíɫəd *rope* Ch t'əmš̌- *two/three etc. together*, t'am'íɫin-*rope.* – IS only Th λ̓'əmx.

*t'aməxʷ *gooseberry.* – See PS ***t'am**; the extension *-xʷ* is CS. Cf. KWA t'ə́mxʷm'əs *gooseberry bush* (LR 350).

*t'anam *to measure.* Sq t'ánamʔn *measure, weigh*, t'ánamtn *a measure, time* Ch t'ánimi- *measure* Ti t'enáwin *moon.* – IS only Li λ̓'ánam'n *try, taste*, λ̓'ánamtn *moon.* Meanings *measure* and *moon, month* associated as in IE (Pokorny 731).

*t'əp *thick (of liquid).* Cx t'ə́pit Ch t'ə́p-.

*t'ap'-us *to close the eyes, be blind.* Cx Se t'áp'us *blind* [Tw t'əpəd/tp'əd *sleep*] Ch ʔact'áps *be blind.*

*s-t'iqs *penis.* Cx t'iqs CV Ti st'iqs CV.

*t'əq' *down, under.* Se t'əq' *to trip*, t'əq'iš̌ *sit down* Sq t'q'ax̌ *fall backward* Cl t'q'əŋ *land (as bird, plane)* Ch t'ə́q'-*down, under(neath).*

*t'əxʷ *to brush, sweep, shake out.* Be t'xʷ *brush, sweep*, t'xʷulmxm *sweep floor* Ld t'íxʷ(i) *brush/shake off* Ch t'ə́xʷ- *brush.* – Cf. Tsimshian t'axʷ *sweep.* IS only Li λ̓'xʷ-*brush, sweep* Th λ̓'əxʷ- *shake out, brush.*

*s-t'əxʷlm *red huckleberry.* Cx t'əxʷʔm NLd st'ít'ixʷ/st'ət'ixʷ SLd st'íxʷib/st'xʷib Qn t'əxʷl'm *Lower* Ch st'əxʷl'm Ch (Oakville dial.) st'ə́x̌ʷlm'.

*t'əx̌(m) *six.* Be t'x̌uɫ Cx t'ə́x̌m Se t'əx̌əm Sq t'ax̌maɫšá? *sixty* Cw t'x̌əm Ck t'x̌əm: Sn t'x̌əŋ Ch t'əx̌ə́m-. – Cf. PS ***t'əx̌**; the use in *six* is CS.

W

*wal *to tip over, spill, capsize.* Be wl *pour, spill* Se wəl *capsize* Sn Sm kʷəl' Sg kʷə́l?ət Cl kʷi?ə́ (actual kʷə́?i), kʷəy'; kʷi? *pour out, tip over,* kʷə́/ə́?ił *be spilling* Lm ?əskʷel?ət Ld gʷal *capsize.* – Cf. PCS ***kʷəł.** IS only Th wéy'es *tip st. over.*

*wəq'íq' *(a type of) frog.* Sq wəq'ə́q' Sn wəq'əq' *tree toad* Cl wə́q'əq's Ld wáq'waq' Tw Ch waq'íq' Ti wəɣéq'. – Cf. QUI wáq'al *frog.*

*wuqʷ *to drift with stream.* Be ?uqʷ Cx giqʷ *drift* [Sl guqʷm *to drag*] Sq wuqʷ *go downstream* Cw Ms wəqʷilm *id.* Ck wəwqʷə́yləm *id.* Nk wuqʷ *drift* Sm waqʷ(ə)ł *downstream* Sn kʷəqʷəl *downstream area* Sg kʷəqʷ *down(river)* Cl kʷə́qʷi *go downstream* [Ld p'əqʷ(ú) *drift*] Tw wuqʷátəb *it drifted away,* wəqʷwił *canoe drifted away* Ti gʷaqʷ-. – IS only Li wúqʷil *go downstream in canoe* Th wuqʷl *id.*

X

*xəq *(high) up.* [Sq šəq *be finished, completed, over,* šəqłalm *be out of breath* Cw šəq *finished (w. work)* Ck xəqłélə́m *spirit dancer makes loud breathy noise at end of dance* Sn šəq *finish*] Ld šə́q *high, up in the air* Tw šəq- *up* (no example) Ch šə́q *clouds.* – The Sq Hl Sn meaning may show the development of Engl. *up* in *eat up,* etc.

*xəwal *to grow.* Sq šə́way [Ld šəgʷá?ac *salmonberry sprouts* Tw šuwə?íc *id.*] Ch šəwál. – See PS ***xaw;** the extension ***-al** is limited to CS.

*x/šay' *(mostly w. final red.) gills.* Sq šá?yay Cw še:y(?) Ck xá:y/xà:y Sn še?i? Ld sšáy'ay' Ch šáy' *fishhead, gills.*

*xay'u? *sexual rival.* Sq šá?yu *co-wife* Cw šá?ye *id.* Sm sáye? *co-wife, spouse of ex-spouse* Ck sxáyə Sn šay'ə? *rival for spouse,* šəyə *co-wife* Ld šayú? *rival, second wife* Tw

154

šáyu *jealous* Ch šayúw- *sideways, on one's side.* – IS only Li (s)xáʔyuʔ *woman's rival in love.*

x^w

*x^{w}ak *to awaken.* Sq x̌^{w}əčx̌^{w}áčayus *"big eye"* Sn x^{w}əčət Sg x^{w}čət Tw ʔasx̌^{w}áč *awake* Ti x^{w}ač. – IS only Li x^{w}ak- (IS has ***qiɫ**).

*x^{w}əl/nitm *white person.* Se Sq x^{w}alítn Cw Ms x^{w}ənítm Ck x^{w}əlítm Sm x^{w}ənitm/m' Sn Sg Cl x^{w}ənitm Ld Tw x^{w}əltəb Ch x^{w}əl/ntm. – IS only Li x^{w}alítn.

x̌

*x̌icʼ *raw.* Be Cx Se x̌icʼ Ck x̌əyçʼ Sm Sn x̌içʼ Cl Ld Tw Ch x̌ícʼ.

*x̌ək^w *tight.* Cx x̌ák^{w}it Se sx̌ək^{w}it Cw x̌ək^w *stuck* Ck x̌ək^w Ch x̌ə́k^w-.

*x̌əlʼ *write.* Cx x̌əlaš Se x̌əlʼə́m Sq x̌əlʔ Cw x̌əlʔels Ck x̌əlʼe:ls Sm x̌ə́lʼət Sn x̌əlʼəlaʔ Cl x̌əyʔ *mark*, x̌iʔə́yu *write* Ld x̌ál(a) Tw ʔasx̌ə́l *written* Ti təx̌élʼəw; x̌iwx̌elʼítn *pencil.*

*x̌aʔliw *horn spoon.* Sq x̌áʔlu Cw x̌éləw Ck x̌eləw Sm Sn x̌elʼəw Sg x̌éʔloʔ Ch x̌á:liwaʔ *dish made of buffalo horn.*

*x̌awas *new.* Cx Sl x̌awʔs Se x̌aws Sq x̌awʔs Cw Ms x̌ewʔs Ck x̌e:ws Sm x̌aw/wʼəs / x̌ə́wəs Sn x̌əwʼəs Sg x̌awʔəs Cl x̌ə́wʼəs Ld x̌awʼs Ch x̌áwas/x̌awás *begin with, first time, at first.*

*x̌ayʼ see ***x/x̌ayʼ**.

x̌^{w}

*x̌^{w}al *to lose (control), give up, fail.* Sq x̌^{w}ay *become senseless, paralyzed, faint* Ld x̌^{w}alʼ *lack control* Ch x̌^{w}al- *lose, give (it) up*, x̌^{w}íl- *fail in health.* – May reflect PS ***ʕ^{w}alʼ**.

*x̌^{w}um *protruding part* (with somatic suffixes in:) Cx x̌^{w}úmɫaɫ *windpipe* Se (s)x̌^{w}úmɫaɫ *Adam's apple and* *thereabouts* Sq x̌ʷúmłnał *windpipe, throat* Cw x̌ʷamłnəł *id.* Ck šx̌ʷəhámélłəł *id.* [Sg Sn x̌ʷaŋn *throat* Sm x̌ʷaŋn *id.* Cl x̌ʷuŋn *throat, siphon of clam*, sx̌ʷuŋəs *tears*] Ch sx̌ʷúmač'a *elbow*, sx̌ʷúmnč *buttocks, pelvis (hips)*.

*x̌ʷumat *paddle* Nk x̌úmet Cl x̌ʷú?ŋət Ld x̌ʷubt Tw x̌ʷúb?at Ch x̌ʷúmat Ti x̌éwət. – IS only Li x̌ʷum't (Th Sh have *tax̌mn).

*x̌ʷaqʷy/qʷix̌ʷ (inv.) *to miss (a shot), guess wrong, etc.* Cw Ck qʷix̌ʷ Sn qʷix̌ʷət Ch x̌ʷáqʷy- *miss, make a mistake.*

*x̌ʷəs *to oil, grease.* Be x̌ʷs Cx x̌ʷəs *oil, grease* Se x̌ʷəs *fat, thick*, x̌ʷástan *marrow, fat* Sq sx̌ʷəs *oil, liquid grease*, x̌ʷastn *fat, hardened grease* Ld sx̌ʷəs *grease.* – IS only Li sx̌ʷəs *fat around stomach.*

y

*yalup *Indian rhubarb, cow parsnip.* Se yálup Sq yúla? Ck yalə/e, yá:le Ch yalp.

*yə-nis *tooth.* [Be ?ica, ?icn-, poss. inversion of *yns; the suff. is -alic] Cx Sl ǯənis Se yənis Sq yənís Cw Ms yənəs Ck yələs Nk yənis Sn Cl Sg čənəs Ld ʒədis Tw yadís Ch yənís-. – See PS *yə- and *-anis.

*yəq-ilx *to crawl.* Be ?ix?aax̌lx Cx ǯəqiš Se yəqíš Sq yəqəy Ck ?əqəyləm/ həqílm *crawl underneath* Ld ʒəqíl Tw biyəqil *he's crawling.* – IS only Li zəqil.

*yaq' *to fall (as tree).* Cx ǯaq' Se Sq yaq' Cw Ck yeq' Sn čeq' *fall down while walking* Sg čeq' Cl čaq' *fall forward on face* Ld ʒáq'(a) Ch yaq'á-.

*yə-xən *lower leg, foot* Be ?ixa, ?ixn- Cx Sl ǯəšn Se yəšən Ld ǯəsəd Tw yašəd Ti yəšən. – See PS *yə- and *-xan.

*yətəwan *salmonberry.* Sq yətuán Ld ʒətgʷad/ʒətgʷəd Tw yitáwad Ch yətwa? Ti yətəgʷn; yətəgʷáni *salmonberry bush.*

*yəw *spirit power (to cure, predict, etc.).* Be syut *supernatural being/phenomenon; song* Cx ǯə́gən *song* Se syəwn *id.* Sq ʔəsyə́wʔ *seer,* siwʔín? *witchcraft,* syə́wan *song,* yəwʔínʔc *understand* Cw Ms syə́wʔə *seer* Ck syə́w:ə *id.* Cw Ms syəʔwin? *inherited spell* Ck syəwi:l *id.,* syúwəl *spirit power, song* Nk siyúwən *id.* Sm syə́wən *spirit song (and its dance),* syə́w'ə *seer* Sn syaw'ə *seer, predict* Sg siyə́wən *spirit dancer's song,* siyəwʔín? *magic* Cl syə́w'ə *seer, predict,* syə́wən *spirit power song/dance* Ld ʒəgʷáʔ *expert, professional, "a great one for"* Tw yəwádaʔb *diagnosis, doctoring, curing* Ch yuw- *wonderful person, gives good luck, great hunter,* yóʔoli- *shoot w. spirit power.* – IS only Li szúwaʔ *clairvoyance,* zəwin' *talk to the water* Th yúweh- *clairvoyant, herbalistic shaman,* ywin' *witch, sorcerer, shaman.*

*yəx̌ (in word for *lizard,* orig. *rock?*) Sq siʔíx̌ix̌as/sʔəyʔíx̌yix̌as *mountain lizard* (syəx̌ás *large rock*) Ch yə́x̌m'c *lizard.*

*yax̌ʷ *to melt.* Be x̌ʷay (inv.) Cx ǯax̌ʷ Se yax̌ʷ Sq yáx̌ʷiʔ *to thaw* Cw Ms Ck yax̌ʷ *id.* Sm čax̌ʷn Sn čəx̌ʷn̩; čax̌ʷn̩ *thaw* Cl čax̌ʷ *melt* Ld ʒáx̌ʷ(a) *thaw, melt* [Tw ʔasyax̌ *melted*] Ch yə́x̌ʷ- Ti cyəx̌ʷ. – IS only Li zax̌ʷ- Th zex̌ʷ-, [zix̌-].

PROTO-INTERIOR-SALISH ROOTS

This list gives roots attested for both North and South Interior Salish.

ʔ

*ʔuʔcxan *lizard.* WSh wʔcxen [wuʔc...] ESh ʔw'cxen [ʔoʔc...] Cb ʔuʔcxn.

*ʔacx̌ *to train in quest for spirit power.* Th ʔécx̌eʔme Sh ʔecx̌m Cb sac'ácx̌aʔəxʷ.

*ʔac'x̌, *c'ax̌ *to look at.* Li ʔac'x̌ *be seen* Th ʔəc'x̌ayn *check net or trapline* Sh c'x̌em Cb ʔac'x̌n Ka ʔac'əx̌ Sp ʔac'x̌m Cr ʔac'x̌.

*ʔukʷ *to carry, haul, take/bring somewhere.* Th ʔesʔúkʷ *delivered,* ʔúkʷume *deliver, transport* Sh ʔukʷm (customary form c'ʔúkʷests) Cv ʔukʷ Ka ʔukʷn Sp ʔúkʷ(u)-: hecʔúkʷstn *I always bring him,* ʔúkʷutntxʷ *you bring her back to where you got her* Cr ukʷ *carry, bring.* – Th and Sp have forms ʔukʷu- and Sh has an extra e in the customary form. ʔu- may be prothetic; if so, a relationship with PS **kʷan* is possible.

*ʔakʷn/l *fish roe.* [Be ʔaqʷm *herring are spawning*] Li kʷúnaʔ Th Sh ʔekʷn Cb ʔakʷn/l Cv ʔikʷn Cr ikʷul (prob. ʔikʷl). – Cf. CAR ʔək'un *fish eggs* (Nater 1977:58).

*ʔa/u̱l *to freeze.* Th ʔalt *icy (ground)* Sh ʔalt *frozen up* Cr or(-t) *be frozen stiff.*

*ʔalkʷ *to store away, keep.* Li ʔalkʷn *watch over sb.* Sh ʔelkʷm *store away* Cb ʔalkʷmn *slave* Ka ʔelkʷm *put away, save* Sp ʔélkʷis *stow, store,* sʔelkʷmn *keepsake* Cr ilkʷ *store new acquisition.*

*ʔanas, *nas *to go, be on one's way.* Li nʼas Th Sh nes Cv nis *be gone, get away, depart* Ka ʔenés Cr enís *leave, set out, go away.*

*ʔapɬ, *pəɬ *having, provided with.* Th pə/eɬ- Sh pəɬ- Ka Sp Cr epɬ-.

*ʔupʼ *to pull up/down w. hook.* Sh ʔupʼsm *hook out fish,* ʔúpʼskeʔ *gaff hook* Sp ʔupʼčstn *long limb w. hook-like projection on end to pull down limbs.*

*ʔapʼx̌ʷ, *pʼax̌ʷ *to choke.* [Th ʔepx̌] Sh ʔepʼx̌ʷ Cb napʼáx̌ʷiʔ Cr pʼáx̌ʷiʔt *cough.*

*ʔuqʷ *ear wax.* ESh cx̌ʔəqʷʔúqʷne Sp snʔóqʷneʔ; snʔoqʷʔóqʷ *id. in both ears.*

*s-ʔasƛʼxʷm *duck.* Sh sʔestʼxʷm Cv "sístl.x̌om" CV Ka sesƛʼxumʼ *mallard duck* Sp sesƛʼxʷm.

*s-ʔistk(ʷ) *winter, cold wind.* – See PS *sutik.

*ʔastkʷ/qʷ *cedar.* Sh ʔestqʷ Cv ʔastkʷ.

*ʔasx̌əmʼ *(fish) backbone.* Sh ʔəsx̌emʼ *fish backbone* Cv ʔasx̌m *backbone* Sp ʔasx̌mʼ *id.*

*ʔiswaɬ *loon.* Th ʔísweɬ Sh ʔísuɬ/ʔísweɬ Cb ʔíswaɬ Cv ʔaʔsíwʼɬ Sp wʼsuʔɬ/ wʼsíwʼɬ. – Cf. PS *ʔus.

*s-ʔatqʷ-ɬp *Ponderosa pine.* Th ESh sʔetqʷɬp Cv sʔatqʷɬp *pine.*

*s-ʔatwn *sandhill crane.* Th Sh sʔetwn Cb sʔatwn Cv sʔitwn *condor, heron.*

*ʔawilʼ *to laugh, smile, joke.* Th ʔeʔúymʼ *laugh, smile* Sh wlʼilm *laugh, sg.* Cb swʼilʼcn *to joke.*

*t-ʔiwl-tk *upstream area, shore.* Sh tʔiwltk *upstream area, interior* Cv tʔiwltk *shore, on shore.* – The same combination of pre- and suffix in Sh tkewltk *far out in the lake,* tqeltk *high* Cv tqiltk *top* (Mattina s.v. -tk). Cf. *wtam-tk.

c

 *ca (red.) *younger sister.* Th céce? Sh céce(?) Cb cáy'a?
id. of woman, cáka? *id. of man* Cv ɫcc?ups; ca?psíw's *be
sisters* Ka ɫcce?ú(ps) Sp ɫcc?ups Cr ccíy'e? *id. of woman.*

 *s-ca? (red.) *crow.* Li scicá? Sh səce? *raven* Ka sca?á?
Sp sc?a?. – A possible CS cognate is Ti "sasa:'a" CV.

 *cu? *to punch.* Li cu?n/cuw'n *to kick* Th cu?tés Sh
c?um (√cu?) Cb cuw'n *id.* Cv c?am Ka cu?úm Sp c?um;
cu?ntés *they hit him* Cr cuw'.

 *cəh *direction, side, half.* Sh cəcxews *half (way, done,
full, etc.)* Cb cəhaw's *half* Cv chntim *run across sb.,* skchikst
right (hand) side, kcahcham/kcahmncút *take turns* Sp swet
ɫu? esčchém *who's next* Cr cih *be next to move.* – For the
occasional shift h > x in Sh see Kuipers1989:20).

 *cək' *to stink.* Sh cxck'ex̌n *smell of armpits* ESh cek't
smell disagreeably Cv ncik'ck'áx̌n *smell of armpits.*

 *cu̲/a̲l *to stretch.* Li cu̲?l̲ *get stretched,* cu̲l̲ləx *stretch
o.s. while reaching* Sh colm *stretch (as gum, rubber),* c?ol
stretched (as sweater after washing) Cv carm *stretch (as
sweater).*

 *s-cuɫm *bull.* [Li cuɫm *red deer skin*] ESh Cb Cv Ka
Sp scuɫm *bull* Cr cúɫum *buffalo,* Nicodemus scúɫm' *bullock.*

 *cuqʷ *to add a length, attach a piece, splice.* Li
cúqʷun' *splice, add another piece of rope,* ncúqʷun' *put a
handle on st.* Th coqʷm *add, increase, extend* Sh cuqʷm *add a
length (of rope)* ESh cucqʷ *head of harpoon* Cv ncqʷcaqʷqn
flint glued to arrow shaft.

 *cəs *to stretch; elongated, thin.* Li cə́sn *stretch* Th
cəstes *id.* Sh cəcícse?t (√cis) *fine, thin, narrow* Cr cas(-t) *be
long, slender, fine,* cis *be made long and slender.* – See *xʷic.

 *cu̲/a̲s *to rattle.* Li sca̲ca̲l's/sca̲ca̲lst *(deerhoof) rattle,*
[nc'ác'səqʷtn *id.* (c'əs *to bump*) Th c'a̲ses *shake rattle*] Sh
cáske? *a rattle,* tkcáspa/e?tn *rattle of rattlesnake* ESh cast *to

rattle Cb c̣úṣkṣtm [Cv caʕsmcáʕs *catchfly*] Sp cos *sound made by deerhoof rattle* Cr cus *snake rattles.*

*citxʷ *house, lodging.* Li Th Sh Cv Ka Sp citxʷ Cr cetxʷ. – Cf. PS *-txʷ and possibly the initial part of PS *cipwn. Cr e is unexplained.

*cwax *creek.* Li cwaw'xʷ; cuw'x *melt away* Th scw/w'ew'xʷ; ʔescw'éx *melted* Sh cwex; cwewxm *water runs down rills on hillside* (ESh *open a ditch*) Cb ccw'áxaʔ Cv cwix *creek, river,* ccwíxaʔ *little creek* Sp cweš *Chimakum Creek,* ccw'éšeʔ *Little id.* [Cr hncéx̣ut (inv.) *stream, river,* Nicodemus hnccx̣ʷút *rivulet, creek,* hnc'éxut *stream, creek*]. – In the Li Th words for *creek* the labialization in xʷ is due to the preceding w.

*cix *to warm up.* Sh cixm *warm st. up (food, a bed),* c'ix *(weather) becomes warm* Cb cixn *warm up (food),* cix *lukewarm (ground, bed)* Cv ncixm *warm st.,* c'ix *become warm* Cr ciš *be heated.* – Cf. cix̌.

*cix̌ *red(hot).* [Th cíx̌es *burn a hole through st.*] Sh cíx̌e *red-breasted merganser* Cb cəx̌ *bright red* Cv cax̌ *blood colored,* kɬcax̌lxʷ *buckskin colored horse,* cix̌cx̌t *very hot,* ncix̌x̌tmnt *warm st.* – Cf. *cix.

*cəʕ *to cry, scream, holler.* Th cʕapeʔme Sh cʕepm Cb caḥcḥápm Cv cacʕáypm Ka caá Sp cácácá *wailing sound* Cr caʕ.

*cəʕʷ NIS *stripe,* SIS *fringe.* Li scuʕʷ *stripe,* cúʕʷɬaʔ *steelhead trout* Th ʔescóʕʷ *striped* Sh cʕʷum *make a stripe,* cəcʕʷum *make furrows,* cʕʷɨniw't *spring salmon* Cb scəʕʷʕʷakst *fingers* Cv kcwcwʕax̌n *fringe on sleeve* Ka esnco:co:ɬníʔut *he has fringes on both sides* Sp hescóʕʷ *it's fringed,* contéxʷ *you fringed it,* scowáčst *finger* Cr caʕʷ *fringe.*

c'

*c'iʔ *deer, meat.* – See PS *c'iʔ; the meaning *deer* is IS.

*c'ək'ʷ stiff. [Th ʔeskʷʼə́c (inv.)] Sh cəkʷcukʷʼ(t); sckʷekst stiff arm Cv Sp c'ukʷʼ Cr c'ekʷʼ.

*c'ələ'ʷ to scratch, claw. Th c'iʕ'ʷetés Sh c'liʕʷm [Cb c'əlx̌n, cix̌ʷn Cv c'lxntim to hook, grab, c'lc'lxúlaʔx̌ʷm scratch the ground Cr c'alx̌ʷ claw, dig claws in, Nicodemus c'lx̌ʷumínn claw]. – None of the SIS forms show a regular reflex.

*c'əl arrow. Sh xc'lmin quiver Ka snc'əlé arrow-point Sp snc'lel'stn arrow(head).

*c'uʔm to weep. Sh c'ʔum Cr c'úʔum (Nicodemus writes two vowels except in the combination c'uʔ-mín- weep for). – There may be a more distant connection with Sh ʔsc'wiq squeal, scream and Cv Sp c'qʷaqʷ cry, weep.

*c'mix̌ʷ peaked. Li (n)c'míx̌ʷlaqin' rooster's comb, bluejay's tuft Cv c'c'm'íx̌ʷyaʔ phlox ("narrowing to a point"). – Cf. PS *c'əm; an extension with -x̌ʷ also in the Tw word quoted there.

*c'ə̓n tight. Li nc'n/n'ə́lusm take aim Sh xc'nosm id. Cv c'nc'ʕant tight, c'nʕap become tight Ka Sp c'an tight (as knot, lid).

*c'u̱/a̱p sour, fermented. Li c'a̱ʔp sour (from fermentation) Th c'apt id., nc'a̱pkʷu homebrew, nc'apym'x̌ʷ yeast bread Sh xc'apkʷm' brew homemade beer Cv nc'upkʷnt make dumplings. – Cf. *c'aq.

*c'əp'q' to adhere, stick to. Li c'əp'q' get stuck (sticky matter) Th c'əq'petés (inv.) stick on Sh cəpq'em id. Ok c'ap'q'w'ícyaʔ burweed Cv kc'əpq'ntim stick on Sp c'p'q'nten id. Cr c'ap'q' id.

*c'aq sour, fermented. Th c'ʔaq get sour, c'aʔqúseʔ fermented berries, nc'áqkʷume make homebrew Sh c'eqm knead, make yeast-bread Cb c'aʔq sour Cv c'aqt id. – Cf. *c'u̱/a̱p.

*c'q'-aɫp fir. Li Th c'q'aɫp Sh cq'eɫp Cb c'q'aɫp Cv cq'iɫp Cr c'áq'eɫp.

*c'əqʷ *to cry, weep.* WSh scəqʷc'iqʷm' *a small owl (cries like baby)* ESh scəqʷc'iqʷ *catbird (bad news bird)* Cv c'qʷaqʷ Ka c'əqʷaqʷ Sp c'qʷaqʷ.

*c'uqʷ *to point.* Li c'uqʷ *do the pointing (in slahal game)* Th c'oqʷm' *id.* Sh cqʷntem *point the right way (in slahal game)* Cb c'uqʷm; c'qʷunn *to name, pronounce* c'úqʷ-ma?/-mn *index finger* Cv c'aqʷm; c'áqʷma? *index finger* Ka c'oqʷm; c'oqʷəmn *index finger* Sp c'oqʷm; sc'oqʷmn/c'qʷmin *first finger* Cr c'uqʷúnts *he pronounces it.* – Cf. PCS *c'u?.

*c'əqʷmus *suckerfish.* Th c'əqʷmus Sh cəqʷmus Cb qʷm'us.

*c'əskik̲, *c'əsqiq (w. final red.) *chickadee.* Th c'ə̣ṣkíkik WSh c'(ə)kíkse? ESh c'qíqe?/cəc'qíq?e Cb c'asqánana? Cv c'əskˤákna?/c'sqáqna? Sp c'sqáqne?. – WSh shows inversion of sk to ks, in ESh and Cv the s is lost; the SIS words contain the suff. -(á)na? *ear, side.*

*c'it' (NIS), **t'ic'** (SIS) *pitch.* Th c'iƛ'áłp; c'əƛ'c'iƛ'ms *get pitch on st.* Sh cit' Cb t'ic' *pitch on young jackpine* Cv t'ic' Cr t'ic' *gum.*

*c'awa(y') *(collar)bone.* Sh c'éwe *collarbone* Cb c'áway' *long bone beads.*

*c'ax *to be ashamed.* Li c'a?x (also *shy*), c'əxc'ax Th c'exm' Sh c'?ex, cəc'exm Cb c'a?x (also *blush*) Cv c'?ax Ka c'e?éš/c'é?š- (also *bashful*) Sp c'eš *bashful,* c'?eš *become id.*

*s-c'axt *brother-in-law (of man).* Li sc'axt Th Sh sc'ext Cb sc'axt Cv sc'ixt Ka sc'eš/st Sp sc'ešt Cr sc'išt.

*c'əx̌ see ***?ac'x̌**.

*c'əx̌əlacn *mink.* Li c'əx̌yacn Th (borr.) c'əx̌lecn Sh c'əx̌lecn Cb c'əx̌əl'icn Cv c'x̌licn Sp c'x̌lecn Fl c'x̌alé? Cr c'ax̌yú?c'n. – Both Li and Cr have y-forms here, Cr -u?c'n is unexplained.

*c'əx̌ʷ I *to act on purpose, promise.* Li c'əx̌ʷn (Mt. Currie x̌ʷəc'n) *to force, coax sb.* Th c'əx̌ʷtes *allow,* c'əx̌ʷʔuy *ready, prepared* Sh c'x̌ʷntes *act on purpose* Cb c'əx̌ʷm *to promise,* c'əx̌ʷc'x̌ʷm *advise, lecture* Cv c'ax̌ʷ *to promise,* kc'ax̌ʷ *do on purpose* Sp čc'x̌ʷnten *have evil designs on sb.* Cr c'ax̌ʷ *be fault of, promise, choose.*

*c'əx̌ʷ II *sand, gravel.* Li c'x̌ʷut *gravel* Th c'əx̌ʷz'úym'x̌ʷ *sandy ground* Sh c'ʕʷyuy'ləx̌ʷ (red. of *c'ʕʷyul'əx̌ʷ) *gravel* Cb c'əx̌ʷəl'ə?x̌ʷul'əx̌ʷ/sc'əx̌ʷc'ix̌ʷl'əx̌ʷ *sand.* – Cf. PCS ***c'ix̌.** – The Sh word clearly belongs here, but ʕʷ is unexplained.

*c'uy *darkness, night.* Sh xc'ʔuy *get dark* Cb sc'úw'i *night* Cv c'uy *dark.*

h

*hamaʔ see ***samaʔ.**

k

*kic *to reach (destination), come upon.* Th kíces Sh kicns; kicx *arrive* ESh skicəc *visitors* Cb kícuʔsn *meet* Cv kic; skicəc *visitors* Ka (kʷ'əł)čic; sčiccn *visitor* Sp čitš; tčicn *meet* Cr čic (also *find*); sčicc *visitors.*

*kah, *kaʔ *to open.* Li kahn *pry st. open,* kahqʷán' *open a lid* Cr čiʔ *open, uncover, unveil.*

*kəl *to look at, see.* Li ké̗l'sas *catch sight of,* kəl'min *look at* Cb kir'n *look at, see* Cv kriʔm *glance at.* – Poss. retracted counterpart of PS ***kal.**

*s-km'xis *bear.* Sh skm'xis *grizzly bear* Cv skm/m'xist *black or brown bear.*

*kən *to help.* Th k(e)néyt *helper* Sh knuxʷm Cv kn'xit Sp čn'šit; čn'šiš *helper* Cr čen'šít.

*s-kint *person.* Th skint, diminutive skikn't *co-wife, second wife of former husband, husband's mistress* Sh skiknt *wife of ex-husband, lover of ex-sweetheart* Cb skint *Indian* Cr sčint *person.*

*kʔəwət, *k'əwət *to walk, step.* Li kʷwatm Th k'wet (k'wilx *sneak up*) WSh kʷwetm ESh k'əwéte (-e < -m) Cv tkʷʔut *walk, pl.* Ka tkuʔút *id.* Sp tkʷʔu(ʔ)t *id.*

*kəx *to go (along) on foot,* ***kx-ap** *to follow, chase.* Th nkxépes *chase out/away (pl. obj.)* Sh xkxepm *chase away (animals),* [nkext *thicket, forest*] Cb kxapn *chase,* nakə́xt *walk on road/trail* Cv kxam *go on foot, follow,* kxan *go along w., follow,* tkxnmncut *id.* Cr češ *accompany,* čšip *chase.*

k'

*k'aʔ *to lie (of round object).* Li k'aʔ *to land somewhere* Th k'eʔtés *set down bulky object* Sh k'ʔem *put, place (as sack of potatoes)* Cb k'ənqin *pillow* Ka č'eʔ *put down (one round object)* Sp č'eʔ *it's a ball,* nč'ʔéneʔ *pillow* Cr č'en' *one round object lies.*

*s-k'il/n *hoary marmot, Rocky Mountain pika.* Li Th sk'il' Sh skik'l' Cb sk'in' [Cr sč'im']. – Borr. in Ck sk'i:l.

*s-k'alp *man's deceased brother's wife; parents-in-law or son/daughter-in-law after death of spouse.* Li (Mt. Currie) sk'álpaʔ *man's deceased brother's wife* ESh sk'ʔalp *id.* Fl sč'eʔélp *parents-in-law or son/daughter-in-law after death of spouse.* – See ***n-qʷic'-tn.**

*k'ələxʷ *to set (of sun), be (dangerously) sick.* Li nk'luxʷ *be in bad shape (of person)* Th k'yuxʷ *(person) is very sick* Sh k'luxʷ *sunset, west,* xk'luxʷ *very sick* Cv k'laxʷ *it gets late/dark* Ka č'elúxʷ *evening, sunset* Sp sč'luxʷ *evening,* sč'luxʷm *dinner,* sč'lxʷtin *the west,* čɫč'lxʷmncut *get out of sight.*

*k'əƛ' *grey, brown, dirty.* Li k'ə́ƛ'k'əƛ' *dirty* Th k'əƛ'k'eƛ' *(very) dirty, dirty grey,* k'éƛ'es *to dirty,* k'əƛ'k'eƛ'éytxʷ *dark grey horse* Sh kətkeƛ't *dirty* Cb ƛ'ək'

165

(inv.) *get dirty* Cv kɫk'aλ'lxʷ *brown horse* Sp čɫč'eλ'xʷ *id.* Cr tč'teɫxʷ *id.*

*k'əm *(stem occurring with many (complexes of) lexical suffixes, sometimes accompanied by local prefixes, to form words expressing parts of the body (but not internal organs), parts of lodgings, and geographical features; its use is markedly less widespread in* Li Th Cr *than in the other* IS *languages).* Li Th Sh Cb Cv k'm-/k'm'- Ka Sp č'm-; stressed only in Sp č'ɫč'im *edge* Cr č'm-, č'é/ám-. Examples: Li k'əm'qin' *top, summit,* nk'əm'qin' *head of valley/river,* k'mus *edge of cliff/sidehill* Th nk'əm/m'qin/n' *top (of tree, mountain),* nk'əmɫniw't *side of body,* nk'əmtem *inside lining for ceiling/wall of house* Sh (t)k'mqin' *roof,* xk'mtem' *inside of house,* sk'mep *foot of tree,* sk'mew's *waist* Cb snk'əmqin *roof,* sk'əmcin *mouth, lips,* sk'maw's *waist* Cv k'mqin *head of river,* sk'miw's *waist,* snk'mikn' *back* Ka sč'əmep *foot of tree,* sč'əmepšn *heel,* sčč'melps *neck* Sp č'mqin *head of river,* sč'mapqn *nape of neck,* snč'mew's *waist* Cr tč'másq'it *sky, heaven,* čsnč'émep *door,* sč'ámaqs *breast.* – The root should not be identified with PS ***k'əm** *grab a handful* (thus Kuipers 1974:212-13, Kinkade 1975:9, see Kuipers 1981:328 fn.4).

*k'am *near, close.* Li k'amləx *sneak along,* Th k'émix *id.* Sh kek'mlx(mns) *sneak up (to sb.)* ESh kək'em *very close* Cv k'ik'm *nearly, almost, pretty soon.* – For the semantics cf. Cb k'il'x *close, near,* k'ilxmn *sneak up to, get close to.*

*k'im *to dislike, hate; (dark?).* WSh ck'imt *disgusted,* ck'imsns *to dislike* ESh ck'im(s) *disgusted,* ck'imsys (< -sns) *dislike* [Cb k'əm' *dark*] Cv k'im' *hate,* [nk'im' *darkness* Sp č'im' *dark* Cr čim' *disdain, turn away fr.,* č'em' *dark (as night)*].

*k'in *dangerous, precarious, causing fear.* Li k'ink'ənt *dangerous* Th k'ənk'ənmins *worry about sb., be concerned of sb.'s welfare* Sh kink'nt *precarious (eg. dangerously close to edge, or ready to blow up)* Cb k'ink'int *dangerous* Cv k'int *afraid* Ka č'int *be afraid for* [Sp č'is *sense of impending* *danger* (also *not up to par, feeling bad-tempered*)] Cr č'in' *be dangerous.*

*s-k'in see ***s-k'il/n.**

*k'ət' *to break off, crack, cut.* Li k'iλ' *to creak, crack (when st. is going to break)* Sh kt'ep *come off (as button)*, kit'm *tear off w. force* Cb k'ə/it'n *break string*, kɨk'ət'p *come off (as button)*, sk'ət'mix *chop wood* Cv k't'ap *get cut* Cr č'et' *cut off completely*

*k'at' *to raise, lift.* Sh ket'm Cv k'at'qnm *raise one's head.* – Cb kλ'ilx *climb a hill ("raise o.s.")* fits semantically, but both consonants deviate. Both would be regular in Sh, and it is possible that contact with a Sh-type dialect has left traces in Cb (cf. next item).

*k'ət'muy'a *eyebrow.* Sh tkət'múy'e Cb k'ət'múy'a (Wordlist k'əλ'múy'a).

*k'əwət see ***k'ʔəwət.**

*s-k'x-us *tear(s).* Li Th sk'xus (k'əx- *shake loose/off*) Sh sk^{w}x^{w}us (labialization automatic) Cv sk'xus.

*s-k'ay'(-t) *spider.* Li sk'ak'yət Th sk'ék'iʔt Sh skek'y' Ka sč'é'ʔit. – Poss. borr. in Sl kíkye.

k^w

s-k^{w}λ'-us *face.* Li Th sk^{w}λ'us Sh sk^{w}t'us Cv sk^{w}λ'us Ka sk^{w}əλ'us Sp sk^{w}λ'us.

*k^{w}um *to save.* Sh k^{w}mum *to flee into the bush (when raid is expected)* Ka kum *save, put away* Sp k^{w}um *save, hide away, get away from.* – Cf. PS **k^{w}um.* Poss. related to Li k^{w}uk^w *get out of a difficult situation*, k^{w}uk^{w}s *save sb.* Th k^{w}uk^{w}stés *id.* Sh k^{w}uk^w *safe, saved*, k^{w}ək^{w}stes *save sb.*, k^{w}ək^{w}sce(c)mx *thank you (lit. you saved me).*

*s-k^{w}imc-xn *rainbow.* Li sk^{w}imcxn Cb sk^{w}əmk^{w}imcxn Cv sk^{w}mk^{w}imcxn [Sp sk^{w}msk^{w}miw't šn Cr skumkumiwtšn]. – Sp and Cr have added a suffix -iw't-, cf. PIS -ɬniw't.

*s-kʷnkʷin-m *wild potato.* Li skʷənkʷin Sh skʷnkʷinm Cb Cv skʷən'kʷin'm Sp kʷn'kʷin'm'.

*kʷus *to gather up (as curtain), pull close.* [Li kʷukʷsəmtáx̌an *unid. large bird (buzzard?)*] Th skʷusp *skirt* Sh kʷusns *gather up (as curtain),* ckʷukʷscn' *drawstring* Cb kʷus- *wrinkled,* skʷusxn *paw,* kʷusuʔsáp *skirt* Sp kʷus *curly,* skʷussn *paw,* kʷskʷussn *walk cautiously* Cr kus *curly; skittish, shy.*

*kʷtun(-t) *big, plentyful.* Sh kʷtunt *plentiful* Cb qʷtunt *big, sg.* Ka Sp kʷtunt *id.,* kʷtənalqʷ *tall.*

*kʷəw, *qʷəw/ʕʷ *to slide, crawl.* Li kʷiwkʷwət *slippery,* kʷiʔəw' *to slip* Th kʷutés *slide st.* Sh kʷwum *id.,* kʷiwlx *drag o.s. along the ground,* qʷiwlx *crawl* Cb qʷəʕʷn *shove, slide,* kʷuwmínct *crawl on belly.* – The other SIS languages have deviant but similar roots: Cv k'ʷx'ʷap *crawl, slither* Ka Sp q'ʷaʕ- *move by sliding* Sp q'ʷix'ʷ *slide* Cr k'ʷaʕ *slide, slip, skid* (Nicodemus gives also q'ʷeʕp *it slid*).

*s-kʷəkʷaw' *rosehip.* Th skʷəkʷew' Sh səkʷew' Cv skʷkʷiw'.

*kʷi/ax *awake, alert.* Li skʷix *alert,* kʷəxkʷix *wild, feral* [Cb kʷaxʷt *awake,* kʷaxʷn *awaken*] Cv kʷxusm *keep awake.*

k'ʷ

*k'ʷul' *to become; do, make, fix.* Li k'ʷul'm Sh k'ʷulm Cv Ka Sp k'ʷul'm Cr k'ʷul'.

*s-k'ʷəlk'ʷalt *(snowy) mountains.* Th k'ʷik'ʷíyt *pinnacle, high mountain* Sh sk'ʷlk'ʷelt *snowy mountains* Ok sk'ʷlk'ʷalt *mountain.*

*k'ʷəƛ' *to become exposed.* Li k'ʷəƛ' *break open (as boil),* nk'ʷəƛ' *break out (as bird fr. egg)* Th kʷ/k'ʷəƛ'k'etés *make st. protrude,* k'ʷəƛ'k'ʷƛ'ə́k' *boil bursts* Sh kʷt'em *dig wild potatoes,* ckʷtek' *rise (sun, moon)* Cb ck'ʷəƛ'p *id. (sun), come off,* sk'ʷəƛ'ptnus *east* Cv k'ʷƛ'am *pull off,* nk'ʷƛ'ntim *take out* *of*, k'ʷƛ'ap *sunrise* Sp k'ʷƛ'ip *appear, come out*, ck'ʷk'ʷƛ'ip *sunrise*, sk'ʷƛ'ptin *east* Cr k'ʷet' *expose, be evident, plain*.

*k'ʷsixʷ *goose*. Li k'ʷsixʷ Th k'ʷesíxʷ Sh Cv k'ʷsixʷ Ka k'ʷəsixʷ Sp k'ʷsixʷ.

*k'ʷuxʷ-s *to be jealous, envious*. Th Sh Sp k'ʷuxʷs.

*k'ʷʕʷəy, q'ʷʕʷəy *small*. Sh k'ʷoyí?(e)se; c/sq'ʷuʕʷy *younger siblings*, cq'ʷʕʷəym-stés *consider inadequate, worthless* Cv k'ʷk'ʷyúma? Ka ɬk'ʷk'ʷoy'úme? *small sg.* Sp k'ʷk'ʷy'úme? [Cr k'ʷiy' *easy, quietly, still*].

<h1 style="text-align:center">1</h1>

*lạc' *to soak*. Th lạ́c'es; l?ac' *soaking wet* Sh lac'm; lac'qnm *moisten the head* Sp nlʕac' *soaked through (as seeping wound or baby's diaper)*. – Cf. *ɬu̧/a̧c, *ɬa̧t'.

*lək' *to tie up, wind (string) around, spin (thread)*. Th yk'əm *wind st. around st.*, Sh lk'em *id., spin (thread)* Cb lək'n *tie up* Cv lk'ntim *id.* Ka Sp lč'nten *id.* Cr leč *bind*.

*lam *to be comforted, pleased, happy*. Li lamn *pacify a child* Th yémes *express affection* Sh lemns *to comfort, console* Cb lamt *glad, happy*, maľn (inv.) *pacify a child* Cv limt *glad, happy* Ka Sp lemt *glad, grateful* Cr lim *be glad, thankful, pleased*.

*liq' *to bury*. Th yiq'm Sh liq'm Cb kalíq'əna?m Cv liq'm Ka laq'm Sp laq'n Cr leq'. – See comment to PS *q'əl-st.

*law-a? *man's father('s brother)*. Sh léw'e *uncle, man's father's brother* Cb lə?aw *man's father* Cv l?iw *id.* Ka l?ew *id.* – Ti lə?ə́h *father of male* corresponds in the initial only but deserves at least a mention because Ti often has cognates of IS relationship terms.

*ləγ *to insert*. Li ləγ'cam' *to cork (a bottle)* Th yγtes Sh lγem Cb liyn *stab, poke, spear* Cr leǯ *stab*.

*ləʕʷ *to rumble.* [Li ləw *fall w. a thud*] Th lʕʷup *rumble,* lwup *knock, hammer, rumble* Sh xłʕʷmtenk *rumbling in stomach* Sp snł'aʕʷm'n'ʔetén'č *growling stomach.*

*laʕʷ *to plunge.* Sh xleʕʷnk *to get under the ice* Ka loó- *dip, fall into a hole,* nlo:pétkʷ *fall in the water through a hole (in the ice)* Sp nlʕʷatkʷntm *he was dunked in the water* Cr laʕʷ *plunge head first,* hnlaʕʷíčtetkʷeʔ *he plunged his hand into water* (Reichard 1938:613, 625).

*lạy *to clatter, rattle.* Sh cłay *eager, excited,* especially in negative expressions: taʔwəs k scłayəs *he doesn't care a hoot* Cr łaymstm.

ł

*łaṭ' *wet, soaked.* Li łəƛ' *get soaking wet* Th łáƛ'es *to wet st., sprinkle, splash* Sh ł'aṭ' *wet,* łəłłaṭ' *id.,* łaṭ'ns *soak,* xłáṭ'le?xʷm *wet the floor* Cb łəṭ' *wet,* łạʔṭ' *soaked* Cv ł'aṭ' *wet.* – Cf. *laċ', *łụ/ạc.

*łəc *to stack, pile up, lay side by side.* Li łəcn *pile up (large objects)* Th łcəm *stack, pile up* [Sh łec'm *to stack*] Cv kłcam *overlap flat items* Sp łcnten *lay side by side* Cr łec *flat objects lie.*

*łac *to pet, stroke.* Sh łecm Cv łcam.

*łụ/ạc I *to drip, soak.* Sh łacm *soak,* cłac *wet,* cxłcap *(baby) has wet behind* Cv łucm *soak,* ł'uc *soaked* Sp łcap *to drip* Cr łac *one drop falls.* – Cf. *lạc', *łaṭ'.

*łụ/ạc II *to pound, smash.* Li łəċ *cave in,* nłcána? *get entombed, house caves in on sb.* Th łact *mashed up* WSh łacm; łackeʔ *pestle* ESh łocm; łockeʔ *id.* Cb łuċt *bruise* Sp łocmn *potato masher.*

*łkap *pot, kettle, bucket.* Th Sh łkep Cb łkap Cv łkap(aʔ) Ka Sp łčep Cr łčip.

*łək' *to break (as rope).* Sh łk'ep *broken (rope), dead* Cr łeč' *string breaks.*

*ɫǝkʷ(-min) *to remember.* Th Sh ɫǝkʷʷmins Cb
nɫǝkʷʷkʷʷminn Cv nɫkʷʷkʷʷmint Ka nɫkʷʷkʷʷumín Sp
nɫkʷʷkʷʷmin; ɫekʷʷl̓sn̓cút *to muse, mull st. over* Cr ɫukʷʷ,
Nicodemus hnɫukʷʷɫukʷʷélgʷesncut *he reminded himself.*

*ɫiq-m̓-aɫp *unid. plant (poison ivy?).* Li ɫǝqɫiqǝq *get
sores from poison ivy,* ɫǝqm̓aɫp *poison ivy* Sh sɫiqt *poison ivy,*
ɫǝqǝmem̓ɫp *id.* Cv ɫɫqm̓iɫp *fireweed.* – The Cv name is the
same as the Li Sh ones, but the semantics cause a difficulty.
See comments to PS *p̓u/an.

*ɫǝqʷ *to put on top, put astride.* Li ɫqʷilx *mount a
horse* Th ʔesɫóqʷ *seated astride,* ɫǝqʷtes *put (astride),* ɫqʷǝp
landed and lying there, ɫqʷiyx *mount a horse* Sh ɫqʷum *heave
st. heavy* (W), *pile up* (E), ɫɫqʷew̓sns *throw st. over a line* Cb
ɫǝqʷn *put away,* snkɫǝqʷmintn *clothesline,* (sn)kɫqʷaw̓sn *id.*
Cv ɫqʷam *store away,* kɫqʷiw̓s *hang draped over* Sp
čɫqʷew̓stn *to drape.* Cr hnɫoqʷílgʷesn *closet, lit. place for
hanging (storing) things.*

*ɫaxʷ NIS *to patch,* ***ɫǝxʷ** SIS *to sew.* Li ɫáxʷan̓ Th
ɫéxʷes Sh ɫexʷm Cb ɫǝxʷm Cr ɫexʷ.

*ɫuxʷ *thicket, bushes.* Li ɫǝxʷɫuxʷ Th ʔcsɫuxʷ; ɫuxʷt
go through bushy area Sh nɫuxʷt *hide o.s. in the bushes* Cv
nɫuxʷt *walk into brush/swamp.*

*ɫǝx̌am *relatives, in-laws.* ESh ɫǝx̌mem *go and* see
*one's beloved in a faraway place (eg. married woman visiting
parents)* Cv ɫx̌mam *live at in-laws,* ɫx̌x̌am *one's in-laws.*

*ɫǝx̌ʷ *pubescence.* Li ɫx̌ʷǝ́x̌ʷm̓ǝx *pubescent (esp. girl)*
Th ɫx̌ʷumx *puberty (of girl), first menses* Sh ɫx̌ʷumǝx *puberty
(of boy or girl)* Sp ɫɫx̌ʷún̓ey *puberty,* hecɫx̌ʷéw̓si *first
menstruation.*

λ̓

*s-λ̓ǝpaʔ *marrow.* Li sλ̓paʔ Th sλ̓epéʔ Sh sλ̓peʔ Cv
sλ̓piʔ.

*ƛ'əpəq *muddy.* Th ƛ'əpqetés *stick st. in mud* Sh sťpeq *muddy,* sťəpqúl'əxʷ *mud* [Cb sƛ'uk'úl'əxʷ *id.*] Cv nƛ'əpqitkʷ *get stuck in mud,* kƛ'pqƛ'pqntim *smear st.* [Sp sƛ'oč'óle?xʷ *mud,* ƛ'oč'ntán *smear w. mud*].

*ƛ'əkʷ see *ƛ'əqʷ.

*s-ƛ'əkʷ *pitchwood.* WSh səstukʷ Cb sƛ'a:ƛ'ə́kʷa? Cv sƛ'ƛ'úkʷa?.

*ƛ'a?kʷilx *shaman.* See PS *kʷəlx and poss. *ƛ'ə?.

*ƛ'əq *to dig up/out.* Li ƛ'əqn Th ƛ'qəm Sh ťqem Cb ƛ'əqn Cv ƛ'qntim Sp ƛ'qasq'l' *dig roots.*

*ƛ'aq *to prick, pin, skewer, stick in.* Li ƛ'áqsa? *barbecue salmon (impaled on stick)* Th ƛ'aqƛ'əqt *thorny, spiny,* ƛ'áqse? *barbecue fish* Sh ťeqm *to pin (as brooch),* ?s(t)ťeq *penetrate, remain stuck (as arrow in flesh),* ťeqxn *awl* Cv nƛ'aq *put st. into st. hollow,* ƛ'áqna? *pocket, sack* Ka ƛ'áqane? *pocket* Sp ƛ'áqist *stick o.s.,* sƛ'ƛ'áqist *a tattoo,* ƛ'áqne? *pocket, bag.*

*ƛ'əqʷ (NIS), *ƛ'əkʷ (SIS) *spot(ted).* Li sƛ'əqʷ *have spot on body,* sƛ'ə́qʷƛ'əqʷ *spotted, variegated* [Th łək- *small spots,* łək- *large spots*] Sh sťuqʷ *spot,* stktəqʷtuťqʷ *spotted, fawn* Cb (ƛ')ƛ'ə́kʷƛ'əkʷ *fawn (spotted)* Cv ƛ'əkʷƛ'akʷ *early fawn* [Sp ƛ'kʷƛ'ukʷ *white-tailed fawn*].

m

*mac'i/a? *to retrieve killed game.* Th méc'i? *receive portion of meat as reward for participating in hunt* Sh méc'e *pack meat of game killed* Cv míc'a? *retrieve killed game.* – Cf. PS *c'i? and possibly *?u/am.

*mc'ac' *a type of groundhog.* Sh smc'ec' Ka mc'ec'.

*mak'p *testicle.* Li mak'p Th Sh mek'p Cb mək'p Sp meč'p. – Cf. PCS *makən.

*məkʷ *snow.* Sh tmukʷtm'/m *snow on trees* Cv mukʷ *id.,* mkʷiwt *mound of snow on ground.* – SIS has a √*makʷ:

Cb smak^wt *snow on ground* Cv mik^wt *be snowed in,* smik^wt *snow* Ka səmeq^wət *id.* Sp smek^wt *id. on ground* Cr mik^w *snow.*

*s-muk^waʔ-xn *spring sunflower.* ESh smúk^weʔxn (WSh cecʼlq, which in ESh refers to the root only) Cv smúk^waʔxn Sp Cr smúk^weʔšn. – Poss. borr. in ESh.

*mal *to appear briefly, be caught a glimpse of.* Sh ʔstmelʼ(x) ESh ʔstmilʼx; mémlet (< *memlmt, red. of *melmt) *shadow flashes by, reflection in water* Sp mel *appear and then disappear (as sb. walking through trees).*

*milʼ *to divide up, share out.* Li nmimlʼm *share out* Sh milm *divide up,* mlxits *share out collective catch of fish* Cv milʼm *id.,* milxt *give st. to sb.* Cr milʼ *distribute (as food at feast).*

*məlk^w *to dislocate, sprain.* Li mlu̦k^w Sh mlok^w Cb mərʼk^w- (source unknown). – Deviant but similar roots in Li məƛʼk^w *slip (off)* Th məƛʼq^w, mƛʼoq^w *dislocate* Cv kʼlmłq^wcnikst *sprain one's wrist,* cf. also Sq Ld pʼətq^w- *sprain,* Ch pʼayə́q^w- *id.* Cf. also Cr (Nicodemus) marʼarʼáxn *have dislocated arm* and comment to *mitʼkʼayaʔ.

*məlk^w *shadow, spirit.* Th sməlek^wózeʔ *spiritual life, soul, ghost* Sh smlk^wék^wye (red. of *smlk^wéye) *shadow* Sp smʼelʼk^wéyʼeʔ *id.*

*məlmət-ałp *white poplar, trembling aspen.* Sh mlməłtełp Cv mlʼmlʼtiłp Sp mʼlʼmʼlʼtełp.

*məli̦n-łp *balsam fir.* Li mə̦lintəp Sh mlenłp Cb mərimłp Cv məriłp Ka (Carson-Flett) manínłp Sp mrinłp Cr (Nicodemus) marámłpalq^w (in the Cr-English part š instead of ł must be an error).. – See PS *mə̦l; the extension *-in is IS.

*mə̦lt *mud, clay, deerlick.* Sh malt *deerlick* Ka malt *mud, clay, earth* Sp malt *dirt.* – See comment under PS *mul.

*maməlt *whitefish.* Li mamlət Th mémit Sh memlt Cv mimlt.

*mulx *cottonwood.* Li mulx *stick* Th Sh Cv mulx Ka Sp Cr mulš.

*məɬq *to collapse, be flattened.* Sh mɬqem *flatten out, crush flat,* mɬeq *collapsed, flattened out* Cb m'm'əɬq *deadfall, trap* Cr maɬq *heavy convex object collapses.*

*s-m/p/p'əƛ'-qin' *mushroom.* Li smə/əƛ'áqaʔ *cottonwood mushroom* Th məƛ'qíʔ *id.* Sh smt'qin', smt'éqeʔ Cb pəƛ'qin' Cv p'ƛ'qin' Ka (Carlson-Flett) p'aƛ'qán Sp p'aƛ'qín.

*s-mʔam *woman, wife.* Li səmʔam *wife,* mamáw's *couple (married, lovers)* Th smʔem *wife,* meʔmʔéw's *married couple* Sh smʔeʔm *wife,* mmews *couple (human),* mmemws *id. (animal)* Cb smʔamm *woman* Cv smaʔmʔím *women (pl. only)* Ka səmʔem *woman, wife* Sp smʔem *woman,* smʔemʔém *id., pl.* Cr smíy'em *woman, wife,* [smém'ulumxʷ *man's younger sister*]. – The derivation with *-aw's (see PS *-was) *mutual, etc.* of the word *couple* from the word *woman, wife* has a parallel in Cv nx̌ʷnx̌ʷiw's *couple* besides Cv nax̌ʷnx̌ʷ *wife.*

*s-min'ip *toad.* Sh smy'nip Cb (Krueger) sminp Cr sm'é:m'ín'ep.

*maʔstm Sh *cross-sex sibling,* SIS *woman's father.* Sh smeʔstm; meʔstméws *siblings and cousins (collectively),* smém'eʔstm *little brother (of girl) or sister (of boy)* Cb (Krueger) maʔástm *woman's father* Cv m'istm'/m *id.* Ka mestm' *id.* Sp m'estm' *id.* – Cf. PIS *saʔstm.

*mit'k'ayaʔ *blood.* Sh mítk'ye Cb məɬk'áyaʔ Cv məɬk'íyaʔ (Vogt 1940b mlk'íʔeʔ), mmátk'yaʔ/mm'átk'yaʔ *blood pudding* Cr mít'č'edeʔ. – The reconstruction is based on the Sh and Cr forms. See comment to PS *pəl'kʷ.

*max *sliver.* Li məxmax *thorny, prickly,* máxakaʔ *have a sliver in one's hand* Th ʔesméx *have a sliver,* mext *get a sliver* Sh mext *have a sliver,* mexkst *id. in one's hand,* tmexm *put sticks through salmon to keep it split open for* *barbecuing,* tmxusm *barbecue salmon* [Cv mxiłp *cedar*] Sp č'łšm'pqin'čst (-šm'- inv.) *have a sliver under one's fingernail.*

*mix (red.) *a type of basket.* Sh mim'x *large cedarbark basket,* mxéxye? (red. of *mxéy'e) *basket* Cr mimš/minš *box.*

*məx̌ʷ *snow.* Li məx̌ʷ *come down heavily (of snow)* Th mx̌ʷəp *snow piles up on ground* Sh scmux̌ʷ *snow,* cmx̌ʷul'əx̌ʷ *there is snow on the ground* Cb smə́x̌ʷəx̌ʷ *snow falling* Ka Sp mx̌ʷup *to snow* Cr max̌ʷ *cover w. snow.*

*may *be nearby, clear, known.* Sh mymey *close by,* meyns *move st. closer* Cb miy *clear, plain* Cv miynt *know, be sure of st.* Sp méye?m *relate, describe,* mistén *know,* hecmíy *it's the truth* Cr miy *make clear, know (an idea).*

*maʕ(ʷ) *to break, smash.* Th má ʕes Cb maʕ ʷn Ok maʕt *broken* Cv maʕ ʷt *id.* Sp maʕ ʷn.

n

*s-naḷək̓ʷ *Clark's nutcracker, grey jay.* Li náḷak̓ʷ Th náľeq̓ʷ Sh snalq̓ʷ Cb Ka snalk̓ʷ Sp snerk̓ʷ.

*nil *contagion, poison.* Sh tnilns *infect sb. with a disease,* tnilt *catch a disease* Cb kanílns *I caught it fr. him* Ka sčəniləmn *poison* (Kinkade IJAL 1967:229) Sp čnilmn *id.* Cr čnilemn.

*s-nina? *(great horned) owl.* Sh snine; ninm *to hoot* Cv snína? Ka sənine? Sp Cr snine?.

*nəq' *to rot.* Li na?q'; na?q'áłc'a? *rotten meat* Th ?esn/n'áq' *rotten,* naq't *rot, rotting, just rotted,* naq'áłc'i? *rotten inside (as wood)* Sh (c)n?eq'; nq'xen *with diseased feet (of horse)* Cb nəq'; na?q' *rotten food* Cv n?aq' *rotten* Ka naq' *id.* Sp naq' *to stink* Cr naq' *organic substance is rotten.*

*nəq̓ʷ *to steal.* Li Th naq̓ʷ Th na/əq̓ʷmén *thief* Sh nq̓ʷum; nq̓ʷcinm *steal food* Cv Ka Sp naq̓ʷ Ka naq̓ʷém'n *thief* Sp naq̓ʷémn *id.,* čnáq̓ʷle?x̌ʷ *tresspass* Cr naq̓ʷ.

*nas see ***?anas.**

*naw' *to blow.* Th new't; néw'es *blow st. (away),* snew't *wind* Sh newt; snewt *wind* Cv niw't; sniw't *wind* Ka né?u; səné?ut *wind* Sp new't; new'n *blow st. away,* snew't *wind* Cr niw'; sniw't *wind.* – Cf. PS ***naw-ilx**.

*nəx̌ʷ I · *female.* Li núx̌ʷa?/nə́n'x̌ʷa? *(female) sweetheart,* snəx̌ʷn'ə́n'x̌ʷ *hen* Th nóx̌ʷe? *(female) sweetheart,* nəx̌ʷnun'x̌ʷ *female bird* Sh nux̌ʷnx̌ʷ *woman,* nx̌ʷnənenəx̌ʷ *female animal* ESh nəx̌ʷnénx̌ʷe Cb núx̌ʷnux̌ʷ *wife* Cv nax̌ʷnəx̌ʷ *id.,* nx̌ʷnx̌ʷiw's *couple (human or animal)* Ka noxʷənxʷ *wife* Sp nóx̌ʷnox̌ʷ *id.*

*nəx̌ʷ II *to be on the move, run* (NIS *of animal or conveyance*). Li nux̌ʷ *to gallop,* nəx̌ʷnəx̌ʷawł *racing canoe/car/wagon* Th nox̌ʷ *animal runs,* nəx̌ʷuyəm'xʷ *car, automobile,* nəx̌ʷnəx̌ʷúse?s *(worms) crawl over berries, fruit* Sh nux̌ʷ *to gallop,* nəx̌ʷuləxʷ *car* Cb nux̌ʷt *go, walk, sg.* Cr nuxʷ *frog swims.*

p

*papa? *(grand)father.* Li spápza? *grandfather* Th spápze? *id.* pep *(grand)father* Sh pépe? *father* (the usual word is qé?ce) Cr pípe? *father.*

*pəc'qʷ see ***p'əc'qʷ**.

*paka? (NIS), ***pakst** (SIS) *put on gloves.* Th péke?me; (pək)péke?(e)ns; spéke? *gloves* Sh spéke? *id.* Cv spikst *id.* Ka pəčpečstm; spečst *glove* Sp spečst *id.,* spčpečst *id., pl.* – The words clearly contain the PS suffix ***-ak-a?/-is(t),** but Th Ka Sp treat ***pak** as a root, which may be due to metanalysis (see Kuipers 1989:30f.). As the existence of a monoconsonantal lexical root in PS is unlikely, the background if this item remains unclear.

*pəkłan *bitter (wild) cherry.* Th pəkłen *bark of id.* Sh pəkłen Cb pə́kłn Cv pəkłán'.

*s-paks(t)-mn *pestle.* Sh spekstxmn *a kind of hammer* (uncertain recording) Cb spaksmn Cr spičsmn. – See comment under ***paka?**.

*pul *to lie, lay, beat up, kill.* Th puysc *beat up, kill,* ʔespúys *killed* Sh pult *to lie,* pəlit *id.,* spulˈtn *bed, lair,* pulsts *beat up, kill* Cv pulst *beat to death* Ka pulsm *hit, kill* Sp pulsm *kill* Cr púlut *kill, injure,* púlusn *I killed him.* – Cf. PS *pul.

*pulˈ-lmˈxʷ *mole.* Li púʔyˈaxʷ *mouse* Th púyˈyeʔxʷ *mole* Sh punˈləxʷ *id.* ESh also splpóla *id.* Cb púlˈyaʔ *gopher, mole* Cv púlˈlaʔxʷ *mole* Cr púlˈye *gopher,* pulyahálˈ *mole.* – See Kinkade 1991:235, who reconstructs PIS *púlyaʔ-ulmˈxʷ, but there is no evidence for the presence of the element (prob. suffix) *-yaʔ in the derivatives with the suffix *earth, soil,* which are limited to IS.

*s-pl-ap *buttocks.* Li splap Th spyep Sh splep Cv splip.

*pəɬ see *ʔapɬ.

*puɬ *to splash, froth.* Li puɬət *to boil, be boiling* Th púɬes *make waves, splash water* Sh puɬ(t) *splash* Cv spʔuɬ *spray* Ka Sp puɬ *splash* Cr puɬ *foam.*

*s-pəƛˈ-qinˈ see *s-m/p/pˈəƛˈ-qinˈ.

*pənˈ see *pˈənˈ.

*pun-ɬp *juniper.* Li punɬ(əp) Th Sh Cb Cv Sp punɬp.

*paq *to "learn one's lesson", tr. punish, take revenge on.* Li paq; paqs *"straighten sb. out"* Th paq *suffer consequences of one's acts,* paqsc *take revenge on* Sh peq; (t)peqsts *give sb. his just deserts* Cv paqq; paqmst *punish.*

*pəs *to break wind.* Li pəsq Cv psam *id., noiselessly.*

*pəst *(other) half/side,* *pəst-awt *area beyond the river/lake.* Th (n)pstewt Sh pəstewt Cb pstawt *across water* Cr péste? *be half, one side.*

*put *to honor, respect, greet.* Sh putns *greet* Cv púta?m *to respect* Sp pútʔem *to honor* Cr púte? *respect, honor, worship.*

*ptakʷl *to tell a mythical or legendary story.* Li ptakʷɬ; sptakʷɬ *legend* Th ptekʷɬ; sptekʷɬ *myth* WSh cptekʷɬ ES scptek^wle (< ...lm), WSh scptek^wɬ(m) *myth, legend* Cv captík^wl *tell stories (myths, fiction).*

*pəw-alxkn *buck deer.* ESh pwélxke (< ...kn) Cv pwalxkn *young id.* Sp pwelščn. – Poss. borr. in ESh. Cf. ***s-x̌^wl'-axkn.**

*pax̌ *to plane, whittle, scrape, scratch.* Li páx̌an' *scrape* Th páx̌es *whittle* Sh pex̌m *id., plane* Cb pax̌n *scratch* Cv pax̌nt *scrape, shave, strike (match)* Sp px̌aʔx̌ *they scratched,* snčpax̌mn *flint stones* Cr pax̌ *rub on rough surface (as strike match).* – Cf. PS ***pax̌.**

*pix̌ *to hunt.* Li Th pix̌m' Sh pix̌m Cv pix̌(m).

*paʕ *faded, grey.* Li pəʕpaʕ *grey(ish),* pəʕp *pale, faded* Th paʕm *to bleach* Sh pʕpeʕt *faded, pale, grey,* [mʕmeʕt *grey*] Cb pəḥ *id.* Sp paʕ *id.* – Cf. PS ***pəq.**

p'

*p'/pəc'q^w *to break/tear off.* Th pc'oq^w *snap off, dislocate (arm, leg)* Sh pəcq^wntes *break off (as branch),* xpəcq^wpus *break one's neck,* pcuq^w *chipped* Sp p'c'q^wum *strip off* [Cr p'əsaq^w *bone breaks*].

*s-p'əlq^w-aqs *turtle.* Sh splq^weqs Ka sp'əl'q^wa(qs) Sp sp'rq^waqs Cr sp'árk^walqs.

*s-p'aƛ'-m *bitterroot (Lewisia rediviva).* Th spiƛ'm ESh spit'm Cb sp'aƛ'm Cv sp'iƛ'm Sp sp'eƛ'm. – Th p points to borrowing from Sh, and Sh i to borrowing from Ok.

*s-p'əƛ'-qin' see ***s-m/p/p'əƛ'-qin'.**

*p'ən' (NIS), ***pən'** (SIS) *to bend, fold.* Li p'an'án *fold* Th p'ən'tes Sh p'new'sns Cb ʔacpən' *bent,* pən'pán'n *fold* Cv paʔpín(n)t *id.* Ka ʔespín' *bent,* pən'nten *bend.* Sp hecpín' *bent, crooked, dented,* hecpepín' *folded* Cr pen' *bend.*

*p'əq^w see PS ***pəq^w.**

*s-p's-aqs *nose.* Li sp'əṣqs Th p'saqs Sh sp'seqs Cv Ka Sp sp'saqs.

*p'ət' *to pour/plop down mushy/wet substance.* Li p'ə́ƛ'n *plop st. down (as wet clothes)* Sh pətat' *hang down around edges (of bread risen too high)* Ka pʕat' *(Carlson-Flett) muddy* Sp pat' *id.,* p't'am *pour gravy-like substance* Cr p'at' *be mushy, pour mushy stuff.*

*p'aw *(to) echo.* Li p'awəw Th Sh p'ewt Cv sp'iwcn/n' Sp p'uw- *echoing, resounding* Cr (Nicodemus) p'ugwílmxʷ/š.

*p'ax̌ *heal over.* Sh p'ex̌t *healed over* Cv p'ʔax̌ Sp p'ʔax̌ *get well* Cr p'aʔx̌ *heal, become well.* – A poss. related root in Th p'x̌íʔx̌aʔt Sh pəpép'x̌eʔt *thin (layer).*

*p'ix̌ *to sear.* Li p'íx̌in' *brand an animal* Th p'íx̌es *sear, brand* Sh p'ix̌m *fry, brand* Cb p'ix̌ *hot* Cv p'íx̌ax̌ *burn one's skin* Sp p'ix̌ *sting, sear.*

*p'ax̌ʷ see ***ʔap'x̌ʷ.**

*p'uy *to wrinkle.* Li p'iʔs Th ʔesp'ís *wrinkled, shriveled up,* p'iʔsetés *cause to shrivel up* Sh p'yusm *frown* Cv p'yus *wrinkled face,* p'uyxn *car,* lit. *wrinkled feet* Sp Cr p'uy *be wrinkled.*

*p'əʕ *to burn (esp. of forest fire).* Li sp'aʕ *burned forest* Th p'aʕt *burned, singed (of flesh),* p'ʕakst *singe one's hand,* p'aʕstés *burn, scald, singe sb.* Sh cp'eʕ *burnt-over terrain* Ka p'aáp *fire (not made by man), it is burning (eg. the forest)* Sp p'aʕntés *burn hair off,* sp'ʕap *forest fire.*

q

*qəc *to shrink.* Li nqcəp *pull a muscle* Th qcəp *shrunk up* Sh qʔic Cb qəcp Cv qcap Sp qcip; sqcmin *spasm* Cr qec.

*qacaʔ, ***qack** *father, elder brother.* Li sqáczaʔ *father,* qack/qə́qcək *elder brother* Th sqáczeʔ *father,* qe/ack *elder brother or male cousin* Sh qéʔce *father,* qeck *elder brother* Cb qack *man's older brother* Cv łqáqcaʔ/qick *man or woman's older brother* (Vogt 1940b qečk) Ka łqáqceʔ *elder brother (of woman),* qecč *id. (of man)* Sp qéceʔ *woman's older brother,* łqáqceʔ *older brother,* qecč *id.* Cr qicč *elder brother.*

*qəl *fresh (as food)*. Th qiyt; qiʔ(n')tés *to wet, dampen* Sh qelt Cb qəlt Cv sqlíłc'aʔ *fresh meat* Cr qel.

*qalt *to reach the top*. Li qayt (borr.) Th qayt Sh qelt Cb katqáltk *on top of* Cv qilt *go over the top/hill,* sqilt *top* Ka qalt Sp qelt Cr qiltč *be inland.*

*qəp *to put st. on st. (mostly to cover or protect)*. Li qəpn Th qəptes; qpey'qs *loincloth* Sh qpem *to bandage,* qəpqintn *kerchief,* qpekst *pot holder* Cv qpqintn *hair, mane,* nqapqn *have a cap on* Sp sqpusl' *feather,* čłqpečstn *pot holder* Cr qep *pad.* – Cf. PCS *qəp'.

*qap *soft, pliable*. Li qəpqap; qápan' *soften* Th qəpqe/ap; qépes *soften* Sh qəpqept ESh qepm *soften hides* Sp qep Cr čip. – Cr has shifted *q to *k.

*qəs *to scratch, tickle*. [Li qəsp *shiver*] Th qsiyx *scratch an itch (of animal)* Sh qəsqism *tickle,* qsep *tickled* Cb qəsn *scratch an itch* Cv qas *scratch,* cqsqsinknt *tickle sb. in the belly* Cr qes *scratch w. nails.*

*qays *to dream, have a nightmare*. Sh qeys *have a nightmare* Cv qiy's *to dream* Ka qéʔis *id.* Sp qey's *id.* Cr qiʔs (Nicodemus) *dream, vision, nightmare.*

q'

*q'ic'qn *stomach, gizzard*. Sh x̌qic'qntn *gizzard* Cb Cv sq'ic'qn *human stomach, gizzard* Sp snq'ic'qn *gizzard.*

*q'əc'w-ayaʔ see qʷəc'w-ayaʔ.

*q'əm *to covet, wish for, crave*. Li q'mál'kʷam *crave st.* Sh qəq'mcnem *speak wishfully of the opposite sex* Cv sk'łq'am *one's wish,* nq'mscin *one's wishing for st.* Ka q'ammscínəmn *covet* Sp č'łq'mnten *wish for* Cr q'em *desire, covet, wish for.* – Cf. PS *q'əm *to swallow,* which via *glutton* and *hungry* can be associated with the present item.

*s-q’apaʔ *sand.* Li sq’áq’paʔ? Th sq’aq’épe? Sh sqéq’pe Cv sq’apínax^w Ka sq’eːpé(ʔeneʔ) Sp sq’p’éneʔx^w Cr sq’epq’eːpíneʔ.

*q’əw *to break (as stick).* Li q’əq’íw’am *break off branches,* q’aw’ *get beaten (in contest)* Th q^wuʔtés *break, snap,* q’íw’es *break (stick) in two,* [q’wisqn *axe*] Sh q’wum *to break, to beat sb. in a game,* x̌q’iwm *break branches to mark the way,* qwq’iw *brittle,* q’iwt *to break, itr.* [Cb q’aw’ísqn *axe*] Ka q’aʔuntén *break st.* Sp hecq^wúw’ *it's broken* (q^w automatically labialized), q’ʔup *it broke* Cr q’ew *break stiff object.*

*q’aw *to cast a spell.* Li q’áwan; sq’aw *be under a spell* Sh q’ewm Cb k’awm Cv q’iwntm *power to kill* Sp q’ewm Cr q’iw *witch.* – Borr. in Sq ʔəsq’əwq’aw *put under a spell by the Lillooet (Mt. Currie or Pemberton) people* (the native word is x̌t’ət).

*q’əx^w *to be proud, conceited.* ESh qəx^wq’éx^weʔt *boast about o.s.* Cb q’əx̌^wq’áx̌^wat Sp q’x^wq’ex^wt Cr q’ex^w. – Poss. borr. in ESh.

*s-q’ax^w *a small owl.* [Th sq’áq’e/ak^w *screech owl*] ESh sq’əq’ex^w *barn owl* Cb sq’ax^wm’ín’aʔ *id.* Cv sq’q’ax^w *screech owl* Sp sq’q’ax^w *pigmy owl.*

*q’ix̌ *strong, hard, tight, tough, grudging, frugal, stingy.* Li q’ix̌ *firm, hard, tough, strong (material),* nq’ix̌c *door is closed* Th q’ix̌t *strong, secure, hard, difficult,* nq’ix̌cn *close/lock door,* q’íq’ax̌t *stingy* Sh q’ix̌m *fasten, tie up solidly,* q’ix̌t *strong, hard, tough, solid, difficult,* x̌q’ix̌cn’s *to lock (door)* Cv q’ix̌q’x̌t *stingy* Ka q’ix̌təmn *miss, regret the loss of st.* Sp q’ix̌t *reluctant,* q’ix̌tmn *be stingy about st.* Cr q’ex̌ *be frugal, grudging.*

*q’əy’ *to make marks, write, draw,* ***q’ay’-w’s(-qn)** *two-point buck ("marks on top (of head)")* Li sq’áq’yas *two-point buck* Sh q’yem’; qəqeq’yəs Cb q’iy’m, nq’iʔq’ay’ú?s/nq’iʔq’áyusqn Ok tq’aq’y’w’sqn (geogr.) *a deer-hunting area* Cv q’y’am Ka q’eʔím Sp q’y’im Cr q’ey’. – Poss. related to PS

*q'al, *q'ay (*make mark = set up a little structure*), and to PS
*q'əyiʔək.

qᵂ

*qᵂəʔ *to tan (soften) hides.* Li qᵂúʔmn *tanning stick* Sh
qᵂʔum *tan hides w. tanning stick* Ka qoʔúp *made soft (of
hides well-tanned).* – A poss. extension in PIS ***qᵂət.**

*qᵂu/aʔ *horseshoe-shaped, hollow, bay.* Th qᵂʔuʔ *bent,
warped (of buckskin, cloth, board),* qᵂuʔtés *bend into corner,
make crooked,* nqᵂuʔqᵂuʔén'i *curved at corner (of basket)* Sh
cqᵂuʔ *horseshoe-shaped, bay,* cx̌qᵂəʔel'xkn *large hollow in
sidehill,* qᵂʔep *gunnysack* Cb qᵂaʔáp *pocket* Cv cnqᵂʔip *bay,*
[ck'łqᵂay' *dead-end gully*] Sp hecqᵂéʔ *puckered,* hecqᵂaʔqᵂéʔ
bulges Cr qᵂiʔ *be hollow.*

*qᵂac *warm.* Li qᵂacləx *warm o.s.* Th qᵂec *(person or
weather is) pleasantly warm* Sh qᵂec *id.* (also *of house, water,
etc.*) Cb qᵂaʔc *hot* Cv qᵂʔac *warm weather,* qᵂacqᵂct *id.* Ka
qᵂec *(comfortably) warm* Sp qᵂec *warm* Cr qᵂic *id.*

*qᵂəl *dust, ashes, powder snow.* Li qᵂul'l' *cloudy* Th
qᵂúy'iʔ *cloud over,* qᵂi(ye)tés *raise dust,* qᵂyəp *get dusty,*
ʔesqᵂíy *powdered* Sh sqᵂlesl'p' *ashes,* s/x̌qᵂlqᵂlul'əxᵂ *id.,*
qᵂlqᵂlul'əxᵂ *dust, silt,* qᵂlem *powder snow,* qᵂuyt *raise dust*
Cb sqᵂəlátkᵂp *ashes,* qᵂułt *dust,* sqᵂu(ʔ)ł *id.* Cv qᵂlmin
ashes, qᵂał *(dust) particles,* qᵂuł *dust* Ka qᵂil *snow is dry,
dusty,* quł *dusty* Sp qᵂl'min *ashes,* qᵂuytn *snowdrift* Cr quł
be dusty, squʔł *dust, dirt,* qoʔł *dust flies about,* [sqᵂniłkᵂəp
ashes].

*s-qᵂəl'ap *black lichen.* Li Ok sqᵂl'ip Cv sqᵂlip Ka
sqᵂəl'a(pqn) Sp sqᵂl'apqn. – Borr. in Ck sqᵂəlip. Because of its
i the Li word looks like a borr. fr. Ok, so that this item is really
SIS. A connection w. PIS ***qᵂəl** is doubtful.

*qᵂliʔt *jackpine.* Li qᵂlítaz' Th qᵂʔit, qᵂiʔtéłp Sh
qᵂəqᵂliʔt Cv qᵂqᵂliʔt Sp kᵂkᵂl'iyt Cr eququl'iʔt *balsam fir,*
Nicodemus qoqol'it *black pine.* – Se qaqlínay *jackpine* has a
vague resemblance to the IS word.

*q^{w}am-q^{w}əm-t *pleasant, good, beautiful.* Li q^{w}amq^{w}mət *funny* Th q^{w}amq^{w}əmt *beautiful, very good (usually spiritual connotation)* Sh q^{w}emq^{w}mt *good-looking, nice (esp. of objects)* Cb q^{w}amq^{w}əmt *good* Cv q^{w}amq^{w}mt *excellent,* q^{w}amq^{w}mqs *excellent food* Ka q^{w}ámqumt *very* Sp q^{w}q^{w}emq^{w}mt *adorable* Cr q^{w}am *pleasant,* Nicodemus q^{w}ámq^{w}amt. – The -q^w of the reduplication syllable blocked the shift *a > i in Cv and Cr, and the second *a* in Cr must be analogical to the first.

*q^{w}an *to be in want, poor, pitiful.* Li q^{w}ənq^{w}ant *poor, destitute,* q^{w}ənmin *want st.* Th q^{w}ənq^{w}ent *poor, pitiful,* q^{w}ənq^{w}ənstes *to pity* Sh q^{w}nq^{w}ent *poor,* q^{w}eq^{w}n't *id.,* q^{w}əq^{w}nstes *to pity,* q^{w}ənen *to want, try hard* Cb q^{w}ə́n'q^{w}ən't *pitiful, poor* Cv q^{w}n'q^{w}an't *id.,* q^{w}n'an' *be pitied* Ka q^{w}ən'q^{w}in't *miserable, poor,* nq^{w}ən'nəmin *to pity* Sp q^{w}n'q^{w}in't *ugly, pitiful,* nq^{w}n'n'min *feel sorry for* [Cr q^{w}ey' *be poor, pitiable, pity,* q^{w}iy'(-t) *have pity for,* Nicodemus q^{w}áy'q^{w}i?t *indigent, pitiful,* snq^{w}ey't *compassion*].

*q^{w}ups-a? *(great-)great-great-grandparent, (gr.-)gr.-gr.-grandchild.* ESh q^{w}úpse? *gr.gr. grandparent* Cb q^{w}úpsa? *id., gr.gr.grandchild* Cv q^{w}úpsa? *gr.gr.gr.grand-mother or -child.* – Poss. borr. in ESh.

*q^{w}asq^{w}ay' *bluejay.* Th q^{w}áq^{w}sq^{w}i (in myths only) Sh (Dog Creek) sq^{w}éq^{w}sq^{w}e, (Canim Lake) q^{w}éq^{w}sqe, (Enderby) q^{w}esqy Cb q^{w}ásq^{w}ay' Cv q^{w}ásqi? Sp q^{w}ásq^{w}i? Cr q^{w}asqn'.

*q^{w}ət *soft, down feathers.* Sh q^{w}tem *soften,* q^{w}ətq^{w}et *soft* Cb q^{w}útq^{w}ut *down feathers.*

*q^{w}əw/ʕ^w see *k^{w}əw.

*q^{w}i/ay *to have plenty.* [Li q^{w}əyn/q^{w}əzn *to use* Th q^{w}əztes *id.*] Sh cq^{w}ey; q^{w}ey'q^{w}yt *rich (of food),* x̌q^{w}yełc'm *eat to one's heart's content, feast* Cb q^{w}áyq^{w}ayt *rich* Cv q^{w}ay *id.,* lut kən q^{w}ay *I'm not rich,* q^{w}a?íls *have enough* Ka q^{w}ey Sp q^{w}ey *frequently, plenty* Cr q^{w}iy (Nicodemus q^{w}iy *he is wealthy*).

*s-q^{w}yic *hare.* Li sq^{w}yic Th sq^{w}oq^{w}yə́c Sh səq^{w}yic Cb sq^{w}q^{w}ícuʔx̌^{w} *snowshoe hare* Ka sq^{w}áq^{w}ciʔ/sq^{w}aq^{w}cíʔ *cottontail rabbit* Cr sq^{w}icmš *id.* – Borr. in Ck sq^{w}iq^{w}əyá:θl *jackrabbit*; the word also resembles Cw Ms sqəqəweθ *hare* Ck sqəweθ, sqíqəwèθ/c *snowshoe hare* Sn s(qə)qəweθ *hare* Sg sqəqəwes *rabbit* Cl qiʔcíʔ *id.*

*q^{w}aʕ, *q^{w}aʕ^w/w *silly, crazy, drunk.* Sh stq^{w}ʕq^{w}eʕs *w. blurred vision* Ok q^{w}aʕ Cv q^{w}aʕ^w Ka q^{w}ew Sp q^{w}e/aw Cr q^{w}eʕ^w.

q^{,w}

*n-q^{,w}ic'-tn *deceased sibling's spouse.* Li (Fountain dial.) nq^{w}ic'tn Th nq^{w}ic'tn *spouse of deceased relative of same sex in same generation* Cv nq^{,w}ic'tn; snq^{,w}ic'tn *replacement husband* Sp nq^{,w}ic'tn *deceased sibling's spouse* Fl nq^{,w}icətn *id.* – The Li and Th forms with plain q^w suggest borrowing from Sh, but no Sh cognate has been recorded. See *s-k'alp.

*q^{,w}əc'w-ayaʔ *chipmunk.* Sh qəc'wéw'ye Cb q^{,w}əc'əw'áy'aʔ Cv q^{,w}q^{,w}c'w'íy'aʔ Ka q^{w}q^{,w}c'uw'é Sp q^{,w}q^{,w}c'w'éy'eʔ Cr q^{,w}c'wíyeʔ.

*q^{,w}aʔk *a river fish (sucker, chub, squawfish).* Li q^{,w}ʔak *bridgelip sucker* Sh q^{,w}eʔk *chub* Cb q^{,w}aʔák *id.* Cv q^{,w}q^{,w}aʔk *small whitefish* Sp q^{,w}eʔč *squawfish.* – Borr. in Ck q^{,w}e:c/q^{,w}əʔec.

*q^{,w}al *to wilt, wither.* Li q^{,w}al *dead trees/bushes* Th ʔesq^{,w}él *withered,* q^{,w}ʔel *become weak, listless,* q^{,w}ʔey *withered, wilted,* q^{,w}ʔil *to wither,* q^{,w}ʔil' *(plant) wilts, (person) becomes tired, listless* ESh Cv Cb q^{,w}ʔil *wilt, dry up.*

*q^{,w}aɫt NIS *backpack, quiver* SIS *to carry on the back.* Li q^{,w}əɫtiʔ *quiver* Th q^{,w}e/alt *backpack* Sh q^{,w}ɫtiʔ *quiver* Cb q^{,w}aɫtmn *carry on the back,* sq^{,w}aɫt *backpack* Cv q^{,w}iɫtm *carry on the back* Ka Sp q^{,w}eɫt *id.* [Cr q^{,w}iʔɫ *move camp, village travels*].

*q'ʷuƛ' *to stuff st. in a hole, gap.* Li q'ʷúƛ'un' Th q'ʷúƛ'es Sh q'ʷut'ns Cb (s)naq'ʷúƛ'xn *socks, footwrappers* Sp nq'ʷuƛ'šn *sock* Cr hnq'ʷut'šn *id.* – Cf. PS **ƛ'aq'ʷ.*

*q'ʷuƛ'-aʔ-xn *to race.* Th nq'ʷəq'ʷúƛ'eʔxn Sh səqʷút'eʔxnm *horse race,* xq'ʷə-q'ʷút'eʔxnm *to race* Cb snq'ʷaq'ʷúƛ'axnəxʷ Ka q'úƛ'eʔš *to race,* k'úƛ'iš *run around, pl.* Sp q'ʷuƛ'š *run, pl.* snq'ʷq'ʷuƛ'štn *racehorse.*

*q'ʷəmp *to be all gone, disappear.* Sh q'ʷmpep *exhausted, all gone,* q'ʷmpesl'p' *be out of firewood* Ka q'omép *run away, pl.* Cr q'ʷen'p *go out of sight, disappear behind hill or horizon,* also *evening.*

*q'ʷmiw's *wild, untamed,* (reduplicated:) *colt.* Li q'ʷmiw's; q'ʷmə́mw'əs *colt* Th q'ʷmiw's *wild horse* Sh q'ʷmiw's; q'ʷmim'ws *colt* Sp q'ʷq'ʷm'ew's *yearling colt* Cr q'ʷəq'ʷm'íw'es *colt.*

*q'ʷit'-s *to smile, nod the head in approval/assent.* Th q'ʷiƛ'sm (borr. fr. Sh) *smile* Sh q'ʷit'sm Cv q'ʷt'sam *nod the head* Ka q'ʷit'əs *id.* Sp nq'ʷit'sm *give approval/assent, nod the head* [Cr ʕʷit's *smile, smirk*].

*q'ʷəx̣ʷ-min-aʔ *dipper bird.* Th sq'ʷox̣ʷmímneʔ Sh sq'ʷəx̣ʷmem'nək Ka q'ox̣om'ín'eʔ *bluejack, a fishing bird,* (Carlson-Flett) q'x̣ʷmíneʔ *dipper bird* Sp q'x̣ʷm'in' *id.*

*q'ʷʕʷəy see ***k'ʷʕʷəy.**

s

*sik' *gopher, ground squirrel.* Sh sisk' Ka Sp sisč' Cr sič'.

*səl I *to peel off.* Th ṣləp Sh slntas Cb sərn Cv srntim.

*səl II (red.) *a type of cricket.* Th ṣəlṣl Sh sal Cb sár'sar Cv sarsr Sp sersr; ʔuɬsér *people who sing and celebrate all summer long,* nsssr'qin' *sing in a high, shrill voice.*

*sul *cold, chilled, frozen.* Sh sulm *freeze st.* Cb sult *be cold (person)* Cv sulm *freeze st.,* sult *frozen numb,* suy't

185

chilled Ka sul *cold, chilly,* súʔi *id.* Sp suln *chill st.,* sult *cold,* suyʼ *chilly* Cr sul *be cold (as body, stove, etc.).*

*samaʔ (poss. ***s-hamaʔ**) *"aliens" (mythical or real).* Li sámaʔ *white person* Th Sh sémeʔ *id.* Sh səmeʔsqíqlmʼxʷ *dwarf* Cv sámaʔ *Frenchman, white person* Sp sémeʔ *French, taboo* Cr hémeʔ *French,* enhémeʔcn *speak French,* – The Cr forms suggest that s- is the nominalizer; in NIS the red. is smsámaʔ, which may be due to metanalysis.

*sinci/aʔ *younger brother.* Th sínciʔ Sh sínce Cb Cv síncaʔ Ka sínceʔ Sp Cr síncaʔ. In Cb Ka Cr *younger brother of male.*

*sun-kʷa *island.* WSh csunkʷm ESh csunkʷe Cb Cv ksunkʷ Ka Sp čsunkʷ.

*səp *to shake off berries from bush,* ***səsəp** *blue- or huckleberry.* Li səpn *shake off berries* Sh spem *id.,* sipm *shake out blanket,* səsep *lowbush blueberry* Cb səsápt *lowbush huckleberry* Cv səsapt *mountain blueberry* Ka (s)sipt *berry like small huckleberry* Sp ssipt *dwarf huckleberry.*

*sipʼayʼ *skin, hide.* Li sipʼázʼ Th sipʼécʼ Sh səspʼey Cb sípʼiʔ Ka səpʼsípʼiʔšn *wear moccasins* Sp sípʼ/pi *tanned hide* Cr sipʼeyʼ *be buckskin.*

*saʔstm *cross-sex sibling-in-law.* Li sʔastm Th sʔestm Sh sʔectm Cb saʔstm Cv saʔstám Sp seʔstém Cr siʔstm (Reichard's and Nicodemus' meanings combined). – See also PIS ***maʔstm.**

*sətk *to twist.* [Li sitkm *make a net*] Sh sətsətkeɫp *peavine* Cb sətkn Cv sətkmstim Cr setč.

*saw *to whisper.* Th nséwʼnʼis *whisper in sb.'s ear* [Sh swsewcnm *ask indirectly, hint one would like to be given st.*] Cv swʼncut Sp swʼimʼt *a whisper,* suʔsuʔntém *they whispered.* – The Sh word may well reflect PS ***saw.**

*sawɫ-kʷa *water.* Sh séwɫkʷe Cb sawɫkʷ Cv siwɫkʷ Ka séuɫkʷ Sp nsewɫkʷm *be in the water* [Cr síkʷeʔ]. – See PS ***səʕʷ.**

*sax *pure, fresh, odorless; abated, numb.* Li səxp *numb*, saʔx *lose taste* Th (n)séxes *to air out, freshen*, nséxcetn *dessert* Sh səxsext *pure, sterilized*, səxex *numb, abated (pain), cold track* Cb səx *fresh, odorless* Cv sxap *aired out*, sxntim *air st. out*, ksixpíc'aʔ *get the chills*, ksaʔxíc'aʔ *cool off (of person).*

*səx̌ʷ *to split/shred.* Li səx̌ʷn *pull off broken branch* Th səx̌ʷtés *split (reeds, rope, willow withes)*, síx̌ʷes *shred* Sp sax̌ʷm *split in little pieces* Cr sex̌ʷ *sound of cracking timbers.*

*sux̌ʷ *to descend.* Li súx̌ʷast *come down (fr. ladder, hill).*, səx̌ʷnas *heavy rainfall* Th sóx̌ʷest *descend*, ʔessóx̌ʷe *downpour* Sh səsux̌ʷnst *descend* Cv sax̌ʷt *go downhill.*

*saɣ/ʕ *to shake (off).* Sh seɣm Cb ksḥaw'sm *shake (a tree).*

*səʕ, *səʕʷ *to drain, strain (a liquid).* Th sʕəp *drain* WSh xseʕ'lkʷm *strain (a liquid)* ESh sʕél'kʷu (u < m) *id.* (Chase dial. sʕél'kʷe), sʔeʕʷ *drained* [Cb səx̌ʷp *drip*] Sp sʕʷop *it melted/dripped*, soʔntén *strain* [Cr saʕʷ *flow*]. – Cf. PS *səʕʷ/w.

t

*təʔ *to pound, crush.* Sh tʔem Cv stʔam.

*takɬ *to reach the bottom of a hill.* Th ntekɬ Sh xtekɬ Cv ntkɬilx.

*tkay' *urine.* Th tkey'; tkey'm *urinate*, ntkey'tn *bladder* Sh tkey; tkey'mn *bladder* Cb tkay'; sntakáyn *urinate*, sntakáy'mn *bladder* Cv tkiʔ Ka tčéʔi *penis* Sp tčey'(m) *urinate*, tečéy *penis, urinary tract*, sntčey'tn *bladder* Cr (Nicodemus) lut hey'ntččiy'ngʷílis *unable to urinate.*

*təkʷ *to tick, beat.* Li təkʷpx̌ʷac *heart is pounding*, ntəkʷpánwas *id.* Cr tukʷ.

*ti/akʷ *to stoke a fire, burn, heat.* Li takʷpm *burn bottom of tree (to fell it)* Th tekʷpm *id.*, tíkʷes *stoke fire, keep* *fire going* Sh t'ikʷ *fire* Cv nta'kʷítkʷ *warm liquid.* – Cf. PS *yəqʷ.

*tikʷ-a' *aunt, father's sister.* Sh tíkʷe'/tí'kʷe/tikʷł Cb tíkʷa' Sp tetíkʷe' *woman's father's sister, woman's brother's daughter* Cr tíkʷe' (Nicodemus: *paternal aunt while father is living*).

*təl'xʷ *to be overcome by difficulties, fail, give up.* Sh tluxʷ *get stuck, give up* Cb til'til'xʷn *be unable,* tíl'til'xʷt *difficult* Cv tilxʷnt *fail, be unable,* tíl/l'tlxʷt *difficult* Sp til'xʷn *be unable,* tl'xʷmist *have a hard time,* til'tl'xʷt/tl'tl'uxʷt *difficult,* tl'xʷncut *be lame.*

*təm' *clouds.* Sh tktmtem(t) *cloudy,* tktmesq't *cloudy day* Cv sktm'tam't *clouds* Sp sčtm'ip *cloud,* čtim' *a cloudy sky* Cr sčtem'p *cloud.*

*ti/amu' *skunk cabbage.* ESh tim'ət Cv stámu'qn Sp tímu' Cr tímu' *fern.* – For the deviating Cr meaning see comment to PS *p'u/an.

*ti'm *snow disappears in spring.* Li ti'əm, təmtim Sh t'imxʷ Cv ta'múla'xʷ Ka tí'im Sp ti'múle'xʷ Cr tim' *ground is clear of snow.*

*s-tum'-kst *thumb.* Th ESh Cv stum'kst.

*s-tməqʷ *thornberry.* Sh stmuqʷ *(berry),* stmqʷełp *(bush)* Sp stm'oqʷ *red thornberry, Columbian hawthorn.*

*s-tunx *man's sibling's child.* Li stunx *niece* Sh stunx, (address:) tunx Cb tunx *man's sister's child* Sp Cr tunš.

*təp (red.) *bee, wasp.* Th stəptəpeyxkn *black wasp* Cv tptpqin *bumblebee.*

*tq'im *strawberry.* Sh tqítq'e Cb tq'im'tq'im' Cv tq'imtq'm Sp q'it'q'm.

*təqʷ *to get dented, arched, hollow in mountains.* Li təqʷ *get dented* Th tqʷəp *id.,* stqʷaw's (geogr.) *a low gap beyond Kanaka mt.* ESh cx(təqʷ)tuqʷ *indented, arched* Sp toqʷ *hole, pocket, bottomland*, ttoqʷ *small hollows in mountains* Cr tətaqʷ *gulch, hollow*.

*taw' *to spoil, wreck.* Li taw'án *ruin st. (by dropping it, or getting it dirty)* Th téw'es *make sb. weary, sickly* Sh twstes *spoil, wreck* Cb tumt *rotten plant or tree.*

*tawm' *navel.* Li táwam' Th tewm'k Cb tawm' Cv (inv.) timw's Sp (inv.) tému? Cr tígʷem'.

*txac' *elk.* Li txac' Th stxec' Sh txec' Cb t'xec' Sp tšec'. – Cb t' unexplained.

*təx̌-cin *tigerlily.* Sh təx̌cin' Cv stəx̌cin. – Poss. to PS *tax̌; an element təx̌ in other plant names: Li tx̌áɬpaz' *Pacific willow,* Th təx̌qin *chocolate tips,* təx̌pé? *red willow berry* Cb tx̌tx̌ay'ɬp *cottonwood.*

*tiʕʷa? (red.) *mint.* ESh təʕʷə?tíʕʷe? Cv tʕʷatíʕʷa?. – PIS status doubtful.

t'

*t'ic' see *c'it'.

*t'i/ac' *to smooth, straighten.* Sh tic'm *to press, iron (clothes)* Cb Cv t'ic'm *id.* Sp t'ecm *id., smooth, straighten* Cr t'ic' *smooth by rubbing.* – Cf. PS *tac.

*t'ak' *to rise (of water), (over)flow.* Li ƛ'ak' *rise (of water)* Th ƛ'ék'es *flood st.* Sh xtek'm *fill w. liquid* Cv t'ík'na? *flood,* kt'ík'na? *water runs over a surface.* – Cf. *t'akʷ.

*t'ak'l(a) *to provide food for travel.* Li sƛ'ak'ɬ *provisions for trip, box lunch* Th ƛ'ék'yens *provide sb. w. lunch,* ?esƛ'ék'ye *have one's lunch with one* Sh sték'le *provisions for travel,* xték'le?tn *lunch box* Cv t'ik'lnt *provide sb. w. grub,* st'ik'l *provisions for trip, box lunch* Sp st'eč'l *lunch* Cr st'ič'l *travel provisions.* – The vague overall similarity to QUI -taqɬ *lunch,* hi:táqɬ *picnic for a trip* may well be accidental.

*t'ak'ʷ *1. to get filled w. liquid; puddle, pool, lake; 2. to rise to the surface, float, emerge fr. the water.* Li nƛ'ak'ʷ *get filled w. liquid; puddle, pool* Th ƛ'eʔk'ʷének *have a bellyful of liquid* Sh t'ek'ʷ *rise to surface of water,* tətk'ʷut (WSh) *pour water on until really soaked,* (ESh) *floating* Cb t'ak'ʷt *lake* Cv t'ik'ʷt *id.,* kɬt'k'ʷitkʷ *float* Ka t'eʔék'ʷ *come out of the water* Sp t'ʔek'ʷ *emerge, come ashore.* – Cf. *t'ak'.

*t'uk'ʷ *to hold/carry in the arms, hug, get an armful of.* Li ƛ'úk'ʷun' *hug* Th ƛ'úk'ʷes *id.* Sh t'uk'ʷns *hug, get an armful of* Cv t'k'ʷw'sikstm (stək'ʷuʔsíkstm) *carry in one's arms.* – The Cv heading is given as t'k'ʷ-, with a reference to t'k'ʷ *put down;* the example has tək'ʷ-; see Intro 3J, end.

*t'aɬ, *t'u/aɬ *sticky, dirty.* Li ƛ'áɬan' *to stick on, weld, glue* Th ƛ'áɬes *id.,* ƛ'aɬt *sticky,* nƛ'eɬstn *bandage, bandaid* Sh t'eɬns *stick on, paste, glue* ESh t'ʔaɬ *decomposing,* t'ətaɬ *decomposed* Cb t'əɬ *dirty,* [t'aɬləxʷ *rubber*] Cv t'iɬnt *glue st.,* t'ɬaɬ *get dirty,* t'ɬap *kneaded* Ka Sp t'iɬ *dirty* Sp t'ɬnten *to dirty, mold, knead,* sct'iɬ *bread dough,* t'eɬ *sticky,* t'eɬn *to stick, plaster* Cr t'oɬ *be lumpy, sticky w. mud,* Nicodemus st'eɬ *blotch.*

*t'am *to grab, press together, bundle up.* Li ƛ'áman *grab* Cv k'ɬt'mʕasm *kiss* Ka t'emčsm *shake hands* Sp hect'ém *bunched,* t'emn *to grab, bunch* Cr t'im *shake hands.*

*s-t'amk-alt *daughter.* Th sƛ'əmkey't *niece* Sh st'mkelt Cb st'ámkaʔ Cv st'mkʔilt Ka st'əmčeʔélt Sp st'mčʔelt (*also:*) *niece (woman's sister's daughter)* Cr st'tímčeʔ.

*s-t'am̓'-alt *cow, cattle.* Li tamált *doe w. horns (hermaphrodite)* Th stm'a/elt, st̓'m'alt Sh stam'ált, st'am'ált Cv st'ámyaʔ *hermaphrodite* Ka st'əm'a Sp st'əm'aʔ Cr st'am'á(ltmš). – Note in Th the exceptional phoneme t'; Sh t' can be pronounced [ƛ'] or [t'] in this word, in ESh [t'] is the norm. The word must be a borrowing in NIS.

*s-t'ənw-ayaʔ *bat (zool.).* Li sƛ'ə/anwín, sƛ'ənwáwy'a Th sƛ'eƛ'n̓ʔúy' WSh st'nwéye ESh stət'nwéye Cv st'nt'an'wáya? (uncertain form) Sp t'en'w'éy'e?. – Cf. PS *s-t'əwin.

*t'up *to twist,* esp. *to spin thread.* Li ƛ'úpun' Th ƛ'úpes Sh t'upm Cv t'upnt, t'apqs Ka t'upm Sp t'upn Cr st'opqs *thread.*

*t'əq *to put down, pile soft material.* Th ?esƛ'áq *bunch, bundle (of cloth, small items),* ?esƛ'əqqín *bundle, stack* Sh stəqt'eq *Indian blanket* Cv t'qntim *put, place st.,* st'qilp *mat, bedding foundation* Ka ?est'áq *it lies (st. soft, as grass, clothes, etc.),* ?esənt'áq *there is tobacco in the pipe,* nt'qem *fill a pipe* Sp t'aq *bushy,* hest'áq *piled up,* t'qntes *pile up* Cr t'aq *bushy stuff lies.*

*t'əqʷ *to strike, slap.* Li ƛ'əqʷn Th ƛ'qʷups *slap on behind* Sh t'qʷum Cb t'əqʷn Cv t'qʷam; t'qʷisxn *hit on the forehead* (but nƛ'qʷups *spank,* poss. borr. fr. Sh or Th) Ka Sp t'qʷum Cr t'aqʷ.

*t'əqʷa? *to sew.* Li ƛ'əqʷ?um Th ƛ'qʷu?tés Sh t'əqʷ?um Cv t'qʷam Ka Sp t'qʷum.

*t'us *(to extract) marrow.* Th ƛ'úses Sh t'usm Cb st'usm *marrow* Cv st'uscn *id.* Sp Cr st'us *id.* – Sh sut'm *to suck* may be an inversion of this root. Cf. **s-ƛ'əpa?.*

*t's-ałp *spruce.* Th ƛ'sełp Sh t'sełp Cv t'st'siłp. – There is a SIS **t'əs in Cb t'əṣ *hard, tough* Cv t'əst'?ast *id.* Ka t'as *id.* Sp t'as *id.,* čt'as *skinny* Cr t'as *thin, skinny,* but the tree name shows no trace of retraction.

*t'əw *to crack,* ***t'əwəq** *to break off.* Li ƛ'əw *to crack (ice, window),* sƛ'uw'q *any kind of slide* Th ƛ'u?ƛ'u?wáq' (geogr.) *"place where there are slides",* [ƛ'y'iqʷ/ƛ'iy'əqʷ *rope or string breaks*] Sh t'weq *cave in, give way suddenly* Cv t'w'qam *break a rope/string* Ka tuw'áq (t irregular) *leaves snap off and fall* Sp t'u?t'w'íč *have finger tips cracked fr. cold,* t'awáq *sound of snapping string/rope.*

*t'əx *sweet.* Li ƛ'əx *sweet, tasty* Th ƛ'əxt Sh t'ext ESh xt'xétkʷe? *sweeten a liquid* Cb t'əx; t'əxt *sugar* Cv t'axt;

st'xaɫq *mountain huckleberry berries*, lit. *sweet fruit* Ka t'iš; st'əša(ɫq) *huckleberry* Sp t'iš *sweet, sugar*, st'šaɫq *huckleberry* Cr t'eš; t'iš *be sweetened*, Nicodemus st'šastq *huckleberry*, lit. *sweet crop*.

*t'uxʷt *to fly*. Sh t'uxʷt *id., sg.*, t'uyxʷt *id., pl.* Cv t'uxʷt; kt'xʷasq't *fly in the sky*, nt'uxʷtmn *airplane* Ka t'uxʷt *fly, sg.* Sp t'uxʷt.

*s-t'yaʔ *hay, grass*. Sh st'yeʔ *hay* Cb st'íyaʔ *id.* Cv st'iyíʔ *(bunch)grass* Sp sx̌sést'yeʔ *sweetgrass* (x̌s- *good*) Cr st'édeʔ *hay, grass, fodder*.

w

*s-wak- (in words for) *lightning*. Sh swekmn'st Cv sw'w'íkiʔst Ka suw'éčən't Sp sʔuw'éčn't.

*wik *to see*. Th Sh wikm Cb wikɫn Ka Sp wičm Cr gʷič(t).

*wakʷ *to stick away, hide*. Li wákʷan' *put st. under one's clothes*, swákʷxal *carry under one's clothes, be pregnant with* Th wákʷes *cuddle st./sb. against one's chest*, ʔeswákʷm *be pregnant*, wákʷukʷ *placed in tomb close to ancestors* Cb wakʷn *to hide* Cv wikʷm *id.* Ka Sp wekʷm *id.*.

*s-wal (red.) *fish*. Li swáwlam *fish (esp. trout) occurring in waters at high location* Th swew'ɫ *(small) fish (other than salmon, sturgeon)*, wéwleme *to fish for small fish in creek, lake (as opposed to river fishing)* Sh swewɫ *fish (generic)*, wewlm *to fish (in any way, w. net, rod etc.)*, [sʕʷíʕʷle *lake trout, "steelhead"*] Ka suw'éʔuɫ *fish* Sp sw'ew'ɫ *id.* – Cf. PS *wəl, *ʕʷəl.

*w'il see *ʔawil'.

*wəlk' NIS, ***wəlk SIS** *frog, toad*. Li wəlik' *sound of frog* Th wlə́k'ze *tree toad* Cb wark *frog* Cr warč *id.* – Borr. in Ck wələ́k' *pacific tree toad*.

*s-wəlm-in'k *gun.* Li swəlmin'k Th swəlwəlmin'k Sh swlmin'k Cb swəlwəlmink /swəlmin'k [Cv nswl'ink *Coyote's son's name*] Ka suːluːləmí(n'č) Sp sululmín'č Cr Nicodemus swlwlmin'č. – See PS *ʕʷəl, *wəl(im).

*wəl-an(k) *stomach, belly.* Li ʕʷəlin Th (n)ʕʷyən Sh wla/enk Ka ʔolín Sp ʔurín. – Ka ʕʷo- > ʔo- as in Sp ʔox̌ʷcínšn'tn s.v. *ʕʷəx̌ʷ.

*wəlq' *to uncover.* Sh wlq'em, [ylq'em] Cr gʷal'q' *uncover pit.*

*wəmax *spirit, life, spirit-power.* Th suméx *life, alive* Sh wmex *to live* Cb sumáx *(spirit) power* Cv sumíx *guardian spirit* Ka suːméš *id.* Sp suméš *spirit power.*

*wəp *hair, fur, cover of grass, weeds.* Li swəpc *beard, moustache, whiskers,* wəpáx̌ʷac *hair on chest* Th ʔeswəp *hairy, furry,* wəpax̌ʷck *hair on chest,* wə/upupqíqne? *brome grass* Sh twupt *furry (animal),* swpcin *beard,* swpuləx̌ʷm *weeds* Cb Cv swəpcin *beard* Cv swpúla?x̌ʷ *hay, grass* Ka suːpcin *beard, moustache,* esču:páx̌ʷcč *have hair on the chest* Sp wup *hairy,* supcín *beard,* supúle?x̌ʷ *grass, hay* Cr gʷep *be hairy, grassy,* sgʷepcn *beard, moustache, whiskers,* gʷəpul'mx̌ʷ *ground is covered with abundant grass.*

*wisx̌ see *ʕʷisx̌.

*wətam-tk *downstream area,* Th Sh wtemtk Cv wtimtk. – Cf. *t-ʔiwl-tk.

*watn *to obtain, get, engage.* Th wətetés/wətntes *do, act on, get, take,* wetn's *engage, hire* Sh sutn (<*swətn) *possession, belonging,* [sew't *animal owned*], twetns *meet sb.,* wwétne *lover of married woman* Cv wtan *obtain, get,* wtntim *put,* cwtntim *take* Cr engʷet (stress?) *belong to.*

*wəx *to comb.* Li wíxin' Sh wxqinm *comb one's hair* Cb swəxmin *a comb* Ka ušqí(nm) *comb one's hair,* sušəmín *a comb* Sp ʔuším; sušmín *a comb* Cr gʷeš.

*wax *to be (present).* Th Sh wʔex Cb ʔacwáx *live somewhere, reside,* snawáxtn *a camp* Cv cwix *to dwell, a dwelling.*

*s-wəy'-numt-mx/xʷ *beautiful, handsome (of person).* Th swiʔnúmt Sh swynumtx, ESh (Chase) swy'numtx, (Enderby) swy'numt Cb swin'úmtəxʷ Cv swiʔnúmt Ka suíʔnumti, *pl.* suiʔwíʔnumti Cr swiʔnúmtmš. – Cv has a suffix -númt *endowed with.*

*s-wyap-mx/xʷ *white person.* Sh swyepmx *white person, Frenchman* Cb suyápənəxʷ; snwiyapənəxʷcínm *English language* Cv swyapyx; wypaym *act like a white man,* nwyapyxcn *in English language* Ka suyápi *white man, American;* pl. suyuyápi Sp suyépi; hecwipscúti *pretend to be a white man* Cr su:yépmš; snwyépmšcn *English language.*

x

*xik' *to miss a target.* Li xik'n Th xík'es Sh xik'm Cb xík'aʔst; xik'ək' *make a mistake* Cv xík'aʔst; xik'k' *having missed* Cr šič'.

*xəmạl/y *fly (insect).* Li xmaz' Th mə̣ze Sh xméye Cv x̌x̌mˤaɬ Cb maɬtxʷ Ka x̌amáɬtn Sp x̌maɬtn Cr haméɬtəmš (Nicodemus hamáɬtəmš).

*xən' *to spread (over), cover.* Th xən'tes *cover w. flat material* Sh xntes *spread out (as empty sack)* Cb kətxən'qintn *lid, cover* Cv txn'ínaʔ *cover w. st. stiff* Ka šən- *shut,* šən'qin'tn *cover, lid* Sp hecšín' *flat object lies* Cr šen' *id.*

xʷ

*xʷəʔ *to raise, lift.* Sh xʷʔim Cv xʷaʔntím Ka kʷəɬxuém (√xʷeʔ).

*xʷc *(in words for)* shoulderblade. Sh xʷcin'əktn Cb xʷcána.

*xʷic *short.* Sh (both W and E) xʷcəcícseʔt Sp xʷxʷíxʷect Cr xʷəxʷic. – The Sh root is cis (see *cəs);

194

disregarding initial xʷ the word parallels eg. Sh qʷəqʷéqʷmeʔt *short (person)*, pəpép'x̌eʔt *thin (layer)*, etc.. The status of xʷ as a (unique) prefix is confirmed by ESh ɬcəcícseʔt *thin (rope)* (in Ka ɬ- appears with diminutive reduplications).

*xʷic' *to give, point to, show*. Li xʷíc'in' *give st.* Th xʷic'm *give away, make donation* Sh xʷic'ns *show* Cv xʷic'nt *give* Ka xʷic'əɬtn *id.* Sp xʷic'š *id.* Cr xʷic' *point toward*.

*xʷal/y *to be absent, missing; debt*. Li xʷaz *mourn, lose st. one treasures*, xʷaz'án *forget about, let st. vanish*, xʷáy'nun *miss, feel the loss of*, xʷyáyawt *owe* Th ʔestxʷec'estés *miss, notice absence of*, xʷyəp *become sad, lonely*, xʷyéyut *credit, what one owes* Sh xʷeym *disappear*, xʷəxʷyewt *absent, not yet there, delayed*, nxʷyewt *sorry, sad*, xʷəxʷyeywt *a loan, credit*, nxʷeymns *feel bad about (a loss)*, nxʷeyns *lose sb. (obj.)'s possession*, lit. *make sb. feel sorry (about the object lost)* Cv xʷlxʷilt *debt(s)* Ka xulxʷilt *debt* Sp xʷlxʷilt *id.*

*xʷul *steam*. WSh sxʷult *warm wind down at the river in the evening* ESh xʷult *heat shimmer*, sxʷult *steam* Cv sxʷul/l' *steam* Sp sxʷʔul' *id.*, xʷul'n *to steam*.

*xʷəli/aʔ *meadowlark*. Li xʷəxʷli Th xʷuxʷʔíy Sh xʷəxʷleʔ Cr xʷéleʔ. – Cf. PS ***xʷiw**.

*xʷlakʷ *whirlwind*. Th Sh xʷəlxʷlekʷm Cr sxʷlikʷ. – Cf. PS ***xʷul** *turn, spin*.

*xʷəƛ̓' *to cut up, whittle*. Li xʷəƛ̓'mináɬ'qs *buckskin coat* Sh sxʷət'mən'elʔqs *id.*, sxʷət'min' *hide, buckskin*, xʷit'ns *cut (up), cut out (as pattern)* ESh xʷt'ekst *knife* Cv xʷƛ̓'am *whittle* Ka Sp xʷƛ̓'im *id.*

*xʷam-qn *roan (horse)*. Th ʔesxʷámqn Sh cxʷemqn Cv Sp Cr xʷamqn, [xʷeméčt *woodpecker*, sxʷuxʷóm'qn' *spoon of antler*].

*xʷap *to unfold, spread (as blanket)*. Li xʷapn' Th xwépes Sh xʷepns Cv xʷipm Ka Sp xʷepm Cr xʷep.

*xʷus *forceful, scary; eager, alert, hurried.* Li xʷə́sxʷəst *strong, forceful (smell, taste, act)* Th xʷusxʷəst *fierce, fearsome,* ʔesxʷús *made (by shaman) to be feared* Sh xʷusxʷəst *scary, awful(ly many),* xʷʔus *eager* Cb xʷusəs *hurry* Cv xʷus *in a hurry,* xʷusxʷst *go fast* Ka xuʔús *wide awake* Sp xʷus *awake, alert* Cr xʷus *arouse.*

*xʷisət *to walk.* Th xʷesít *walk, travel* Sh xʷəset *go about, travel (short distance)* Cv xʷist *walk (along)* Ka Sp xʷist *id., sg.* Cr xʷist *travel, go about.*

*xʷət *to come to the end, be exhausted, finished.* [Li nxʷətp *to go around,* sxʷətpaszánuxʷ *year*] Th xʷətpetés *to complete, finish off* Sh xʷtep *reach the end, come to an end* Cr xʷet *be exhausted, come to end.*

*xʷʔ(it) *much, many.* Li Th xʷʔit Th xʷeʔlscút *have plenty of everything,* xʷeʔɬscʼemʼ *(fish) has lots of bones* Sh xʷʔit; xʷeʔsqléwʼ *rich* Cb xʷiʔít Cv xʷʔit; xʷʔasqʼt *many days,* xʷaʔcín *say a lot* Ka xuʔít; xuʔétkʷ *much water* Sp xʷʔeyt; nxʷeʔúleʔxʷ *many loaves of bread.*

*s-xʷuʔt *vagina.* Sh Ka sxʷuʔt.

*xʷay see ***xʷal/y.**

*xʷuy *to go.* Li nxʷuytm *go ahead* Th xʷuyʼ Sh xʷuyt *to exit* Cv Ka Sp Cr xʷuy.

*s-xʷuynt *ice.* Sh sxʷuynt Cb sxʷuyntk Ka sxʷuyəmtkʷ Sp sxʷuyntkʷ Cr sxʷúdent (Nicodemus also sx̌ʷ...).

*xʷy-aqs *to spear.* Sh xʷyeqs *make a hole in the ice,* sxʷyeqs *spear for making a hole in the ice* Cb sxʷiyáqs *war spear.*

x̌

*x̌əc *to bet.* Th x̌cəm Sh x̌cem Cb x̌əcm Cv x̌cx̌camʼ Ka x̌cx̌cimʼ *gamble* Sp x̌cx̌ciʔm *id.* Cr x̌ac. – Cr *a* due to red. x̌ácx̌acmʼ (Nicodemus), see comment to ***qʷam-qʷəmt.**

*n-x̌al *to be afraid.* Sh nx̌lstes *to scare,* nx̌elmns *be afraid of,* nx̌eł(t) *afraid* Cb nax̌áł *afraid* Cv nx̌ilmst *be afraid of,* nx̌ił *afraid* Ka nx̌eləmn *be afraid of,* nx̌eł *afraid* Sp henx̌éli *he is afraid,* nx̌eł *he was afraid* Cr x̌ał *scare,* hnx̌ił *afraid.*

*x̌əlit *to ask, invite.* Li x̌lit *invite to a feast* Th x̌i(ye)tés *ask, request* Sh x̌litns *invite, call towards one,* x̌litx *ask for* Cb x̌əlitn *call, invite* Cv x̌litm *ask* Ka x̌alítm *ask, invite* Sp x̌litm *invite (along).*

*s-x̌alwiʔ *husband.* Th x̌áy'wi Sh sx̌élwe Cb sx̌álwi Cv sx̌ílwiʔ Ka sx̌éluiʔ Sp sx̌élwiʔ.

*x̌əlax̌ʷ *tooth.* Li x̌aláx̌ʷzaʔ *yellowbells* Th x̌yex̌ʷ; x̌əlx̌lel/l'x̌ʷ *corn, maize* Sh x̌lex̌ʷ; x̌lx̌lelx̌ʷ *corn* Cb x̌əlax̌ʷ; x̌əl'x̌əl'ax̌ʷ *corn* Ka x̌aléx̌ʷ Sp x̌lex̌ʷ; x̌x̌l'x̌l'ex̌ʷ (poss. error for -x̌ʷ) *tiny teeth, ear of corn* Cr x̌élex̌ʷ. – Borr. in Se x̌lx̌əl'alx̌ʷ *corn.*

*s-x̌aƛ'-(m-)xn *leggings, pants.* Sh sx̌et'mxn Cb sx̌aƛ'mxn Cv sx̌iƛ'xn Cr sx̌it'mšn.

*x̌əm' *dry.* Li x̌əm'p *dry out* Th ʔesx̌əm ESh tx̌əm'ep *(berries) dry up on bush,* tx̌mp'úseʔ *id.* Cb x̌əm' Ka Sp x̌am' Sp x̌mip *dried.* – Cf. PS *x̌aw.

*x̌əmạl see *xəmạl/y.

*x̌əp *to pile up flat objects.* Li x̌əpn Th x̌pəm Sh x̌pem [Cb x̌ax̌əpaʔ *flat cornhusk bag*] Cv x̌píc'aʔm *pile limber objects (eg. blankets) flat* Sp hecx̌pmilš *they're all piled up,* nx̌pmew's *it's layered, doubled* Cr x̌ep.

*x̌ap *to chew, crunch, gnaw.* Sh x̌epm Cr x̌ip *gnaw to destroy (as beaver, mouse, squirrel).*

*x̌əp' *to sew/lace up, fasten together.* Th x̌p'əm *sting, stick w. pin or needle* Sh x̌p'em *stitch up, join together* Cv tx̌p'iwnt *sew up* Sp x̌p'nten *to baste,* x̌p'min *lace* Cr x̌ep' *button, fasten together, sew.*

*x̌aq' *to pay a reward.* Li x̌aq' *pay for job or service* Th x̌áq'm *pay* Sh x̌eq'm *pay for cure* Cb x̌aq'n *pay* Cv x̌aq'm *id.* Ka x̌aq' *pay for work or favors received* Sp x̌aq'n *pay* Cr x̌aq' *pay reward.*

*x̌əs(-t) *good.* Th x̌əst *pleasant, tasty* ESh x̌əx̌sekst *good shot, marksman* Cb x̌əst Cv x̌ast; x̌saqs *good food* Ka x̌es *feel good,* x̌est *good,* x̌seɫx̌ʷ *good house* Sp x̌is *feel good, be well,* x̌est *good* Cr x̌es *be well, good,* x̌est *good.*

*x̌iw' *raw.* Li (s)x̌iw' Th ʔesx̌íw' Sh cx̌iw Cb ʔacx̌íw' Cv cx̌iw' Sp hecx̌íw' Cr x̌iw'.

*x̌əy I *to heat.* [Li x̌əz'p *throw off sparks*] Sh x̌yem; x̌yx̌eyt *hot,* tx̌yesxnm' *to heat stones* Cr sx̌íyeʔst *cooking stones.*

*x̌əy II, NIS *x̌yum *big, large.* Li Th x̌zum Sh x̌yum Cr x̌áy'x̌iy' *one is large.*

*x̌y-awt *one period (day, year) removed.* Th piʔx̌áwt *tomorrow,* spiʔx̌áwt *yesterday* Sh pəx̌yewt *yesterday, tomorrow* (depending on proclitic) Cb t'x̌yawt *last year,* t'x̌yawtwíl'x *next year* Cv t'x̌iwtwílx *next year, a year from now.*

*x̌əʕ *breeze, draught.* Th x̌ʕəp *breeze starts up* Sh x̌ʕx̌eʕt *draughty, windy,* x̌ʕilx *become windy-cold,* x̌ʕusm *fan the face* Cb sx̌aʕp *south wind,* cx̌aʕpmíx *wind blowing* Cv x̌ʕap *air,* x̌x̌aʕúsnt *fan sb.* Ka x̌a *cool,* x̌aáp *get cool, wind cools* Sp x̌aʕ *drafty,* x̌ax̌aʕústn *fan* Cr x̌aʕ *to fan,* x̌eʕigʷ(-t) *be full of holes so air can pass through,* sx̌aʕp *breeze.*

x̌ʷ

*x̌ʷəc' *to force, coax, insist.* x̌ʷəc'n *force, coax sb.,* x̌ʷə́c'x̌ʷc'ət *pushy* Th x̌ʷəc'tes *coax, force sb.,* x̌ʷə́c'x̌ʷəc't *forceful, stubborn* Sh x̌ʷc'ilx *insist (on doing st.),* x̌ʷicx̌ʷəc't *forceful, persistent* Cb x̌ʷəc'x̌ʷəc'n'aw'áx̌ʷ *argue with e.o.* [x̌ʷc'am *break st. (as stick)* Cv nx̌ʷec'cín' *I ate food behind his back*].

*s-x̌ʷľ-axkn *buck deer.* Li sx̌ʷl/ľaxkn Th sx̌ʷy'exkn Sh sx̌ʷlexkn Cb sx̌ʷəľakn Cv sx̌ʷľixkn Sp sx̌ʷľeščn' Cr sx̌ʷaľíscn.

*x̌ʷiƛ' *to crack, break st. (wood, branches).* Sh x̌ʷit'm *crack st.* Cv x̌ʷiƛ'nt *break st.* Sp č'ɫx̌ʷiƛ'is *he broke sticks for gambling.*

*x̌ʷən-t *fast.* Th x̌ʷənt; x̌ʷənstes *speed st. up* Sh x̌ʷent; x̌ʷn'stes *speed st. up* [Cv sx̌ʷnitkʷ (geogr. *Kettle Falls,* nx̌ʷntkʷitkʷ (geogr.) *Columbia river*] Cr x̌ʷen *hurry to get at,* (Nicodemus) x̌ʷent *to hurry.* – Cf. the KWA forms quoted under PS ***ląxʷ, x̌ʷạl**.

*x̌ʷup-t *weak, stupid, useless (person).* Li sx̌ʷuptxʷ *weak, stupid* Sh sx̌ʷuptx *dumb, stupid, good-for-nothing* Cb x̌ʷupt *stupid* Cv x̌ʷupt *weak,* sx̌ʷuptx *id., useless (person)* Ka Sp x̌ʷupt *lazy, indolent* Cr x̌ʷup *be inefficient, careless,* x̌ʷupt *inept.*

*x̌ʷt-aɫp *cow parsnip, Indian rhubarb.* Sh x̌ʷtaɫp *Indian rhubarb* Cb x̌ʷux̌ʷtáɫp *cow parsnip* Cv x̌ʷx̌ʷtiɫp *Indian rhubarb/celery* Ka x̌ʷteɫp (Carlson-Flett) *cow parsnip, Heracleum lanatum, rhubarb* Sp x̌ʷx̌ʷteɫp *id.*

*x̌ʷəy *sharp.* Li x̌ʷə́zx̌ʷəz; nx̌ʷzusm *sharpen (a blade)* Th x̌ʷəzx̌ʷə́zt; nx̌ʷzúses *sharpen* Sh x̌ʷyx̌ʷeyt; x̌ʷyusm' *sharpen* Cb x̌ʷíyx̌ʷiyt Cv x̌ʷyx̌ʷayt Ka x̌ʷix̌ʷí Sp x̌ʷix̌ʷíyt.

*(s-)x̌ʷəʕʷ(-al-mxʷ) *fox.* Li (s)x̌ʷʕʷalxʷ Th x̌ʷeyxʷ WSh x̌ʷʕʷelmx ESh x̌ʷʕʷélexʷ (< -mxʷ) Cb sx̌ʷəʕʷx̌ʷʕʷ Cv x̌ʷʕʷilxʷ Ka x̌ʷa:x̌ʷaá Sp sx̌ʷóx̌ʷo Cr sx̌ʷéʕʷx̌ʷeʕʷ, (Nicodemus) sx̌ʷéʕʷx̌ʷeʕʷ. – Borr. in Ck sx̌ʷəwel

y

*yukʷaʔ *wart.* Li zəʔuʔkʷ Th sc'əc'úxʷeʔ Sh s(y)əkʷeyúkʷeʔ Cb syuʔyuʔkʷúl Cv syaʔyá(ʔ)kʷaʔ, sy'ay'ákʷaʔ Sp sy'ey'úkʷeʔ.

*yul *thick (cylindrical).* Th zuyt *stout, stocky, of large diameter* Sh yult *thick (as rope),* yul(l)qʷ *thick (tree, pole)* Cv yult *thick tree,* yulp *thick rope.*

*yəlxʷ *to wrap, cover.* Th ʔeszʔíxʷ *wrapped,* ziʔxʷetés *to wrap* ESh ylxʷum *wrap st. around st.* Cv ylxʷntim *cover, wrap* Sp yeĺxʷn *cover, drape,* niĺxʷús *one of his eyes is covered.*

*yəƛ̓ *to rub.* Li zəƛ̓n *rub st. on a washboard* Th zəƛ̓tes *rub, scrub, scour* Sh yt̓em *id.* Cb yəƛ̓usn *sharpen (blade).*

*yənixʷ *waterhemlock, poison parsnip.* Th znixʷ *waterhemlock (Cicuta douglasii)* Sh ynixʷ *id.* Cb yənixʷ *poison parsnip* Cv ynixʷ *wild parsnip (poisonous).*

*yaq̓ *to peep, peer.* Li záq̓il Th (n)záq̓ix *peep over (st. high)* Sh yeq̓lx *peep over (as into well)* Cr daq̓ *peer through cracks.*

*yis-t *to camp overnight, spend the night.* Sh (c)yist; ʔex k yistəxʷ *goodnight, sleep well* Cr des *camp (Nicodemus sdest to camp, camping),* sídist *night passes, spend night.*

*yəʕ I *to gather (esp. of people); many, all.* Li (n)ziʔzəʕ *each, every one,* [zəʕpiw's *Sunday*] Th zaʕt *assembled, having arrived at a place (people),* zaʕpə́m *assemble, gather (things) in a particular place,* zʕəm *assemble (things),* zʕəp *gather at a spot (esp. just arrived)* Sh cyʕap *arrive (from far)* Cb syaʕʕ *gathering, meeting,* yaʕpqín' *lots, many* Cv yaʕ *people (have)gather(ed),* cyaʕp *arrive here,* cyaʕ / yayáʕt *all* Ka iyaʔmstén *I gather it,* esiyáʔ *all, every* Sp yaʕ *gathered,* hecyáʔ *it's everything* Cr yaʕ *assemble, be many, gather, crowd,* y̓aʕpqin' *be many, much.*

*yəʕ II *war spear.* Sh xyeʕ *lance (6-8 ft. long)* Cv nyaʕ *war spear.*

*yəʕʷ *strong, intensive, violent.* Th zoʕʷzóʕʷt/zuʔzúʔt *strong* Sh yʕʷyuʕʷt *id.,* yʕʷilx *exert o.s., do one's utmost* Cb yáʕʷyəʕʷt *hard (work, rain)* Cv ywyaʕʷt *strong* Ka yo:yót *id.* Sp yoyót *id.,* yoyoscút *exert o.s.*

γ

*γac (red.) *sparrowhawk.* ESh γeγcγəc *kestrel, sparrowhawk* Cv γγʼicγc.

*γəl *strong, vigorous.* Li ʕálʕəl Th γəlγelt/ʕelγəlt/ʕəlʕal/ʕəlʕilt; ʕliyx *run as fast as one can* Sh γlγalt *strong, brave,* γlγəláłcʼe *brave* Ka élʼi(st) *try hard* Cr ȝarʼ *firm, strong.*

ʕ

*ʕat (red.) *unid. bird of prey.* Li ʕatʕət *a large mountain bird* Sh ʕetʕət *mosquito hawk (?)* Cb háthat *bull hawk (prairie falcon or pigeon hawk?).*

*ʕəc *to tie, knot.* Li ʕəcn Th ʕactés Sh ʕcem (also *knit nets*) Cb hacn Cv ʕacám Ka aác-, yesa:cím *I tie it* Sp ʕacntés *he tied it* Cr ʕec.

*ʕələxʷ *stiff, frozen.* Sh ʕluxʷ *stiff (material)* Cb halʼxʷ *freeze.*

*ʕiƛ' *to take a bite.* Li ʕíƛ'in Cb ʔachaƛ'stús *gnaw,* shhəƛ'mix *id.* Cv ʕaƛ'ám. – Cf. PS *x̌iƛ'.

*ʕiw/ʕʷ *to pile up by throwing, dump.* [Li ʕawʼilx *get together, have a meeting*] Th ʕíwes *pile up* Sh ʕiwns *id.,* ESh xʕiʕʷntm *pl. are put in jail* Cr ʕigʷ *throw pl. objects.* – There is a √*ʕay in Li ʕázan Sh ʕeym *pile up.*

*ʕəx̌ I *to lace up.* Li ʕəx̌n *lace up hide for tanning on frame* Th ʕax̌tés Sh ʕx̌em *string up (a hide)* Cv cʕax̌ *laced,* kʕax̌á/íc'aʔ *lace on the outside* Sp ʕax̌ntén *bind up,* ʕax̌ic'aʔtn *hide stretcher* Cr ʕax̌ *wrap string evenly.* – Cf. *ʕʷəx̌ʷ.

*ʕəx̌ II *to scratch.* Th ʕáx̌leʔxʷ *to harrow,* ʕx̌əp *harrowed* Sh ʕx̌ntes *make furrow for planting* Cv ʕax̌nt *to scratch,* ʕáx̌laʔxʷnt *harrow the soil.*

ʕʷ

*ʕʷisx̌, *wisx̌ *robin.* Sh wswísx̌a Cb sx̌ax̌w'ísx̌aʔ/x̌ax̌w'ísx̌ax̌w'is Cv ʕʷisws Cr wésx̌ax̌.

*ʕʷəx̌ʷ, wəx̌ʷ *to lace up.* Th ʔeswóx̌ʷ *woven/laced back and forth,* wox̌ʷetés *lace up (shoes)* ESh tʕʷx̌ʷikn'xn *shoelaces* Sp ʕʷox̌ʷ *strung up,* ʕʷox̌ʷntén *string (a wire),* ʔox̌ʷcínšn'tn *moccasin string* Cr ʕʷax̌ʷ *stringlike object extends.* – Cf. *ʕəx̌ I. Sp ʕʷo- > ʔo- in ʔox̌ʷcínšn'tn paralleled by Ka ʔolín s.v. *ʕʷəl-an(k).

LEXICAL SUFFIXES

Salish has a number of suffixes for most of which an original (often somatic) meaning can be established, these meanings being extended and/or transferred in different ways in the individual languages. Their relation to the root is limitative (goal-object, shape, instrument, locality, manner, etc), sometimes they play the role of classifiers, in a few cases they have been grammaticalized (see comment to PS *-mix, *-was). In the lists which follow only the original meanings and some common extensions are given. Where possible, suffixes are quoted in their stressed form.

Between root and suffix a connective element *-(a)l- or (less often) *-aw- may appear; in the y-languages the former has the shape -ay- or -i-, and these y-forms are widespread in Salish (cf. Intro 3C).

PROTO-SALISH SUFFIXES

*-cin (-ucin, -uc, -c) *mouth,* see PCS *cucin. Be -uc *oral, orifice,* nu-√-uc *mouth,* -ał-uc *door(way)* Cx -usin Sl -u:θn Se -ucin Sq -c Cw -ay-cin, -aʔc *edge* Ck -a:θil, -a:y-θíl Sm -aθn, -ay-θn, -ay:-sə(-tn) Sn -aθin Cl -ucn Ld -ucid Tw -ucad Ch -ucin, -acn Ti -(u)cin ~ Li -c, -cin; -acín' *to eat,* -ał'-c *food* Th -ucin, -ce, -c Sh Cb Cv Ka Sp Cr -cin.

*-íc'aʔ *hide, blanket, clothes.* Be -l-ic' *exterior surface, skin, bark, side,* -ul-iic/-ul-ic' *clothing* Sl -ic'a *vêtement* Sq -ay-c'a(ʔ), -ic'a *clothes* Cw -ə/iç'eʔ *strands or fibre, cloth* Ck -ic'ə/e *clothes* Sn -iç'əʔ *cloth* Cl -c'aʔ in łuc'áʔŋ *take off clothes* Ld -ic'aʔ *clothe, wear, support from shoulder,* -al-ic'aʔ *clothing,* -ul-ic'aʔ *blanket* Tw -ic'a *blanket, garment,* -ul-ic'a *blanket,* -al-c'a in ʔaskʷtəx̌álc'a *ripped clothes* Ch -ic'a *blanket, clothes,* -al-ic'a *blanket* Ti (Haeberlin) -ic'a *id.* ~ Li -ic'a *clothing, covering, skin* Th -ic'eʔ *outer covering* Sh -ic'eʔ

203

hide, surface Cb -ic'a? *body (outside)* Cv -ic'a? *body cover, outside cover* Ka -ic'e? *all around* Sp -ic'e? *blanket, outside covering* Cr -ic'e? *all around, all over.* – Cf. PS *c'i? and QUI -c'a *blanket, clothes.*

*-ak, *-ák-a?, *-ak-is(t) *hand, lower arm.* Be -ak Cx -čis in ?úpa?ǯa?čis *mittens, gloves* Se -ači Sq -ač Cw -cə/es Ck -cəs Sm -čis, -səs Sn -sis (improductive also -čəs) Cl -cis Ld -ači? Tw -ači Ch (Tenino dial.) -aka, -aki, -ika, -ka Ti -ači(?) ~ Li -aka?, -akst Th -eke? *digit, branch,* -ekst *hand* Sh -ekst; -eke? *branch, antler, implement* Cb -akst, -aks(n) Cv -ikst Ka Sp -ečst Cr -ičs *hand entire,* -ičt *hand, finger.*

*-ik(n) *back.* Be -ik Cx -ag-ič, -ičin Sl -ag-ič Se -il-ič Sq -č, formative -ičn Cw -əcn Ck -(əw-)ic Sm -íč, -əw-eč, -ew-əč Sn -ew-ič Cl -əw'-ič, -u?-eč, -əw-e?č Ld -w-ič; -ič *surface, covering* Tw -ičə/ad Ch -ičan Ti -ičn ~ Li -ikn (less productive than n-√-k *back, middle*) Th -ikn' Sh Cb -ikn Cv -ik(n') Ka Sp -ičn/n', -ič Cr -ičn'.

*-kʷa see -qʷa.

*-kʷup *fire(wood).* Cx -ał-kʷup in qʷə́natkʷup *ashes* Sl -aw-kʷəp Se -ikʷup, -akʷup, -ičup Sq -ikʷup (productive), ši-čəp *firedrill,* yəqʷ-l-čp *put wood on the fire* Cw Ck -əl-cəp Sm -ečəp Sn -čəp Ld -čup, -(al-)icup Tw -čup, -ay-qʷp *wood* Ch -ičap Ch (Tenino dial.) -ikp ~ Li -(í)kʷp, xʷuľ-kʷəp *to drill fire* Sh xʷul-əkp *match* Cb -kʷp, -at-kʷup Cv xʷul-kp *firedrill* Cr -kʷəp.

*-lup see ***-nup.**

*-alaq *wind, weather.* Se λ'əqmálaq *north wind,* q'i?xʷaláq *south wind,* čawaláq *east wind,* kʷasálaq *warm weather,* č'əmálaq *cold weather* [Ch łə́čiyaq- *wind blows*] ~ Ka chałq *south, southern* Sp s?anłq *summer.*

*-í/álaqs *clothes.* Tw -ilaqs in yalbílaqsəd *cedar bark skirt* Ch -ilqs *skirt* ~ Li -aľ(a)qs Th -eľqs Sh -eľqs Cb -alqs Cv -alqs *dress, woman's clothes* Ka Sp -alqs Cr -aľqs.

*-i/als(t) *stone, rock, round object.* Be -lst Sl -ays Se -als in xiy'áls *stone, rock,* sc'úmals *whetstone* (but cacxíls *pebbles*) Sq -uy?s *large object, piece, chunk* Cw -als *round object (as eggs, potatoes, oranges),* k'wǝnt'als *rock, basalt* Ck -a:ls *spherical object, fruit* Sm -als *round thing, rock, fruit* Ld -ilc *round object* Tw -ilas *hard, round object,* q'wǝl?ílas *cooking stone* Ch -is, -i?s, a?s *round object* Ti (Haeberlin) -a:ls *stone* [M.T. Thompson -e/alč *round thing*] ~ Li -alc, -al'st Th -als̩; -elst *knife,* -ey?st/-i?st *stone* Sh -elst; -qn-i?st *shot,* ESh scǝcǝméye?st *buckshot* Cb -a?st *stone* Cv -i/a?st *arrow, bullet* Cr -els *round object (?),* -i?st *rounded surface, rock.*

*-i/al(t) *child.* Be -lt Se -ǝlt in mǝna?ǝlt *give birth,* -al-il in yašǝnalít *pack baby on back* Sq -ay?ł, -íał, [-ułł] Ck -ǝł, [-a:łł Sm -a:ł, -ay'ł Sn -ał] Cl -ay't, [-ú?ił] Ld -i?ł Tw -ał, -i?l- in bidí?lǝb *leave/abandon a baby* Ch -aył, -ayl-, -i(?)ł [Ti -ǝ?uł] ~ Li -alt, n-√-il't; -ay'ł (borr. fr. Sq) Th -il't, -iyt, -il'eh Sh -elt, -il't, -il'e Cb -alt Cv -il(a?)t Ka Sp -elt Cr -ilt.

*-átc'i/a? *meat, body.* Ld -ałc'i *meat* Tw -ałc'i in st'alátc'i *venison* (lit. *sliced meat*) Ch -(ał-)c'i *meat, flesh, body, game* ~ Li -ałc'a *meat, inside of body; mind, thoughts* Th -ełc'i? *body, carcass, flesh, meat; seat of emotions and intelligence* Sh -ełc'e *meat, game, inside; character* Cb -ałc'a? in ntǝlátc'a?n *clean fish or game* Cv -itc'a? *single enclosure, body,* lqítc'a?n *pluck feathers.* – Cf. PS *c'i?.

*-ałp *tree, bush, plant.* Be -ałp (but p'anítp, see PS ***p'u/an**) Cw Ms Ck -ǝłp Sm -i/ełč Sn Cl -iłč Ch -(n)ł, -ay-nł ~ Li -ałp (improductive) Th -ełp, -eł, -unł Sh -ełp Cb -ałp Cv -iłp Ka Sp Cr -ełp. – Cf. PCS -*ay'.

*-mix^w, ***-mix** *life force, "mana", person(s), animals, world, land, river; woman's breast, milk,* ***-ul-mix^w** *earth, land, ground,* see PS ***tmix^w**, ***qal-mix^w**. Be -mx *inhabitant, native of,* -al-mx *breast,* -ul-mx *land, ground, floor,* staltmx *chief* Cx túmiš *man,* tátčumix^w *animal,* ?íq^wumix^w *sweep floor* Sl -umiš *appearance,* -mix^w *floor, bottom* Se -umiš *resemble,* stúmiš *man,* tatčúlmix^w *animal,* q'ǝlq'ǝlúlmix^w *dew,* cilúlmix^w *floor* (but ?íq^wmix^wtn *broom,* cf. Cx) Sq

-mixʷ, -miš *people, tribe,* stə́lməxʷ *Indian, person* Cw
-(əl-)məxʷ *group, people; breast, milk* Ck -məxʷ *people,
person,* -a:-məxʷ *person,* -a:l-məxʷ *tribe,* słeq'əmək *a large
portion of the earth* Sm -(el-)ŋəxʷ *being, living thing, person
(?)* Sn -ŋəxʷ *being; breast* Cl -(ay-)ŋ(ə)xʷ *in* ʔəcłtayŋxʷ
person, niyac'á?uŋəxʷ *different people;* sqəyayŋəxʷ *any large
tree,* st'ayŋ(ə)xʷ *medicine,* č'ac'áy'ŋəxʷ *milk a cow* Ld -bixʷ
homogeneous group, -al-bixʷ *earth, land; milk, teat, suckle,*
[-ulgʷədx *land*] Tw -bixʷ *people,* -al-bixʷ *settlement, people,*
-u/al-bəš *ground, floor,* -al-bəš *milk* in sqʷistálbəš (qʷist
cow) Ch -(ał/y-)tmš *land, country,* -(u/a)-mš *place,* qʷumš
breast of female, milk Ti (Haeberlin) -uš *people,* -e/ouš *place,*
(Thompson) -e/əw'š, -iw'əš *id.* ~ Li -məx *person,* -al-mixʷ
earth, land, soil; breast, udder, -ul-m'əxʷ/-lumxʷ/-ul'axʷ
earth, land, soil, [-ał-məx *belly, sack*] Th -emx *person,
people,* -emxʷ *teat, breast,* [-eł-mx *looseweave basket, bag*],
-ule?xʷ/-ul'exʷ/-uye?xʷ *land, earth, ground,* -uym'xʷ *id.* Sh
-m(ə)x *person, people,* xp'e?m'xʷm *to milk,* cxłp'e?m'xʷ *to
nurse,* -ul'əxʷ, -ule?xʷ *land, ground, soil* Cb -mixʷ *person,
man,* -(ə)xʷ *resident,* -tsamxʷ *breast,* -ul'əxʷ *land, ground,
soil* Cv -mix *person,* -ula?xʷ *earth, land,* [-ilxʷ *person; coat,
body covering*] Ka Sp -ule?xʷ *ground* Sp -ixʷ, -iš *people,
residents* Cr -əmx *people,* -il-mx *person, man,* -ul'əmxʷ
ground. – Grammaticalized in the 1 sing. object suffix of the
causative paradigm Se Sq -mš Ld -bš NSt -ŋəs Tw -beš Ch -mš
Ti -wəš Li -mx and in the 3 pl. subject suffix in the WSh
progressive form ʔex γ-s-√-mx *they are ...ing* (cf. the use of
French *on* (< Latin *homo*) for 1st person sg. eg. in *on s'en fiche,*
or in *on se défend* in answer to the question *ça va?,* and for
general 3rd person). The suffix includes the t- of the
independent form in the Cb Sp Cr forms under PS *qal-mixʷ
and in Be staltmx *chief* (for the meaning cf. Ka iləmíxʷ *id.* vs.
Ch ʔílamiš- *Indian*), see PCS *tal-mixʷ.

*-áni/a? *ear (side),* see PS *t'ana?. Be -ik-an; -an
temple, collarbone Cx Sl -a?na Se -ana Sq -ay-a?n, -ay-an Cw
-ən'ə Ck -é:lí:-ye, -əle Sm -əné?, -ən' Ld -(a)di?, --əl-di? Cl -a?n,
-ay-n Tw -adi Ch -án'(i)-, -a?n', -na? Ti -áni?, -án'i ~ Li

n-√-((a)l-)ana? Th -en'i(h) Sh -ene Cb -ə/ana? Cv -ina? Ka -ene?, -əne? Sp -ene? Cr -ine?, ene?.

*-anak *belly, stomach, anus, buttocks, tail; excrement,* see PS ***mnak**. Be -ank *vertical aspect of body (front side),* -nnak *excrements* Cx -nič *tail, anus, buttocks* Sl -nič *buttocks, rear, root* Se -nač *bottom (in any sense), buttocks* Sq -nač (formative) Cw -nə/eč *bottom, base, root,* -əl'-nəč *droppings* Ck -(ə́)ləc *bottom,* -ələc *dung* Sm -nəč *bottom, tail* Sn -neč *tail, rear end* Ld -(a)dəč *abdomen, belly* Tw -adač *belly,* tə́l-nəc *manure* Ch -inači-, -nč, (Tenino dial. -naki-, -nk) *rump, buttocks, hips* Ti (Haeberlin) -aneč *belly* ~ Li -an'(a)k, -ana?k, -ank *belly, inside, hillside* Th -ene(?)k, -enk *belly* Sh -enk *belly, hollow, curved surface,* -en'ək *dung (of herbivores),* kʷə́ł-nek *id. (of carnivores)* Cb -ank *belly, flat surface* Cv -ink *stomach, inside, side, sidehill* Ka -enč *stomach* Sp -eneč *id., wall* Cr -inč *hollow, belly.*

*-nup, *-lup *ground, foundation, floor.* Sq -(ay-)nup; łx̌ənptn *floor* Cw -ənəp Ck -iləp Sm (borr.) -ənəp [Sn -ənəkʷ Cl -ənəkʷ, -ənukʷ-] Ld -(i)dup Ch -inp ~ Li -ay'lup/ -an'lup/-ał'nup/-ilap Th -eyep Sh -ił'əp Cv -ilp Cr -ilup.

*-anis *tooth,* see PCS ***yə-nis**. [Be al-ic] Sl -nəs Se -nis, -ul-nis Sq -ans Cw -əl-nəs Ck -əlís, -ə́l:əs Sm -ə́nəs Sn -nəs Cl -i?-nis Ld -dis Tw -adis, -ads, -al-dis Ch -yanisi, -(ya)ns; -nis *mouth, jaw, cheek* Ti (Haeberlin) -ans ~ Li -qan'is; -anis *edge* Th -enis Sh x-√-en's [Cv -is, -ys Ka Sp -eys] Cr -ins.

*-ánaxʷ *season, salmon, year, weather,* see PS ***kanaxʷ**. Be -l-a(n)xʷ *years* Cx Sl ǯanxʷ *fish, salmon* Se syanxʷ *dog salmon* Sq -aw-anəxʷ*year(s),* hi-ú-nəxʷ *(period of) big waves* Cw -əwu:nxʷ *years,* heylénxʷ *autumn* Ck təmhilélxʷ *id.* Cl qʷqʷa?án'xʷ *call for bad weather* Ld -(al-)adxʷ *year,* ?uládxʷ *catch salmon,* s?uládxʷ *salmon (generic)* Ch -anuxʷ *years,* -alaxʷ *id., sky, weather* ~ Li -l-anxʷ, -inxʷ *weather, wind,* -as-z-anəxʷ *year* Th -s-z-enxʷ *id.* Sh -t-y-enxʷ-m *years* Cr -inxʷ *weather.* – Cf. KWA hnxʷila *fish for humpback salmon* (LR no. 2457). Sh Cv Sp

-nuxʷ *be caught, affected by some (usually natural) phenomenon)* do not belong here.

    *-ap *bottom, base, rear.* [Sl -ay-ip *cuisse*] Ck -əp in sθiyəp *loincloth* Sm -(əw-)eč *bottom, rump, tail* Sn -ew'eč *bottom* Cl xʷikʷʷuʔáčŋ *diaper* Ld -ap *bottom, base, buttocks* Tw -ap *rear end, behind, tail* Ch (Tenino dial.) -ap *base,* [Ch -aps *backside, buttocks*] ~ Li -ap *back part* Th -ep *bottom,* -épeʔ *hip, buttocks, stump* Sh -ep *buttocks, bottom, under, behind* Cb -ap *base, bottom* Cv -ip *id.* Sp -ep(st) Cr -ip *bottom (non-somatic), after, behind.* – Cf. ***-up-s, *-up-aʔ.**

    *-up-s, *-úp-aʔ *tail,* see PS ***s-up-s, *s-up-aʔ.** Sq -iʔ-ups Tw -ups in qʷʷilʔúpsəbəd *tail,* x̌ítups *eagle-tail fan* Ch -ups, -ips, -(y)al-ps; -apsi- *backside, buttocks* Th -upeʔ; -ups *anus* Sh -ups, -upeʔ Cb Cv Ka Cr -ups. – Cf. ***-ap.**

    *-aps(m) *neck.* Be -apsm *(side of) neck.* Sq -apsm Cw -əpsə/em Ck -əpsm Sm Sn -ečsŋ Cl -ačšŋ Ld -apsəb Tw -apsab Ch -apsm Ti -əhsəw ~ Li (Haeberlin 277) -apsm Th -eps, -epsém, -epsm, -épse Sh -eps Cb -al-ps Cv -ips Ka -el-ps Sp -elps(t) Cr -eps *neck all around,* -il-ps *back of neck.*

    *-qin *head (hair, top; throat, voice, language).* See PCS ***-iqʷ,** which is used for *head* in Be Cx Se Sq Cw Sm Sn (and also in Li), ***qin** occurring productively with other meanings and with the meaning *head* in individual words only. Cx -qin *tongue, language,* x̌ʷə́ƛ'qin *pillow* Sl -qin *langue (organe, instrument de communication)* Se -qin-m *speak (a language),* x̌ʷəƛ'qín *pillow* Sq -qin *hair; throat, language* Cw -qe/ən *throat, voice, etc.* Ck -əql *id.,* -qə́yl *on top* Sm -qin' *id.* Sn -qən *hair, pharynx* Ld -qin Tw -qəd; -al-qəd *hair* Ch -aqi *voice, talking, language* Ti -íqín ~ All IS -qin (improductive in Li).

    *-qs(n) *nose (point, end),* see PCS ***məqsn.** Be -l-x̌s Sq -qs Cw -qs(n), -əl-qsn Ck -əqs(l), -əl-qs(l) Sm -(ə)qs(n), -él-əqsn Sn Cl -əqsn Ld -qs Tw -ə/aqs Ch -qs Ti -qs, Haeberlin also -čs ~ Li -aqs Th Sh -eqs Cb -əl-qs Cv Ka -(a)qs Sp -aqs Cr -i/aʔqs; -al-qs *end.*

*-qʷa, *-kʷa *water,* see PS *qʷuʔ and PIS *sawɬkʷa. Cx Se -kʷu Sq -aɬ-qʷu; staqʷ *water, river,* ʔáyaɬqʷ *beach* Cw -əɬ-qə, -əɬ-cə Ck -əɬ-ce *unclear liquid* Sm -eɬ-sə/e, -aɬ-s *id.* Sn -eɬ-sə Ld -aɬ-qʷu Tw -akʷ, -(al-)qʷu Ch -či, -iɬ-či Ch (Tenino dial.) -ki, -kʷu Ti -qi, -qe, -aɬ-qi ~ Li -(at-)kʷaʔ, -at-qʷaʔ Th -kʷu, -et-kʷəw Sh -(et-)kʷe Cb -(at-)kʷ Cv -(it-)kʷ; -al-qʷaʔ *rivershore* Ka Sp -(et-)kʷ Cr -kʷeʔ.

*-us I *face,* see PCS *mʔus. Be -us Cx -us; -aw-us *eye* Sl -aw-əs *id.* Se -us; -al-us *eye* Sq -us; -ayʔ-us *eye* Cw -as; -al-əs *eye* Ck -a(:)s; -a:l-əs *eye* Sm -a(:)s Sn -as Cl -us; -aʔy-ús *eye* Ld -us; -al-us *eye* Tw -us; -ay(a)s *eye* Ch -us Ti -us; -ay(i)s *eye* ~ All IS -us.

*-us II *fire.* Be -al-us Sm -əw's(əʔ) Sn -əw'sə [Ti --ay(i)s] ~ All IS -us.

*-ásk'ay' *throat, breath, (voice, song),* see PS *ʔask'ay'. Ti -e/usč'ey' *breath* ~ Li n-√-ask'aʔ *song* Th -esk'iʔ *id.* Sh -esk'e *name* Cb -ask'iʔt *breath* Cr -isč'ey't *breath, voice.* – Cf. QUI -iskʷa *language.*

*-txʷ *lodging; (skin or bark covering of lodging > sheet, plumage, etc.; frame of lodging > rib)* see PS *ʔuɬ-(t)xʷ. Be ʔastxʷ *be inside,* ʔustxʷ *go inside,* caltxʷ *bark of red cedar* Cx qáʔqiyawtxʷ *log cabin,* ʔíy-atxʷ *roof* Sl -aw-txʷ Se -aw-txʷ, -aɬ-txʷ, -uɬ-txʷ; ʔíl-atxʷ/ʔil-ál-atxʷ *roof* Sq -awʔ-txʷ Cw -ə/ew'-txʷ Ms -ew-txʷ Ck -txʷ, -á(:)w-txʷ, -ál-txʷ, -el-txʷ Sm -ew-(t)xʷ Sn -ew'-txʷ Cl -aw'-txʷ, -uʔ-txʷ Ld -txʷ, -al-atxʷ, -al(ʔ)-txʷ, -ay-txʷ, --agʷ-txʷ *neighbor,* -al-xʷ *(animal) hide* Tw -al-txʷ, ʔalʔ-txʷ *he's in the house* Ch -utxʷ, -u/al-itxʷ, -lwil-txʷ Ti -txʷ, -aɬ-txʷ, -is-txʷ ~ All IS except Cb has citxʷ *house* (Cr cetxʷ); Cb stxʷul *house,* txʷúlc'aʔtn *sweathouse* seem to contain the item as a root-element. Li -atxʷ; -al-txʷ *outside surface, skin; rib,* -alxʷ *family* (xʷʔít-alxʷ *have a karge family*), -aw'-txʷ *house* (borr. fr. Sq) Th -eɬxʷ; -ey-etxʷ *fur, plumage, foliage; rib* Sh -eɬxʷ; -el'-txʷ *sheet-like object, skin, bark; rib* Cb -aɬxʷ Cv -iɬxʷ, diminutive -iɬ-aʔ-xʷ, -alxʷ *coat, body covering,* -ilxʷ *id., person (as member of a tribe or family group)* Ka -eɬxʷ; -elxʷ *skin, hide,* sənkʷélixʷ *guests,*

209

family (?) Sp -eɬxʷ *skin, hide, house,* -(el-)ixʷ/-(el-)iš *people, residents,* snkʷélixʷ *people, tribe* Cr -iɬxʷ; -ilxʷ *hide, skin, mat, covering.*

*-wil *canoe,* see PS *wil. Be -u/aɬ Sl -əgəɬ Sq -wiɬ Cw -əw-ɬ, -əxʷəɬ Ck -awəɬ, -aɬ, -əwi:ɬ Sm -əwəɬ, -aɬ Cl -əkʷɬ Cz wiɬ, wil- Ch -wil-, -wiɬ Ti -egiɬ, ekɬ ~ Li -wiɬ, -aw(i)ɬ Th -ewíɬ, -éwɬ Sh -əwíl', əw'iɬ, -ew'l, -ewɬ Cb -wíl Cv -iwl-, -iwɬ Ka -eul, -éʔuɬ Sp -ew'l, -ew'ɬ, -wiɬ Cr -gʷil.

*-was. The occurrences of this suffix are best summed up in three groups: (1) ***-iws** *body* (limited to CS), (2) ***-was**, ***-aws**, ***-i/al-was**, **-*i/an-was** *chest,* and (3) a suffix homophonous with (2), meaning *pair, mutual, middle, half* (see PS *was).

Group (1). *body.* Cx Sl Se Sq -iws Ck -i:ws Sm -iws, -ikʷ(ə)s Sn -iw's, -ikʷəs Cl -ikʷs, -iws Ch -iws *meat*; IS only Li -al'-iw's.

Group (2). *chest* Be -alus Cx Se Sq -inas Cw -inəs Ck -i:ləs Sm Sn Cl -inəs; Sm Sn -enkʷəs *stomach* Cl yénəwəs *heart* Ld -idgʷas; yədwas *heart* Tw yadwás *id.* (see PS *yə-) Ti (Haeberlin) -al-i-gas *breast* Ti yingas CV *heart* Si "ye:nega:'s" CV *id.* (see PS *yə-) ~ Li n-√-anwas *heart, inside, mind,* pt-ínus-m *think* Th -eynəws *interior,* -inus *mind* Sh -ews *surface (table, shelf, road),*-eləs *chest, character, floor,* pt-inəs-m *think* Cb -ələwas [Sp -els *front, feeling*] Cr -i/el-gʷes *heart, stomach; property,* [-elwís *about (locally)*].

Group (3). *pair, mutual, middle, half.* Be -n-al-us (inv. < *-l-an-us) *pieces, (being) between,* ɬnus *two* Sq ʔán?us *id.* Ld -gʷas, -waʔs *pair* Tw -ayalwəs, -ilwəs *together* Ch -alawas, -élawas *middle, junction,* -alaws *group of interconnected members,* -uws *middle,* [-niwš, -uš, wš *reciprocal*] Ti -i/agʷas *middle, center* ~ Li ʔán'was *two,* n-√-in'was *middle,* -aw's *id.; collective,* -əl'-was *in half, in/down the middle* Th -ew's *waist* Sh -ews *half, middle, mutual* Cb -aw's *middle, center* Cv -iw'(a?)s *id.* Ka -e?us *middle, between,* [-elis *reciprocal*] Sp -ew's(t) *middle, half, center* Cr -iw'es *between, together, be in contact.* –

Grammaticalized in the Sq reciprocal suffix -nəw'as *each other.*

    *-xan *foot, leg,* see PCS ***yə-xən.** Cx Sl Se -šin Sq -šn Cw -š(e)n Ck -xl Sm -s/šn Sn -sn Cl -sán Ld -šad Tw -(al-)šəd Ch -šan Ti -šn ~ Li -xn, -xín (in words for footwear), -xán in s̩k̩ʷə̩lk̩ʷə̩lxán *swan* (Fountain dial.) Th -xn, -xe, -x Sh -xen Cb -xn Cv -xan Ka Sp Cr -šin.

    *-xʷc- *tongue,* see PS ***tixʷc.** Be -aliixc in ƛ'qalii(x)cm *stick out one's tongue* Sq -al-xʷcał (independently məqálxʷcał *tongue*) Ck -ə́xʷθə̓ł Sm -(í-)xʷsə̓ł Tw sdəxʷcáč *tongue* Li -alxʷcał (borr. fr. Sq) Th -íxʷec'k' (<-ixʷa?ck) *palate, roof of mouth (tongue* is tə́łe?) Sh -ixʷe?ck Cr -ipłtixʷcč. – For Sh inserted ***-a?-** cf. Cv -isa?xn *rocks* vs. Sh -esxn *id.* In Th the glottalization has been transferred to the final consonants.

    *-áx̌an *arm (side).* Cx -ax̌an, [-ay-ix̌] Se -l-ax̌an Sq -ay-ax̌a?n *arm;* -ax̌an *side* Cw -ə̓l'-ex̌n; -ə/ex̌n *side* Ck -ə̓l-éx̌l Sm Sn -ex̌n Cl -i?-ax̌n Ld Tw -ax̌ad Ch -ax̌an ~ Li -ax̌an Th -ex̌n, -éx̌e Sh -ex̌n, -epst-x̌n Cb Cv Ka -ax̌n Sp Cr -ax̌n,

    *-áx̌ʷac *chest,* see PS ***tax̌ʷac.** Tw -ax̌ʷac in šaw?áx̌ʷac *collarbone,* staláx̌ʷac *animal thorax* Ch -ax̌ʷc ~ Li -ax̌ʷac Th -ax̌ʷck Sh (Haeberlin 277) t-k'm-ax̌ʷck *collarbone* Cv -ax̌ʷck Ka -ax̌ʷcč Sp -ax̌ʷcčt.

    *-áyan *net, (fish)trap,* see PS ***?ax̌ʷ-ayan.** Sq -ay?i(n), -i?an? Cw -e?yən Ms -ə̓l'yən Ck -e꞉yəl, -iyəl, -əwyəl Cl ?ə̓kʷ'áy(ə)n *scoopnet* Ld -aȝad Tw biwəqʷʷi?ad (stress?) *river gillnet* Ch -yan in ?áx̌ʷyanm *set out a large net* Cz ?ax̌ʷyn *fishing net* ~ Li -ayən Th -ezn, -eyn Sh -ey'n Cb məl'-áy'ən *bait,* ?áx̌ʷin *net (seine)* Cv ?ax̌ʷyn *id.* Cr -idən in kʷu-kʷe?-ídən *thou gottest a nibble.*

PROTO-COAST-SALISH SUFFIXES

*-λ'ak *belly,* see PCS λ'ak. Sl -λ'ač Ch -λ'ači-, -λ'č, Tenino dial. -λ'k, -λ'č.

-aq/-aq' *crotch, sexual organs.* Be -aax̌ Sl -aq' Sm -əq [Ld -aq *forked* eg. λ'iλ'pəq *underpants* (λ'əp *beneath*)] Ch -aq Ti -ə?əq, -eq'. – IS only Li n-√-il'-ə/aq *crotch,* n-√-aq *buttocks, behind, bottom.* – Cf. PS *s-pəlq.

*-iqʷ *head.* Be -iix̌ʷ Cx Sl -iqʷan Se -iqʷ(an) Sq -qʷ Cw -i/a?qʷ Ck Sm -iqʷ, -(əl-)i(?)qʷ Sn -iqʷ Cl -eqʷ Ld -al-iqʷ *hat* Tw -i(l)-qʷad. – IS only Li -qʷ *head, top, hair,* -il'-qʷ *head.* – Cf. PS *-qin.

*-ay' *tree, bush, plant.* Cx Sl Se -ay Sq -ay? Tw -ay Ti -i. – IS only Li -az'. Cf. PS *-aɬp.

PROTO-INTERIOR-SALISH SUFFIXES

*-ul *habitual.* Li Th Sh -uɫ Cb -ul in kɫƛ’a?ƛ’a?anmúl *jealous*, ḷ̣əmḷ̣əmmuḷ̣ *thief* Cv -uɫ Sp -uɫ in qʷl’qʷl’tuɫ *he talks a lot* Cr -ul. – To be distinguished from Li -?úl Th Sh -?úy *real.*

*-alk’ *string, rope.* Li -alk’ (also *surface*) Th -eyk’ Sh -el’k’ (also *skin, blanket*) Cr -əl’č̓ in spígʷəl’č̓ *man's belt.*

*-alqʷ *elongated cylindrical object (tree, log, stick).* Li Th -alqʷ Sh -elqʷ (also *rope, line, furrow*) [Cb məlk’ʷal’qʷ *bracelet*, -alqʷ-akst *forearm*] Cv -al(a?)qʷ Ka Sp Cr -alqʷ.

*-alxkn *quality of, relation to.* Li -alxkn, -ayxkn Sh -el’xkn Cv -ilxkn Sp -elščn (see PIS ***pəwalxkn**).

*-ɫniw’t *side of body.* Li -aɫniw’t; root-element in n-ɫniw’t *id.* Sh -ɫníw’t Cb -alniw’t Cv -ɫníwt Ka -ɫní?ut Sp -ɫniw’t Cr -eɫniw’ *position alongside,* [-aɫq’iw’t *shoulder*].

*-aɫq *harvest (berries, roots).* Th Sh -eɫq Cb -ɫq in snak’ʷúnɫqtn *farm, garden* Cv -aɫq, -áɫa?q Ka Sp -aɫq [Cr -stq]. – On the coast, Sq has -alč in ciqʷálč *dig potatoes* (Sh t’qeɫq *id.*).

*-aɫqʷəlt *throat.* Li -u/aɫqʷəlt Sh -eɫqʷl’t Cv -aɫqʷl(t) *mouth, throat, neck.*

*-ín’ak *weapon for shooting.* Li -in’(a)k Th -in’(e)k Sh -inək; ck’ʷinək *bow*, swlmin’k *gun* Cb -ink; swəlmin’k/swəlwəlmink *gun* Cv -ink, sck’ʷink/ck’ʷin’k *bow* Ka Sp -in’č.

*-ápla? *handle, attachment, rule.* Li -apl’, -ápla? *cheek*, -ápl’a-xn *heel* Th -epye? *cheek*, -epye?-xn *heel* Sh -íple? *handle* in tk’míple? *id.*; *rule, law, order* eg. tk’ʷnmíple? *institute a law*; -eple?-xn *heel* Cb -ápəla? *handle*, tk’ʷánpla?an *I led him w. a rope or by the hand*, tx̌áq’pla?an *I paid for it*;

k'm-ápələʔ-xn *heel* Cv -iplaʔ *handle* in tk'míplaʔ *id.*; *to order*, tkʷlstíplaʔntsn *I sent for you*; -ip(aʔ)ɬ-xn *heel*.

*-sqáx̌aʔ *domestic animal*, esp. *horse*, see PS *s-qax̌aʔ. Sh -sqéx̌eʔ Cv -sqáx̌aʔ Sp -sqáx̌eʔ. – Li Th have the independent word only, Sh both the word and the suffix, SIS the suffix only. Cr does not have the word, but Cr esčíčeʔ *horse* is also used as a lexical suffix.

*-ús-aʔ *berry, small round object*, see PS *ʔus-aʔ. Li -ús(aʔ) Th Sh -úseʔ Cv -úsaʔ *circular, spherical*.

*-ú/ásləp' *(fire)wood*, see PS *li/ap'. Li -usləp' Th -u/esyep' Sh -eslʼp' *house- or campfire* Cv -islp'. – Root-element in Cv slip' *wood* Cr slip' *woody*.

*-ásq'it *day, sky*, see PS *q'ilt, *q'iyt. Li -asq'ət Th Sh -esq't Cb Cv -asq't Ka -ásq'at Sp -asq't Cr -asq'it.

*-ast'ya *grass*. Sh Sp -ést'ye. – Cf. PIS *s-t'yaʔ.

*-aswəɬ *fish*. Li -ásuɬ Th (inv.) -eɬus Sh -esəɬ Cr -ísgʷeɬ (-ásweɬ after retracted p'at' in p'at'ásweɬ *trout*). – Cf. PS *wəl.

*-awt *position, area (?)*. Th Sh -ewt Cb -awt (see PIS *pəst).

*-útyaʔ *crude, makeshift*. Th -utye *simple, rustic, crude* Sh tqʷəqʷlx-uty-m' *to stumble (without falling)* (qʷiwlx *to creep*) Cb kaɬqəlxútiy'aʔ *ride horseback, sg.,* kay'ər'xútiy'aʔ *id., pl.* Cv -utyaʔ *approximation, hand-made, makeshift* Sp -utyeʔ *around*. – Prob. *-út-yaʔ, with the unstressed form of *-ú/áyaʔ.

*-ú/áyaʔ *playingly, pretending, substitute*. Li -az', -uz' Th -ec'é(h) Sh -éy'e, -úy'e Cv -áyaʔ Cr -íyeʔ.

CENTRAL SALISH ROOTS

This list gives roots attested for minimally Squamish in the north down to and including Twana in the south.

*ʔal *be inside, at home; house.* Cx ʔáyaʔ *house, home,* ʔaɬtxʷ *inside* Se ʔélwim *house, home,* ʔaɬtxʷ *inside of house* Sq ʔaytxʷ *be at home* Sn ʔeʔləŋ *house* Cl ʔaʔyəŋ *id.* Ld ʔálʔal *id.* Tw ʔaltxʷ *he's in the house.* – Cf. PS *ʔal.

*ʔəli see ***həli**.

*ʔisaw *to chew.* Sq ʔísawʔn Tw ʔisáwac. – IS only Li. ʔísaw'-.

*ʔut' *to stretch.* Sq ʔut' Cw ʔat'ət *stretch, pull bowstring* Ck ʔát'- Sn ʔat' *slingshot* Cl ʔut't Tw ʔut'.

*ʔəxʷal-mixʷ *settlement, village.* Sq ʔúxʷumixʷ Cw Ms Ck Nk xʷélŋəxʷ *Indian* Sg ʔəxʷelŋəxʷ *id.* Cl ʔəxʷiy(ə)ŋəxʷ *person* Tw ʔaxʷálbixʷ *one-house permanent settlement.* – IS only Li ʔúxʷalmixʷ *person.*

*s-cəqay *sockeye salmon.* Cx sə́qayʔ Se scə́qay Sq scə́qi Cw θə́qey (Hukari θə́qiʔ) Sn θəqəy' Sg səqeʔ (= iʔ) Cl scə́qiʔ Ld scəqiʔ (stress?) / scəqí Tw scə́qay. – IS only Li scqaz' *barbecued salmon, dried and stored away.*

*s-c'ək'ʷ *worm.* Sl ç'íç'ik'ʷ Se sc'ic'k'ʷ Sq sc'ək'ʷ Cw sç'ək'ʷ *worm, bug* Ck sç'ək'ʷ/k'ʷ *id.* Sn sç'ək'ʷ Sg sc'aq'ʷ (prob. k'ʷ) Cl Ld Tw sc'ək'ʷ.

*c'əq' *to drip, leak (as roof).* Se c'əq'náčaɬtxʷ *rainwater (coming through/from roof)* Cw ç'q'əm *drip* Ck ç'(ə)q'ə́m, ç'áq'm *dripping, leaking* Nk c'qes *water soaked* Sn ç'(ə)q'ŋ̊ Sg c'əq'ŋ̊ Cl c'ə́q'ŋ̊ Tw c'əq'.

*c'is *to peck, nail.* Se c'ísit *to nail* Sq c'ísinʔ *id.. c'istn horn, antler, nail* Cw Ck Sn ç'ísət *to nail* Sm c'istn *horn, antler* Sn sç'istn *antler* Sg cestn (prob. c') *id., c'isn nail, spike* Ld c'əs *to peck, nail. c'ís(i) to nail* Cl c'əs *hit* Tw c'ə́stəd *nail*

215

[Ch cúsi- *to/a nail*]. – Cf. PS *c'əs; the meaning *peck, nail* is CS.

*čəwat *clever, in good shape.* Se čə́wat *able to, good at* Sq (ʔəs)čəčəwʔát *clever, able* Cw scəwʔet *know how* Ck sčəwat *smart, intelligent* Sm sčuw'ét *smart, know how to* Sn čəwet *clever, resourceful* Sg sčoʔét Ld čəwá(ʔ)t *know how to, be good at* Tw čuʔwát *it's o.k.*, bičuʔwatábčəd *I'm getting well.*

*č'am'-ay-iqʷ *great-grandparent/-grandchild.* Cx č'áč'əmʔiʔqʷ Se sč'ámiqʷ Sq sč'ámʔiqʷ Cw Ms sc'áʔməqʷ Ck sc'a:məqʷ Sn č'am'əqʷ Sg č'ə́ʔməqʷ Cl č'aʔməqʷ Ld sč'ábiqʷ Tw č'ábʔiqʷ. – Cf. PCS *-iqʷ and p. 221 *c'əp'. IS only Th sc'ác'ma(ʔ)qʷ *gr. gr. grandmother.*

*hakʷ *to remember.* Cx hákʷʷat Se hakʷʷát Cw hekʷʷ Ck hékʷʷələs Nk hékʷʷen *think* Sn hekʷʷ Sg héʔekʷʷ Cl hakʷʷ Tw hákʷʷəc.

*həli/ʔəli *life, spirit.* Sq sʔə́li *dream, vision, guardian spirit* Cw Ms helíʔ *live* Ck helí: *id.* Cw Ms sʔə́lye *lay spirit power* Ck sələyé *id.* Cw Ms Ck šxʷəlí *life, soul* Ck sxʷayəlxʷ *id.* (alternative of šxʷəlí) Sm he/əlí *alive,* səlí *soul,* sʔə́y/y'lə *guardian spirit* Sn Sg həli *alive* Cl shəyi *soul, life spirit* Ld həlíʔ *live, be alive* Tw həlí *id.,* shəlí *soul, vitality.*

*kʷam (w. suff. *bottom* or *earth*) *root.* Cx Se kʷəʔə́mnač Sl kʷə́ʔmnəč [Sq t'kʷʷámyəxʷ] Cw Ck kʷə́mlə́xʷ Sn kʷə́mləxʷ Ld qʷəbəláxʷ Tw kʷábələxʷ *cedar root* [Ti kʷʷagʷə́ʔ(ə)s]. – IS only Li [ƛ'akʷʷáml'axʷ Th k'əm'y'éxʷ]; note the parallel deviating Sq and Li initials.

*s-ɬaw-in *bedmat.* See PS *ɬaw. – IS only Li sɬaw'ín' *bedding, blanket*; the root is all-Salish, the extension *-in is CS.

*ƛ'u/ac' *to tie, tight(en).* Sq ƛ'uc'- *be packed tightly* Sn ƛ'ç'aləs *tight weave* Ld ƛ'ac' *cinch,* ƛ'úc'(u) *tie, knot* Tw ƛ'uc'úd *tie/knot it!,* ƛ'ác'apad *belt.* – Cf. PS *lu/ac'.

*mut *to carry/lift on arms/hands.* Cx Se mútut Tw butúd (*imp.*).

*pala? *one.* Cx Sl páʔa Cx páya *always* Sl páʔyeʔ *id.*
Tw pálʔawləs *a hundred* [Qn LCh paw CV Si higʷí CV Ti
higí CV]. – IS only Li pálaʔ Th péyeʔ.

*paləqʷ *to boil.* Sl paːloqʷ [Cx páluqʷ] Tw pəlʔə́qʷad
(*imp.*).

*pən *to bury.* Cx pə́naš Se pənáš Sq pənt Cw pənət Ck
piːlt Sn čə́nət Ld pəd Tw ʔaspə́d *buried.*

*q'əməs *mushroom, fungus.* Ck q'ə́mːə/ə́s *mushroom*
Tw k'əbə́s *a large white edible id.* – IS only Li sq'ə́m's *pine
mushroom,* q'əm'salqʷ *tree fungus.* Th q'á/ém'es *pine
mushroom,* q'am'eséyqʷ *oyster mushroom.*

*q'əw *to howl.* Cx q'ə́gim Se q'əwím Sq q'əwm Cw
q'eʔwəm Ck q'áːw Ld q'əwab/q'əwahəb Tw biq'ə́wab *it's
howling.*

*s-qʷmay *dog.* Sq sqʷmayʔ Cw Ms sqʷmey (Hukari
Cw sqʷmeyʔ) Ck sqʷəmeːy [Cl sqməy'] Nk sqʷəmmey Ld
sqʷə/ubáy Tw sqʷəbʔay.

*s-qʷə(t)xm *fog.* Sq sqʷətšm Ck sqʷətxm Ld sqʷə́šəb
(also *smoke*) Tw sqʷəšəb.

*s-qʷum-ay' *head, brain.* Sq sqʷúmayʔ *head* Sn
sqʷaɲiʔ *id.* Tw sqʷúbay *brain.* – See PS ***qʷum;** the
extension with -ayʔ is CeS.

*s-tal-ikn *back, spine.* Sq stayʔč *back* Tw stáličad
spine, səxʷtáʔličad *id.*

*s-tayał *nephew, niece.* Sq stáyał Tw stáʔyił *deceased
sibling's child, nephew.*

*t'al *to put st. across.* Cx t'ayʔš *blanket* Se t'áłat *put
across,* st'alš *blanket* Sq t'át'ał *loom,* t'áłiqʷ *raft* Ck t'ə́łcəstəl
loom Ld t'át'ał *id.,* t'áł(a) *put crossways,* t'áłiʔqʷəb *across
(two) canoes* Tw t'áłikʷ *id., watertruck.*

*t'iliqʷ *strawberry.* Se t'ə́liqʷ Sm Sn t'il'əqʷ Sg t'eʔləqʷ
Cl t'éʔyəqʷ SLd t'iləqʷ Tw t'íliqʷ. – IS only Cb t'iləqʷ (PIS
*tq'im).

217

*t'əq-t'q (in name of) *vine maple*. Sq t'əqt'qay? Ld t'əqt'qac Tw t'əqt'qay.

*xʷal-mixʷ see ***ʔəxʷal-mixʷ**.

*xʷu/ay *to sell*. Cx xʷúǯum (*active-itr.*), xʷáʔǯis (*tr.*) Se xʷúyum, xʷayíš Sq xʷúyum Cw xʷayəm Ck xʷəyə́m Sn xʷəyəm Sg xʷayəm; šxʷimélə *store* Cl xʷuyəm Ld xʷúyub Tw x̌ʷúyub.

*x̌əɬ *hurt, sick, angry*. Se x̌əɬ *hurt* Sq ʔəsx̌əx̌íɬ *extremely* Cw Sn x̌əɬ *hurt* Ck x̌əx̌ə́ɬ *id*. Cl x̌əɬ *ache, hurt* Ld x̌əɬ *sick* Tw x̌əɬ *angry*.

*x̌ʷiɬ'm *rope, string, twine, thread*. Cx Sl x̌ʷíʔlm Se x̌ʷíx̌ʷəlm Sq x̌ʷilʔm Cw Ms x̌ʷəyʔlm? Ck x̌ʷə́y:lm Nk xʷíylim Sn x̌ʷiɬ'm/x̌ʷiɬ'm'/x̌ʷəy'lm Sg Cl x̌ʷeʔlm Ld Tw x̌ʷíləb. – The word has been recorded as Chinook Jargon (J. Powell), the source may be Salish. IS only Li x̌ʷiɬ'm.

*s-x̌ʷiš(š)n *deer*. Sq sx̌ʷiʔšn Tw sx̌ʷíššəd.

*s-x̌ʷayam *myth*. Cx x̌ʷáx̌ʷaʔǯam? Se sx̌ʷax̌ʷəyám Sq sx̌ʷəx̌ʷiʔám? Cw sx̌ʷəyʔém? Sm sx̌ʷíyim' Sn Sg sx̌ʷiʔém' Cl sx̌ʷiʔám'; x̌ʷiʔám' *narrate* Ld sx̌ʷiʔáb Tw sx̌ʷəx̌ʷiʔáb. – Here prob. belongs Sq sx̌ʷáyʔx̌ʷay *a type of mask* Ck sx̌ʷá:yx̌ʷəy *masked dance ceremony* Cl sx̌ʷə́yx̌ʷi *id*.

*yəc *to tell, report*. Sq yəcm Cw yəθəs Ck yə́θəst Sn yəθasəŋ Cl yəcm *recite, tell (legend)* Ld yə́cəb Tw biyə́cəb *he's preaching*.

*yašn *to carry on the back*. Cx ǯášin *backpack* Se syašn *id.*, yašənalíɬ *pack baby on back* Tw ʔasyášnəm *packing st.*, yayášniɬ *carrying baby on back*.

*yəx̌ʷala? *eagle*. Sq yəx̌ʷála? Cw Ms yə́xʷəle Ck yə́xʷələ Ld yəx̌ʷ(ə)lá? Tw yəx̌ʷə́lə. – IS only Li yox̌əlá CV.

LOCAL COAST SALISH
LILLOOET / THOMPSON ELEMENTS

The existence of CS elements in Li and Th was mentioned Intro 5, and in the PS, CS and CeS lists of etymologies reference has been made to Li and Th borrowings.[1] Here words are listed which according to our criteria do not qualify for PS, CS or CeS status but which are found in both CS and Li and/or Th.

As regards the influence of CS, the cases of Li and Th are quite different, and not only in that CS loans in Li are much more numerous than in Th. Th grammar rather closely parallels that of Sh, whereas in Li the influence of CS is not limited to lexicon. In morphology Li has the suffixes -c *mouth* (as in Sq, vs. IS -cin), -az' < -ay' *tree* (as in Cx Se Sq, -i in Tw Ti, vs. IS -aɫp), -q^w *head* (as in Sq, cf. Be -iix̌^{w}, vs. IS -qin), -mx in the 1 sg. obj. suffix of the originally causative paradigm (as in most of CS, absent in IS), -ap in the 2 pl. obj. suffix with 3rd pers. subj. (as in Be Se Sq, absent in IS), -wit for 3d pl. obj. in all forms and 3 pl. subj. with 2nd pers. obj. forms (Sq -wit, absent in IS), -muɫ for 1 pl. obj. in the neutral paradigm (as in most of CS, absent in IS). In syntax Li shares with the neighboring coast languages the adding of tr. subj. endings to enclitics, the proclitic element ʔə to refer to the actor with a pass./itr. verb, the element k^{w}ə introducing subordinate clauses. In Li there has been a fusion of Coast and Interior dialects, though the IS element clearly predominates (out of the 373 exclusively IS etyma that have been established Li takes part in 286; in 10 of these it is the only representative of NIS). That this fusion is at least partly due to intermarriage is suggested by the nursery word túta *go to sleep* which must reflect Sq Se ʔítut *sleep* (Li ʕ^{w}uy't, other IS *ʔitx), cf. also the loanwords k^{w}tamc *husband* (Be Sq Tw; – IS *sx̌alwi/a), (s)xáʔyuʔ *woman's rival in love*

---

[1] The headings under which these Li and/or Th words are found are listed at the end of this section.

(Sq Cw Ck Sm Sn Ld), scutáɫ *son-in-law* (Se Sq Hl St; – IS *snak'ɫxʷ), száʔtən *widow(er)* (Se Sq Hl St; – IS *sɫwalmt).

The words specified in the first paragraph above are summed up in three lists. List 1 gives the cases in which Be participates, List 2 those found minimally from Sq down to Ld, List 3 words with a more limited distribution in CS. Obvious loans from IS into Ck, the easternmost of the Hl dialects, are not included.

LIST 1

*cixʷ *to reach.* Be cxʷyakm *reach for st.* Sq cixʷ *arrive, reach (a place)* ~ Li cixʷ *id.,* cixʷakaʔmín *reach for st.* – Cf. PIS *kic-, a root not found in Li. For Sq cáx̌ʷam *reach for st.* see PS *caʕʷ.

*c'laʔ *a type of basket.* Be c'la ~ Li c'laʔ Th c'əy'eh-. – Cf. HEI c'lá KWA c'liʔ (LR no. 749) HAI c'la: *spruce-root basket* (Lincoln-Rath 1986) Tsimshian c'əlá: (Nater 1977).

*məc' (*mə̣c' ?) *to squeeze.* Be mnc'; mnc'aqʷ's *squeeze berries (to extract juice)* [Cx mət'k' *mash*] Se məc'qʷat *crush* ~ Li mə̣c'n *put st. under st. heavy.* – For Be n see under PS *pə̣t.

*nəqʷ *sun, fire, warm.* Be niix̌ʷ/niiqʷ- *fire* Sq nuqʷ *noon,* snəqʷm *sun* ~ Li nəqʷ *(comfortably) warm,* nəqʷnuqʷ *id.,* "snuqum" CV *sun.* – Cf. PS *yəqʷ.

*nwas *two.* Be ɫnus/ɫwaas- Sq ʔánʔus ~ Li ʔán'was. – See PS *was and suff. -was. For another numeral see *x̌əʔúcin in List 3.

*paqʷu, *p'aq'u *to be scared, afraid.* Be paax̌u, paaqʷu- Se p'aq'ús *deadfall, Indian trap* Sq (ʔi)p'áqʷaɫ ~ Li páqʷuʔ; p'áq'uɫ *cache* Th páqʷuʔ-. – Semantically cf. English "fear" and Old Saxon va:r *ambush.*

*p'uqʷ *grey, faded, mouldy.* [Be puux̌ *mouldy,* spuux̌altswa *grey blueberry (vaccinium ovalifolium)*] Cx

220

p'úqʷp'uqʷ *greyish berries* Se p'uqʷúm *grey, faded* – Li
p'əqʷp'uqʷ *grey(ish brown),* p'úp'uqʷ *highbush blue
huckleberry, grey blueberry.*

*s-qala *red huckleberry.* Be sqala Ck sqe:lə ~ Li
sqaʔəl'.

*qałayu *gaffhook.* Be qałayu Cx Sq q̓áłayu ~ Li
q̓áłayu *big gaffhook.* – Cf. HEI Gáλáyú KWA Gaλa *fish w.
hook* NWAK Gaλ- *to gaff, hook, crochet* (LR no. 2184).

*qʷup *hair.* Be sqʷup- Cx qʷupusin *moustache* Se
qʷupm *hairy* ~ Li qʷuʔpəqʷ *bushy, messy hair.*

*tiqʷ *mud(dy).* Be stqʷ *mud* Sq tiqʷ *id.* ~ Li tiqʷ
muddy.

LIST 2

*ʔac *surface.* Sq sʔacus *face,* nəxʷʔácač *palm of hand,*
sʔacq *bottom* Cw Ms sʔaθəs *face* Ck sʔa:θəs *id.* Sm sʔasəs *id.*
Sn sʔaθəs *id.* Cl sʔacs *id.* Ld sʔácus *id.* ~ Li nʔacáka? *palm
of hand,* nʔacq *bottom.*

*ʔəx̌c' *backbone.* Sq (nəxʷ)ʔə́x̌c'č Ld sx̌əx̌c' *backbone
of fish* ~ Li ʔə́x̌c'.

*c'əp' *gr. gr. gr. grandparent/-child.* Sq c'əp'iʔə́qʷ Cw
Ms ç'ə́p'ayəqʷ Ck ç'ə́p'ayáqʷ/ç'ə́p'ayəqʷ/ç'ə́p'iyəqʷ Sm
ç'/c'ə́p'ayəqʷ Sn ç'ə́p'əyəqʷ Ld c'əp'yiqʷ ~ Li c'əc'p'a?
grandfather. – Cf. CeS *č'am'-ay-iqʷ.

*kəs *to send (a person).* Sq čəšn; sčə́šn *messenger* (š
by assimilation) Ld čəs *send on errand* ~ Li skəsn *messenger.*

*k'əλ'a? *stone, rock.* Cw (Nanaimo dial.) "tlátsa" CV
(inv.) Nk "tsî̓tla" CV Ld č'ə́λ'ə? ~ Li k'ə́λ'a.

*s-kʷiqaq *robin.* [Cx č'ə́qč'əq] Sq skʷqaq Cw Ms Ck
skʷqeq (Galloway Ck skʷakʷqe:q) Sn kʷəsqəq Ld skʷəqiq
[Ch swísq'q', wísq'aq'-] ~ Li skʷiqəq.

*k'atl *devil's club.* [Se č'ə́ʔatay] Sq č'átiay? ~ Li k'átlaz' Th k'étye?. – Kinkade 1955:33 quotes from a J.P. Harrington MS a Lower Ch form which shows initial č'at- and possibly the l/n interchange (Intro 3D).

*ƛ'aɫm *salt.* Cx Se Sq ƛ'aɫm Sm ƛ'eɫn̯' Sn ƛ'eɫn̯ ~ Li ƛ'aɫm. – For other IS see PS *c'u/al.

*mu/al'sm *blueberry sp.* Cx Se mal'sm Sq mul?sm Cw Ms mal'sm Ck ma(:)lsm Sm mal'sn̯' Sn mal'sn̯ Ld bul'cəb ~ Li mạl'ṣm Th məlṣm.

*maqa? *snow.* Sq máqa? Cw Ms Ch méqe Sm n̯éqe/ə Sn n̯eqə Ld báqʷu ~ Li máqa?. – Th Sh have wuxʷ-, see also IS *məx̌ʷ.

*nəh, *na(?) *to name, call.* Cx nan; nə́ʔit *mean, call, tell* Sl nan *name* Se nat *tell*, nə?it *id.* Sq nan; snəh/sna? *a name* Cw Sm sne *id.* Sn nəhi:mət *ancestral name,* netn̯ *name sb.* Cl nat *id.* Ld dáʔ(a) ~ Li nahən Th ne(h)- *name, pronounce,* netés *call by (particular) name.*

*nəp *to put in.* Cx nə́piš *insert* [Sq txʷnəp *hit upon,* nəw'n *put into*] Ld sdəpač *parcel* ~ Th nəptes.

*nat *night, 24-hr period,* Cx Se nat *night* Sq snat *id.* Cw Ms snet *id.* Ck sle(:)t *id.* Sm (s)net *id.* Sn snet *id* Cl ʔəsnat *id.* Nk nê'tox *yesterday* Ld dat *day, 24-hr period,* dádato *tomorrow* (Snyder) ~ Li natxʷ *yesterday.*

*s-paʔc *black bear.* Cw Ms spéʔeθ Ck spe:θ Sg Sm spéʔes Sn speʔəθ NLd spaʔc ~ Th spéʔec.

*q'əməs *mushroom, fungus.* Ck q'ə́m:əs/q'ə́m:ə́s *big white edible mushroom* Tw k'əbə́s *a large white mushroom* ~ Li sq'əm's *pine mushroom,* q'əm'salqʷ *tree fungus.*

*q'ayx̌ *cascara.* Cw q'ey'x̌əɫp Ck Sn q'eyx̌əɫp NLd q'ayx̌əc ~ Li q'ay'x̌ɫəp/q'ay'ɫəp /q'ə́ʔx̌ɫəp/q'aq'ɫəp Th q'áyx̌eɫp.

*qʷɫiʔ-xn *shoe (white man's).* Sq qʷɫiʔšn Ck qʷəɫ(l)i:xl Sm qʷɫiʔšn Sn qʷɫəy'šn Ld qʷɫiʔšəd ~ Li qʷɫiʔxn.

*t'ilm *to sing.* Se Cw Ms t'ilm Ck t'i?ílm (Elmendorf-Suttles) / t'ilm (Galloway) Sm Sn t'ilm Cl t'iyəm Ld t'ílib ~ Li ƛ'ilm.

*x̌ák'i?t *fireweed.* Sq x̌ač't Ck x̌ec'ət ~ Li (s)x̌ak't; x̌ək'tn'aɬp *goldenrod* Th sx̌ə́k'i?t. – Kinkade 1995:45 quotes a NLd x̌áč'tac (Ld -ac *plant*).

LIST 3

*s-?ac'á?məs *woman's shoulder blanket.* Sq s?ac'ám?əs Ck s?aç'aːməs *shawl* ~ Th c'əc'a?məs *id.*

*?umik *(to go) upstream.* Sq tx^w?úmič *go upstream* ~ Li ?úmik *id.*

*?əpən/l-xn *lizard, salamander.* Se ?i?plx̌n *salamander* (word not generally known) Sq ?əpn'x̌n *id.* ~ Li ?ə́/ápəlsa(?) *id. ("water lizard").*

*?iw'as *to fish w. line.* Se yə́was *jig for ocean-floor fish* Sq ?iw?ás *fish w. line in river* ~ Li ?í?w'as *fish w. rod.*

*?ux^w-al-mix^w *Indian, tribe, village.* Sq ?úx^wumix^w *village* Sg ?əx^welŋəx^w *id.* Cl ?əx^wiy(ə)ŋəx^w*village* ~ Li ?úx^walmix^w *person.* – Related forms in Cw Ms Nk x^wə́lməx^w *Indian* Ck x^wə́lmə́x^w *id.* – IS only Li ?úx^walmix^w *person, Indian.* Cf. PS ***qal-mix^w** and comment given there.

*(s-)ca?cqay *sprout, young shoot (esp. of thimbleberry)* Se scácqay Sq scá?cqay Cw Ms sθe?θqəy Ck sθeθqəy [Sn θéθq'i] ~ Li cí?cqaz'.

*cawas *level, even.* [Se syawás] Sq cuás ~ Li cwas Th cuwes-; cuwesxə́n *measure one shoe against the other.*

*caw'in *coho salmon.* Cx sə?n Sq cáw?in Cw θe?wən Sm Sn sew'ən ~ Li cá?win. – Cf. NWAK ӡw'n *coho (silver) salmon* (LR no. 619), NOO cox^w-, cow'it *coho salmon.*

*c'ap' *busy, excited.* Cx c'áp'aw? *busy,* c'áp'it *id.* Se sc'ap'ít *id.* Sq c'ic'áp' *to work* ~ Th c'ep'- *frantic.*

*c'iq' *mud.* Cx c'íc'iq' Se sc'íc'iq' Sq sc'iq' [Ck sç'iql Cl c'əqᵂc'qᵂ *dirty*] ~ Li c'i?q' *get dirty.*

*s-c'uqᵂay' *spring salmon.* Sq sc'úqᵂi *fish (generic)* Cw Ms sç'áqᵂey? Ck sç'á:qᵂi *fish (generic)* Sm sç'/c'áqᵂi? Sn sç'aqᵂi? Nk sc'úqᵂəy' ~ Li sc'úqᵂaz'.

*hi?qᵂin *lamp, light, torch.* Se hiyqᵂí?n Sq hi?qᵂín Sn či?əqᵂn *lightbulb* ~ Li hi?qᵂín *candle.* – See PS *yəqᵂ and Intro 3K.

*haw *warm.* Cx hágat *warm st. up* Se háwat *id.* ~ Li haw; háwan *warm st.*

*huy-a? *to get ready.* Sq huyá? *leave, depart* ~ Li xᵂ/huzá? *get ready.* – See PS *huy. Cf. also Li hú maɬ *goodbye* and Sq huy maɬáɬ *id.*

*s-kasnəkm *illegitimate child.* Sq skasnəkm ~ Li skasənkm.

*k'aca *storage box.* Se k'áča *basket w. lid* ~ Li k'áca? *storage box,* k'ə́k'ca? *small id.,* k'əck'ə́k'c?aqᵂ *unid. bush, tops of which look like* k'ə́k'ca?. – Cf. HAI k'àac'i *box for transporting fine sand or oolichans* (LR no. 1472 and Lincoln-Rath 1988:220). The correspondence Se č - Li c can result from borrowing in either direction (Li c is phonetically [č]), but the Li form is closer to the HAI one. The difference c - c' between the Salish and HAI words is unexplained.

*k'ih *to rise, raise.* Se č'iyt *to lift* Sq č'ih- ~ Li k'ih-. – Many derivatives in both Sq and Li.

*k'im *cold, to freeze.* Cx Se č'əm *cold* ~ Li k'ímaľc *freeze,* sk'ímaľc *ice* (-aľc *rock, hard substance*). – See PS *k'ay.

*k'ət(xᵂ) *to cut, sever, carve.* Cx Se č'ətt *cut* Sq č'ətxᵂ *carve* ~ Li k'ətn *poke,* k'ətxᵂan *cut off* Th k'ət(e)tés *wedge st. (sharp) in ground at an angle,* k'ətxᵂetés *sever,* k'tuxᵂ *severed, cut off.* – Cf. Ck xə́t'kᵂe:ls *carve wood* Sm xə́t'kᵂn̦ *id.* Sn xt'kᵂən̦ *id.*

*k'əxʷaʔ *lacrosse.* Sq k'ə́xʷaʔ (borr.) ~ Li k'ə́xʷaʔ *id., hockey.*

*s-kəy'a-mx *porcupine.* Se skə́y'amx ~ Li (Fountain dial.) skíyʔamx.

*k'yaq *salmon weir.* Sq č'iaq Ck c'iyéq ~ Li sk'zaq *fishtrap.*

*kʷəs *to spray.* Se kʷəst *squirt, spit* ~ Li kʷis *to drop, rain.*

*kʷut *to pout.* Se kʷutucínm ~ Li kʷútqsam'.

*kʷ̓uləxʷ *dog salmon.* Cx kʷ̓úʔuxʷ *smoked/dried fish* Se skʷ̓úluxʷ *dried fish* [Sq kʷ̓áʔlaxʷm Qualicum (geogr.)] Cw Ms kʷ̓aʔləxʷ Ck kʷ̓a:ləxʷ Sg kʷayəx (prob. kʷ̓ayəxʷ) Sm Sn kʷ̓al'əxʷ ~ Li kʷ̓al'xʷ Th kʷ̓úluʔxʷ.

*kʷ̓uƛ' *salt water, ocean.* Se kʷ̓úƛ'um *salty (taste)* Sq kʷ̓uƛ'kʷ *salt water* Cw Ms Ck kʷ̓áƛ'kʷa *sea* Ck (Galloway kʷ̓áƛ'kʷe) ~ Li kʷ̓uƛ' *sea, ocean.*

*ləc' (red.) *gall, bile (color).* Sq ləlʔc' *bright yellow* Ck lələ́c' (borr.) *gall(bladder)* ~ Li ləl'c' *bile.*

*lam *liquor.* Sq lam Cw Ck lem ~ Li lam. – CJ lum, Zenk lam fr. English *rum.*

*ləs *bottom, lower part.* Sq ləs; sləsc *lower lip,* etc. ~ [Li lə̣s *cave in*] Th ləs-/lə̣s- *low.* – The retraction in Th and poss. Li points to borrowing.

*ləqʷay' *clothes.* Sq yəqʷáyʔ ~ Li ləqʷaz' *blanket, clothing, dress.*

*ɬasm *Indian rice.* Sq ɬasm ~ Li ɬasm.

*ɬəx̌ *vegetation.* Se ɬəx̌aš *hide in vegetation* ~ Li ɬəx̌p *overgrown, grown into sticks.*

*ɬəwqim *blueberry sp.* Cx ɬə́wqim Se ɬəwqím Sq ɬəwqím? Cw Ms ɬəwʔqim? Ck ɬəwqi:m Sm ɬəw'qim' ~ Th ɬuʔqím'.

*s-ƛ'əɬalm *grizzly bear.* Sq sƛ'əɬalm ~ Li sƛ'aɬálm.

225

*mic *to sit/squat down.* Sq mícincut *squat* ~ Li míca?q *assume a sitting position* Th míce/a?q *id.*

*məx̌ *gap, divide.* Cx məx̌ičt *divide (as mass of loose things)* Se sməx̌lus *w. parted hair* ~ Li sməx̌ *be in the middle (between others)* Th məx̌- *gap.*

*nəp *to be on the trail/road.* [Se nunpiwánm *think*] Sq nəxʷsnə́n?p *walk right on trail* ~ Li nə́pnəp *be (walk, stay) on the road.*

*niw *spouse (address form).* Sq nə́wa ~ Li niw Th nínw'e.

*nəx̌ *to abrade/cut lightly.* Se nəx̌t *strike (as match)* ~ Li nəx̌m *cut one's skin lightly (to draw blood).*

*puc *to soak.* Se púcut *put under the tap* ~ Li pu?c *get soaked, get soft in water.*

*pəs *to air.* Se pəsxʷ ~ Li pəsq *to fart.*

*paxələqʷ *yellow cedar.* Cw pašələqʷ Ms paxələqʷ Ck pa:xələqʷ Sm Sn pašələqʷ ~ Li páxlaqʷ.

*p'ak' *hot.* Sq p'ač *hot* ~ Li (Fountain dial.) p'ák'am *heat soaked salmon* Th p'ek'kstm *warm the hands (said of child).*

*p'əqʷ *pimples.* Se p'əqʷiws *have measles* ~ Th p'əqʷnweɬn *cause skin eruptions,* p'oqʷt *have measles.*

*p'ə̣sk'a *hummingbird.* Ck p'ə́sk'e/pə́sk'e/písk'e ~ Li p'ə̣́sk'a? Th p'ə̣́sk'e?. – This may be a borrowing from a non-Salish language.

*p'astən *unid. plant.* Se p'əstə́nay *goat's beard* ~ Li p'astn' *false azalea.*

*qal'q *wild rose.* Sq qal?q; qál?qay *(the bush)* Cw qel'q, qel'qəɬp Ms qelqəɬp Ck qe:lqəɬp Sm qə́l'əq, qəl'qi/eɬč ~ Li qəl'q, qəl'qaz'.

*qtin' *(dipnet for fishing in) pool in river.* Sq qtin? *pool in river where fish swim around* ~ Li sqtin' *big dipnet.*

*qaw *to lean against, sleep with.* Cx qáʔgust *lean st. against st.,* qáʔgusʔim *lay with* Se qǝw'it *to sleep, share bed with* ~ Li qáwam *have sexual intercourse.*

*q'ǝmul-ay', *q'ǝmul-aɫp *maple, lit. paddle tree.* Se q'ǝmulay' Sq q'mlay? Ms q'ǝmǝlǝtp Ck q'ǝmǝw:ɫp Sm q'ǝmǝniɫč ~ Li q'ǝm'laz' Th q'ám'neɫp.

*q'ǝpxʷ/q'ǝp'xʷ/q'ǝpkʷ/q'ǝp'kʷ *to crunch (when chewed).* Cx q'ǝp/p'xʷim, q'ǝp'k'ʷim *make crunching noise (as when chewing candy)* ~ Th q'ǝpq'ǝpkʷlehéɫp *highbush cran- or squashberry (after clicking sound when chewed).* – Cf. PS *q'ap'x̌ʷ/xʷ.

*q'aw I *to lose (contest), pay.* Sq q'áwat *pay,* q'áwaɫns *punish* Ck q'áwet *pay* Sn q'ewǝt *id.* [Cl q'aʔyúst *id.*] ~ Li q'aw *get beaten (in contest),* q'áwǝn *beat (in contest).* – Ck á instead of expected é is unexplained.

*q'aw II *to attach by string.* Se q'aw'ínastn *suspenders* ~ Th q'áwqes.

*q'ǝwis-qin *axe.* Se q'ǝwísqin ~ Li (n)qʷwisqn' Th q'wisqn.

*q'ǝwat *stick (esp. for beating rhythm).* Cx q'áʔgat/q'áʔgay *walking stick* Se q'ǝwa *id.* Sq q'ǝwat *stick for beating rhythm* Sn q'ǝwǝt *id., drumstick* ~ Li q'watm *to drum.*

*q'awax̌ *(red.) chocolate lily.* Se sq'áq'awx̌ ~ Li q'áq'w'ǝx̌ Th q'áw'e/ax̌.

*q'ax̌ *to bend backwards.* Se q'áx̌at ~ Li q'ax̌lǝx *curl up* Th q'á/éx̌es *bend,* q'éx̌etm *(person) gets bent over backwards (fr. convulsion).*

*q'xʷaʔ-wiɫ *war/racing canoe.* Sq q'xʷawʔɫ *West coast or Chinook canoe* Cw Ms Ck q'xʷǝwǝɫ *Nootka type canoe* Sm Sn q'x̌ʷǝw'ɫ *big, resp. racing canoe* [Ld x̌ix̌q'wíɫ/ x̌íx̌q'ǝwiɫ *racing canoe*] ~ Li q'x̌ʷuʔɫ *war canoe.* – The x̌ʷ in Sm Sn Li may be due to assimilation. The Ld form is derived from x̌ix̌q' *compete.*

*qʷmčuľs *cranberry sp.* Sq qʷmčul?s Cw Ms qʷəm?cals Ck qʷəmča:ls Sm qʷəmčaľs Sn qʷəm'čaləs ~ Li qʷəmçaľṣ Th qʷəmcens.

*qʷul *digit.* Sq qʷuy- in níx̌qʷuy?ač *finger,* níx̌qʷuy?šn *toe* ~ Li sc'qʷúḷaka? *thumb,* sc'qʷúḷaxn *big toe,* x̌zum qʷúḷxn *id.,* sqʷḷúḷa?xn *hoof.* – The Li retraction points to borrowing.

*qʷiqʷəɫ *mountain ash.* Ck qʷiqʷəɫ Sm qʷaqʷiɫč *arbutus* ~ Th qʷiqʷíɫ *(fruit),* qʷiqʷiɫéɫp *(bush).*

*qʷn-aɫp *Indian hellebore.* Se qʷənaɫp Sq qʷnaɫp Sn qʷənəɫp ~ Li qʷnaɫp Th qʷneɫp. – Of the languages for which the word is attested only Th has -eɫp as a productive suffix (Se -ay Sq -ay? Sn -iɫč).

*qʷ?up *crabapple.* Se Sq qʷ?up Cw Ms Ck qʷə?ap Sg qʷá?ap ~ Li qʷ?up Th qʷ?ep.

*qʷəy (mostly red.) *copper.* Cx qʷə́?is Se qʷə́yqʷiy Sq qʷə́yqʷi, sqʷa?íls Ck qʷíqʷi ~ Th ?estqʷəqʷzéy'st. – The Th word means *blue stone* (see PS *qʷay); the PS suffix -i/alst is recognizable in the Cx and 2nd Sq form. A root *qʷəl occurs in Ck sqʼʷəl *a metal found in mines, used for arrowheads* Li sqʼʷəl *copper* Th qʷiy *id.*

*saliq' *to dangle.* Se saliq'ím *dangle, hang down* ~ Li salləq' *be carried around dragging/dangling.*

*səl/nəy *lowbush Oregon grape.* Sq sə́l?yáy? *(bush)* Cw Ms sə́nəy?əɫp *(id.)* Ck sə́líy; sə́líy?əɫp Sm sə́ni? Sn səni? ~ Li sə́ləy' Th sə́ni?.

*sasq'əc *Sasquatch.* Ms sesq'əc Ch se:sq'əc ~ Li sásq'əc.

*su/an (red.) *to stagger.* Se sansúnum ~ Li sən'san'ám.

*tak(əm) *total.* Cx táčam? *be visible, showing,* táčaymixʷ *tribe* ~ Li takm *all.*

*tuɫ-k-ist *stone maul.* Sq ntə́ɫčis Cw Ms Ck štə́ɫcəs ~ Li túɫkis Th túɫkist.

*təx̣ʷaʔč *bow (for shooting)*. Sq táx̣ʷaʔč Cw Ms táx̣ʷac Ck táx̣ʷa:c ~ Li táx̣ʷʔac. – Borr. by Li (IS has *ckʷinʼk, see PS ***cəkʷ** and PIS -inʼak), which identified CS č with NIS c (phonetically č). The CS word may contain PS ***-ak** *hand* and PS ***təx̣ʷ** *straight, settled*.

*təm *season of (time when fish come, berries ripen, etc)*. Sq Ck təm- ~ Li təm.

*təmɬ-apsm *woodpecker sp*. Sq tmɬəpsm Cw Ms táməɬəpsm Ck təm(:)ə́ɬəpsm Sn təmətečsŋ ~ Th tə/ə́mɬapsm prob. *northern flicker*. – See PCS ***təmɬ**, **PS *-apsm**. Th retraction as common in borrowings.

*təmus *"velvet" (originally prob. a kind of fur)*. Sq támus Ck támə́s Sm təmsə́ləqn ~ Li tə̣ms. – Li retraction points to borrowing. The Sm suffix -ələqn means *wool, soft covering, hair*.

*tʼəq *to stick/press/glue together*. Cx tʼəqt *stick st. on st.* ~ Li ƛ̓əqp *pressed together* Th ƛ̓əqpetés *glue st*.

*tʼəqʼ *to snap (shut), trip sb*. Se tʼəqʼ *to trip*, [tʼəqʼiš *sit down* Sq tʼqʼax̣ *fall backward*] ~ Li ƛ̓əqʼpan *spring a trap* Th ƛ̓qʼəp *snap shut*.

*waʔ *to continue*. Sq wə́ʔu; wa (clitic:) *continuous, progressive* ~ Li waʔ *be busy with*.

*s-wiʔ *eulachon*. Sq swiwʔ, swíʔu Cw Ms swiʔwə Ck swi:wə Sn swiwʼə ~ Th swíwe; wíweme *to fish for eulachon*.

*wac *to defecate*. Se wač *excrements* ~ Li wac; swac *excrements*. – For the Se - Li correspondence č - c see comment under ***kʼaca**.

*wul *tule*. Sq wəl Cw wəlʔ (Elmendorf-Suttles), wu:lʼ (Hukari), Ms wi:lʔ Ck wo:l Cw Ms wí:lʔeɬ *tule mat* Ck wə́w:leɬ *id*. Sn skʷaləlʼ *tule* ~ Th wul *id*.

*xaʔ *high, top, upward*. Cx šaʔ *climb* Se šaʔ *id*. ~ Li xaʔ *high* Th xeʔ *(area) above, top, upward*.

*xat *lead*. Sq šat *shot, lead*, šátaχan *sinker line* Cw
šet *lead, shot, gun shell* Ck xat *lead*, xətaləqətl *sinker line* Sm
Sn šet *bullet, sinker* Cl šat *lead* ~ Li xat *lead weight*. – Borr.
fr. English *shot* (the Sq √šat *dive* is attested elsewhere only in
Cw štem *swim underwater (as fish/seal)*). The borrowing must
have started on the coast.

*xiw *to thread on string, put on spit*. Se šəw'íwat *id.
of beads, clams* ~ Li xíwin *put a stick into/through st*.

*xʷic' *to sway, rock (baby)*. Se xʷíc'it *rock (baby)* Sn
xʷəç'n̩ *stagger* ~ Li xʷic'qs *jump up (as end of board, log)*,
xʷi/əc'amáya *seesaw*.

*x̌cəm *cedar box*. Sq x̌cəm Cw x̌θəm? Sn x̌θəm ~ Li
x̌ə́cm. – Cf. KWA x̌cəm (LR no. 2382).

*x̌-k'i-t *this/near side*. Sq x̌č'ítaχan *(the) near side* ~ Li
x̌k'it *this side*. – See PS ***k'ih, k'i-t**. The prefixed x̌- is found
only here.

*x̌ət' *skunk cabbage(?)*. Se x̌ət'x̌ət'tan *unid. plant* ~ Li
x̌əƛ' *skunk cabbage*.

*x̌ə?úcin *four*. Sq x̌ə?úcn Cw Ms x̌a?áθn Ck x̌a?áθl ~
Li x̌ʷ?úcin. – See comments to PS ***x̌əc**.

*x̌ʷuqʷ *to pole up (in canoe)*. Se x̌ʷúqʷsam Sq
x̌ʷúqʷcut; sx̌ʷuqʷtn *canoe pole* Ck x̌ʷaqʷət; sx̌ʷaqʷtl *canoe
pole* Sn x̌ʷaqʷət; sx̌ʷaqʷn *canoe pole* Cl x̌ʷuqʷn *id.* [Tw
x̌ʷuqʷ- *pull*] ~ Li x̌ʷuqʷtn *canoe pole*.

*s-x̌ʷuqʷ-ɬnaɬ *kerchief* (***-ɬnaɬ** *neck*). Se sx̌ʷúx̌ʷqʷɬaɬ
Sq sx̌ʷə́qʷnaɬ *handkerchief* Ck sx̌ʷə́qʷəlɬəl Sm sx̌ʷix̌ʷqʷɬnəl
anything worn around neck ~ Li sx̌ʷuqʷɬəl.

*x̌ʷu?qʷ *sawbill duck*. Sq x̌ʷuhqʷ *loon* CwMs Ck
x̌ʷa:qʷ Sg x̌aq' Sn x̌ʷa?əqʷ Cl x̌ʷú?uqʷ ~ Li x̌ʷu?qʷ

*x̌ʷ?it *wedge*. Cx x̌ʷə́?it Se sx̌ʷə?it Sq x̌ʷ?it Cw Ms Ck
x̌ʷə?it ~ Li x̌ʷ?it.

*yumač *spring salmon*. Se yúmač Sm yaməč Nk
yúmač CV NLd yubəč ~ Li zúmak.

*yuh *careful, alert, warned.* Sq yuh *be careful,* yan? *warn* Cw ya:t *warn* ~ Li zuhən *id.*

*s-yə/al-m-čis *fingerring.* Sq slmčis Ck siyáləmcəs Sm s(xʷ)yə́ləmčis Sn sxʷyeləmčəs ~ Li syalməc. – See PS yə̣l and -ak, etc.. Here Li borrowed fr. Ck.

*s-yaq-c *wife, woman.* Se syáqcuw *wife* ~ Li (Mt. Currie dial.) syáqca? *woman.* – For ***-c** see comment to PS ***?imac.**

*s-ya?tn *widow(er).* [Cx ǯaťtn] Se syatn Sq sya?tn Cw Ms sye?tn Ck sye(:)tl Sm siyé?tn n sye?tn Cl sya?tn ~ Li sza?tn. – See the IS equivalents under PS ***ɬaw(-al).**

*yawap *sail.* Cx yáwap *material, cloth* Sq yáwap *sail* ~ Li yáwap *sail.* – Cf. NWAK yw- *wind, draft* (LR no. 1571), HAI yúp'iq *mast.*

*yaxən *to carry on the back.* Cx ǯášin *backpack* Se syašn *id.* ~ Li szaxn *itr.,* szaxəns *tr.*

References to Li and/or Th borrowings in preceding lists are found under the following headings:

Both Li and Th: PCS *?asxʷ, *?ay', *cataw, *c'iwq', *kʷəl, *ɬəx̌ʷ, *ƛ'əp, *məl(al)us, *maqʷam, *mu?t, *(s-)mayac, *p'akʷ, *s-ləway' (s.v. PS *ləw/ʕʷ), *sa?q, *ťəxʷ, *wuqʷ, *yəw, *yax̌ʷ; CeS *kʷam, *pala?, *q'əməs.

Li only: PS k'aɫu?, *ɬaw, *ʕi/al; PCS *?itk'/q'əp, *?ax̌ic, *cucin, *cal'aɬ, *k'əyuya, *kʷac, *kʷ-tam-c, *liq, *ƛ'?imin, *maqin, *məxk'/kn, *p'a/uqʷ, *qəl, *qəm, *qəp', *qiw'x̌, *qəx̌, *q'a/il, *q'a?may?, *qʷaliɬ, *qʷənis, *qʷas-tan, *qʷʸix̌, *ťanam, *xay'u?, *xʷak, *xʷəl/nitm, *x̌ʷumat, *x̌ʷəs, *yəq-ilx; CeS *?isaw, *?əxʷalmixʷ, *s-cəqay, *s-ɬaw-in, *x̌ʷil'm, *yəx̌ʷəla?; suffixes PS *-txʷ; PCS *-aq, *-iqʷ, *-ay'.

Th only: PS *yəʕ; PCS *s-(c)x̌al-m, *c'əkʷa?, *kʷʸukʷ, *ɬik', *s-ɬan-ay', *qalx, *ťəm(x), *wal; CeS *č'əm'-ay-iqʷ.

INDEX OF NON-SALISH ELEMENTS

NORTH WAKASHAN

INDEX OF NON-SALISH ELEMENTS

BIBLIOGRAPHY

ABBREVIATIONS:

AL   Anthropological Linguistics.

CMM   National/Canadian Museum of Man/Civilization. Canadian Ethnology Service. Mercury series.

ICS(N)L International Conference on Salish (and Neighboring) Languages. [The Papers of the *ICS(N)L* are not subject to peer review].

IJAL   International Journal of American Linguistics.

LR   Lincoln-Rath 1980 (see under OTHER LANGUAGE SOURCES below).

UCPL   University of California Publications in Linguistics.

UMOPL University of Montana Occasional Papers in Linguistics.

SELECTED GENERAL AND COMPARATIVE STUDIES:

Boas, F., Haeberlin, H. 1927 Sound shifts in Salishan dialects. *IJAL 4*:117-36.

Czaykowska-Higgins, E., Kinkade, M.D. (eds.) 1998 Salish languages and linguistics. *Salish languages and linguistics. Theoretical and descriptive perspectives.* 1-68. Berlin-New York. [Does not supersede Thompson's 1979 account of the history of phonological reconstruction].

Galloway, B.D. 1982 Proto-Central Salish phonology and sound correspondences. MS.

Kinkade, M.D. 1973 The alveopalatal shift in Cowlitz Salish. *IJAL 39*:224-31.

___. 1988 Proto-Salishan colors. In Shiply, W. (ed.) *In honor of Mary Haas: From the Haas festival conference on Native American linguistics.* Berlin.

___. 1990 Prehistory of Salishan languages. *Papers 25th ICNSL* 197-212. Vancouver.

___. 1991[1] Proto-Salishan mammals. *Papers 26th ICSNL* 233-8. Vancouver.

___. 1993 Salishan words for 'Person, Human, Indian, Man'. In Mattina, A., Montler, T. (eds.) *American Indian ling-*

uistics and ethnography. In honor of Lawrence C. Thompson. UMOPL 10:163-83.

___. 1995 Transmontane lexical borrowing in Salish. *Papers 30th ICSNL* 28-46. Victoria.

___. 1998 Origins of Salish lexical suffixes. *Papers 33rd ICNSL* 266-95. Seattle.

Kinkade, M.D., Sloat, C. 1972 Proto-Eastern Interior Salish vowels. *IJAL 38*:26-48.

Kuipers, A.H. Towards a Salish etymological dictionary. [I]. *Lingua 26* 1970:46-72; II. *Lingua 57* 1982:71-92; III. *Papers 30th ICSNL* 199547-54; IV. *Papers 31st ICSNL* 1996:203-10; V. *Papers 33rd ICSNL* 1998:296-306.

___. 1973 About evidence for Proto-Salish *r. *Dutch contributions to the 8th ICSL (Eugene, Or.)* 1-12. Leiden.

___. 1981 On reconstructing the Proto-Salish sound system. *IJAL 47*:323-35.

Newman, S. 1977 The Salish independent pronoun system. *IJAL 43*:302-14.

___. 1979[1] A history of the Salish possessive and subject forms. *IJAL 45*:207-23.

___. 1979[2] The Salish object forms. *IJAL 45*:299-308.

___. 1980 Functional changes in the Salish pronominal system. *IJAL 46*:155-67.

Pokorny, J. 1959 *Indogermanisches etymologisches Wörterbuch, Bd. I*. Bern-München.

Reichard, G.A. A comparison of five Salish languages. Parts I-IV *IJAL 24* 1958:239-300; *25* 1959:8-15, 90-96, 154-167, 239-253; *26* 1960:50-61.

Swadesh, M. 1950 Salish internal relationships. *IJAL 16*: 157-67.

___. 1952 Salish phonologic geography. *Language 28* 1952: 232-48.

Thompson, L.C. 1979 Salishan and the Northwest. In Campbell, L., Mithun, M. (eds.) *The languages of Native America*. 692-765. Austin.

Thompson, L.C., Thompson, M.T., Efrat, B.S. 1974 Some phonological developments in Straits Salish. *IJAL 40*:182-96.

Vogt, H. 1940[1] *Salishan studies. Comparative notes on Kalispel, Spokan, Colville, and Coeur d'Alene.* Oslo 1940.

SALISH LANGUAGE SOURCES:

GENERAL

Haeberlin, H. 1974 Distribution of the Salish substantival [lexical] suffixes (M.T. Thompson, ed.) *AL 16*:219-350.

Boas, F. 1925 *Comparative Salishan vocabularies.* American Philosophical Society Library, Boas collection, Manuscript #Boas B63c, S2, Pt 3. Philadelphia.

BELLA COOLA

Nater, H.F. 1977 *Stem-list of the Bella Coola language.* [Gives cognates in Salish and other languages].

___. 1984 *The Bella Coola language. CMM Paper 92.* Ottawa. [Suffixes p. 75ff.]

___. 1990 *A concise Nuxalk-English dictionary. CMM Paper 115.* Hull, Quebec.

COMOX-SLIAMMON

Davis, J. 1970 *Some ʔAyʔaӠuθəm words.* MS. [188 words].

Grenier, L. ,Bouchard, R. 1971 *Sliammon word list no. 1 and 2.* (tape with transcription). [266 words, in list 2 ordered in semantic categories].

___. 1971 *How to write the Sliammon language.* (tape with transcription).

Hagège, 1981 C. *Le Comox Lhaamen de Colombie britannique.* Amerindia, no. spécial 2. Paris.

Timmers, J.A. n.d. *Comox stem list.* MS.

SECHELT

Timmers, J.A. 1977 *A classified English-Sechelt word list.* Lisse.

SQUAMISH

Kuipers, A.H. 1967 *The Squamish language. Grammar, texts, dictionary.* The Hague.

___. 1969 The Squamish language. Grammar, texts, dictionary, Part II. The Hague.

____. 1989 *A report on Shuswap with a Squamish lexical app-endix.* Paris.

Walker, C.I. 1973 *An English-Squamish dictionary.* MS.

HALKOMELEM

Elmendorf, W.W., Suttles W. 1960 Pattern and change in Halkomelem Salish dialects. *AL 2*:1-32.

Galloway, B. D. 1980 *Tólméls ye siyelyólexwa. Wisdom of the Elders.* Sardis B.C. [Includes classified word list].

____. 1993 *A grammar of Upriver Halkomkelem. UCPL 96.* Berkeley. [Suffixes p. 202f.]

____. n.d. *English-Halkomelem dictionary.* MS.

Hukari, T.E. 1995 *Dictionary of Hul'qumi'num'.* Cowichan tribes.

NOOKSACK

Galloway, B.D. 1982 (see above under GENERAL).

____. 1993 Nooksack reduplication. In Mattina, A., Montler, T. R. (eds.) *American Indian linguistics and ethnography in honor of Laurence C. Thompson. UMOPL 10*:93-112.

STRAITS

Galloway, B.D. 1990 *A phonology, morphology and classified word list for the Samish dialect of Straits Salish. CMM Paper 116.* Hull, Quebec.

Mitchell, M.R. 1968 *A dictionary of Songish, a dialect of Straits Salish.* [Unpublished M.A. thesis U. of Victoria]. [Comparison with related dialects and languages suggests some possible recording errors in this valuable early account; these are indicated in the text].

Montler, T.R. 1991 *Saanich, North Straits Salish classified word list. CMM Paper 119.* Hull, Quebec.

____. 2000 *Klallam classified word list.* [Internet] http:// www. ling.unt.edu/~montler/Klallam/WordList/KlIntro.htm.

LUSHOOTSEED

Snyder, W.A. 1968 *Southern Puget Sound Salish. Texts, place names and dictionary.* Sacramento.

Bates, D., Hess, T.M., Hilbert V. 1994 *Lushootseed dictionary.* Seattle.

TWANA

Drachman, G. 1969 *Twana phonology.* Columbus.

Thompson, N.R. 1979 *Twana dictionary (student version).* Shelton, Wash.

TSAMOSAN

Kinkade, M.D. 1991[2] *Upper Chehalis dictionary. UMOPL 7.*

TILLAMOOK

Thompson, M.T. n.d. *Tillamook-English dictionary, with English-Tillamook glossary.* MS [work in progress].

LILLOOET

Van Eijk, J. 1987 *Dictionary of the Lillooet language.* MS.

THOMPSON

Thompson, L.C., Thompson, M.T. 1996 *Thompson River Salish dictionary. UMOPL 12.*

SHUSWAP

Kuipers, A.H. 1974 *The Shuswap language. Grammar, texts, dictionary.* The Hague-Paris.

___. 1975 *A classified English-Shuswap word list.* Lisse.

___. 1983 *Shuswap-English dictionary.* Leuven.

___. 1989 *A report on Shuswap, with a Squamish lexical appendix.* Paris.

Palmer, G. 1975 Shuswap Indian ethnobotany. *Syesis* 8:29-81.

Williams, C. 1999 *Re Splatsínac re cwqeqwlútns.* Enderby.

COLUMBIAN

Kinkade, M.D. n.d. *Classified word list for B.C. Indian languages. Columbian Salish version.* MS.

___. 1975 The lexical domain of anatomy in Columbian Salish. In Kinkade, M.D., Hale, K.L., Werner, O. (eds) *Linguistics and Anthropology: in honor of C.F. Voegelin* 423-43. Lisse, The Netherlands.

___. 1981 *Dictionary of the Moses-Columbia language.* Nespelem, Washington.

OKANAGAN-COLVILLE

Mattina, A. 1985 *The golden woman. The Colville narrative of Peter J. Seymour.* Tuscon, Arizona. [The glossary gives a number of Shuswap cognates].

___. 1987 Colville-Okanagan dictionary. UMOPL 5.

Mattina, A, DeSautel, M (eds.) 2002 *Dora Noyes DeSautel ła? kłcaptík"ł. UMOPL 15*. [Contains a glossary].

KALISPEL–SPOKANE–FLATHEAD

Carlson, B.F., Flett, P. 1989 *Spokane dictionary. UMOPL 6*.

Sloat, C. 1965 *An English to Kalispel supplement to Vogt's dictionary*. MS.

Vogt, H. 1940² *The Kalispel language. An outline of the grammar with texts, translations and dictionary*. Oslo.

COEUR D'ALENE

Nicodemus, L.G. 1975 *Snchitsu'umshtsn. The Coeur d'Alene language. Vol. I: The grammar. Coeur d'Alene-English dictionary. Vol. II: English-Coeur d'Alene dictionary.* Spokane.

Reichard, G.A. 1938¹ Coeur d'Alene. In Boas, F. (ed.) *Handbook of American Indian languages, vol. 3*. Glückstadt-Hamburg-New York. [Suffixes p. 601f.]

___. 1938² Stem-list of the Coeur d'Alene language. *IJAL 10*:92-108.

Sloat, C. n.d. *A concordance to the translations in Reichard's Coeur d'Alene*. MS.

OTHER LANGUAGE SOURCES:

Boas, F. 1918 *Kutenay tales*. Washington.

___. 1947 *Kwakiutl grammar, with a glossary of the suffixes*. Philadelphia.

Kortlandt, F.H.H. 1975 Tones in Wakashan. *Linguistics 146*: 31-34.

Lincoln, N.J., Rath, J.C. 1980 *North Wakashan comparative root list. CMM 68* Ottawa.

___. 1986 *Phonology, dictionary and listing of roots and lexical derivates of the Haisla language of Kitlope and Kitimat. CMM 103*.

Powell, J.V., Woodruff, F. 1976 *Quileute dictionary. Northwest Anthropological Research Notes Vol. 10 no.1 Pt. 2* Moscow, Idaho.

Rath, J. C. 1981 *A practical Heiltsuk-English dictionary, with a grammatical introduction. CMM 75* Ottawa.

Sapir, E., Swadesh, M. 1939 *Nootka texts. Tales and ethnological narratives, with grammatical notes and lexical materials.* Philadelphia.

The Shorey Book Store, 1973 *Dictionary of the Chinook Jargon or Indian trade language of the North Pacific coast.* Facsimile reprint SJS 5. Seattle.

Vink, H. 1974 A reverse dictionary of Kwakiutl suffixes. *Dutch contributions to the 9th ICSL (Vancouver)* 76-98. Leiden.

Zenk, H. 1993 A basic Chinook Jargon lexicon. *28th ICSNL:* 393-88. Seattle.